ARCO

CORRECTION OFFICER

12th Edition

Eve P. Steinberg

Twelfth Edition

Macmillan General Reference
A Simon & Schuster Macmillan Company
1633 Broadway
New York, NY 10019-6785

Macmillan Publishing books may be purchased for business or sales promotional use. For information please write: Special Markets Department, Macmillan Publishing USA, 1633 Broadway, New York, NY 10019-6785.

An ARCO Book

ARCO is a registered trademark of Simon & Schuster, Inc.
MACMILLAN is a registered trademark of Macmillan, Inc.

Library of Congress Number: 98-88340

ISBN: 0-02-862807-1

Manufactured in the United States of America

10 9 8 7 6 5 4 3 2 1

CONTENTS

What Is a
Correction Officer?

CORRECTION OFFICERS, under the direct supervision of a high-ranking officer, are responsible for the custody and security, as well as the safety and well-being, of adult and juvenile offenders in federal, state, and larger municipal correctional facilities.

Owing to their close contact with inmates, Correction Officers may participate as members of corrections teams of caseworkers, psychiatrists, psychologists, teachers, and others working to help the individual inmate.

Because of the emphasis on the rehabilitation of inmates, Correction Officers in some correctional facilities lead or participate in group counseling sessions to help inmates adjust to life in the institution and to prepare them for life "outside," after their release.

They may be assigned a wide variety of tasks, some dealing almost exclusively with institutional security involving little or no inmate contact, such as manning a wall or gate post or making periodic rounds of assigned areas checking for faulty bars, gates, locks, doors, and for nonpermissible articles, such as drugs or firearms.

Correction Officers must remain constantly alert for signs of disorders, tensions, and unusual behavior and rule infractions among inmates. They attempt to break up fights or other disturbances and report incidents and violations of regulations to their supervisors. In addition to security and custodial responsibilities, Correction Officers may actively participate as team members in the classification process of new inmates. They interview each new inmate to create good inmate-officer relationships and closely observe the inmate's conduct, response to authority, overall attitude, and relationship with other inmates, as well as abnormal behavior, and report results to their supervisors, verbally or in writing.

Correction Officers may be required to administer first aid in emergencies or censor inmates' mail.

Correction Officers work in maximum, medium, and minimum security correction facilities. The facility may be a penitentiary or prison, usually located outside of metropolitan areas, or a smaller facility, such as a prison camp, detention center, correctional center, treatment center, or prerelease center located in a city or town. Men and women are usually housed in separate institutions, although some facilities have separate sections for men and women under one roof.

In emergency situations, such as riotous inmate behavior and attempted escapes, a Correction Officer may be required to use firearms, chemical agents, and other emergency equipment. Because institutional security is a 24-hour responsibility, Correction Officers may be required to work nights, holidays, weekends, and overtime during emergencies. They usually work an 8-hour day, 40-hour week. Correction Officers must have the ability to stand and walk for long periods of time.

JOB REQUIREMENTS

Because Correction Officers are an important link in the offender rehabilitation process, persons considering such employment should be tuned in to the needs of people in trouble and have an interest in helping them overcome their problems.

High school graduation or its equivalent or qualifying work experience is required for employment in most penal systems. Applicants should be at least 21 years old and in good health. Many states require applicants to pass a civil service examination. Other states require applicants to have some experience in corrections or related work, for example, military service. Education above the high school level may be substituted for general experience by the U.S. Office of Personnel Management for employment in the federal prison system. Many universities and community colleges now offer courses in criminal justice.

Most states require that applicants meet certain height and weight requirements and have good vision and hearing.

The federal government, as well as almost every state and a few localities, provides training for Correction Officers based on guidelines established by the American Correctional Association. Some states have special training academies. All states and local departments of correction, however, provide informal on-the-job training. Experienced officers receive inservice training to keep abreast of new ideas and procedures.

OPPORTUNITIES

Employment of Correction Officers is expected to increase much faster than the average for all occupations through the year 2000 as additional officers are hired to supervise and counsel an increasing inmate population and to relieve tensions in already crowded correctional institutions. Expansion and new construction of correctional facilities are also expected to create many new jobs for Correction Officers. Increasing public concern about the spread of illegal drugs—resulting in more convictions—and the adoption of mandatory sentencing guidelines calling for longer sentences and reduced parole for inmates will also spur demand for Correction Officers. Rapid growth in demand coupled with job openings resulting from the need to replace experienced workers who retire or transfer to other occupations should mean favorable job opportunities for Correction Officers.

Employment of Correction Officers is not usually affected by changes either in economic conditions of the overall level of government spending because security must be maintained in correctional institutions at all times. Even when corrections budgets are cut, Correction Officers are rarely laid off.

With additional education, experience, or training, qualified officers may advance to Correction Sergeant or other supervisory, administrative, or counseling positions.

Applying for Correction Officer Positions

The first step towards securing a position in corrections is to pick up an announcement for the opening and to read it carefully. The announcement will give you a great deal of information about the job, how to apply, and how to qualify.

The announcement generally includes a job description and various requirements concerning age, citizenship, residency, and education. Often, the announcement also includes medical and physical requirements, aspects of character which may be disqualifying, and a description of the examination. Application procedures and deadlines are stated on the announcement. Sometimes the application form will accompany the announcement.

You can get the announcement for an open exam in the personnel office for the jurisdiction in which you wish to apply. City applications are usually available at the city hall. County applications are generally available at a county office. The nearest Office of Personnel Management is likely to have state announcements along with the federal announcement. If no announcement is available, the position probably is not accepting applications at that particular time. Someone in the personnel office may be able to predict when hiring will begin for the position again. You may consider applying to another jurisdiction, if you are qualified. By gaining training and experience working as a Correction Officer in one jurisdiction, you make yourself a very attractive candidate for positions in the jurisdiction of your choice when hiring reopens. The person with a corrections background also gains qualifying experience for many other positions in law enforcement.

The following pages give you a good sampling of representative Correction Officer announcements at the city, county, state, and federal levels. We have included several announcements because of the wide variation in requirements. Read the announcements carefully. Salaries, training programs, working conditions, and medical requirements all vary; physical requirements are tested in different ways. And, of course, the written examinations tend to be unique for each jurisdiction. Requirements and testing procedures are always subject to change. Be sure to request current announcements from jurisdictions that interest you to get the most accurate, up-to-date information.

Most application forms, on the other hand, are very similar. They ask personal questions, educational questions, and work history questions. Since the applications do not different significantly, we have not included city, county, or state application forms in this chapter. The federal application, on the other hand, is lengthy and detailed. Since there is no written examination for applicants who wish to be Correction Officers in the federal system, the application form itself is the medium for qualification. The federal examiners assign weights to answers to questions on the federal application and rank candidates according to the quality of their responses. We have included the entire federal application since it serves in lieu of an exam.

Sample Announcements

SAMPLE CITY ANNOUNCEMENT

Notice of Examination for Correction Officer

Salary: The rate is subject to negotiated change. In addition, there is an annual uniform allowance, holiday pay, and contributions by the City to Welfare and Annuity Fund and City-paid health insurance. After appointment, incumbents will receive salary increments for five years.

Job Description: Under supervision, maintains security within correctional facilities and is responsible for the custody, control care, job training, and work performance of inmates of detention and sentenced correctional facilities, and performs related work.

Examples of Typical Tasks: Supervises inmate meals, visits, recreational programs, and other congregate activities; inspects assigned areas for conditions which threaten safety and security; conducts searches in order to detect contraband; completes forms and reports; maintains appropriate log books; communicates with other area Correction Officers to exchange pertinent information; issues verbal orders, announcements and explanations to inmates; observes inmates and makes recommendations concerning medical and/or psychiatric referrals; safeguards Departmental supplies and equipment; escorts inmates within and outside of the facility; responds to unusual incidents and disturbances; enforces security procedures in accordance with Department guidelines; requests medical assistance for inmates when necessary; counts and verifies the number of inmates present in assigned areas; verifies identification of inmates; supervises inmates of either sex.

Other Job Factors: Listed below are examples of physical activities that Correction Officers perform and environmental conditions in which their activities are conducted. This is not a comprehensive listing, only an indication of some of the job factors.

Stands for up to eight-and-one-half hours continuously; walks up several flights of stairs; uses physical force to break up fights; when assigned a double tour, works 17 hours continuously; works outdoors in all kinds of weather; lifts heavy objects; moves heavy items; is exposed to fumes from disinfectants and sanitary supplies; wears bulletproof or radiation protective vest; is subject to close contact with inmates.

Correction Officers are required to change tours or work overtime, and to work rotating tours and shifts, including nights, Saturdays, Sundays, and holidays.

Qualification Requirements

Candidates must possess a four-year high school diploma or its educational equivalent.

License Requirement: On the date of appointment, possession of a valid unrestricted New York State driver's license is required. Employees must maintain such license during their employment.

English Requirement: Candidates must be able to understand and be understood in English (See General Examination Regulation E.9).

Proof of Identity: Under the Immigration Reform and Control Act of 1986, you must be able to prove your identity and your right to obtain employment in the United States prior to employment with the City of New York.

Citizenship Requirement: United States citizenship is required at the time of appointment. All qualification requirements mentioned above must be met by the date of appointment.

Character Background: Proof of good character and satisfactory background will be absolute prerequisites to appointment. The following are among the factors which would ordinarily be cause for disqualification: (a) conviction of an offense, the nature of which indicates lack of good moral character or disposition towards violence or disorder, or which is punishable by one or more years of imprisonment; (b) repeated convictions of an offense, where such convictions indicate a disrespect for the law; (c) discharge from employment, where such discharge indicates poor behavior or inability to adjust to discipline; (d) dishonorable discharge from the Armed Forces; and (e) persons who have been convicted of petit larceny.

Medical, Psychological, and Physical Qualifications: Eligibles must pass medical and psychological tests. Eligibles will be rejected for any medical condition which impairs their ability to perform the duties of the position in a reasonable manner, or which may reasonably be expected to render them unfit to continue to perform those duties in a reasonable manner. All employees must be medically, psychologically, and physically fit to perform the full duties of the position, and must continue to meet prescribed standards throughout their careers. Periodic testing may be required. Medical standards are available at the Application Section of the Department of Personnel, 18 Washington Street, New York, NY 10004.

Candidates may be required to pass a qualifying physical test.

At the time of appointment, candidates will be required to provide documentation of immunization for rubella, measles, whooping cough, diphtheria, and chicken pox.

Drug Testing: For both titles, a drug screening test will be conducted as part of a pre-employment screening process. Drug tests will also be administered to all Probationary Correction Officers during Academy Training and again as part of the medical examination at the end of probation. All employees may again be drug tested on a random basis after their probationary periods are completed. Any member of the NYC Department of Correction found in possession of, or using illegal drugs, will be terminated.

Test Information

Test Description: Written, multiple-choice test, weight 100. The written test may include questions requiring any of the following abilities: written comprehension, written expression, memorization, problem sensitivity, number facility, deductive reasoning, inductive reasoning, information ordering, spatial orientation, and visualization.

The passing score will be determined after an analysis of the results.

Applicants may be summoned for the test prior to a review of their qualifications.

Test Date: The multiple-choice test is expected to be held on Saturday, June 15.

Admission Card: Applicants who do not receive an admission card at least 4 days prior to the tentative test date must appear at the Examining Service Division of the Department of Personnel, 2 Washington Street, Manhattan, 17th floor, during normal business hours on one of the 4 days preceding the test date to obtain an admission card.

Application Information

Application Period: From February 7 through March 26. Application forms may be obtained in person or by mail from the Application Section, New York City Department of Personnel, 18 Washington Street, New York, NY 10004. Properly completed **ORIGINAL** application forms (**NO COPIES**) must be submitted only by mail to the **New York City Department of Personnel, Bowling Green Station, P. O. Box 996, New York, NY 10274-0996.** Application must be postmarked no later than the last date of the application period.

Application Fee: Payable by money order ONLY. Money orders should be made payable to the New York City Department of Personnel. The social security number of the candidate and the number(s) of the examination(s) for which he or she is applying must be written on the money order. Cash and checks will <u>not</u> be accepted. The applications fee will be waived for a New York City resident receiving public assistance who submits a clear photocopy of a current Medicaid card along with the application. Applicants should retain their money order receipt as proof of filing until they receive notice of their test results.

Appointment Information

Investigation: Candidates are subject to investigation before appointment. At the time of investigation, candidates will be required to pay a fee for fingerprint screening.

At the time of investigation and at the time of appointment, candidates must present originals or certified copies of all required documents and proof, including, but not limited to, proof of date and place of birth by transcript of record of the Bureau of Vital Statistics or other satisfactory evidence, naturalization papers if necessary, proof of any military service, and proof of meeting educational requirements.

Any willful misstatement of failure to present any documents required for investigation will be cause for disqualification.

Probationary Period: The probationary period is 24 months.

As part of the probationary period, probationers will be required to successfully complete a prescribed training course. In accordance with City Personnel Director's Rules and Regulations, probationers who fail to complete successfully such training course, at the close of such training course, may be terminated by their agency head.

Firearms Qualification: Candidates must qualify and remain qualified for firearms' usage as a condition of employment for the duration of their tenure. A firearms qualification test will be administered annually to determine qualification.

Residency Requirement: The New York State Public Officers Law requires that any person employed as a Correction Officer in the New York City Department of Correction must be a resident of the City of New York or of Nassau, Westchester, Suffolk, Orange, Rockland, or Putnam counties.

Promotion Opportunities: Employees in the title of Correction Officer are accorded the opportunity to be promoted to the title of Captain (Correction) and from that title to Warden (Correction) at several levels.

Special Arrangements

Accommodations are available for applicants who provide satisfactory proof of disability. Applications for accommodations must be submitted as early as possible and in no event later than 30 work days before the test or part of a test for which accommodation is requested. Consult General Examination Regulation E.10 for further requirements.

The Department of Personnel makes provisions for candidates claiming inability to participate in an examination when originally scheduled because of the candidate's religious beliefs. Such candidates should consult General Examination Regulation E.11.2 for applicable procedures in requesting a special examination. Such requests must be submitted no later than 15 days before the scheduled date of regular examination.

City Department of Personnel Correction Officer

Physical Fitness Test

In order to become a Correction Officer, candidates must pass a qualifying physical fitness test. Candidates will be called to take the physical fitness test as the needs of the service require and may be called at any time during the life of the list. Candidates will be *called* in order of final rating.

Medical evidence to allow participation in the physical fitness test may be required, and the Department of Personnel reserves the right to exclude from the physical test any eligibles who, upon examination of such evidence, are apparently medically unfit. Eligibles will take the physical test at their own risk of injury, although efforts will be made to safeguard them.

Candidates must complete the *entire* course consisting of six events in not more than *42 seconds* (men); *52 seconds* (women).

Candidates who do not complete successfully event 3 will be penalized 8 seconds (men); 9 seconds (women). This penalty will be added to the time required by the candidate to complete the course. Candidates who do not complete successfully event 3 should proceed immediately to the next event. Candidates must remember that they have only *42 seconds* (men); *52 seconds* (women) to complete the course.

CANDIDATES WHO DO NOT COMPLETE SUCCESSFULLY EVENT 5 WILL FAIL THE TEST. IN ORDER TO COMPLETE SUCCESSFULLY EVENT 5, CANDIDATES MUST MEET *ALL* THE CONDITIONS DESCRIBED BELOW FOR THIS EVENT.

DESCRIPTION OF EVENTS

1. Run up 33 steps.
2. Run approximately 43 yards following a designated path, including at least four 90° turns, to a wood box.
3. Push the box, weighing approximately 100 pounds, forward a distance of approximately five yards and then back to its original position.
4. Run approximately 10 yards to a dummy, weighing approximately *125* pounds (men), *120* pounds (women), which is hanging with its lowest point approximately three feet above the floor.
5. Raise the dummy so as to remove it from its hook, and carry it approximately two yards to a bench. Place the dummy onto the bench under control. *You must not drop or throw it down.*

   (Failure to meet all of the conditions for this event will result in failure in the test as a whole.)
6. Run approximately 10 yards to the finish line.

   Candidates who fail the test on their first trial will be allowed a second trial on the same date.

SAMPLE COUNTY ANNOUNCEMENT

Personnel Office Announces
Civil Service Examination
CORRECTION OFFICER

Written Examination Date: **April 23**
Last File Date: **April 6**

Completed applications must be postmarked no later than the last filing date, or if not mailed, applications must be delivered to the above address no later than 5:00 p.m. on the last filing date.

Duties

Under supervision of a higher ranking officer, a Correction Officer is responsible for the custody and security of inmates of the Department of Corrections on an assigned shift. Correction Officers supervise the movement and activities of inmates; make periodic rounds of assigned areas; conduct searches for contraband; maintain order within the facility; and prepare reports as necessary. They advise inmates on rules and regulations governing the operation of the facility and assist them in resolving problems. Correction Officers have a high degree of responsibility for their actions and decisions. Officers may be required to carry firearms in the performance of certain duties and to perform other related work as required. Correction Officers may supervise inmates assigned to work details, and are expected to cooperate in facilitating the prisoner rehabilitation program. They may also participate in the training of other Correction Officers.

Minimum Qualifications

Education: By the date of examination, either: (A) Graduation from a standard high school; (B) possession of a high school equivalency diploma.

Age: Candidates must be not less than 20 years 6 months of age on the date of the written examination. Eligibility for appointment is 21 years of age.

Driver's License: Possession of a valid driver's license at time of probationary and permanent appointment.

Residence: There are no residence requirements to participate in the examination, but preference in appointment may be granted to eligibles who have been residents of the County at least 30 days immediately prior to the effective date of probationary appointment.

Medical and Physical Qualifications: *Visual* acuity must be binocular vision of 20/40 with or without the use of corrective lenses and *not less* than 20/100 unaided. Candidates who are successful on the written portion of the examination are subject to a *medical examination and physical agility examination* at a later date. Details on the other medical and physical requirements and content of the agility examination as set by the County Personnel office will be made available to candidates at a later date.

Background Investigation: All applicants will be subject to a pre-employment background investigation and a criminal record search TO BE CONDUCTED BY THE APPOINTING AUTHORITY. Conviction of a felony *will* bar appointment. Conviction of a misdemeanor or other violation of law *may* bar examination and/or appointment. A person adjudicated a youthful offender may be disqualified from appointment. Because of the nature of this position, successful candidates will undergo a thorough investigative screening to determine suitability for appointment as a Correction Officer. Failure to meet the standards set for the investigative screening may be required to submit a fee determined by the State Division of Criminal Justice Services to conduct a criminal record search. The refusal of any candidate to submit the required fee shall, in itself, constitute a declination of a valid offer of appointment. Candidates will be instructed at the appropriate time when and how to submit payment.

As part of the background investigation process, the candidate may be required to participate in substance abuse testing designated by the Appointing Authority, and thereafter may be required to participate in such testing on a periodic basis during the twelve (12) month probationary period after appointment. Evidence of substance abuse may lead to disqualification from appointment or termination from employment.

Psychological Screening—Candidates who achieve a passing score on the written test may be required by the Appointing Authority to participate in a psychological screening process. Failure to meet the standards set for this screening may contribute to disqualification.

Training Requirements: Successfully complete a 12-week pre-service training program at the county training Academy. Correction Officers are granted peace officer status under provisions of Section 1.20 of the State Penal Law, subject to the mandatory training requirements under Article 2 of the State Criminal Procedure Law. These training requirements include, but are not limited to, the following: (1) Firearms qualification course. (2) Peace Officer certification course, which meets criteria established by the Municipal Police Training Council. (3) State Basic Correction Officer Test, administered under the auspices of the State Commission of Correction. All appointees will be required to serve and satisfactorily complete a 52-week probationary period. During this time, job performance will be periodically reviewed and carefully evaluated. Failure to meet training and/or performance standards while on probation may result in termination of employment at any time.

NOTE: IN ACCORDANCE WITH LAW, A CORRECTION OFFICER IS A PEACE OFFICER AND MUST BE QUALIFIED TO HOLD SUCH OFFICE. CANDIDATES MUST BE U.S. CITIZENS AT THE TIME OF PROBATIONARY APPOINTMENT.

Subject of Examination

The *WRITTEN TEST* is designed to test for knowledge, skills, and/or abilities in such areas as:

1. *Memory for Facts And Information.* These questions are designed to test how well the candidates can recall information presented. The candidates will be presented with information describing or depicting prison scenes or other facts. They will have a short time to memorize the information before it is collected by the monitor. They will then be asked to recall specific details.

2. *Reasoning Clearly And Making Sound Decisions Related to Security And Control Of Inmates And General Officer-Inmate Relations.* This subtest is a sampling of fundamental concepts and/or their application to situations in the Correction field.

   The subtest will deal with, but will not necessarily be restricted to, such areas as relations with inmates, other officers including superior officers, and the general public. This subtest will not require the candidate to have any prior knowledge of rules, regulations, or procedures of any correction facility.

3. *Understanding And Interpreting Written Material.* These questions are designed to test how well the candidates comprehend written material.

   The candidates are provided with brief selections and are asked questions relating to the selections. All the information required to answer the questions is presented in the selections; the candidates are not required to have any special knowledge relating to the content area covered in the selections.

4. *Preparing Written Material.* These questions are designed to test how well the candidates can express themselves in writing. Particular emphasis is placed upon two major aspects of written communication: How to clearly and accurately express given information, and how to present written material in the most logical and comprehensive manner.

NOTE: Upon passing the written part of the exam, you will be scheduled to appear for a medical exam. At that time, you will be required to show proof of the following documents:

- High school diploma or GED
- Birth certificate
- Residency (one month prior to the date of the written exam and one month prior to the date of your physical exam)
- Driver's license (Part I and II include convictions)
- Citizenship certificate (if you are a naturalized U.S. citizen)

IF YOU DO NOT HAVE ORIGINAL COPIES OF THE ABOVE DOCUMENTS, BEGIN TO SECURE THEM NOW. YOU WILL NOT BE PROCESSED UNLESS YOU HAVE THEM ON THE DATE OF YOUR PHYSICAL EXAM.

Insurance Benefits:

Health: Hospital/Major Medical.

Dental: Coverage plan through the Tri-County Federation of Police.

Prescription Drugs: Full coverage PCS Plan $3 service charge.

Optical Plan: Full coverage to employees and their dependents.

Life Insurance: After 1 year of employment in the State Retirement System. Addition coverage at low-cost premiums through COBA + Special Line-of-Duty Death Benefits— County Government ($100,000) and Federal Government ($50,000).

Leave Benefits:

12 days — Paid holidays

10 days — Annual leave

15 days — After 1 year of service

20 days — After 15 years of service

5 days — Personal leave per year

12 days — Sick leave

Occupational Injury Benefits

Other Benefits:

Credit Union: Payroll deduction savings and loan program.

Consumer Buying Power: Discount purchasing plan.

Disability Insurance: Optional coverage through COBA.

Retirement Plan: State Retirement System (Tier 4).

Work Schedule:

Shift assignments (7-3, 3-11, 11-7) are made at the discretion of the Division administrator. Correction Officers work a 3-2/3-3 work schedule, with three successive days off every other week. Attendance on the three "pay-back" days per year for in-service training and/or firearms requalification is mandatory.

Personnel Office—Investigation Section

REQUIREMENTS FOR INVESTIGATIVE SCREENING
WHEN YOU APPEAR FOR THE INVESTIGATIVE SCREENING AT THE MEDICAL
EXAMINATION SUBMIT SATISFACTORY EVIDENCE OF THE FOLLOWING:

1. Date and place of birth (birth certificate, baptismal certificate showing date and place of birth, school record, naturalization certificate).

2. Proof of residence (utility bills, tax receipts, leases, copy of tax return, W-2 forms, mortgage payments, rent receipts—ONE MONTH PRIOR TO DATE OF WRITTEN TEST *AND* at the present time).

3. High school graduation or equivalency diploma as claimed on the application.

4. Discharge papers and DD-214, if you served in the Armed Forces.

5. A valid state driver's license—Part I and Record of Convictions.

6. Personal History Statement *must be completed* and signed and brought with you to screening.

7. Passport-size picture (color or black and white).

ONLY ORIGINAL DOCUMENTS LISTED ABOVE ARE ACCEPTABLE. FAILURE TO SURRENDER THESE DOCUMENTS AND TO SUBMIT THE NECESSARY EVIDENCE WILL DISQUALIFY CANDIDATE UNTIL THEY ARE SUBMITTED.

County Personnel Office Medical Standards for Correction Officer

Acceptable Weight in Pounds According to Frame (Men)

A Height (in bare feet) Feet	Inches	B Small Frame	C Medium Frame	D Large Frame
5	2	128-134	131-141	138-150
5	3	130-136	133-143	140-153
5	4	132-148	135-145	142-153
5	5	134-140	137-148	144-160
5	6	136-142	139-151	146-164
5	7	138-145	142-154	149-168
5	8	140-148	145-157	152-172
5	9	142-151	148-160	155-176
5	10	144-154	151-163	158-180
5	11	146-157	154-166	161-184
6	0	149-160	157-170	164-188
6	1	152-164	160-174	168-192
6	2	155-168	164-178	172-197
6	3	158-172	167-182	176-202
6	4	162-176	171-187	181-207

Acceptable Weight in Pounds According to Frame (Women)

A Height (in bare feet) Feet	Inches	B Small Frame	C Medium Frame	D Large Frame
4	10	102-111	109-121	118-131
4	11	103-113	111-123	120-134
5	0	104-115	113-126	122-137
5	1	106-118	115-129	125-140
5	2	108-121	116-132	128-143
5	3	111-124	121-135	131-147
5	4	114-127	124-138	134-151
5	5	117-130	127-141	137-155
5	6	120-133	130-144	149-159
5	7	123-136	133-147	143-163
5	8	126-139	136-150	146-167
5	9	129-142	139-153	149-170
5	10	132-145	142-156	152-173
5	11	135-148	145-159	155-176
6	0	138-151	148-162	158-179

NOTE: Although the above tables commence at specified heights, no minimum height requirement has been prescribed. These tables of height and weight will be adhered to in all instances except where the Civil Service examining physician certifies that weight in excess of that shown in the table (up to a maximum of 20 pounds) is lean body mass and not fat. Decision as to frame size of a candidate shall be made by the examining physician.

THE FOLLOWING TESTS WILL BE PART OF THE PHYSICAL EXAMINATION:

VISION

HEARING

SEROLOGY

URINALYSIS

CHEST X-RAY TO BE TAKEN AT A LATER DATE

BLOOD PRESSURE

A color perception test will not be part of the examination since color blindness is not a disqualifying condition. **VISUAL ACUITY STANDARDS:** The minimum acceptable standard of visual acuity (uncorrected) shall be 20/100 binocular vision, total vision corrected to 20/40. Candidates for whom visual acuity is recorded at 20/100 will be required to be re-examined at the county Medical Center at a later date. Vision at the time of such exam must be between 20/20 and 20/100 for candidate to be qualified.

Correction Officer Physical Fitness Test

In order to become a Correction Officer, candidates must pass a qualifying physical fitness test.

Medical evidence to allow participation in the physical fitness test may be required, and the Department of Personnel reserves the right to exclude from the physical test any eligibles who, upon examination of such evidence, are apparently medically unfit. Eligibles will take the physical fitness test at their own risk of injury, although efforts will be made to safeguard them.

Candidates must complete the *entire* course consisting of seven events in not more than *65 seconds*.

NOTE: In accordance with the requirements of the Americans with Disabilities Act, there are some differential standards for women and older candidates in terms of time and weight lifting.

CANDIDATES WHO DO NOT SUCCESSFULLY COMPLETE EVENTS 3, 5, and 6 **WILL FAIL THE TEST.**

DESCRIPTION OF EVENTS

1. Run up approximately 40 steps.
2. Run approximately 40 yards following a designated path including at least four 90° turns, to a sandbag.
3. Push the sandbag, weighing approximately 100 pounds, forward a distance of approximately five yards and then back to its original position. (Failure to meet all of the conditions for this event will result in failure in the test as a whole.)
4. Run approximately 10 yards to a dummy, weighing approximately 110 pounds, which is hanging with its lowest point approximately 3 feet above the floor.
5. Raise the dummy so as to lift the attached ring off the metal pipe. Allow the dummy to slide onto the floor. *You must not drop it or throw it down.* (Failure to meet all of the conditions for this event will result in failure in the test as a whole.)
6. Step up approximately 18 inches and walk across a 12-foot beam by placing one foot in front of the other until you reach the other end. (You must be in control at all times and falling off the beam will result in failure of the test as a whole.)
7. Run approximately 10 yards to the finish line.

Candidates who fail the test on their first trial will be allowed a second trial on the same date after a rest period.

CANDIDATES WHO DO NOT SUCCESSFULLY COMPLETE ALL THE EVENTS IN THEIR PROPER SEQUENCE WILL FAIL THE TEST.

SAMPLE STATE ANNOUNCEMENT #1

Opportunities in Government

Correction Office Trainee
Correction Office Trainee (Spanish Speaking)

The Positions: Correction Officer positions are located throughout the state in the various facilities of the State Department of Correctional Services. As a Correction Officer, under the direct supervision of a high ranking officer, you would be responsible for the custody and security, as well as the safety and well-being, of criminal offenders in State correctional facilities and correction camps. As a Correction Officer (Spanish Speaking), you would be assigned to a facility with a heavy concentration of Spanish-speaking inmates.

As a Correction Officer, you would also supervise the movement and activities of inmates; make periodic rounds of assigned areas; conduct searches for contraband; maintain order within the facility; and prepare reports as necessary. You would advise inmates on the rules and regulations governing the operation of the facility and assist them in resolving problems. You would have a high degree of responsibility for your actions and decisions. You may also be required to carry firearms in the performance of certain duties and to perform other related work as required.

THERE ARE NO REQUIREMENTS FOR ADMISSION TO THE EXAMINATION.

If you pass the written test, you will be contacted, in rank order, to complete a background investigation, a physical/medical examination, and psychological evaluation. You must successfully complete each of these in order to be eligible for appointment.

It will be necessary for you to come to the state capital on two separate days, at your own expense, in order to complete these activities.

Background Investigation: If you pass the written test, you will undergo a thorough background investigation to determine your suitability for appointment as Correction Officer. Conviction of a felony will bar appointment. Conviction of misdemeanors or violations of law may bar appointment. A person adjudicated a youthful offender may be disqualified from appointment. Failure to meet the standards for the background investigation will result in disqualification.

Physical/Medical: If you pass the written test, you must meet the physical/medical standards for Correction Officer. These include binocular visual acuity not less than 20/20 with or without correction (if correction is required, binocular visual acuity not less than 20/40 without correction) and satisfactory hearing. You will also be required to pay a medical laboratory fee.

Psychological Screening: If you pass the written test, you will also be required to participate in a psychological screening process. Failure to meet the standards set for this screening will result in disqualification.

AT THE TIME OF APPOINTMENT: You must meet the following requirements:

Minimum Age: You must be at least 21 years old. (If you are less than 20 years of age at the time of the written test, you are unlikely to become appointable before the eligible lists are superseded by eligible lists resulting from the next examinations for these titles.)

Education: You must be a high school graduate or have a high school equivalency diploma (issued by an appropriate State education authority). Diplomas issued through a home study course and not by an appropriate educational authority are not acceptable.

Written Test To Be Held APRIL 23, Applications MUST be Post-marked No Later Than MARCH 7
A Processing Fee Must Accompany Your Application

NOTE:

1. In accordance with State law, a Correction Officer is a peace officer and must be qualified to hold such office and must be a U.S. citizen.

2. If you pass the written test for Correction Officer (Spanish Speaking) and are considered for appointment, you will be required to demonstrate your proficiency in the Spanish language. Proficiency must be at a level that will assure your ability to perform the duties of the position properly.

3. If you apply for Correction Office Trainee (Spanish Speaking), we urge you to apply for both examinations.

4. All appointees will be employed as Trainees.

SELECTION: There will be a written test which you must pass in order to be considered for appointment. The written test will be designed to test for knowledge, skills, and/or abilities in such areas as: reasoning clearly and making sound decisions related to security and control of inmates and general officer-inmate relations; understanding and interpreting written material; preparing material; and memory for facts and information.

TRAINEESHIP: Please notify the Department of Civil Service if you change your mailing address after filing for the examination. You will be required to participate in, and satisfactorily complete, all requirements of a 12-month training program before you can advance to Correction Officer. As part of the program, you will attend the Correctional Services Training Academy. Training at the Academy will include academic courses in such areas as emergency response procedures, interpersonal communications, legal rights and responsibilities, security procedures, and concepts and issues in correction. Successful completion of the weapons training course is mandatory for continued employment. Trainees will also receive rigorous physical training to develop fitness, strength, and stamina. Failure to maintain the required academic standing, to qualify with weapons, or to qualify in meeting the physical standards will result in termination of employment. Formal Academy training will last six weeks, followed by a six-week period of on-the-job training. At that point, you will be assigned to a correctional facility for full duty. A probationer who fails to meet the training standards while at the Academy may be terminated because of such failure.

PROBATION: All appointees will be required to serve and satisfactorily complete a 52-week probationary period. During probation, performance will be periodically reviewed and carefully evaluated. A probationer who fails to meet the performance standards may be terminated at any time.

STATE RESIDENCE NOT REQUIRED: If you are appointed from a list, you may be required to furnish the appointing authority with acceptable documentation establishing your identity and eligibility for employment in the United States.

FEES: File one processing fee. The required fee must accompany your application. Send check or money order payable to the Department of Civil Service and write the examination number(s) and your social security number on your check or money order. Do not send cash. As no refunds will be made, you are urged to compare your qualifications carefully with the requirements for admission and file only for those examinations for which you are clearly qualified. You are responsible for payment of a clinical laboratory test fee if medical examination is required prior to appointment.

EXCEPTION TO FEE REQUIREMENT: An exception to both the processing fee and the clinical laboratory test fee, when required, will be made only for persons receiving Supplemental

Social Security payments or public assistance (Home Relief or Aid to Dependent Children), provided Foster Care, or certified Job Training Partnership Act eligible through a state or local social service agency, and for those who are unemployed and primarily responsible for the support of a household. Individuals wishing to claim this waiver of fee on the basis of Supplemental Social Security, Home Relief, or Aid to Dependent Children must certify on their applications that they are receiving public assistance and must indicate the type of assistance they are receiving, the agency providing the assistance and their case numbers. Persons claiming this waiver through the Foster Care or Job Training Partnership Act Certification must specify the program and name of their contact agency. Such claims are subject to later verification and, if not supported by appropriate documentation, are grounds for barring appointment.

NOTE: Fingerprints are sometimes required at the time of appointment. When they are required, the fee involved must be paid by the appointee.

It is the policy of the Department of Civil Service to provide for and promote the equal opportunity for employment, compensation, and other terms and conditions of employment without discrimination because of age, race, creed, color, national origin, sex, sexual orientation, disability, or marital status.

State Correction Officer Fact Sheet

Annual salary advancements are based on performance evaluations. Employees are also eligible for pay raises as negotiated by their certified bargaining agent (Council 82—AFSCME—AFL-CIO). Negotiations are currently underway between the State and Council 82—AFSCME—AFL-CIO which may result in higher starting salaries.

Other:
Additional compensation is provided through a pre-shift briefing premium payable each payroll period in addition to base salary.

Inconvenience pay program to employees who work four (4) hours or more between 6:00 p.m. to 6:00 a.m.

Location pay for employees working in certain urban countries and specified major cities.

Insurance Benefits:

HEALTH:
Health insurance for individual coverage (Empire Plan or various health maintenance organizations) is provided at low or no cost to the employee. Additionally health insurance is provided for employees with dependent coverage at low cost. Correction Officers can select from several health insurance options to obtain the coverage which best suits their needs. There is a 28-day waiting period before coverage takes effect for new employees.

PRESCRIPTION DRUG:
Prescription drug coverage is provided through the health insurance plan selected. Under the Empire Plan there is a co-payment charge per prescription. Prescription coverage under a health maintenance organization varies according to the individual plan.

DENTAL:
The full premium of dental coverage is currently provided through Group Health Incorporated. No deductible is required. Benefits are available to new State employees only after the completion of six (6) months of employment

LIFE:
Life insurance available at reduced premiums through your certified bargaining agent (Council 82—APSCME—AFL-CIO).

Leave Benefits:

ANNUAL LEAVE:
Earned at the rate of one half day pay per period. Bonus days credited for up to seven years of service on anniversary date. Additional bonus days provided in union contracts. Forty days **MAXIMUM** accumulation.

PERSONAL LEAVE:
Five days of leave are granted on date of employment for use each year. It is NOT cumulative. On anniversary date unused personal leave is lost and five new days are provided.

SICK LEAVE:
Earned at the rate of one half day per pay period. Accumulation of sick leave from year to year is allowed with a maximum leave accrual of 225 days. Absences due to illness or death in the employee's immediate family may be chargeable to sick leave not to exceed 15 days per calendar year.

WORKER'S COMPENSATION LEAVE:
An employee necessarily absent from duty because of an occupational injury will be granted compensation leave with pay without charge to leave credits for up to six months.

HOLIDAY OBSERVANCES:
There are twelve days which are observed as holidays by the State. Correction Officers required to work on a holiday shall receive at their option either (a) additional compensation, or (b) a compensatory day off.

Retirement:

GENERAL:
If you are a new State employee, you must contribute three (3) percent of your gross earnings toward the support of your retirement benefits. Membership is mandatory for permanent full-time employees. Interest accumulates on all contributions to the retirement fund. Normal retirement age is 62 under this plan; however, you may retire at one-half pay after 25 years service as a Uniformed Correction Officer. Deductions for Social Security are separate from contributions made to the Employee's Retirement System.

DEATH BENEFITS:
Ordinary and accidental death benefits are payable on your behalf to your survivors through application to the Retirement System.

Other Benefits:

CREDIT UNION:
Payroll deduction savings and loan feature.

CONSUMER BUYING POWER:
Available through your certified bargaining unit.

UNIFORMS:
A professional uniform is furnished and replaced as needed by the employer. The annual uniform maintenance allowed may be increased each year if negotiated.

EDUCATION AND TRAINING:
Training reimbursement is available for higher education. Continuous on the job training is available as an enhancement to promotional opportunities.

ID Cards, Badges, and Fingerprinting

Required of all employees. Mandatory fee for fingerprinting. Have ID card with you at all times. Badges are provided by the Department to all Correction Officers. Correction Officers are Peace Officers under Section 1.20 of the Criminal Procedure Law.

Reassignment

Upon completion of training, new Correction Officers are assigned to facilities based upon the staffing needs of the Department. Thereafter, employees may request, in preference order, to be reassigned on the basis of seniority to other facilities. The waiting time for a transfer depends upon the length of existing reassignment lists and Correction Officer turnover.

Minimum Age for Appointment

Candidates must be twenty-one years of age on or before the date of their appointment.

Department of Civil Service—Medical Review Unit Statement of Physical and Medical Requirements for Correction Officer Trainee

NOTE: Candidates are required to meet the physical and medical requirements stated below and in the announcement, at the time of the medical examination, at the time of appointment, and at appropriate intervals thereafter.

1. **Height and Weight**—Will not interfere with the candidate's ability to perform the essential functions of the position. All candidates will be evaluated for stamina and vigor to demonstrate their physical fitness through tests of strength, agility, flexibility, and endurance.

2. **Speech**—Must be free of speech pathology which would interfere with the ability to communicate clearly.

3. **Vision**—Distant visual acuity should be correctable to better than, or equal to 20/30 (Snellen) in each eye; if correction is required, binocular visual acuity not less than 20/70 without correction. Binocular peripheral vision should not be less than 170 degrees.

4. **Color Vision**—Perception of color is deemed acceptable if the candidate correctly reads nine (9) or more of the first thirteen (13) plates of the 24-plate edition of the Ishihara Test. If the candidate's color perception is deemed unacceptable through the use of said test and he/she believes the results to be incorrect, such an individual may at his/her own expense take the Farnsworth-Munsell 100-Hue Test. (a) The test must be taken under the supervision of an ophthalmologist having the proper equipment and utilizing the standards established by the Municipal Police Training Council. (b) If the candidate takes and completes the Farnsworth-Munsell 100-Hue Test, the specialist shall certify in writing whether or not the candidate meets the required color perception standards. (c) Both eyes should be examined together and scored as such. (d) If a candidate fails the initial test, he/she must, upon request, be immediately retested and the lower total error score used for purposes of qualification. A total error score of not more than 124 is deemed acceptable. (e) The use of any lens by an officer candidate in order to meet the color perception standard is not acceptable.

5. **Hearing**—The average hearing level (HL) for the three (3) test frequencies of 500, 1000, and 2000 Hz will not exceed 25 dB in either ear, and no single hearing level will exceed 30 dB at

any of these 3 test frequencies in either ear. Hearing loss at 3000 Hz will not exceed 40 dB HL in either ear. Use of hearing aids is permitted as long as they are self-contained and fit within (auricular) or behind or over (post-auricular) the ear. Candidates with hearing aids, at their own expense, must provide evidence from a licensed audiologist, using functional gain or real ear measurements, that their aid(s) meet the stipulated manufacturers standards. *Recourse Testing*: If the candidate's pure tone screening test is deemed unacceptable, such candidates may at his/her own expense have an audiological evaluation administered by a NYS licensed audiologist, including: 1. hearing sensitivity, 2. speech discrimination in quiet, 3. speech discrimination in noise. Testing should be performed in a sound-treated environment meeting the 1969 ANSI or any subsequent standard. The CID W-22 word lists should be presented at 50 dB HL via a calibrated speed audiometer through a single speaker stationed at 0 degrees azimuth with the candidate seated at approximately 1 meter (39 inches) from the speaker. Speech (hearing) discrimination testing in a background of broad-band noise should be conducted in the same sound field environment. Again, using a different version of one of the CID W-22 word lists presented at 50 dB HL, a competing noise should be simultaneously presented at 40 dB HL (S/N=+10) through the same speaker (0 degrees azimuth) as the test words or through a separate speaker located at 180 degrees azimuth. The minimal acceptable standard of speech (hearing) discrimination shall be a score no poorer than 90% in quiet and 70% in noise on tow of the pre-recorded versions of the CID W-22 word lists. An open-test response format should be utilized with the candidate responding in writing.

6. **Cardiovascular**—Candidate must have a functional and therapeutic cardiac classification no greater than NYS Class IA. This determination must be made clinically or by cardiac stress test. Candidates with uncontrolled high blood pressure will be restricted pending remediation.

7. **Respiratory System**—The respiratory system must be free of chronically disabling conditions that would interfere with the candidate's ability to perform the essential functions of the position.

8. **Diabetes**—Candidates who are diabetic must provided evidence of satisfactory medical control. Candidates will be evaluated on a case-by-case assessment as to the control of diabetes and presence and severity of symptoms and complications.

9. **Neurological Health**—Candidates must be free of neurological disorders that would interfere with the candidate's ability to perform the essential functions of the position. Candidates with any type of epilepsy or seizure disorders must provide evidence of one-year seizure free history with or without drug control.

10. **Musculoskeletal Health**—Candidates must have no defects, deformities, or disorders that will interfere with the candidate's ability to perform the essential functions of the position. The use of prostheses or braces is allowed as long as the candidate can perform the full range of duties of the position and no security risk is posed.

11. **General Medical Statement**

    A. Candidates must be free of any medical condition, including alcohol abuse, and/or psychiatric disorder, that would jeopardize the safety and health of inmates, the public, and/or other employees, or would clearly interfere with the ability to perform the essential functions of the position.

    B. Candidates may not have a medical problem that prevents them from working mandatory unscheduled overtime.

    C. Candidates found to be abusing legal drugs or using illegal drugs will be disqualified.

State Department of Civil Service
Correction Officer Trainee
Agility Test Description

The test will consist of the seven (7) elements described below, which are essential for the satisfactory performance of the duties of a Correction Officer.

All elements are scored on a pass/fail basis and candidates must satisfactorily complete each element of the test in order to successfully complete the test. Candidates who fail the test will not be appointed to the position. Unsuccessful candidates will be considered for retesting at a future date.

Element I

Stair Climb: This task consists of safely going up and down one flight of stairs.

Element II

Ladder Ascent: The candidate safely climbs to a height of approximately 12 feet, the ladder encased by a standard industrial safety cage with an interior dimension of approximately 30 inches, until the designated rung is touched. The candidate then descends to the floor in a safe manner.

Element III

Suspended Dummy Raise: A rescue dummy simulating a body weighing 120 pounds is hanging by a rope. The dummy must be raised vertically (3 inches) until the noose pressure is off the neck and held there for a period of five (5) consecutive seconds. The dummy must be raised by facing it and using hands and arms (as in a "bear hug").

Element IV

Body Transport: A 160-pound dummy is placed on a blanket. The candidate must pull the weighted blanket a total distance of 30 feet.

Element V

Obstacle Vault: This task consists of getting over a three-foot-high obstacle in a safe manner. Hurdling or diving is not permitted.

Element VI

Door Lock and Unlock: This task consists of properly unlocking a standard use security cell door, using the assigned key, going through the door, and relocking the same door.

Element VII

Load and Unload: This task consists of properly loading and unloading a weapon, 4-inch revolver, observing all specified safety regulations. Live ammunition will not be used.

Three-Minute Step Test: In addition the agility test includes an element to screen for cardiovascular disease: For 3 minutes, the candidate will lift one foot at a time while stepping on and off a 12-inch bench at a rate of 24 times per minute. The candidate must keep pace with a metronome set at 96 beats per minute. After the 3 minutes of stepping, the candidate will sit down and relax without talking. A 60-second heart count will be taken starting 5 seconds after the completion of stepping. There is no pass/fail on this test. Instead, EHS medical staff will consider the results of this test along with other aspects of the examination to determine if a candidate is capable of performing the essential duties of a Correction Officer Trainee.

SAMPLE STATE ANNOUNCEMENT #2

Correctional Officer I

SALARY:

CLOSING DATE: OPEN AND CONTINUOUS

POSITION DUTIES: This is the beginning level of security work in an adult correctional facility. Positions are available at various penal institutions throughout the state.

Minimum Qualifications

Within six months of submitting the application, each candidate must:

Be 21 years old and possess a high school diploma or General Education Development (GED) certificate.

Selection Process

Candidates who meet the minimum qualifications will be admitted to the examination for this classification.

Candidates are required to attain a converted score of not less than 70 on a scale of 100. Successful candidates will be ranked by score and placed on the employment list in a tentative status only, subject to further evaluation of a comprehensive background investigation, proof of citizenship or resident alien status, a physical examination, and an oral interview to be conducted by the hiring agency.

Examination

The written examination will consist of items designed to test the candidate's visual and associative memory, as well as their reading comprehension skills.

Information for Candidates

APPLICATIONS: Applications may be obtained by mail or in person from the Department of Personnel. Your application is part of the examination process. Answer each question fully and clearly. Photocopies of the application form are acceptable.

QUALIFICATIONS: You must possess the minimum qualifications stated before you can be selected for a State job. However, if you are scheduled to complete an educational or licensing requirement within six months of the date of the application you may participate in the examination process. Permanent State employees may also complete necessary experience requirements within six months of the date of their application. Credit will be give for relevant part-time, temporary, or volunteer experience based on the number of hours worked per week. You must include on your application the time you spent in such activity. You are required to be a citizen or national of the United States or an alien lawfully admitted for United States permanent residence, or an alien authorized under United States Immigration and Nationality Act to be hired in the position for which you have applied.

ELIGIBILITY: Applicants meeting the minimum qualifications will be notified when and where to appear for written, oral, or demonstration examinations. If the examination is an evaluation of relevant training and experience, a notice will be sent if further information is needed. Candidates are ranked according to the examination score and remain eligible for consideration for at least one year from the date of the examination.

PHYSICAL EXAMINATION: Eligible candidates may be required to pass a job-related physical examination.

Important Information on Applying for State Government Positions

Application

1. State Merit System examinations are scheduled at various times during the year, and are announced through use of newspaper ads and other recruiting activities. When an examination is announced, applicants should file an application with the Department of Personnel by the announced closing date. File a separate application (Form MS100) for each position in which you are interested.

2. Applications will only be accepted for positions currently on the Department of Personnel's testing schedule. Candidates interested in positions not on the examination schedule will need to have their names and addresses placed in an "Interest File" for those positions in which they are interested. Information on the "Interest File" is available by calling the Application Control Unit of the Department of Personnel. As examinations are announced, applicants will be mailed postcards notifying them to file their applications by the closing date.

3. You may obtain applications forms by calling or writing the Department of Personnel.

4. You may file *clear* photocopies of your application if the original application is up to date. Each copy must have on it the correct position title and your original signature. Photocopies must be of standard size paper (8.5" by 11"). Reduced copies will not be accepted.

5. Your application is part of the examination process. Answer each question fully and clearly. The information you give is used to determine whether you are accepted for the examination. In some cases, it is used to determine your test score.

Qualifications

1. You are required to be a citizen or national of the United States or an alien lawfully admitted for United States permanent residence, or an alien authorized under United States Immigration Reform and Control Act of 1986 to be hired in the position for which you have applied.

2. Effective July 1, 1982, amendments to the law governing the Office on Aging and Pensions System allows persons age 70 and older to participate in Merit System examinations and be considered for appointment subject to the provisions of Article 64A. Persons age 70 or older appointed after July 1, 1982, are excluded from becoming members of the Pension System.

3. You *must* possess the minimum qualifications stated on the job specification sheet. Exceptions are not made; however:

    (a) if a high school diploma or a college degree is required and you will be getting one within six months after the test date, you may be admitted to the examination.

    (b) unless otherwise stated on the job specification sheet, if a license, certificate, or associate membership is required and you have applied for one and are in the process of getting it, you may be admitted to the examination.

    (c) if you are a promotional candidate and will meet the experience requirements within six months after your experience is evaluated by the Department of Personnel, you will be admitted to the examination. (A promotional candidate is a permanent State employee who has completed an original three- or six-month probationary period by the test date. Candidates who have been reinstated are also considered promotional.)

All requirements must be complete before any candidate can be selected for a State position.

4. If you are a State employee and your job duties are different from those listed for your assigned classification, your "acting" experience can be accepted as qualifying. However, it must be verified by your supervisor and processed through your agency's personnel department.

5. You will be given credit for part-time or temporary work based on the number of hours worked. It must total the full amount of experience required. You will also be given credit for civic, welfare, service, and organizational activity which meets the experience qualifications. You need not have been compensated for it. You must include on your application the time you have spent in such activity.

Examination

1. You must pass an examination to qualify for a position. The purpose of the examination is to set up a list of persons eligible to fill positions. An examination is scheduled when the list of eligibles for that position does not have enough names from which agencies can choose. To be notified for the examination, you must file an application before the closing date. Closing dates are announced in the classified section of newspapers and some county papers and on bulletins posted in state agencies. If your application is received in the office of the Department of Personnel by 5:30 p.m. on the closing date and you qualify for the position, you will be notified for the next scheduled test about eight to ten days before the test date.

2. Special test arrangements and accommodations are arranged for handicapped candidates, providing the Department of Personnel is notified *in advance* of the type and extent of the handicap. It is the applicant's responsibility to contact the Department of Personnel to request a special test date, *after* he/she receives test notice.

3. Most State Merit System examinations are written, oral, and/or demonstration of skill. For some positions, the examination may be a rating of your education and experience based upon the information stated on your application. The content of an examination is based on the job duties and the level of responsibility of the job.

4. If you miss an examination because of illness or personal reasons, a special examination will *not* be arranged. If you do not appear to take an examination, you must file a new application if you wish to be notified for the next examination. If you cannot take examinations on *Saturday because of religious affiliation*, or *because you are in the military reserve* and have been called to active duty for summer encampment or emergency reasons, an alternate test date may be set for you. Your request for an alternate test date must be made in writing. If you are a military reservist, you must also submit a copy of your official orders.

5. At the time of the examination, you will be asked about your "area of availability." Some applicants want employment only in a certain location. Other applicants will consider employment anywhere in the state. Eligible lists may be established by area or on a statewide basis. It depends on agency needs, the salary level of the position, and whether the position is used by one department only or one area only. When lists are established on an area basis, eligibles are listed by score within each area.

6. Veterans' preference points, which you may be entitled to receive, will be added to your final earned passing score. Detailed information concerning eligibility will be found on the application (Form MS 100). Copy of DD214 must be submitted to the Department of Personnel in order to receive Veteran's Preference. Promotional candidates *do not* receive veterans' preference but do receive seniority credit.

Selection

1. You receive your Notice of Test Results from the Department of Personnel. The next contact comes from a State agency which will do the hiring. When a State agency has a vacant position, the agency may select from among the top five eligibles who are interested in the position or the agency may elect to select from the top five promotional candidates within their own organization. Eligibles are ranked in order of test score. If eligibles are hired, those further down on the lists move up and become eligible for consideration.

2. All eligibles will receive an initial one year of eligibility on the Certification of Eligibles List. However, to ensure the availability of appropriate eligible lists, each list will be reviewed after being in effect for ten months. The review will be for the purpose of possible extension of the eligible list.

SAMPLE STATE ANNOUNCEMENT #3
Department of Correction

Greetings:

The Department of Correction employs over 1,400 employees in 105 job classifications. There are over 850 Correctional Officers currently serving the State in an expanding career field that is a very important part of the criminal justice community.

Corrections is an exciting career field for an individual who is sincerely interested in professional opportunity and growth. It is an area where a person can take advantage of an extensive training program that can be directly applied to career advancement.

Correctional Officers are highly trained professionals providing an important service to the community. Statewide employment opportunities are now available.

I welcome your interest in pursuing a career with the State Department of Correction.

Sincerely,

Commissioner

As a Correctional Officer your responsibilities include security, supervision of inmates and maintaining order in an institutional facility.

You may be assigned to a variety of different posts to carry out these responsibilities. Examples are:

- —Transporting inmates
- —Control room
- —Visiting room
- —Gatehouse
- —Motorpool
- —Housing unit
- —Outside patrol
- —Security for inmate in private medical facility
- —Mailroom
- —Central supply
- —Laundry
- —Educational building
- —Road crew
- —Canine unit

While working these various posts, you will be exposed to all levels of security.

- Excellent Benefits
- Promotional Opportunities
- Uniform Provided

- Statewide Vacancies
- 216-Hour Training Course

MUST PASS:

Written examination

Oral interview

Medical exam

Background investigation

All phases of training

Individuals who pursue a career in the Correctional Officer series, and who possess related vocational work experience, may take advantage of openings in the following areas:

Cook

Building Maintenance Mechanic

Auto Mechanic

Group Leader

Storekeeper

Trades Instructor

Department of Correction

DATE OF POSTING: CLOSING DATE: Continuous
POSTING NUMBER: LOCATION: All Counties

Open To: Department of Correction Employees & Applicants

CLASSIFICATION AND PAY GRADE:

Class Code: 45724   Pay Grade: 07
Class Title: Correctional Officer   Salary:

MINIMUM QUALIFICATION:

Possession of High School Diploma or General Equivalent Diploma (GED).

GENERAL DESCRIPTION:

Responsible for security, supervision of inmates, and maintaining order in an institutional facility. May be required to maintain control and custody of inmates during transport.

KNOWLEDGE, SKILLS, AND ABILITIES:

Ability to learn and apply facility and departmental policies, procedures, rules, and regulations; ability to acquire and apply skill in the use of weapons, self-defense and prescribed procedures for dealing with violent or abusive inmates; ability to learn the attitude and group habits of persons in custody; ability to observe and effectively enforce rules appropriate to the security setting; ability to supervise the activities of inmates in assigned tasks; ability to act quickly and effectively in emergencies; ability to follow written and oral instructions; ability to establish and maintain effective working relationships with other officers and staff personnel; ability to apply training, instructions, procedures and judgment in all aspects of the work; ability to learn and apply the proper handling of sentry dogs as required by work assignment; ability to learn and apply the methods and techniques of custodial care of sentry dogs as required by work assignment.

SPECIAL REQUIREMENTS:

Must be 21 years of age at time of application. Prior to institutional assignment, candidates must successfully complete all phases of a six-week Correctional Office Basic Course. This course is administered by the Department of Correction at the Staff Training Academy. Coursework includes physical, classroom and hands on training. Instruction is provided in the areas of inmate supervision, defensive tactics, riot control, weapons, report writing and emergency medical training.

LICENSES, REGISTRATIONS, AND/OR CERTIFICATES:

Eligibility for possession of a valid Class "A" operator's license or equivalent as issued by the Department of Public Safety at the time of application and possession of such license at the time of appointment and during the tenure of employment in this class as required by work assignment.

EXAMINATION REQUIREMENTS:

1. Written Examination Components

	Number of Questions	Percentage of Total Scene
Vision Memory	20	20%
Associative Memory	15	15%
Writing Ability	25	30%
Reading Comprehension	34	35%
TOTAL	94	100%

2. Writing sample

   In the near future, a writing sample will be added to the existing examination. This will be graded Pass/Fail and will be administered at the same time as the existing exam. Individuals will be required to pass both sections for further consideration.

Personal Information for New Applicants

Position Title: Correctional Officer

Pay Grade: 7

Starting Salary: $_____ while in training course. When assigned to institution, includes $1,200/year hazardous duty pay.

Shift Differential: 5% for working any hours between 6:00 PM and 8:00 AM.

Probationary Period of Six Months: Union membership optional after probationary period. Dues will be paid by Union members; service fee will be paid by nonmembers.

Hours Per Week: 40

Holidays: Twelve (12) standard per year and any other that the Governor may designate. Specific scheduling depends on date and holiday observance and individual work schedule.

Vacation: Seniority prevails. Scheduling is done by the Duty Captain. Accrued at a rate of $1\frac{1}{4}$ days per month. Rate increases with length of service. Maximum accrual: two times annual accrual.

Insurance:

Life: $2,000 fully paid Educators Mutual Life Insurance
$100,000 fully paid, Line of Duty Life Insurance.
Optional Metropolitan Life Insurance:
to be paid by the employee, equal to your annual salary rounded to the next highest thousand.
Approximate cost of under $8.00 per month.

Health: Blue Cross Blue Shield—Eligible for enrollment immediately upon employment of group rates. **MUST BE PAID ENTIRELY BY THE NEW EMPLOYEE FOR A PERIOD OF THREE MONTHS.** After three (3) months of satisfactory employment, the State will pay for 80% of the monthly premium. Any optional coverage will be paid by the new employee.

Available Plans:

> Basic
> Comprehensive
> First State Health Plan
> HMO
> Total Health Plus

Dental: Voluntary—Eligible for enrollment immediately upon employment or during group enrollment. Employee is responsible for paying **FULL** premium.

> Individual—$4.83 semimonthly
> Family—$11.81 semimonthly

The plan benefits emphasize preventive dental care; semi-annual exams, cleaning, X-rays, and fluoride treatments are provided at no charge. Other listed services are provided at 30% to 50% below the State's average dental cost.

Pension: The State offers a pension plan for all full-time and regular part-time employees. This is a contributory program with vesting after 10 years of earned credit service.

State Employee Credit Union: All full-time State employees are eligible to join. Membership fee of $6.00 paid by the employee. Payroll deduction available for the regular contributions.

Blood Bank: Full-time State employees are eligible for group coverage. Annual dues paid by the State. To maintain membership employees must give blood, designate a donor, or donate $35.00 once every 3-5 years. Unlimited blood supply for employee and immediate family.

Employee Assistance Program: (STEP) A program designed to help any employee who is experiencing personal difficulties on the job with regard to alcohol, drugs, emotional difficulties, marriage/family conflicts, financial, or legal issues.

Career Progression:

Correctional Corporate	Pay Grade 08
Correctional Sergeant	Pay Grade 09
Correctional Lieutenant	Pay Grade 11
Correctional Staff Lieutenant	Pay Grade 13
Correctional Captain	Pay Grade 15

SAMPLE STATE ANNOUNCEMENT #4

Correction Officer

Annual Starting Salary:	Salary Group: CC01	Application Closing Date: NO CLOSING DATE	Exam No.:

SALARY INCREASES ANNUALLY AFTER COMPLETION OF 13-WEEK TRAINING PERIOD.

General Statement of Duties: Participates in formal training course in correctional work; upon completion of formal training is assigned to an institution or center and performs, with increasing independence, custodial and rehabilitative duties in a wide variety of assigned posts on any shift; carries out regulations and directions pertaining to custody of inmates; supervises conduct of inmates in daily work or leisure activities maintaining order and discipline; maintains constant surveillance of assigned area to detect and prevent introduction of contraband, misconduct of inmates or other violation of rules, regulations or directives; instructs inmates in proper work or personal habits; performs administrative or clerical work as necessary to process or control movement of inmates, authorized personnel or materials; serves as security escort for inmates within and outside of facility; may be required to physically restrain inmates; participates in directed treatment activities as required; evaluates and reports on inmate progress; does related work as required.

Minimum Qualifications Required

Special Legal Requirement: Applicants must be at least eighteen (18) years old. The Appointing Authority may require possession of a current state Motor Vehicle Operator's License at time of appointment.

Physical Requirement: General good health, free from any disease or injury which would impair health or usefulness, with sufficient strength, stamina, agility, and visual and auditory acuity to perform all the duties of the class. (A complete medical and physical examination will be required of all candidates.)

The Written Examination Will Cover These Areas: Ability to follow oral and written instructions; ability to observe and remember important details from work related scenes and photographs; ability to read, understand, and apply job related rules and regulations; ability to analyze situations quickly and accurately; ability to work under pressure; job related interest and preference as they compare to successful Correction Officers.

To Apply for the Examination: Interested candidates should call the State Testing Center to make an appointment to take the exam. An application package will be sent to you which you must complete and bring to your scheduled examination appointment.

DO NOT MAIL YOUR APPLICATION FOR THIS EXAM.

Test Administration: Test administrations will be given on a regular continuous basis on weeknights and/or at various locations around the state on Saturdays.

ALL CANDIDATES WILL BE SCHEDULED BY APPOINTMENT ONLY.

THE NAMES OF SUCCESSFUL CANDIDATES WILL BE PLACED ON AN EMPLOYMENT LIST AND REMAIN THEREON FOR A PERIOD OF ONE YEAR. UNSUCCESSFUL CANDIDATES MAY APPLY TO RETAKE THIS EXAM SIXTY (60) DAYS AFTER THEY ARE TESTED.

THE EXAMINATION WILL BE COMPOSED OF THE WRITTEN TEST, WHICH WILL COMPRISE 100% OF THE FINAL EARNED RATING. THE SELECTION PROCESS WILL ALSO INVOLVE AN ORAL INTERVIEW, A PHYSICAL EXAMINATION AND A BACK-GROUND INVESTIGATION CONDUCTED BY THE DEPARTMENT OF CORRECTIONS.

Promotional Opportunities☐Paid Vacation☐Sick Leave with Pay☐Health Services☐Paid Health Insurance☐Major Medical☐Group Insurance☐Longevity Pay☐12 Paid Holidays☐Excellent Retirement Benefits

Job Openings

Openings for examinations with closing dates may have been filled on a provisional basis until an employment list is produced. Information on the availability and status of immediate openings may be obtained by calling the State Recruitment/Test Center.

Applications

Application Form No. PLD-1 is available from the Recruitment/Test Center of the Personnel Division, Department of Administrative Services, or at any one of the offices of the State Job Service.

Anticipated Eligibility

Candidates engaged in qualifying experience or training but lacking up to six (6) months of the required experience and training will be admitted to the examination but must meet the minimum requirements before appointment. Anticipated eligibility may not apply to those examinations announced without a closing date and administered at least once a month.

Admission to Examination

Admission to an examination may be conditional. Applications may be reviewed for minimum requirements after the examination.

List Usage

Examination results may be used to make original appointments into State service and to promote current permanent State employees. Most lists remain in effect for one (1) year and may be extended for up to an additional two (2) years.

The Personnel Division may postpone the date of any examination. If postponed, notices will be mailed to candidates before the last test date.

Individuals appointed must serve a working test period, in accordance with the provisions of the State Personnel Act or appropriate labor contract. The working test period serves as the final phase of the examination.

Appeal

If your application is rejected, you may appeal by writing to the Personnel Division, Department of Administrative Services within seventeen (17) days of receiving a rejection notice. Your appeal will be heard by a panel, appointed by the Direction of Personnel and Labor Relations, consisting of a Personnel Officer from each of three State agencies with more than one hundred employees. A hearing will take place within sixty (60) days of the date we receive your appeal.

SAMPLE STATE ANNOUNCEMENT #5

Entry Level Security Exam (Correction Officer 8)

Beginning Pay: $

Duties: Including, but not limited to: guarding, supervising, and participating in the custody and security of prisoners in correctional facilities.

Qualification requirements:

Education: 15 semester (or 23 term) college credit hours in one or a combination of the following areas: correction, criminal justice, psychology, sociology, educational psychology, family relations and/or guidance and counseling, pastoral counseling, social work, and law enforcement.

Transcript *must* be presented at the time of application.

Experience: No specific type of amount is required.

Before being hired as a Corrections Officer 8, applicants must pass a physical agility test and a background check conducted by the State Department of Corrections.

Scheduling information: *All* applicants must submit a Civil Service application each time they want to take the exam. Applicants must indicate their qualifying education on the application and specify their interest in the Corrections Officer Exam in the Job Interest portion of the application, or the application will be returned.

Applicants must possess the required educational coursework and must submit transcripts documenting possession of these prerequisites to Civil Service *at the time of application*. Photocopies are acceptable.

If your college transcripts are not submitted with your application, you will not be scheduled for the examination. Applicants may take this exam only once within a twelve-month period.

Applications may be submitted at any time. Applicants will be scheduled for Civil Service examinations based on the hiring needs of the state. Examinations *may* be limited for specific locations in the state.

Examination information: This examination consists of three video-based exam sections. It evaluates skills, knowledge, and abilities related to critical elements of security positions. Each section is scored independently. *A passing score for each section is required to pass the examination.* If you fail the first section, the remaining two sections will not be scored. If you pass the first two and fail the third section, you will still fail the examination. All three section scores must be passing scores. *You must achieve a passing score on all sections of the examination to have your name placed on the employment list.*

	Approximate Examination Time
Section 1: Human Interaction	1 hour and 20 minutes
Section 2: Reading Comprehension	15 minutes
Section 3: Incident Observation Report Writing	30 minutes

Because this is a video based examination, no late admissions will be allowed.

The successful completion of the examination does *not* guarantee a job or an interview.

SAMPLE FEDERAL ANNOUNCEMENT

U.S. Department of Justice
Federal Bureau of Prisons

Correctional Officer

The Bureau of Prisons is an Equal Opportunity Employer

(Revised 4/1996)

Opportunities in the Federal Government
Announcement No. 431 GS-5/6

(Open Until Further Notice)

Submit forms to:

Federal Bureau of Prisons
Examining Section
10010 Junction Dr., Suite 217 South
Annapolis Junction, MD 20701

Salary and Promotion

Correctional Officers are appointed at the GS-5 and GS-6 levels. Salaries of federal employees are adjusted periodically. A strong internal merit promotion system allows excellent advancement opportunities.

Duties

Enforcing the rules and regulations governing the operation of a correctional institution and the confinement, safety, health, and protection of inmates. This may, at time, require arduous physical exertion to subdue unruly inmates who may be armed or assaultive.

Supervising the various work assignments of inmates.

On occasion, Correctional Officers are required to carry firearms and participate as members of the corrections team of Caseworkers, Psychiatrists, Psychologists, Teachers, and others working to help the individual inmate.

Where the Jobs Are

Vacancies may exist in the correctional institutions shown on the Geographic Availability List that is included in the application package.

Benefits

Insurance: You may elect to be covered by group life insurance and health insurance for which the government shares in the cost.

Retirement: Your retirement coverage entitles you to retire at 50 after 20 years or at any age *after* 25 years of Federal law enforcement service. Retirement at age 57 after 20 years of service is mandatory. Retirement contributions and Federal and state taxes are deducted.

Mandatory General Requirements
Citizenship:

Must be a U.S. citizen.

Age:

At time of appointment, applicants must not have reached their 37th birthday unless they have previously served in a Federal civilian law enforcement position covered by special civil service retirement provisions, including early or mandatory retirement. The maximum entry age limit has been established under the authority of Public Law 100-238, and the age limit constitutes an exception to normal age discrimination prohibitions contained in section 15 of the Age Discrimination in Employment Act.

Employment Interview:

All qualified candidates will be subject to an employment interview prior to final selection. Interviews will be held within the general area (approximately 250 miles, round-trip) where the applicants resides. All candidates must pay expenses to the interview site and to their first employment location.

Physical Examination:

All applicants are subject to satisfactory completion of a physical examination.

Security Investigation:

All applicants are subject to satisfactory completion of a Full Field Security Investigation.

Training:

All applicants must successfully complete training provided by the Bureau as follows:

200 hours of formal training within the first year of employment.

120 hours of specialized training at our residential training center located at Glynco, Georgia, within the first 60 days after appointment. The required training includes tests in academics, firearms, and self-defense. All applicants appointed on or after **January 1, 1997,** must also successfully complete physical ability testing.

Miscellaneous Information:

Correctional Officers are required to work weekends and rotating shifts. Additional pay is given for evening, Sunday, and holiday work. Work is performed inside and outside depending on the nature of the assignment. A uniform clothing allowance is provided by the Bureau of Prisons.

Basic Qualification Requirements
No Written Test is Required

Applicants must possess the knowledge, skills, and abilities required for correctional work, and, in addition, demonstrate the possession of personal attributes important to the effectiveness of correctional officers such as:

- Ability to meet and deal with people of differing backgrounds and behavioral patterns.
- Ability to be persuasive in selling and influencing ideas.
- Ability to lead, supervise, and instruct others.
- Ability to reason soundly and to think out practical solutions to problems.
- Ability to make decisions and act quickly, particularly under stress.
- Poise and self-confidence, and ability to remain calm during emergency situations.

GS-05

Full four (4) year course of study in any field leading to a bachelor's degree from an accredited school or possession of a bachelor's degree.

OR

The equivalent of at least three (3) years of full-time general experience performing duties such as providing assistance, guidance and direction to individuals; counseling individuals; responding to emergency situations; supervising or managing; teaching or instructing individuals; or selling products or services (*persuasive commissioned sales*).

Examples of occupations where general experience may have been gained:

- Teacher or instructor
- Counselor
- Worker with juvenile delinquents
- Parole/probation worker
- Welfare/social worker
- Firefighter
- Nurse
- Clergyman
- Emergency medical technician
- Air traffic controller
- Supervisor or manager
- Persuasive salesperson in commissioned sales (*e.g., automobile, insurance, etc.*)
- Security guard
- Children's day care facility worker

GS-06

Nine (9) semester hours or fourteen (14) quarter hours of graduate study, from an accredited school, in Criminal Justice, Criminology, Social Science, or another field of study related to the position such as law.

OR

The equivalent of at least one (1) year of full-time specialized experience performing duties such as ensuring individuals confined in a correctional or mental health facility adhere to the rules and regulations; responding to domestic disturbances; or apprehending and arresting individuals violating the law. Examples of occupations where specialized experience may have been gained:

- Correctional Officer
- Detention Officer
- Police Officer

- Border Patrol Agent
- State Trooper
- Sheriff
- Park Ranger
- Deputy Sheriff supervising inmates in a jail
- Mental Health Residential Facility Worker

NOTE: COMBINATIONS OF EDUCATION AND EXPERIENCE EQUIVALENT TO THE REQUIREMENT AT EACH GRADE LEVEL ARE ACCEPTABLE. PERTINENT UNPAID OR VOLUNTEER EXPERIENCE IS ACCEPTABLE. QUALIFYING PART-TIME EXPERIENCE THAT IS LESS THAN 35 HOURS PER WEEK MUST BE PRO-RATED ON THE BASIS OF A 40 HOUR FULL-TIME WORKWEEK.

Prorating of Education Substitited for Experience

Education *successfully completed* in an accredited college, university or resident school level may be substituted as indicated below.

Thirty (30) semester hours or forty-five (45) quarter hours of undergraduate study is equivalent to nine (9) months of general experience.

A full four-year course of college study (*120 semester hours or 180 quarter hours*) leading to a Bachelor's Degree may be substituted for three (3) years of general experience and is fully qualifying for grade GS-5.

Nine (9) semester hours or fourteen (14) quarter hours of graduate study in Criminal Justice, Criminology, Social Science, or another field of study, related to the position such as law, is fully qualifying for grade GS-6.

Basis of Rating

Qualifications and rating are based on responses reported by the applicant in Block 17 on the Qualifications and Availability Form "C," therefore, respond accurately and completely to each question to ensure that you will get proper credit.

How to Apply

- Submit an application form or resume reflecting the **REQUIRED INFORMATION, SEE ENCLOSURE FOR INFORMATION THAT IS REQUIRED.**

 APPLICATIONS OR RESUMES THAT DO NOT REFLECT ALL THE REQUIRED INFORMATION WILL NOT BE PROCESSED.

 Keep your original application or resume in case you are contacted for an interview. Send the examining section a clear, legible copy bearing an original signature and date.

- OPM Form 1203 AW, Form C *(Qualifications and Availability Form).*

 APPLICATION FORMS CAN BE OBTAINED FROM:

 Federal Bureau of Prisons
 National Recruiting Office
 Room 460
 320 First Street, N.W.
 Washington, DC 20534
 Telephone No. (202) 307-3204

In addition, **IF APPLICABLE,** submit the following:

A. **IF YOU ARE CLAIMING 10 POINT VETERAN PREFERENCE,** submit Standard Form 15 and letter from Veteran's Administration and/or branch of the military (*dated within last 12 months*).

B. **IF YOU HAVE SERVED IN THE MILITARY,** submit DD Form 214.

C. **IF YOU HAVE REACHED YOUR 37TH BIRTHDAY,** submit a copy of Standard Form 50 showing initial appointment to a civilian law enforcement position covered by special Civil Service retirement provisions.

D. **IF YOU HAVE BEEN CONVICTED OF A FELONY OFFENSE,** submit proof of relief of firearms disabilities that expressly authorizes you to possess a firearm.

Length of Eligibility

Initial eligibility period is **12** months.

Eligible competitors who have not been appointed must submit up-to-date information on their qualifications at intervals of not less than **10** and not more than **12** months, if they wish to remain active on the register.

Department of Justice (DOJ) Surplus or Displaced Employees Requesting Special Selection Priority Consideration

If you are currently a DOJ employee who has received a Reduction in Force (RIF) separation notice or a Certificate of Expected Separation, you may be entitled to special priority selection under the Department of Justice's Agency Career Transition Assistance Program (CTAP). To receive this priority consideration you must:

1. Be a current DOJ career or career conditional (tenure group I or II) competitive service employee who has received a RIF separation notice or a Certificate or Expected Separation (CES) *and,* the date of the RIF separation has not passed *and* you are still on the rolls of DOJ. You *must* submit a copy of the RIF separation notice or CES along with your application.

2. Be applying for a position that is at or below the grade level of the position from which you are being separated. The position must not have a great promotion potential than the position from which you are being separated.

3. Have a current (or latest) performance rating or record of at least fully successfully or equivalent. This *must* be submitted with your application package.

4. Be currently employed by DOJ in the same commuting area of the position for which you are requesting priority consideration.

5. File your application by the vacancy announcement closing date and meet all the application criteria and conditions of employment (e.g., submit all required documentation, age requirement, Integrity Interview, Panel Interview, Physical, Vouchering, etc.).

6. Be rated well-qualified for the position. (Score must be 86 or above.)

Displaced Employees Requesting Special Selection Priority Consideration under the Interagency Career Transition Assistance Program (ICTAP)

If you are a displaced Federal employee, you may be entitled to receive special priority selection under the ICTAP. To receive this priority consideration you must:

1. Be a displaced Federal employee. You *must* submit a copy of the appropriate documentation such as a RIF separation notice, a letter from OPM or your agency documenting your priority consideration status with your application package. The following categories of candidates are considered displaced employees.

    A. Current or former career or career-conditional (tenure group I or II) competitive service employees who:

        1. Received a specific RIF separation notice; or

        2. Separated because of a compensable injury, whose compensation has been terminated, and whose former agency certifies that it is unable to place; or

        3. Retired with a disability and whose disability annuity has been or is being terminated; or

        4. Upon receipt of a RIF separation notice retired *on* the effective date of the RIF and submit a Standard From 50 that indicates "Retirement in lieu of RIF"; or

        5. Retired under the discontinued service retirement option; or

        6. Was separated because he/she declined a transfer of function or directed reassignment to another commuting area.

    OR

    B. Former Military Reserve or National Guard Technicians who are receiving a special Office of Personnel Management (OPM) disability retirement annuity under section 8337(h) or 8456 of title 5 United States Code.

2. Be applying for a position at or below the grade level of the position from which you have been separated. The position must not have a greater promotion potential than the position from which you were separated.

3. Have a current (or last) performance rating or record of at least fully successful or equivalent. This *must* be submitted with your application package. (This requirement does not apply to candidates who are eligible due to compensable injury or disability retirement.)

4. Occupy or be displaced from a position in the same local commuting area of the position for which you are requesting priority consideration.

5. File your application by the vacancy announcement closing date and meet all the application criteria and conditions of employment (e.g., submit all required documentation, age requirement, Integrity Interview, Panel Interview, Physical, Vouchering, etc.).

6. Be rated well-qualified for the positions. (Score must be 85 or above.)

DEAR CORRECTIONAL OFFICER APPLICANT:

The Bureau of Prisons Examining Section uses an automated rating system to process applications for the Correctional Officer Register. This system requires applicants to record responses to multiple choice questions on a computerized form (*Qualifications & Availability Form [Form C]*).

FORM "C" IS A SELF REPORTING EXAMINING INSTRUMENT. QUALIFICATIONS AND RATINGS ARE BASED ON THE RESPONSES YOU REPORT, THEREFORE, RESPOND ACCURATELY AND COMPLETELY TO EACH OF THE OCCUPATIONAL QUESTIONS. IT IS EXTREMELY IMPORTANT FOR APPLICANTS TO FOLLOW DIRECTIONS CAREFULLY AND PROVIDE ONLY ONE RESPONSE THAT MOST ACCURATELY REFLECTS YOUR EDUCATION AN/OR EXPERIENCE, TO EACH QUESTION. ALSO, IT IS EXTREMELY IMPORTANT TO THOROUGHLY READ THE ENCLOSED CORRECTIONAL OFFICER ANNOUNCEMENT 431 AND THE "IMPORTANT NOTICE" PRIOR TO COMPLETING FORM C. THE "IMPORTANT NOTICE" PROVIDES INSTRUCTIONS ON HOW TO PROPERLY EVALUATE YOUR

EDUCATION/EXPERIENCE. THESE INSTRUCTIONS MUST BE FOLLOWED IN ORDER TO ACCURATELY REPORT YOUR QUALIFICATIONS ON FORM C. IF THE INSTRUCTIONS ARE NOT FOLLOWED, YOUR NOTICE OF RESULTS WILL NOT REFLECT AN ACCURATE EVALUATION OF YOUR QUALIFICATIONS FOR THE POSITION. YOU MUST ALSO SUBMIT AN APPLICATION OR RESUME REFLECTING THE INFORMATION ON THE "REQUIRED INFORMATION" SHEET.

We appreciate your interest in employment with the Federal Bureau of Prisons. Please do not hesitate to call the Examining Office at (301) 317-5250 or 5251 if you have any questions or if we can be of further assistance.

Important Notice

Qualifying Military Experience Is Evaluated on the Same Basis as Qualifying Civilian Experience

Examples: Experience as a Military Correctional Specialist is evaluated on the same basis as a Civilian Correctional Officer; experience as Military Security Policeman with arrest power is evaluated on the same basis as a Civilian Police Officer with arrest power. Supervisory experience (*whether military or civilian*) is evaluated on the same basis, etc.

Calculating Education Credit

- Education must have been received from an accredited college, university, or resident school.
- Credit is not allowed for courses that were not successfully completed.
- 30 semester hours or 45 quarter hours of *undergraduate* study is equivalent to 1 year of education or 9 months of *general* experience.
- A full four-year course of college study (120 semester hours or 180 quarter hours) leading to a Bachelor's Degree may be substituted for 3 years of *general* experience and is fully qualifying for grade G2-5. (*Credit for a Bachelor's Degree is allowed only if you currently possess the degree or expect to receive it within 9 months.*)
- 9 semester hours or 14 quarter hours of *graduate* study in Criminal Justice, Criminology, Social Science, or another field of study *directly related to the position* such as law, is fully qualifying for grade GS-6.

Calculating Experience Credit

- "Full-time" experience is considered to be 35-40 hours per week.
- "Part-time" experience (*less than 35 hours per week*) must be **PRORATED** based on a 40-hour workweek.

  EXAMPLE: A. Supervisory experience at 20 hours per week for **1** year = **6** months credit allowed.

- Credit is *not* allowed for additional experience, that was gained during the same time frame that is in excess of 40 hours per week.

  EXAMPLE: A. Supervisory experience at 50 hours per week for **1** year = only **1** year credit allowed even though more than 40 hours per week were worked.

  B. Teacher experience at 30 hours per week for 1 year *plus* security guard experience at 20 hours per week for the same year = only **1** year credit allowed because both jobs were worked during the same time frame.

- **Credit is not allowed for internship experience required for a degree.**

- *Equivalent* of 3 years of "full-time" experience means:

The amount of experience, *PRORATED* "part-time" OR "full-time" OR a combination of both, equates to 3 full years. **IT DOES *NOT* MEAN THAT YOU CAN ONLY CREDIT "FULL-TIME" EXPERIENCE**.

EXAMPLES: A.   Supervisory experience at 20 hours per week for 6 years = 3 years credit allowed. (The 6 years of "part-time" experience, when PRORATED, is *equivalent* to 3 years of "full-time" experience.)

                    B.   Counselor experience at 40 hours per week for 2 years = *2 years credit allowed* PLUS Supervisory experience at 20 hours per week for a 2 year period *DIFFERENT* from the time frame for the counselor experience = *1 year credit allowed*. TOTAL: 3 years credit allowed (2 years of "full-time": experience combined with "part-time" experience, when PRORATED, is *equivalent* to 3 years of "full-time" experience.

Calculating Combined Undergraduate Education and General Experience Credit

To combine your undergraduate education and general experience, you must convert each to a percentage and then add them together. Follow Step 1 (Undergraduate Education), Step 2 (General Experience), and Step 3 (Combining Undergraduate Education and General Experience) below. **NOTE: The combined total of your undergraduate education and general experience MUST EQUAL AT LEAST 100% in order to qualify.**

STEP 1—UNDERGRADUATE EDUCATION

Successfully completed education that has not led to a degree is credited on its relationship to 120 semester hours, since 120 semester hours of *progressive* study is equivalent to four years of undergraduate education and meets the basic requirements.

Compare your semester hours to the 120 total semester hours needed and convert it to a percentage. Compute the percentage by using the following formula:

FORMULA: YOUR NUMBER OF UNDERGRADUATE SEMESTER HOURS: 120

(If your school is on a quarter system, you may convert quarter hours to semester hours by using the following):

$$\frac{(2 \times \#\text{Qtr hrs} = \text{Semester hours})}{3 \qquad\qquad 1}$$

EXAMPLES:

If you have 30 semester hours, 30 ÷ 120 = .25 (25%)

If you have 60 semester hours, 60 ÷ 120 = .50 (50%)

If you have 90 semester hours, 90 ÷ 120 = .75 (75%)

If you have 120 semester hours, 120 ÷ 120 = 1.00 (100%)

Thus, 30 semester hours of progressive study is comparable to one year of undergraduate education, 60 semester hours of progressive study is comparable to two years of undergraduate education, and 90 semester hours of progressive study is comparable to three years of undergraduate education.

STEP 2—GENERAL EXPERIENCE

Note that it is not enough to just have experience, it must be the **right kind** of experience. Study the description of general experience on the Announcement 431, decide if your experience corresponds to any of the descriptions, then convert your general experience to a percentage. Determine your percentage of qualifying general experience that will be combined with your percentage of undergraduate education by using the formula below:

FORMULA: YOUR NUMBER OF MONTHS OF GENERAL EXPERIENCE ÷ 36

EXAMPLES:

If you have 6 months of the right kind of general experience, $6 \div 36 = .166$ (16.6%)

If you have 26 months of the right kind of general experience, $26 \div 36 = .72$ (72%)

If you have 32 months of the right kind of general experience, $32 \div 36 = .888$ (88.8%)

STEP 3—COMBINING UNDERGRADUATE EDUCATION AND GENERAL EXPERIENCE

Now take your percentage of undergraduate education and your percentage of general experience and add them together. In order to meet requirements through a combination of education and experience, **the total of the two percentages must be at least 100%.** You do not meet the requirements if your total is less than 100%.

EXAMPLE 1:

Undergraduate education totaled 62 semester hours. (Formula: $62 \div 12 = .516$ or 52%)

General experience totaled 18 months. (Formula: $18 \div 36 = .500$ or 50%)

Total: 52% = 50% = 102% (**100% or more = Qualified**)

EXAMPLE 2:

Undergraduate education totaled 30 semester hours. (Formula: $30 \div 120 = .025$ or 25%)

General experience totaled 20 months. (Formula: $20 \div 36 = .555$ or 56%)

Total: 25% + 56% = 81% (**Less than 100% = Not Qualified**)

To combine your graduate education and specialized experience, you must convert each to a percentage and then add them together. Follow Step 1 (Graduate Education), Step 2 (Specialized Experience), and Step 3 (Combining Graduate Education and Specialized Experience) below.

STEP 1—GRADUATE EDUCATION

Determine how many years of graduate level study you possess. (Refer to the instructions above on "Graduate Education"—Defining an Academic Year.)

STEP 2—SPECIALIZED EXPERIENCE

Experience is credited based on its relationship to one year of specialized experience. Note that it is not enough to just have experience, it must be the *right kind* of experience. Study the descriptions of specialized experience on the Announcement 431, decide if your experience corresponds to any of the descriptions, then convert your specialized experience to a percentage if it is less than a year. Since one year of specialized experience equals 100%, compute your qualifying experience as a percentage of the one year of specialized experience required by using the following formula:

FORMULA: YOUR NUMBER OF MONTHS OF SPECIALIZED EXPERIENCE: 12

EXAMPLES:

If you have 3 months of the necessary specialized experience: $3 \div 12 = .25$ (25%)

If you have 6 months of the necessary specialized experience: $6 \div 12 = .50$ (50%)

If you have 9 months of the necessary specialized experience: $9 \div 12 = .75$ (75%)

STEP 3—COMBINING GRADUATE EDUCATION AND SPECIALIZED EXPERIENCE

Now take the percentage of graduate education and your percentage of specialized experience and add them together. In order to meet requirements through a combination of education and experience, *the total of the two percentages must be at least 100%*. You do not meet the requirements if your results total less than 100%.

EXAMPLE 1:

Your *graduate education* totaled 33%

Your *specialized experience* totaled 50%

TOTAL: 33% + 50% = 83% (LESS THAN 100% = NOT QUALIFIED)

EXAMPLE 2:

Your *graduate education* totaled 83%

Your *specialized experience* totaled 33%

TOTAL: 83% + 33% = 116% (100% OR MORE = QUALIFIED)

Required Information

(Must Be Typed or Printed Legibly in Ink)

JOB INFORMATION

- Announcement number, title, and grade of the job you are applying for.
- Full name, mailing address (include ZIP code), and home and work telephone numbers (include area codes).
- Social Security Number and birth date.
- Citizenship. (Most Federal jobs require United States citizenship.)
- Veteran's preference. (Form SF-15, Claim for 10-point Veteran's preference and supporting proof if you are claiming preference.)

EDUCATION

- High school name, city, and state (ZIP code if known) of high school where you earned diploma or GED (give dates).
- College
  - name, city and state (ZIP code if known),
  - majors,
  - type and year of any degrees, or
  - if no degree, show courses and credit hours earned (indicate semester or quarter).

WORK EXPERIENCE

- Give the following for each job related paid or non-paid civilian or military work experience. (Do not send job descriptions.)
  - job title (and series and grade if Federal job),
  - duties and accomplishments,
  - employer's name and address,

- supervisor's name and telephone number,
- starting and ending dates,
- hours worked per week, and
- salary
- Indicate if we may contact your current supervisor.

APPLICATIONS OR RESUMES THAT DO NOT REFLECT ALL THE REQUIRED INFORMATION WILL NOT BE PROCESSED.

Questionnaire for Correctional Officer GS-007-5/6

Instructions

In this booklet you will be asked to provide information regarding your education and experience as it relates to the work of a Correctional Officer. Please use a #2 pencil to mark your responses on the Qualifications & Availability Form (Form C). Return the Form C and any additional forms requested to our office.

Enter the following to complete the Form C:

Section 1:	Your name
Section 2:	Correctional Officer
Section 3:	431
Section 4:	0007 C
Section 5:	Leave blank
Section 6:	05 or 06 (the lowest grade you will accept) - GS-5 is the lowest grade covered
Section 7:	Self explanatory - Parts A through D; See instructions for Part E
Section 8:	001
Section 9:	See the **Geographic Availability Form** for instructions
Section 10-16:	Self explanatory
Section 17:	See the **OCCUPATIONAL QUESTIONS**
Section 18:	Leave blank
Section 19:	Enter the code(s) that correspond to the foreign language(s) you speak fluently. If you do not speak any of these foreign languages fluently, **LEAVE THIS BLOCK BLANK.**

01-Spanish   03-Chinese   05-Japanese
02-Arabic   04-French

Section 20:	Date of birth
Section 21:	Enter 001 if you are female
Section 22:	Omit
Section 23-26:	Self explanatory. If you answer yes to number 2, 3, or 4, in item 24, provide a detailed narrative explanation of the circumstances, names and addresses of courts and individuals involved, dates, and locations with the Form C.

WARNING!!! YOUR ANSWERS WILL BE VERIFIED AGAINST THE NARRATIVE INFORMATION YOU PROVIDE IN YOUR RESUME OR APPLICATION AND INFORMATION YOUR REFERENCES PROVIDE. ADDITIONALLY, A BACKGROUND INVESTIGATION WILL BE CONDUCTED THAT INCLUDES CHECKS WITH LAW ENFORCEMENT ORGANIZATIONS, FORMER EMPLOYERS, CO-WORKERS, SCHOOLS, REFERENCES, NEIGHBORS, ETC. FALSIFYING YOUR BACKGROUND, EDUCATION, AND EXPERIENCE IS CAUSE FOR NOT HIRING YOU AND BARRING

YOU FROM APPLYING FOR FEDERAL EMPLOYMENT. THEREFORE, CAREFULLY
ENTER THE INFORMATION THAT ACCURATELY REFLECTS YOUR ACTUAL EM-
PLOYMENT AND/OR EDUCATIONAL BACKGROUND.

Employment Availability

INSTRUCTIONS FOR COMPLETING SECTION 7 (EMPLOYMENT AVAILABILITY,
PART E), OTHER EMPLOYMENT QUESTIONS (OEM) ON THE QUALIFICATIONS
AND AVAILABILITY FORM (FORM C).

Question 1:   Are you currently a Department of Justice (DOJ) employee who has been
declared surplus **AND** requesting special priority selection consideration under
the DOG Agency Career Transition Assistance Program (CTAP)?

A=YES   B=NO

Question 2:   Are you a displaced federal employee who is requesting special priority selection consideration under the Interagency Career Transition Assistance Program
(ICTAP)?

A=YES   B=NO

(**NOTE:** If your answer is **YES** to either questions 1 or 2, you must meet the CTAP or ICTAP
eligibility requirements **AND** submit supporting proof documentation. Refer to the Special Selection Consideration Provisions for Surplus or Displaced Federal Employees section of the vacancy
announcement for additional information.)

Geographic Availability Form

INSTRUCTIONS FOR COMPLETING SECTION 9 (GEOGRAPHIC AVAILABILITY)
ON THE QUALIFICATIONS & AVAILABILITY FORM (FORM C).

The listing of the geographic codes on the reverse side of this sheet are separated into
two columns. You may select only one (1) location from column 1. This will be considered your first choice location preference. Enter the three digit location code number
that appears in column 1 in the three spaces designated as number 1 in section 9 on
Form C. Blacken the corresponding oval below each number you have entered.

You may select two (2) locations from column 2 (you do not have to select any from this
column if you do not want to be considered for other than your first choice location). If
you wish to select one (1) location from column 2, enter the corresponding three digit
location code number in the three spaces designated as number 2 in section 9 on Form
C. Blacken the corresponding oval below each number you have entered. If 2 selections
are made from column 2, the second selection location code number should be entered
in the three spaces designated as 3 in section 9 on Form C, and the corresponding oval
below each number you have entered should be blackened. APPLICANTS MAY BE
REFERRED TO THEIR SECOND AND THEIR CHOICE LOCATION PREFER-
ENCES ONLY WHEN THERE ARE INSUFFICIENT FIRST CHOICE APPLICANTS
AVAILABLE FOR THOSE LOCATIONS.

YOU MAY SELECT A MAXIMUM OF THREE LOCATIONS.

SELECT ONLY THOSE LOCATIONS WHERE YOU ARE WILLING TO ACCEPT
EMPLOYMENT.

IF YOU REFUSE EMPLOYMENT CONSIDERATION AT ANY LOCATION THAT
YOU INDICATE YOU ARE AVAILABLE FOR, YOUR NAME WILL BE REMOVED
FROM THE REGISTER OF ELIGIBLE CANDIDATES.

You may select only one (1) location from column 1 (First Choice), and up to two locations from columns 2 (Second Choice). Blacken the corresponding oval(s) in clock 9 on the Qualifications & Employment Availability Form (Form C).

	COLUMN 1	COLUMN 2		COLUMN 1	COLUMN 2
Ashland, KY-FCI	001	051	Fort Worth, TX-FMC	042	092
Englewood, CO-FCI	002	052	Tucson, AZ-FCI	043	093
Morgantown, WV-FCI	003	053	Rochester, MN-FMC	044	094
El Reno, OK-FCI	004	054	Duluth, MN-FPC	045	095
Lompoc, CA-USP	005	055	Loretto, PA-FCI	046	096
Milan, MI-FCI	006	056	Oakdale, LA-FCI	047	097
Petersburg, VA-FCI	007	057	Los Angeles, CA-MDC	048	098
Seagoville, TX-FCI	008	058	Marianna, FL-FCI	050	100
Tallahassee, FL-FCI	009	059	Fairton, NJ-FCI	101	201
Dublin, CA-FCI	010	060	Sheridan, OR-FCI	102	202
Lexington, KY-FMC	011	061	McKean, PA-FCI	103	203
Oxford, WI-FCI	012	062	Jesup, GA-FCI	104	204
Miami, FL-FCI	013	063	Pensacola, FL-FPC	105	205
Bastrop, TX-FCI	014	064	Yankton, SD-FPC	106	206
Memphis, TX-FCI	015	065	Coleman, FL-FCC	107	207
Talladega, AL-FCI	016	066	*Taft, CA-FCI (10/96)	108	208
Atlanta, GA-USP	017	067	Bryan, TX-FPC	109	209
Leavenworth, KS-USP	018	068	Lompoc, CA-FPC	110	210
Lewisburg, PA-USP	019	069	El Paso, TX FPC	111	211
*Forrest City, AZ-FCC (9/96)	020	070	*Yazoo City, MS-FCI (10/96)	112	212
Marion, IL-USP	021	071	Las Vegas, NV-FPC	113	213
Terre Haute, IN-USP	022	072	Waseca, MN-FCI	114	214
Ray Brook, NY-FCI	023	073	Seymour Johnson, NC-FPC	115	215
Otisville, NY-FCI	024	074	*Elkton, OH-FCI (10/96)	116	216
Danbury, CT-FCI	025	075	*Seatac, WA-FDC (10/96)	117	217
La Tuna, TX-FCI	026	076	Oakdale II, LA-FDC	118	218
Sandstone, MN-FCI	027	077	Three Rivers, TX-FCI	119	219
Terminal Island, CA-FCI	028	078	Schuylkill, PA-FCI	120	220
Texarkana, TX-FCI	029	079	Manchester, KY-FCI	121	221
Boron, CA-FPC	030	080	Guaynabo, PR-MDC	122	222
Big Springs, TX-FCI	031	081	Florence, CO-FCC	125	225
Eglin, FL-FPC	032	082	Estill, SC-FCI	126	226
Phoenix, AZ-FCI	033	083	Allenwood, PA-FCC	127	227

	COLUMN 1	2		COLUMN 1	2
Montgomery, AL-FPC	034	084	Brooklyn, NY-MDC	128	228
Safford, AZ-FCI	035	085	Miami, FL	129	229
Chicago, IL-MCC	036	086	Ft. Dix, NJ-FCC	130	230
San Diego, CA-MCC	037	087	Greenville, IL-FCI	131	231
New York, NY-MCC	038	088	Pekin, IL-FCI	132	232
Alderson, WV-FPC	039	089	Cumberland, MD-FCI	133	233
Springfield, MO-MCFP	040	090	Carse-FMC (Ft. Worth, TX)	134	234
Butner, NC-FCC	041	091	Beckley, WV-FCI	135	235
Oklahoma City, OK-FTC	136	236	*Beaumont, TX-FCC (8/96)	137	237

*Anticipated to open dates

Occupational Questions

(Enter Responses in Section 17 on Form C)

1. Choose one statement from the descriptions below that best describes you. Darken the oval corresponding to that statement in Section 17 on the Form C. **Please select only one letter.**

   A. I am under the age of 37.

   B. I am 37 years of age or older, and I have held a Federal civilian law enforcement position covered by special civil service retirement provisions. A copy of my Standard Form 50 showing my previous appointment is enclosed with my application package.

   C. I am 37 years of age or older, and I have not held a Federal civilian law enforcement position. **STOP HERE.** You do not meet a condition of employment based on Public Law 100-238 that allows the establishment of a maximum entry age limit.

2. Choose one statement from the descriptions below that best describes you. Darken the oval corresponding to that statement in Section 17 on the Form C. **Please select only one letter.**

   A. I have never been convicted of a felony offense.

   B. I have been convicted of a felony offense, but I have proof of relief of firearms disabilities that expressly authorizes me to carry a firearm. Proof of relief of firearms disabilities is enclosed with my application package.

   C. I have been convicted of a felony offense, and I do not have proof of relief firearms disabilities. **STOP HERE.** You do not meet a condition of employment based on the Omnibus "Crime Control and Safe Streets Act" that prohibits felons/ex-felons from possessing firearms.

From the responses below, select the one that most closely and accurately describes the **HIGHEST** level of education and/or experience you possess and demonstrates your ability to perform correctional officer work. Reference Correctional Officer Announcement 431 to review the Basic Qualification Requirements for the GS-5 and GS-6 grade levels prior to making your selection. **Please select only one letter** (A, B, C, D, E, F, G, H, *or* I).

   A. I have completed at least 9 semester hours or 14 quarter hours of graduate level education in criminal justice, criminology, social science or another field of study related to the position such as law.

B. I will complete within nine months at least 9 semester hours or 14 quarter hours of graduate level education in criminal justice, criminology, social science or another field of study <u>related to the position</u> such as law.

C. I have completed at least 4 years of undergraduate study leading to a Bachelor's Degree.

D. I will complete within nine months at least 4 years of undergraduate study leading to a Bachelor's Degree.

E. I have completed the equivalent of at least 1 year of full-time work experience performing duties such as ensuring individuals confined in a correctional or mental health facility adhere to the rules and regulations; responding to domestic disturbances; or apprehending and arresting individuals violating the law. **See the "IMPORTANT NOTICE" to determine if you meet the requirements of this response.** Examples of occupations where this experience may have been gained:

Correctional Officer

Detention Officer

Police Officer

Border Patrol Agent

State Trooper

Sheriff

Park Ranger

Deputy Sheriff supervising inmates in a jail

Mental Health Residential Facility Worker

F. I have completed the equivalent of at least 3 years of full-time work experience performing duties such as providing assistance, guidance and direction to individuals; counseling individuals; responding to emergency situations; supervising or managing, teaching or instructing individuals; or selling products or services (persuasive commissioned sales). **See the "IMPORTANT NOTICE" to determine if you meet the requirements of this response.** Examples of occupations where this experience may have been gained:

Teacher or instructor

Counselor

Worker with juvenile delinquents

Parole/probation worker

Welfare/social worker

Firefighter

Nurse

Clergyman

Emergency medical technician

Air traffic controller

Supervisor or manager

Persuasive salesperson in commissioned sales (e.g., automobile, insurance, etc.)

Security guard

Children's day care facility worker

G. I have a combination of graduate education of the type described in A or B and experience of the type described in E that totals 1 year. **See the "IMPORTANT**

NOTICE" on how to combine education & experience and to determine if you meet the requirements of the response.

H.   I have a combination of undergraduate education of the type described in C or D and experience of the type described in F that totals 3 years. **See the "IMPORTANT NOTICE" on how to combine education & experience and to determine if you meet the requirements of this response.**

I.   I do not have any education or experience as described above.

4.   From the responses below, select only one letter that contains the provision which most closely and accurately described the **HIGHEST** level of education and/or experience you possess. Reference Correction Officer Announcement 431 to review GENERAL EDUCATION/EXPERIENCE at the GS-5 grade level and SPECIALIZED EDUCATION/ EXPERIENCE at the GS-6 grade level prior to making your selection. **Please select only one letter** (A, B, C, *or* D).

A.   I have completed, or will complete within nine months, 9 semester hours or 14 quarter hours of graduate level education in criminal justice, criminology or law.

OR

I have completed the equivalent of at least 1 year of full-time work experience performing duties such as ensuring individuals confined in a correctional or mental health facility adhere to the rules and regulations; responding to domestic disturbances; or apprehending and arresting individuals violating the law. **See the "IMPORTANT NOTICE" to determine if you meet this provision.** Examples of occupations where this experience may have been gained:

> Correctional Officer
>
> Detention Officer
>
> Police Officer
>
> Border Patrol Agent
>
> State Trooper
>
> Sheriff
>
> Park Ranger
>
> Deputy Sheriff supervising inmates in a jail
>
> Mental Health Residential Facility Worker

OR

I have a combination of the type of graduate education and experience as described above. **See the "IMPORTANT NOTICE" on how to combine education & experience and to determine if you meet this provision.**

B.   I have completed, or will complete within nine months, 9 semester hours or 14 quarter hours of graduate level education in a social science.

OR

I have completed, or will complete within nine months, at least four years of undergraduate study leading to a Bachelor's Degree in criminal justice.

OR

I have completed the equivalent of at least 6 months of full-time work experience performing duties such as ensuring individuals confined in a correctional or mental health facility adhere to the rules and regulations; responding to domestic disturbances; or apprehending and arresting individuals violating the law. **See the "IMPORTANT NOTICE" to determine if you meet this provision.** Examples of occupations where this experience may have been gained:

Correctional Officer

Detention Officer

Police Officer

Border Patrol Agent

State Trooper

Sheriff

Park Ranger

Deputy Sheriff supervising inmates in a jail

Mental Health Residential Facility Worker

OR

I have a combination of the type of education and experience as described above. **See the "IMPORTANT NOTICE" on how to combine this education & experience and to determine if you meet this provision.** Examples of occupations where this experience may have been gained:

Teacher

Counselor

Worker with juvenile delinquents

Parole/probation worker

Welfare/social worker

Firefighter

Nurse

Emergency medical technician

Air traffic controller

OR

I have a combination of the type of education and experience as described above. **See the "IMPORTANT NOTICE" on how to combine this education & experience and to determine if you meet this provision.**

D. I have completed or will complete within nine months, at least four years of study leading to a Bachelor's Degree in any field *other than* criminal justice, law, social science, or criminology.

OR

I have completed the equivalent of at least 3 years of full-time work experience performing duties such as supervising or managing co-workers or subordinates in a non-correctional environment; selling products or services to the public (persuasive commissioned sales); or maintaining security of buildings or property. **See the "IMPORTANT NOTICE" to determine if you meet this provision.** Examples of occupations where this experience may have been gained:

Supervisor or manager

Persuasive sales person in commissioned sales (e.g., automobile, insurance, etc.)

Security guard

Children's day care facility worker

OR

I have a combination of the type of education and experience as described above. **See the "IMPORTANT NOTICE" on how to combine this education & experience and to determine if you meet this provision.**

5. Select **one** response that most accurately describes your level of experience and ability to supervise:

    A.   I have ensured individuals confined in a correctional or mental health facility adhere to the rules and regulations.

    B.   I have supervised or managed co-workers, subordinates or detainees in a non-correctional environment.

    C.   I have led work teams or work crews.

    D.   I have no experience supervising, managing or leading individuals.

6. Select **one** response that most accurately describes your level of experience and ability to communicate verbally.

    A.   I have routinely provided verbal instructions directly to individuals confined in a correctional or mental health facility.

    B.   I have verbally conveyed the views of organizations or individuals to second parties; counseled or advised individuals who need guidance or direction; or verbally coordinated team efforts.

    C.   I have verbally conveyed work assignments, instructions and training directly to individuals in a non-correctional environment.

    D.   I have no experience demonstrating the ability to communicate verbally.

7. Select **one** response that most accurately describes your level of experience and ability to react to a crisis situation.

    A.   I have resolved or prevented serious disturbances or provided emergency assistance to individuals confined in a correctional or mental health facility. This may have included breaking up fights or resolving arguments among individuals before the situation escalates.

    B.   I have occasionally resolved or prevented potentially serious disturbances or provided emergency assistance to individuals in a non-correctional environment. This may have included providing health care to patients in hospital emergency rooms, responding to domestic disturbance calls or fighting fires.

    C.   I have met production quotas or deadlines.

    D.   I have no experience demonstrating the ability to react to crisis situations.

RETURN TO THE INSTRUCTIONS FOR COMPLETING SECTIONS 18 THROUGH 26 OF FORM C.

READ BEFORE COMPLETING BLOCK 17 ON FORM C

PLEASE NOTE THAT THE *HIGHEST* GRADE LEVEL OR CORRECTIONAL OFFICER POSITIONS COVERED UNDER ANNOUNCEMENT 431 IS *GS-6*, AND THE *LOWEST* GRADE LEVEL IS *GS-5*.

In response to questions 3 and 4 of the "Occupational Questions," applicants are instructed to select the one statement that most closely and accurately describes the *HIGHEST* level of education and/or experience they possess.

Therefore, you must compare your education and/or experience to the descriptions and examples of qualifying duties, for each grade level, in order to determine your *HIGHEST* level of education and/or experience. If you possess qualifying education and/or experience described for both the GS-5 and GS-6 grade levels, respond to questions 3 and 4 of the "Occupational Questions" by selecting one statement for each question that describes the qualifying education and/or experience you possess for the GS-6 grade level.

EXAMPLE: An applicant's qualifications include both a Bachelor's Degree in Criminal Justice and at least one full year of full time Correctional Office experience.

The Bachelor's Degree is qualifying education for the GS-5 (LOWEST) grade level.

The Correctional Officer experience is qualifying experience for the GS-6 (HIGHEST) grade level.

Thus, this applicant should respond to question 3 and 4 of the "Occupational Questions" by selecting the one statement, for each questions, that describes/lists Correctional Officer experience, because it is the applicant's *HIGHEST* level of education and/or experience (qualifying for the GS-6 grade level).

PLEASE REFERENCE CORRECTIONAL OFFICER ANNOUNCEMENT 431 TO REVIEW THE DESCRIPTIONS AND EXAMPLES OF QUALIFYING EDUCATION AND/OR EXPERIENCE FOR EACH (GS-5 AND GS-6) GRADE LEVEL *PRIOR* TO RESPONDING TO QUESTIONS 3 AND 4 OF THE "OCCUPATIONAL QUESTIONS."

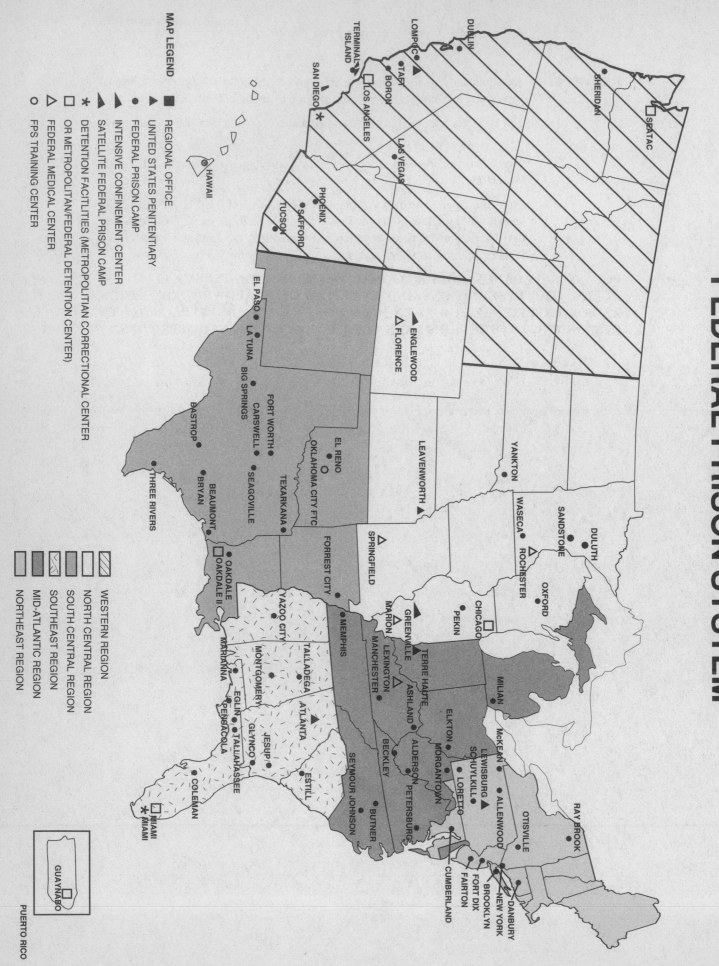

FEDERAL PRISON SYSTEM

MAP LEGEND

- ■ REGIONAL OFFICE
- ▶ UNITED STATES PENITENTIARY
- • FEDERAL PRISON CAMP
- ◤ INTENSIVE CONFINEMENT CENTER
- ◣ SATELLITE FEDERAL PRISON CAMP
- ✻ DETENTION FACILITIES (METROPOLITIAN CORRECTIONAL CENTER OR METROPOLITAN/FEDERAL DETENTION CENTER)
- □ FEDERAL MEDICAL CENTER
- △ FPS TRAINING CENTER

WESTERN REGION
NORTH CENTRAL REGION
SOUTH CENTRAL REGION
SOUTHEAST REGION
MID-ATLANTIC REGION
NORTHEAST REGION

PUERTO RICO
GUAYNABO

U.S. OFFICE OF PERSONNEL MANAGEMENT
QUALIFICATIONS & AVAILABILITY FORM

FORM APPROVED
OMB No. 3206-0040

FORM C

PRINT YOUR RESPONSE IN THE BOXES AND BLACKEN IN THE APPROPRIATE OVALS.

USE A NO. 2 PENCIL

DO NOT FOLD, STAPLE, TEAR OR PAPER CLIP THIS FORM.
DO NOT SUBMIT PHOTOCOPIES OF THIS FORM.
We can process this form only if you:
- Use a number 2 lead pencil.
- Completely blacken each oval you choose.
- Completely erase any mistakes or stray marks.

EXAMPLES

CORRECT MARK

INCORRECT MARKS

1 YOUR NAME: _____

2 JOB APPLYING FOR: _____

3 ANNOUNCEMENT NUMBER: _____

FOLLOW THE DIRECTIONS ON THE "FORM C INSTRUCTION SHEET"

4 OCCUPATION (OCC)

5 CASE NO. (CNO)

6 LOWEST GRADE (LAG)

7 EMPLOYMENT AVAILABILITY

ARE YOU AVAILABLE FOR:

	YES	NO		YES	NO
A) full-time employment		(FTE)	D) jobs requiring travel		(TRV)
-40 hours per week?	Y	N	away from home for		
			-1 to 5 nights/month?	Y	N
B) part-time employment of	(PTE)		-6 to 10 nights/month?	Y	N
-16 or fewer hrs/week?	Y	N	-11 plus nights/month?	Y	N
-17 to 24 hrs/week?	Y	N			
-25 to 32 hrs/week?	Y	N	E) other employment questions		
C) temporary employment			(see directions)		(OEM)
lasting	(TMP)		Question 1?	Y	N
-less than 1 month?	Y	N	Question 2?	Y	N
-1 to 4 months?	Y	N	Question 3?	Y	N
-5 to 12 months?	Y	N	Question 4?	Y	N

8 (OSP) OCCUPATIONAL SPECIALTIES

9 (GFP) GEOGRAPHIC AVAILABILITY

2109418

OPM FORM 1203-AW (7-92)

★U.S. GOVERNMENT PRINTING OFFICE: 1995-398-363

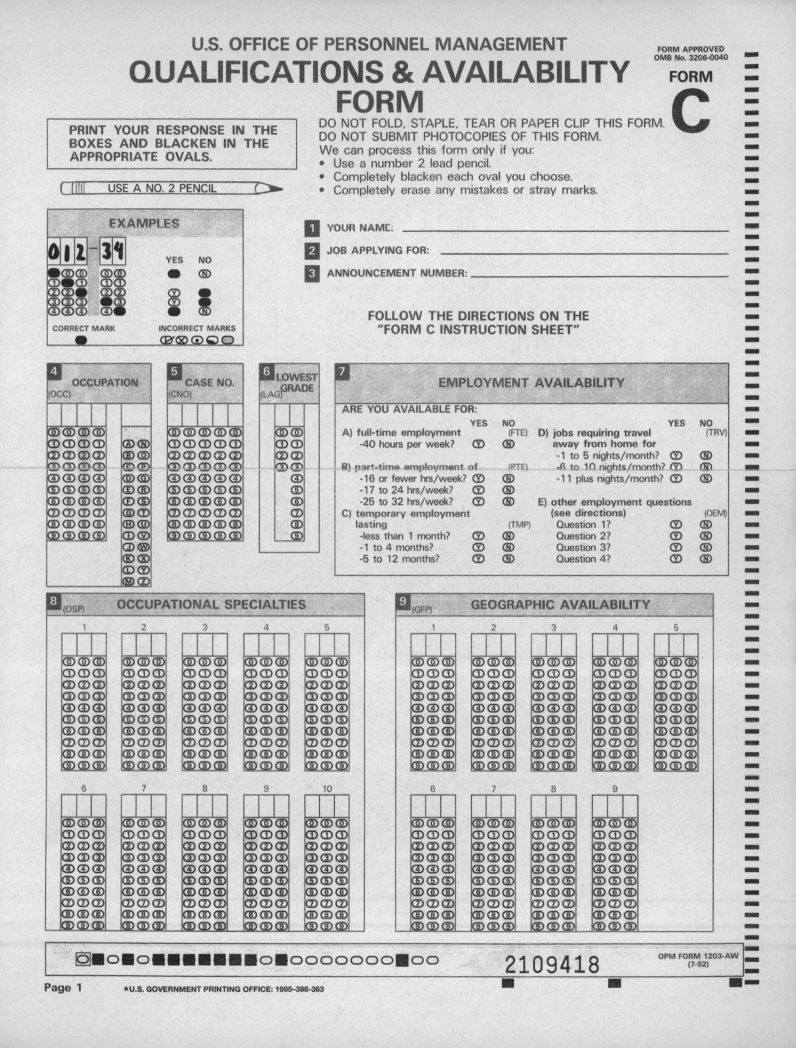

10 FIRST NAME (FNM)   MI (MIN)   LAST NAME (LNM)

11 SOCIAL SECURITY NUMBER (SSN)

12 TELEPHONE NUMBER (TEL)   AREA CODE   CONTACT TIME (TCT)

○ Day

○ Night

○ Either

13 STREET, ADDRESS (HOUSE NUMBER AND STREET AND APT. NO., WHERE YOU WANT TO RECEIVE MAIL.) (ADR)

LEAVE BLANK COLUMN BETWEEN NUMBER, STREET, NAME, ETC.

14 CITY (CTY)

15 STATE CODE (STE)

IF OUTSIDE THE U.S.A. BLACKEN "OV" AND PRINT COUNTRY HERE

USE STANDARD STATE CODES

16 ZIP CODE + 4 (ZIP)   OPTIONAL

17 (OCQ) OCCUPATIONAL QUESTIONS

1 (A)(B)(C)(D)(E)(F)(G)(H)(I)	41 (A)(B)(C)(D)(E)(F)(G)(H)(I)	81 (A)(B)(C)(D)(E)(F)(G)(H)(I)	121 (A)(B)(C)(D)(E)(F)(G)(H)(I)
2 (A)(B)(C)(D)(E)(F)(G)(H)(I)	42 (A)(B)(C)(D)(E)(F)(G)(H)(I)	82 (A)(B)(C)(D)(E)(F)(G)(H)(I)	122 (A)(B)(C)(D)(E)(F)(G)(H)(I)
3 (A)(B)(C)(D)(E)(F)(G)(H)(I)	43 (A)(B)(C)(D)(E)(F)(G)(H)(I)	83 (A)(B)(C)(D)(E)(F)(G)(H)(I)	123 (A)(B)(C)(D)(E)(F)(G)(H)(I)
4 (A)(B)(C)(D)(E)(F)(G)(H)(I)	44 (A)(B)(C)(D)(E)(F)(G)(H)(I)	84 (A)(B)(C)(D)(E)(F)(G)(H)(I)	124 (A)(B)(C)(D)(E)(F)(G)(H)(I)
5 (A)(B)(C)(D)(E)(F)(G)(H)(I)	45 (A)(B)(C)(D)(E)(F)(G)(H)(I)	85 (A)(B)(C)(D)(E)(F)(G)(H)(I)	125 (A)(B)(C)(D)(E)(F)(G)(H)(I)
6 (A)(B)(C)(D)(E)(F)(G)(H)(I)	46 (A)(B)(C)(D)(E)(F)(G)(H)(I)	86 (A)(B)(C)(D)(E)(F)(G)(H)(I)	126 (A)(B)(C)(D)(E)(F)(G)(H)(I)
7 (A)(B)(C)(D)(E)(F)(G)(H)(I)	47 (A)(B)(C)(D)(E)(F)(G)(H)(I)	87 (A)(B)(C)(D)(E)(F)(G)(H)(I)	127 (A)(B)(C)(D)(E)(F)(G)(H)(I)
8 (A)(B)(C)(D)(E)(F)(G)(H)(I)	48 (A)(B)(C)(D)(E)(F)(G)(H)(I)	88 (A)(B)(C)(D)(E)(F)(G)(H)(I)	128 (A)(B)(C)(D)(E)(F)(G)(H)(I)
9 (A)(B)(C)(D)(E)(F)(G)(H)(I)	49 (A)(B)(C)(D)(E)(F)(G)(H)(I)	89 (A)(B)(C)(D)(E)(F)(G)(H)(I)	129 (A)(B)(C)(D)(E)(F)(G)(H)(I)
10 (A)(B)(C)(D)(E)(F)(G)(H)(I)	50 (A)(B)(C)(D)(E)(F)(G)(H)(I)	90 (A)(B)(C)(D)(E)(F)(G)(H)(I)	130 (A)(B)(C)(D)(E)(F)(G)(H)(I)
11 (A)(B)(C)(D)(E)(F)(G)(H)(I)	51 (A)(B)(C)(D)(E)(F)(G)(H)(I)	91 (A)(B)(C)(D)(E)(F)(G)(H)(I)	131 (A)(B)(C)(D)(E)(F)(G)(H)(I)
12 (A)(B)(C)(D)(E)(F)(G)(H)(I)	52 (A)(B)(C)(D)(E)(F)(G)(H)(I)	92 (A)(B)(C)(D)(E)(F)(G)(H)(I)	132 (A)(B)(C)(D)(E)(F)(G)(H)(I)
13 (A)(B)(C)(D)(E)(F)(G)(H)(I)	53 (A)(B)(C)(D)(E)(F)(G)(H)(I)	93 (A)(B)(C)(D)(E)(F)(G)(H)(I)	133 (A)(B)(C)(D)(E)(F)(G)(H)(I)
14 (A)(B)(C)(D)(E)(F)(G)(H)(I)	54 (A)(B)(C)(D)(E)(F)(G)(H)(I)	94 (A)(B)(C)(D)(E)(F)(G)(H)(I)	134 (A)(B)(C)(D)(E)(F)(G)(H)(I)
15 (A)(B)(C)(D)(E)(F)(G)(H)(I)	55 (A)(B)(C)(D)(E)(F)(G)(H)(I)	95 (A)(B)(C)(D)(E)(F)(G)(H)(I)	135 (A)(B)(C)(D)(E)(F)(G)(H)(I)
16 (A)(B)(C)(D)(E)(F)(G)(H)(I)	56 (A)(B)(C)(D)(E)(F)(G)(H)(I)	96 (A)(B)(C)(D)(E)(F)(G)(H)(I)	136 (A)(B)(C)(D)(E)(F)(G)(H)(I)
17 (A)(B)(C)(D)(E)(F)(G)(H)(I)	57 (A)(B)(C)(D)(E)(F)(G)(H)(I)	97 (A)(B)(C)(D)(E)(F)(G)(H)(I)	137 (A)(B)(C)(D)(E)(F)(G)(H)(I)
18 (A)(B)(C)(D)(E)(F)(G)(H)(I)	58 (A)(B)(C)(D)(E)(F)(G)(H)(I)	98 (A)(B)(C)(D)(E)(F)(G)(H)(I)	138 (A)(B)(C)(D)(E)(F)(G)(H)(I)
19 (A)(B)(C)(D)(E)(F)(G)(H)(I)	59 (A)(B)(C)(D)(E)(F)(G)(H)(I)	99 (A)(B)(C)(D)(E)(F)(G)(H)(I)	139 (A)(B)(C)(D)(E)(F)(G)(H)(I)
20 (A)(B)(C)(D)(E)(F)(G)(H)(I)	60 (A)(B)(C)(D)(E)(F)(G)(H)(I)	100 (A)(B)(C)(D)(E)(F)(G)(H)(I)	140 (A)(B)(C)(D)(E)(F)(G)(H)(I)
21 (A)(B)(C)(D)(E)(F)(G)(H)(I)	61 (A)(B)(C)(D)(E)(F)(G)(H)(I)	101 (A)(B)(C)(D)(E)(F)(G)(H)(I)	141 (A)(B)(C)(D)(E)(F)(G)(H)(I)
22 (A)(B)(C)(D)(E)(F)(G)(H)(I)	62 (A)(B)(C)(D)(E)(F)(G)(H)(I)	102 (A)(B)(C)(D)(E)(F)(G)(H)(I)	142 (A)(B)(C)(D)(E)(F)(G)(H)(I)
23 (A)(B)(C)(D)(E)(F)(G)(H)(I)	63 (A)(B)(C)(D)(E)(F)(G)(H)(I)	103 (A)(B)(C)(D)(E)(F)(G)(H)(I)	143 (A)(B)(C)(D)(E)(F)(G)(H)(I)
24 (A)(B)(C)(D)(E)(F)(G)(H)(I)	64 (A)(B)(C)(D)(E)(F)(G)(H)(I)	104 (A)(B)(C)(D)(E)(F)(G)(H)(I)	144 (A)(B)(C)(D)(E)(F)(G)(H)(I)
25 (A)(B)(C)(D)(E)(F)(G)(H)(I)	65 (A)(B)(C)(D)(E)(F)(G)(H)(I)	105 (A)(B)(C)(D)(E)(F)(G)(H)(I)	145 (A)(B)(C)(D)(E)(F)(G)(H)(I)
26 (A)(B)(C)(D)(E)(F)(G)(H)(I)	66 (A)(B)(C)(D)(E)(F)(G)(H)(I)	106 (A)(B)(C)(D)(E)(F)(G)(H)(I)	146 (A)(B)(C)(D)(E)(F)(G)(H)(I)
27 (A)(B)(C)(D)(E)(F)(G)(H)(I)	67 (A)(B)(C)(D)(E)(F)(G)(H)(I)	107 (A)(B)(C)(D)(E)(F)(G)(H)(I)	147 (A)(B)(C)(D)(E)(F)(G)(H)(I)
28 (A)(B)(C)(D)(E)(F)(G)(H)(I)	68 (A)(B)(C)(D)(E)(F)(G)(H)(I)	108 (A)(B)(C)(D)(E)(F)(G)(H)(I)	148 (A)(B)(C)(D)(E)(F)(G)(H)(I)
29 (A)(B)(C)(D)(E)(F)(G)(H)(I)	69 (A)(B)(C)(D)(E)(F)(G)(H)(I)	109 (A)(B)(C)(D)(E)(F)(G)(H)(I)	149 (A)(B)(C)(D)(E)(F)(G)(H)(I)
30 (A)(B)(C)(D)(E)(F)(G)(H)(I)	70 (A)(B)(C)(D)(E)(F)(G)(H)(I)	110 (A)(B)(C)(D)(E)(F)(G)(H)(I)	150 (A)(B)(C)(D)(E)(F)(G)(H)(I)
31 (A)(B)(C)(D)(E)(F)(G)(H)(I)	71 (A)(B)(C)(D)(E)(F)(G)(H)(I)	111 (A)(B)(C)(D)(E)(F)(G)(H)(I)	151 (A)(B)(C)(D)(E)(F)(G)(H)(I)
32 (A)(B)(C)(D)(E)(F)(G)(H)(I)	72 (A)(B)(C)(D)(E)(F)(G)(H)(I)	112 (A)(B)(C)(D)(E)(F)(G)(H)(I)	152 (A)(B)(C)(D)(E)(F)(G)(H)(I)
33 (A)(B)(C)(D)(E)(F)(G)(H)(I)	73 (A)(B)(C)(D)(E)(F)(G)(H)(I)	113 (A)(B)(C)(D)(E)(F)(G)(H)(I)	153 (A)(B)(C)(D)(E)(F)(G)(H)(I)
34 (A)(B)(C)(D)(E)(F)(G)(H)(I)	74 (A)(B)(C)(D)(E)(F)(G)(H)(I)	114 (A)(B)(C)(D)(E)(F)(G)(H)(I)	154 (A)(B)(C)(D)(E)(F)(G)(H)(I)
35 (A)(B)(C)(D)(E)(F)(G)(H)(I)	75 (A)(B)(C)(D)(E)(F)(G)(H)(I)	115 (A)(B)(C)(D)(E)(F)(G)(H)(I)	155 (A)(B)(C)(D)(E)(F)(G)(H)(I)
36 (A)(B)(C)(D)(E)(F)(G)(H)(I)	76 (A)(B)(C)(D)(E)(F)(G)(H)(I)	116 (A)(B)(C)(D)(E)(F)(G)(H)(I)	156 (A)(B)(C)(D)(E)(F)(G)(H)(I)
37 (A)(B)(C)(D)(E)(F)(G)(H)(I)	77 (A)(B)(C)(D)(E)(F)(G)(H)(I)	117 (A)(B)(C)(D)(E)(F)(G)(H)(I)	157 (A)(B)(C)(D)(E)(F)(G)(H)(I)
38 (A)(B)(C)(D)(E)(F)(G)(H)(I)	78 (A)(B)(C)(D)(E)(F)(G)(H)(I)	118 (A)(B)(C)(D)(E)(F)(G)(H)(I)	158 (A)(B)(C)(D)(E)(F)(G)(H)(I)
39 (A)(B)(C)(D)(E)(F)(G)(H)(I)	79 (A)(B)(C)(D)(E)(F)(G)(H)(I)	119 (A)(B)(C)(D)(E)(F)(G)(H)(I)	159 (A)(B)(C)(D)(E)(F)(G)(H)(I)
40 (A)(B)(C)(D)(E)(F)(G)(H)(I)	80 (A)(B)(C)(D)(E)(F)(G)(H)(I)	120 (A)(B)(C)(D)(E)(F)(G)(H)(I)	160 (A)(B)(C)(D)(E)(F)(G)(H)(I)

18 (JBF) JOB PREFERENCE

01 ○	06 ○	11 ○	16 ○	21 ○	26 ○	31 ○	36 ○	41 ○	46 ○	51 ○	56 ○	61 ○	66 ○
02 ○	07 ○	12 ○	17 ○	22 ○	27 ○	32 ○	37 ○	42 ○	47 ○	52 ○	57 ○	62 ○	67 ○
03 ○	08 ○	13 ○	18 ○	23 ○	28 ○	33 ○	38 ○	43 ○	48 ○	53 ○	58 ○	63 ○	68 ○
04 ○	09 ○	14 ○	19 ○	24 ○	29 ○	34 ○	39 ○	44 ○	49 ○	54 ○	59 ○	64 ○	69 ○
05 ○	10 ○	15 ○	20 ○	25 ○	30 ○	35 ○	40 ○	45 ○	50 ○	55 ○	60 ○	65 ○	70 ○

19 LANGUAGES

(LNG)

(0)	(0)	(0)	(0)	(0)	(0)
(1)	(1)	(1)	(1)	(1)	(1)
(2)	(2)	(2)	(2)	(2)	(2)
(3)	(3)	(3)	(3)	(3)	(3)
(4)	(4)	(4)	(4)	(4)	(4)
(5)	(5)	(5)	(5)	(5)	(5)
(6)	(6)	(6)	(6)	(6)	(6)
(7)	(7)	(7)	(7)	(7)	(7)
(8)	(8)	(8)	(8)	(8)	(8)
(9)	(9)	(9)	(9)	(9)	(9)

20 DATE BLOCK

(SDF)

M	M	D	D	Y	Y
(0)	(0)	(0)	(0)	(0)	(0)
(1)	(1)	(1)	(1)	(1)	(1)
	(2)	(2)	(2)	(2)	(2)
	(3)	(3)	(3)	(3)	(3)
	(4)		(4)	(4)	(4)
	(5)		(5)	(5)	(5)
	(6)		(6)	(6)	(6)
	(7)		(7)	(7)	(7)
	(8)		(8)	(8)	(8)
	(9)		(9)	(9)	(9)

21 OTHER INFORMATION

(MSC)

(0)	(0)	(0)	(0)	(0)	(0)	(0)	(0)	(0)
(1)	(1)	(1)	(1)	(1)	(1)	(1)	(1)	(1)
(2)	(2)	(2)	(2)	(2)	(2)	(2)	(2)	(2)
(3)	(3)	(3)	(3)	(3)	(3)	(3)	(3)	(3)
(4)	(4)	(4)	(4)	(4)	(4)	(4)	(4)	(4)
(5)	(5)	(5)	(5)	(5)	(5)	(5)	(5)	(5)
(6)	(6)	(6)	(6)	(6)	(6)	(6)	(6)	(6)
(7)	(7)	(7)	(7)	(7)	(7)	(7)	(7)	(7)
(8)	(8)	(8)	(8)	(8)	(8)	(8)	(8)	(8)
(9)	(9)	(9)	(9)	(9)	(9)	(9)	(9)	(9)

22 SPECIAL KNOWLEDGE

(SPK)

(0)	(0)	(0)	(0)	(0)	(0)	(0)	(0)
(1)	(1)	(1)	(1)	(1)	(1)	(1)	(1)
(2)	(2)	(2)	(2)	(2)	(2)	(2)	(2)
(3)	(3)	(3)	(3)	(3)	(3)	(3)	(3)
(4)	(4)	(4)	(4)	(4)	(4)	(4)	(4)
(5)	(5)	(5)	(5)	(5)	(5)	(5)	(5)
(6)	(6)	(6)	(6)	(6)	(6)	(6)	(6)
(7)	(7)	(7)	(7)	(7)	(7)	(7)	(7)
(8)	(8)	(8)	(8)	(8)	(8)	(8)	(8)
(9)	(9)	(9)	(9)	(9)	(9)	(9)	(9)

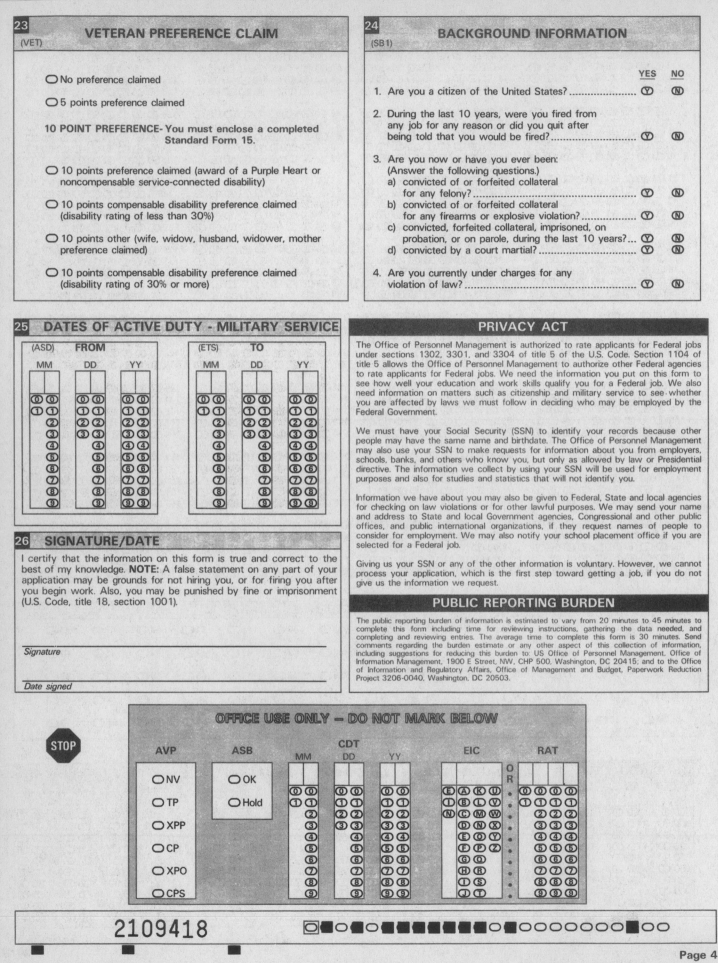

23 VETERAN PREFERENCE CLAIM
(VET)

○ No preference claimed

○ 5 points preference claimed

10 POINT PREFERENCE- You must enclose a completed Standard Form 15.

○ 10 points preference claimed (award of a Purple Heart or noncompensable service-connected disability)

○ 10 points compensable disability preference claimed (disability rating of less than 30%)

○ 10 points other (wife, widow, husband, widower, mother preference claimed)

○ 10 points compensable disability preference claimed (disability rating of 30% or more)

24 BACKGROUND INFORMATION
(SB1)

	YES	NO
1. Are you a citizen of the United States?	Ⓨ	Ⓝ
2. During the last 10 years, were you fired from any job for any reason or did you quit after being told that you would be fired?	Ⓨ	Ⓝ
3. Are you now or have you ever been: (Answer the following questions.)		
a) convicted of or forfeited collateral for any felony?	Ⓨ	Ⓝ
b) convicted of or forfeited collateral for any firearms or explosive violation?	Ⓨ	Ⓝ
c) convicted, forfeited collateral, imprisoned, on probation, or on parole, during the last 10 years?	Ⓨ	Ⓝ
d) convicted by a court martial?	Ⓨ	Ⓝ
4. Are you currently under charges for any violation of law?	Ⓨ	Ⓝ

25 DATES OF ACTIVE DUTY - MILITARY SERVICE

(ASD) **FROM**   (ETS) **TO**

MM   DD   YY   MM   DD   YY

26 SIGNATURE/DATE

I certify that the information on this form is true and correct to the best of my knowledge. **NOTE:** A false statement on any part of your application may be grounds for not hiring you, or for firing you after you begin work. Also, you may be punished by fine or imprisonment (U.S. Code, title 18, section 1001).

Signature
_____

Date signed
_____

STOP

OFFICE USE ONLY – DO NOT MARK BELOW

AVP   ASB   CDT   EIC   RAT
                        MM   DD   YY

AVP: ○ NV   ○ TP   ○ XPP   ○ CP   ○ XPO   ○ CPS

ASB: ○ OK   ○ Hold

2109418

Training

Corrections work is challenging, interesting, difficult, and worthwhile. It is also risky. Prison populations include many individuals with a history of violent behavior and disregard for human life. Correction Officers who work with these individuals must be highly trained both in procedures for maintaining their own safety and in techniques for "correcting" inmates in their charges.

No Correction Officer recruit is issued a uniform and a key ring and sent into a cellblock. All jurisdictions carefully train and supervise recruits to be certain that these new employees are fully capable of performing all of their duties before they are given full responsibility. The training programs vary greatly from jurisdiction to jurisdiction and from region to region. Some systems rely heavily on classroom instruction and lengthy, formal training programs. Others offer relatively little formal training but have extensive apprenticeship programs by which a new recruit is assigned to work full time alongside a seasoned Correction Officer. Self-defense and firearms training are part of every program.

The Federal Prison System trains all of its recruits at its centralized training facility in Glynco, Georgia. There, in a campus setting, prospective Federal Correction Officers receive classroom instruction in correction law, psychology, philosophy of rehabilitation, and rules managing prison-type situations among their fellow classmates with instruction and feedback from specially qualified instructors. Their judgment is heightened with challenging assignments, and their marksmanship is sharpened on the firing range. A few weeks of this intensified training does much to prepare recruits for further on-the-job training under careful supervision at prison locations.

Many states, counties, and large cities offer similar academy-type training, often in combination with other programs. The instructors at the state, county, and city academies have often received their training at the federal facility in Glynco. As the federal government assists the states by training the trainers, so many states offer assistance to counties and cities by sharing their facilities and expertise. New York State, for example, offers a two-week classroom program at its central facility in Albany to supplement the hands-on, participatory training offered by county and city training facilities.

Here are some highlights of the New York State Basic Training Program for County Correction Officers. The format and methodology of your own training may be quite different, but the topics covered and the breadth of instruction will be similar.

THE CORRECTION OFFICER'S ROLE AND STRESS   4 HOURS

This presentation examines correctional stress and the correctional stressors associated with its existence. Observable signs of stress are discussed, as well as possible methods of dealing with and/or reducing stress.

ESSENTIAL SERVICES   7 HOURS

The United States Constitution guarantees certain fundamental rights to all citizens of the United States. In the discussion of Essential Services in Corrections, correctional requirements will be examined to illustrate how such requirements translate into a minimum standard of services which a jail must provide for inmates to insure a safe, secure, and humane environment. The following Essential Services will be discussed in detail: Food Service, Medical Care, Personal Hygiene, Inmate Mail, Telephone Calls, Commissary, Visitation, Recreation, Access to Courts, Inmate Packages, Published and Printed Materials, Access to Media, Library, and Religious Practices.

INTERPERSONAL COMMUNICATIONS   7$\frac{1}{2}$ HOURS

The most effective tool Correction Officers have at their disposal is their communication skill. This course will acquaint officers with various issues relative to nonverbal and verbal communications. Also, different communication climates will be explored and related to different correction situations.

Officers will also be instructed in ways in which they can influence the behavior of inmates; that is, how they can get an inmate to move from point "A" to point "B." Issues such as motivation, attitudes, and environment of a correctional facility will be looked at to see how they affect officer/inmate interaction.

SPECIAL INMATES   4 HOURS

This segment will deal with the detection and proper handling of special prisoners who require medication, close scrutiny, and strict supervision. Such types include the alcoholic, mentally ill, drug addict, suicidal, diabetic, epileptic, and homosexual. Alcoholics Anonymous, suicide prevention, and counseling are discussed, among other intervention techniques, for reducing anxiety among individuals who experience mental or emotional stress while incarcerated.

This segment will also deal with inmates in the 16 to 20 year age bracket. Trainees will become familiar with the characteristics of young offenders and what motivates them. Personality traits and characteristics will be explored in order to give the line officer insight into how to respond to these individuals.

SECURITY SKILLS   7$\frac{1}{2}$ HOURS

Trainees will discuss the following topics: population counts, inmate movement and control, searches, firearms, key control, dangerous material control, inmate supervision, tool control, administrative segregation, discipline, and grievance procedures.

Trainees will be acquainted with generally accepted codes of inmate conduct. Inmates' responsibility in adherence to a code of conduct will be explored, and the privileges available to inmates who act responsibly will be discussed.

Trainees will also be introduced to the nature of discipline and the objectives that effective discipline can obtain, the handling of serious and minor infractions of facility rules, and how to reprimand an inmate properly. Also, introduction will be made to the informal and formal resolution of complaints. Procedures for the filing and keeping of records and appeals procedures will be explored. There will also be a discussion of how proper use of a grievance procedure will minimize conflict.

FIRE PREVENTION   3$\frac{1}{2}$ HOURS

This will not be hands-on nor how-to-prevent-fire presentation. It will, however, familiarize trainees with first aid, fire protection equipment, and, most importantly, spell out the hidden, dangerous shortcomings of the basic instruments. Through a video presentation and visual transparencies, trainees will also focus on the factors of rapid fire spread, heat flow, the major problems in dealing with fire situations in jails today, developing good professional role attitudes between county jail administrations and the county fire personnel, and, most importantly, the need for good fire prevention practices.

HOSTAGE SURVIVAL   4 HOURS

Trainees will be given an overview of hostage survival techniques. Emphasis will be placed on the dynamics that take place while an officer is held hostage and what officers can do to prepare for and survive a hostage situation.

OBJECTIVE OBSERVATION & REPORT WRITING   7 HOURS

This class acquaints the trainees with the ease with which preconceived assumptions and prejudices can negatively affect their performance on the job. The trainees will receive instruction relating to problems in perception that will enable them to safeguard their own objectivity while performing their duties. Trainees will have the opportunity to relate these concepts to the technical areas of report writing.

The balance of this class will deal with the actual writing of a report. Problems often encountered by officers, as well as certain report writing pitfalls, will be discussed. Participants will be asked to write a report based on a video presentation of a jail incident, and the reports will be critiqued in class.

LEGAL ISSUES $7\frac{1}{2}$ HOURS

Topics which will be discussed are Corrections and the U.S. Constitution, Courts, Correction Law, Correction Standards, and Rights and Liabilities of Correction Personnel.

TRANSPORTATION OF INMATES   2 HOURS

Trainees will receive instruction in generally accepted methods of transporting prisoners. Special problems which may arise during transport procedures are spelled out. Equipment and tactics for accomplishing prisoner transport are displayed and explained.

CRIME SCENE PRESERVATION $1\frac{1}{2}$ HOURS

Participants will be given instruction in how to secure a crime scene and preserve and collect evidence. Proper handling and recording of evidence will be stressed.

STANDARD FIRST AID (MODULAR SYSTEM) $3\frac{1}{2}$ HOURS

Trainees will receive instruction in the following topics: Emergency Action Principles, Respiratory Emergencies, First Aid for Wounds, First Aid for Burns, First Aid for Sudden Illness, and Emergency Rescue and Transfer. Trainees successfully completing the requirements of this segment, including satisfactory testing, will receive American Red Cross certification.

Trainees not presenting proof of current accredited Standard First Aid (or better) certification will be required to attend this training segment. Trainees will be provided with approved American Red Cross Modular Books, which must be returned at the completion of this training segment, and a Workbook, which may be retained by the trainees. Trainees will be required to spend a minimum of four hours in independent study outside of the formal classroom, reading the Modular text material and completing the Workbook, prior to this formal lecture segment.

Test-Taking Techniques

The first step towards a test is preparing for it. You have a good start by purchasing this book. The previous exam sample and the model exam which we have included offer you a chance to experience many different kinds of questions covering a variety of subjects and different styles. Since Correction Officer exams vary so, and since we cannot predict which exam you will take, it is important that you become familiar with the whole possible range.

Set aside a portion of time each day to study. Choose a study spot that is well lighted and free from distractions. Read through this book up to this part, if you have not already done so, so as to set the stage. Let yourself get excited about the job.

Since the Correction Officer exam of each jurisdiction is unique, there is not much point to trying any one of the models before you begin your study of test topics. Each of the chapters which follow gives you real help with a question area. Give equal time to each area until you begin to recognize your own strengths and weaknesses. Then devote extra time to the areas that need it most. You may find it helpful to return to these chapters after taking the model exams so as to further refine your skills.

Your study time should always be in blocks of at least one hour. When you get to the exams, it would be best to complete each in one sitting. If that is impossible, do not divide any exam into more than two parts.

Time yourself accurately when answering the exams. Part of your test preparation is learning to pace yourself and learning to think under the pressure of time. Never look ahead at the answers until you have fully completed the exam.

When you do look at the answers and score yourself, look at the explanation as well. You can learn a great deal from the explanations, even from the explanations for the answers you have answered correctly. The explanations often amplify the thinking that went into the correct answer choice. Thoughtful, complete preparation with this book should give you the skills and the confidence you will need on exam day.

Your last minute preparations for any exam are based strictly on common sense. They include getting a good night's sleep and leaving home early enough so that you do not need to rush or worry. It is a good idea to wear a watch to your exam so that you can keep track of your own time and pace yourself. Be sure to bring your admission card and whatever identification was specified in the literature you received. Unless you were informed that pencils would be supplied, bring at least two sharpened #2 pencils with clean erasers.

Once all examinees are seated in the examination room, the test administrator will hand out forms and give instructions as to how to fill them out. Listen carefully and follow all instructions. Ask questions if necessary. The administrator will tell you of the procedure that will be followed when the exam begins. He or she will tell you how to recognize the start and stop signals, what to do if all your pencils break or if a page seems to be missing from your test booklet. The instructions will be step-by-step and should be very clear, but if you are uncertain about anything, do not hesitate to ask. No one keeps a record of who asks questions, even questions that seem to be foolish.

When the exam begins, the key word is READ. READ every word of every question. Be alert for exclusionary words which might affect your answer—words like "not," "most," "all," "every," "except."

READ all the choices before you mark your answer. It is statistically true that most errors are made when the correct answer is the last choice. Too many people mark the first answer that seems correct, without reading through all the choices to find out which is best.

The following list consists of important suggestions for taking your exam. Read the suggestions right now, before you continue. Read them before you attempt the model exams. Read them once more the evening before you take your exam.

1. Blacken your answer space firmly and completely. ● is the only correct way to mark the answer sheet. ◑, ⊗, ⊘, and ∅ are all unacceptable. The machine might not read them at all.

2. Mark only one answer for each question. If you mark more than one answer you will be considered wrong even if one of the answers is correct.

3. If you change your mind, you must erase your mark. Attempting to cross out an incorrect answer like this ● will not work. You must erase any incorrect answer completely. An incomplete erasure might be read as a second answer.

4. All of your answering should be in the form of blackened spaces. The machine cannot read English. Do not write any notes in the margins.

5. MOST IMPORTANT: Answer each question in the right place. Question 1 must be answered in space 1; question 52 in space 52. If you should skip an answer space and mark a series of answers in the wrong places, you must erase all those answers and do the questions over, marking your answers in the proper places. You cannot afford to use the limited time in that way. Therefore, as you answer each question, look at its number and check that you are marking your answer in the space with the same number.

6. Try to answer every question. If you are unsure of an answer you mark, put a check next to the question in the question booklet. Then, if you have time, you can quickly spot those questions to which you would like to give some extra thought.

7. Guess if you must. If you do not know the answer to a question, eliminate the answers that you know are wrong and guess from among those remaining. Most Civil Service examination scores are based only upon those questions that are answered correctly. That is, there is no penalty for a wrong answer. This means that even a wild guess is better than a blank space. A wild guess gives you a 20% or a 25% chance to be right, depending on the number of choices. If the space is blank, you have no chance at all. Ask the test administrator if there is a guessing penalty or if only right answers count. If the answer is "rights only," then guess.

8. If your exam has a guessing penalty, ignore this advice. Otherwise, if you notice that time is about to run out and you have not completed all the questions, mark all remaining questions with the same answer. Some will probably be correct. In doing this, choose an answer other than (A). (A) is generally the correct answer less often than the other choices.

9. Stay alert. Concentrate. Be sure to mark the letter you mean.

10. If you finish before time is up, do not daydream. Check to be sure that each question is answered in the right space and that there is only one answer for each question. Return to the difficult questions and rethink them.

Preparing for Your Exam

As you have learned from reading the various announcements, each jurisdiction which administers a Correction Officer exam seems to have a somewhat different idea of what skills and abilities should be tested and of how to go about testing them. The exams cover far too many subjects for us to give you detailed instruction in all of them. Furthermore, many exam subjects do not lend themselves to instruction. Judgement and Reasoning, for instance, tend to be natural strengths which may be enhanced by life's experiences but which cannot be taught.

Other subjects lend themselves more readily to further discussion and to suggestions for tackling the questions. The next few chapters explore some of the types of questions which appear on Correction Officer exams, one type at a time. Our approach to each type of question is different because the demands made by each type of question are different.

MEMORY AND OBSERVATION—This chapter concentrates on improving your powers of observation. It points out what to look for and how to look for it. The exercises direct your attention to details and help you to focus your concentration as you must when taking an exam and when serving as a Correction Officer.

Take your time with these exercises. Try to anticipate the questions you might be asked about each photo. Train yourself to notice the details in these exercises, and you should feel more confident when faced with memory and observation questions on your exam.

READING COMPREHENSION—There is a real system to use in approaching reading comprehension passages and questions. This chapter will teach it to you.

ENGLISH USAGE AND GRAMMAR—Test makers hope to be able to predict an applicant's ability to write clear and intelligent reports and memoranda on the basis of the applicant's mastery of English usage and grammar. This chapter gives you a crash refresher course. If grammar is troublesome for you, give this chapter extra time and attention.

Observation and Memory

Memory is a very individualized skill. Some people remember details of what they see and hear, others remember only the most obvious facts. Some people memorize easily, others find memorizing very difficult. Some people remember forever, others forget in a short time. Some people can memorize in a systematic manner, others are haphazard in their methods or have no method at all.

We really cannot tell you how to memorize. We can, however, teach you how to look at photographs and point out the details on which you should concentrate.

Photograph for Exercise 1—*The Auto Body Shop*

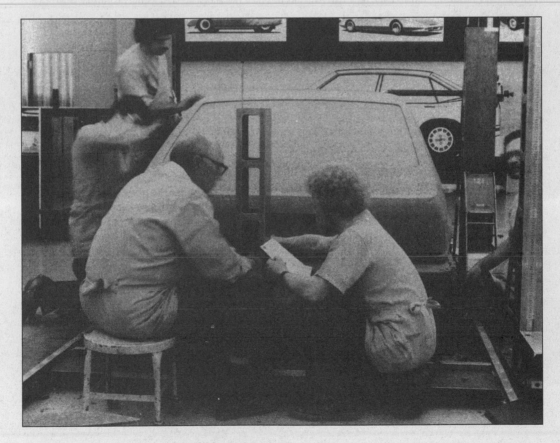

(Photograph courtesy of General Motors)

EXERCISE 1

Let us begin by looking together at the photograph of the Auto Body Shop. Start with the people:

1. How many people are in the photograph?

2. How many men? How many women?

3. What do the people appear to be doing?

4. Are the people all working together? If not, how many are working alone? How many together? Is the man on the right working?

5. Note the clothing. Dark pants, dark socks, light shirts crossed across the chest and tied in back. The two men in the foreground have on the same shoes, but the other visible pair of shoes is different.

6. Note glasses. Which men wear them?

7. Note hair. Which men have dark hair? Which light? Can you describe the hairstyles of the light-haired men?

8. One man is sitting on a stool. Which man? How many legs does the stool have? Of what does the stool appear to be made? Does it move on casters?

9. Which of the men have beards? Mustaches?

10. Is anyone wearing a watch? Who?

Observe the action:

11. What does the man in the right foreground have in his hand? What is he probably doing?

12. What does the man who is standing appear to be doing? What about the man kneeling beside him?

13. What might be the relationship of the older man to the younger ones?

Note the background:

14. There are pictures of cars on the walls. Parts of how many cars are visible? How many tires are shown?

15. What else can be seen on the walls? Telephone? Calendar? Bookcase?

16. Is the car on which the men are working up on a lift?

17. How many levels of floor are visible? Is the floor clean?

18. There is a number on one piece of equipment. Did you notice the number? Remember it!

A good question writer could easily develop ten questions based upon these observations. Would you have noticed everything and made note as well about what was not there at all?

In looking at a photograph, focus first on the people. Notice their clothing, physical features, and activities. Count, but also make note of which person or persons are wearing what, doing what, interacting with whom and so on. Then notice the prominent objects. Next, turn your attention to the background, floors, walls, etc. Finally, start at the left side of the photograph and move your eyes slowly to the right, noticing special details such as numbers, calibrations, dirt spots, unidentified objects, etc. If you work very hard at noticing, you are likely to remember what you noticed, at least for the duration of the exam.

Photograph for Exercise 2—*Time Out for Refreshments*

(Photograph courtesy of The Coleman Company, Inc.)

EXERCISE 2

Let us look at the photograph called "Time Out for Refreshments."

1. The people in the picture are . . . number, sex, age.

2. The people are wearing . . . notice the boy's belt, label on jeans (even if you cannot read it, you should notice that it is there), long-sleeved plain shirts.

3. Notice hair color, type (curly or straight), and length.

4. Note that no shoes are visible; neither person wears glasses nor a watch nor hat.

5. What is the boy doing? What is the girl doing?

6. Who is standing? Who sitting? On what?

7. On what is the soda can resting? On what is the cooler resting?

8. What else is on the table? Notice the lantern, covered pot, box, and coffeepot.

9. How many slats make up the table? The bench?

10. What is on the ground? Snow? Sand? Gravel? Lawn? rocks? Flowers? Wild grasses?

11. The day is . . . Cold? Warm? Rainy? Cloudy? Sunny? Where is the sun in the picture?

12. In the background are (is) . . . Mountains? Trees? Water? Boats? Tents? More grass? Other people? Animals?

13. What can you see in the sky? What is on or in the water? What else is there on the land?

14. Does the cooler have a handle on top? Where? Is it all one color? How many colors? Describe the design of the cooler.

15. Where is the fill valve on the lantern?

16. Does the coffeepot have a handle?

17. Does the tent have a visible window?

18. Describe the end of the bench? Squared off? Rounded? Other?

How did you do with this photograph? Are you developing skill at noticing everything?

Photograph for Exercise 3—*Ship to Shore*

(Photograph courtesy of The Coleman Company, Inc.)

EXERCISE 3

Study the photograph titled "Ship to Shore." On a plain piece of paper make as comprehensive a list as you can. Try to notice every detail on which you could possibly be quizzed. When you have completed your list, compare it with ours which follows. If you noticed everything that we did, you are becoming very observant. Perhaps you found details that we missed. If so, congratulate yourself and keep up the good work.

(On the actual exam, you will not be permitted to write any notes. You will have to make observations and hold them as mental notes only. This exercise, however, will be more effective if you jot down everything you see.)

Here is our list:

1. There are four people in the photograph, two adults and two children.
2. Two people are in a canoe, a man and a child.
3. The man in the canoe is sitting in the stern (rear) and is paddling on his left side.
4. The child in the canoe is in the bow (front) and is paddling on his right side.
5. The child in the canoe is blonde, the man dark-haired. Both are wearing garments with long sleeves.
6. A woman and a little girl are standing on the shore.
7. The little girl is blonde; the woman's hair is darker.
8. Both the woman and the girl are wearing jackets. The little girl's jacket is a winter jacket with a fleece-lined hood.
9. In the foreground is a cooler with white top, white handle, and drainage valve.
10. On top of the cooler is a soda can.
11. Also in the foreground is a light colored tent of modified Quonset shape.
12. A door flap of the tent is rolled back.
13. The opening of the tent is screened.
14. The water is calm.
15. The bank is grassy.
16. The body of water is lined with trees and shrubs.
17. Not visible: sky, end of body of water, background beyond the treeline, other people, and animals.

By now you should be getting pretty good at this activity.

Photograph for Exercise 4—*Beauty Culture Classroom*

EXERCISE 4

Complete this chapter by studying the final photograph of the Beauty Culture Classroom. Make this exercise an observation and memory exercise rather than just an observation exercise. Study the photograph for five minutes. Make mental notes of as many details as you possible can, but do not do any writing while you look at the photo. Then close the book and write as many details as you can remember. When you have written all that you can remember, draw a line on your paper and reopen the book. Add to the list details which you forgot and details which you previously overlooked. Then compare your list with ours.

1. The scene is a classroom. The students are women; the instructor is a man.

2. The students are all seated; the teacher is standing.

3. The teacher has dark, curly hair. He wears white pants and a white knit, collared sport shirt with some dark stripes.

4. The teacher wears a watch on his left wrist and a bracelet on his right. He has something in each hand.

5. The teacher has some slender object in each breast pocket.

6. The teacher is not wearing glasses. He is clean shaven. His mouth is closed.

7. Parts of thirteen students are visible.

8. The class is racially mixed.

9. The students are wearing a uniform which consists of white short-sleeved blouse with cuffs on the sleeves and wide pointed collar, dark slacks, and dark overblouse vest.

10. Footwear is not part of the uniform though low white shoes seem to be favored.

11. One student is wearing a long-sleeved print shirt under her uniform blouse. That student is black and wears glasses.

12. Most students are seated on folding chairs with writing arms. One student is sitting in a chair without an arm. That student is closest to the camera. She has her notebook open on her lap, wears her hair in a bun, has side combs in her hair and loop earrings, is wearing white shoes, and has a watch on her left wrist and a ring on one finger of her left hand.

13. The students all appear to be very attentive.

14. While some students are holding a pen or pencil, none appear to be writing, and some even have notebooks closed.

15. There is a cane leaning on the wall right next to the door.

16. The room lighting is not visible.

17. The floor is made of square tiles.

18. On the floor in the foreground can be seen parts of three suitcases or large briefcases and two large plastic bags with something dark inside each.

19. Beside the teacher is a low table. On that table is a model of a woman's head and a spray bottle.

20. Behind the low table is a white cabinet with two doors. On top of the cabinet is a book and two small unidentifiable objects.

21. Part of a second white cabinet is visible beside the first.

22. In the left background is a sink with a depression in its front rim.

23. On a shelf behind the sink is a stack of unidentifiable objects.

24. Pasted on the wall over and around the door are sixteen separate pictures. Some of these feature only one woman, some have a number of smaller snapshots on a standard size background.

25. The largest number of separate heads one can count in any of these pictures is seven (top picture of far left group).

26. The part of the room to the right is deeper than that on the left.

27. There is a dark-colored, molded shape chair behind the instructor.

28. Two students are supporting their chins with one hand. One student is using her left hand, the other her right.

29. Of all the students, only one is obviously wearing glasses.

30. One student is wearing high-heeled open shoes.

This was a very difficult exercise. The classroom is cluttered and the photograph filled with details. Your own exam, which will ask only a few questions about each photograph, is unlikely to quiz you about truly unimportant details nor about features of the photographs which did not reproduce clearly. After your experience with these exercises, however, you should know how to look at photographs and how to commit important details to memory.

How to Answer Reading Questions

The key to success with reading questions is not speed but comprehension. Civil service exams are not, as a rule, heavily speeded. There is ample time in which to complete the exam, provided that you do not spend excessive time struggling with one or two "impossible" questions. If you are reading with comprehension, your mind will not wander, and your speed will be adequate.

Between now and the test day, you must work to improve your reading concentration and comprehension. Your daily newspaper provides excellent material to improve your reading with the first paragraph or two. Read with a pencil in hand. Underscore details and ideas that seem to be crucial to the meaning of the article. Notice points of view, arguments, and supporting information. When you have finished the article, summarize it for yourself. Do you know the purpose of the article? The main idea presented? The attitude of the writer? The points over which there is controversy? Did you find certain information lacking? As you answer these questions, skim back over your underlinings. Did you focus on important words and ideas? Did you read with comprehension?

As you repeat this process day after day, you will find that your reading will become more efficient. You will read with greater understanding, and will "get more" from your newspaper.

One aspect of your daily reading that deserves special attention is vocabulary building. The most effective reader has a rich, extensive vocabulary. As you read, make a list of unfamiliar words. Include in your list words that you understand within the context of the article but that you cannot really define. In addition, mark words that you do not understand at all. When you put aside your newspaper, go to the dictionary and look up every new and unfamiliar word. Write the word and its definition in a special notebook. Writing the words and their definitions helps seal them in your memory far better than just reading them, and the notebook serves as a handy reference for your own use. A sensitivity to the meanings of words and an understanding of more words will make reading easier and more enjoyable even if none of the words you learn in this way crops up on your exam. If fact, the habit of vocabulary building is a good lifetime habit to develop.

Success with reading questions depends on more than reading comprehension. You must also know how to draw the answers from the reading selection and be able to distinguish the best answer from a number of answers that all seem to be good ones, or from a number of answers that all seem to be wrong.

Strange as it may seem, it's a good idea to approach reading comprehension questions by reading the questions — not the answer choices, just the questions themselves — before you read the selection. The questions will alert you to look for certain details, ideas, and points of view. Use your pencil. Underscore key words in the question. These will help you direct your attention as you read.

Next, skim the selection very rapidly to get an idea of its subject matter and its organization. If key words or ideas pop out at you, underline them, but do not consciously search out details in the preliminary skimming.

Now read the selection carefully with comprehension as your main goal. Underscore the important words as you have been doing in your newspaper reading.

Finally, return to the questions. Read each question carefully. Be sure you know what it asks. Misreading of questions is a major cause of error on reading comprehension tests. Read all the answer choices. Eliminate the obviously incorrect answers. You may be left with only one possible answer. If you find yourself with more than one possible answer, reread the question. Then skim the passage once more, focusing on the underlined segments. By now you should be able to conclude which answer is best.

Reading comprehension questions may take a number of different forms. In general, some of the most common forms are as follows:

1. **Question of fact or detail.** You may have to mentally rephrase or rearrange, but you should find the answer stated in the body of the selection.

2. **Best title or main idea.** The answer may be obvious, but the incorrect choices to the "main idea" question are often half-truths that are ideas or even offer a supporting idea quoted directly from the text. The correct answer is the one that covers the largest part of the selection.

3. **Interpretation.** This type of question asks you what the question means, not just what it says.

4. **Inference.** This is the most difficult type of reading comprehension question. It asks you to go beyond what the selection says, and to predict what might happen next. Your answer must be based upon the information in the selection and your own common sense, but not upon any other information you may have about that subject. A variation of the inference questions might be stated as, "The author would expect that . . ." To answer this question, you must understand the author's point of view, and then make an inference from that viewpoint based upon the information in the selection.

5. **Vocabulary.** Some civil service reading sections, directly or indirectly, ask the meaning of certain words as used in the selection.

Let's now work together on some typical reading comprehension selections and questions.

Selection for Questions 1 to 4

The recipient gains an impression of a typewritten letter before beginning to read the message. Factors that give a good first impression include margins and spacing that are visually pleasing, formal parts of the letter that are correctly placed according to the style of the letter, copy that is free of obvious erasures and overstrikes, and transcript that is even and clear. The problem for the typist is how to produce that first, positive impression of her work.

There are several general rules that a typist can follow when she wishes to prepare a properly spaced letter on a sheet of letterhead. The width of a letter should ordinarily not be less than four inches nor more than six inches. The side margins should also have a desirable relation to the bottom margin, as well as the space between the letterhead and the body of the letter. Usually the most appealing arrangement is when the side margins are even, and the bottom margin is slightly wider than the side margins. In some offices, however, a standard line length is used for all business letters, and the secretary then varies the spacing between the date line and the inside address according to the length of the letter.

1. The best title for the preceding paragraphs is

    (A) "Writing Office Letters"

    (B) "Making Good First Impressions"

    (C) "Judging Well-Typed Letters"

    (D) "Good Placing and Spacing for Office Letters"

2. According to the preceding paragraphs, which of the following might be considered the way that people quickly judge the quality of work that has been typed?

    (A) by measuring the margins to see if they are correct

    (B) by looking at the spacing and cleanliness of the typescript

    (C) by scanning the body of the letter for meaning

    (D) by reading the date line and address for errors

3. According to the preceding paragraphs, what would be definitely undesirable as the average line length of a type letter?

    (A) 4"

    (B) 5"

    (C) 6"

    (D) 7"

4. According to the preceding paragraphs, when the line length is kept standard, the secretary

    (A) does not have to vary the spacing at all because this also is standard

    (B) adjusts the spacing between the date line and inside address for different lengths of letters

    (C) uses the longest line as a guideline for spacing between the date line and inside address

    (D) varies the number of spaces between the lines

Begin by skimming the questions and underscoring key words. Your underscored question should look more or less like this:

1. The <u>best title</u> for the preceding paragraphs is:

2. According to the preceding paragraphs, which of the following might be considered the way that people <u>quickly judge the quality</u> of work that has been typed?

3. According to the preceding paragraphs, what would be definitely <u>undesirable</u> as the <u>average line length</u> of a type letter?

4. According to the preceding paragraphs, <u>when the line length is kept standard</u>, the secretary

Now skim the selection. This quick reading should give you an idea of the structure of the selection and of its overall meaning.

Next read the selection carefully and underscore words that seem important or that you think hold keys to the question answers. Your underscored selection should look something like this:

The recipient gains an impression of a typewritten letter before beginning to read the message. <u>Factors that give a good first impression</u> include <u>margins and spacing that are visually pleasing</u>, formal parts of the letters that are <u>correctly placed</u> according to the style of the letter, copy that is <u>free to obvious erasures and overstrikes</u>, and transcript that is <u>even and clear</u>. The problem for the typist is how to produce that first, positive impression of her work.

There are several general rules that a typist can follow when she wishes to prepare a properly spaced letter on a sheet of letterhead. The width of a letter should ordinarily <u>not be less than four inches, nor more than six inches</u>. The side margins should also have a desirable relation to the bottom margin, as well as the space between the letterhead and the body of the letter. Usually the most appealing arrangement is when the <u>side margins are even</u>, and the <u>bottom margin is slightly wider</u> than the side margins. In some offices, however, a <u>standard line length is used for all business letters</u>, and the secretary then <u>varies the spacing between the date line and the inside address</u> according to the length of the letter.

Finally, read the questions and answer choices, and try to choose the correct answer for each questions.

The correct answers are: 1. (**D**), 2. (**B**), 3. (**D**), 4. (**B**). Did you get them all right? Whether you made any errors or not, read these explanations.

1. (**D**) The best title for any selection is the one that takes in all of the ideas presented without being too broad or too narrow. Choice (D) provides the most inclusive title for this passage. A look at the other choices shows you why. Choice (A) can be eliminated because the passage discusses typing a letter, not writing one. Although the first paragraph states that a letter should make a good first impression, the passage is clearly devoted to the letter, not the first impression, so choice (B) can be eliminated. Choice (C) puts the emphasis on the wrong aspect of the typewritten letter. The passage concerns how to type a properly spaced letter, not how to judge one.

2. (**B**) Both spacing and cleanliness are mentioned in paragraph 1 as ways to judge the quality of a typed letter. The first paragraph states that the margin should be "visually pleasing" in relation to the body of the letter, but that does not imply margins of a particular measure, so choice (A) is incorrect. The passage makes no mention of errors, only the avoidance or erasures and overstrikes, so choice (D) is incorrect.

3. (**D**) This answer comes from the information provided in paragraph 2, that the width of a letter "should not be less than four inches nor more than six inches." According to this rule, seven inches is an undesirable line length.

4. (**B**) The answer to this question is stated in the last sentence of the reading passage. When a standard line length is used, the secretary "varies" the spacing between the date line and the inside address according to the length of the letter. The passage offers no support for any other choice.

Let us try another together.

Selection for Questions 5 to 9

Cotton fabrics treated with the XYZ Process have features that make them far superior to any previously known flame-retardant-treated cotton fabrics. XYZ Process-treated fabrics are durable to repeated laundering and dry cleaning; are glow-resistant as well as flame-resistant; when exposed to flames or intense heat form tough, pliable, and protective chars; are inert physiologically to persons handling or exposed to the fabric; are only slightly heavier than untreated fabrics; and are susceptible to further wet and dry finishing treatments. In addition, the treated fabrics exhibit little or no adverse change in feel, texture, and appearance and are shrink-, rot- and mildew-resistant. The treatment reduces strength only slightly. Finished fabrics have "easy care" properties in that they are wrinkle resistant and dry rapidly.

5. It is most accurate to state that the author in the preceding selection presents

    (A) facts but reaches no conclusion concerning the value of the process

    (B) a conclusion concerning the value of the process and facts to support that conclusion

    (C) a conclusion concerning the value of the process unsupported by facts

    (D) neither facts nor conclusions, but merely describes the process

6. The one of the following articles for which the XYZ Process would be most suitable is

    (A) nylon stockings

    (B) woolen shirt

    (C) silk tie

    (D) cotton bedsheet

7. The one of the following aspects of the XYZ Process that is not discussed in the preceding selection is its effects on

    (A) costs

    (B) washability

    (C) wearability

    (D) the human body

8. The main reason for treating a fabric with the XYZ Process is to

    (A) prepare the fabric for other wet and dry finishing treatment

    (B) render it shrink-, rot-, and mildew-resistant

    (C) increase its weight and strength

    (D) reduce the chance that it will catch fire

9. The one of the following that would be considered a minor drawback of the XYZ Process is that it

    (A) forms chars when exposed to flame

    (B) makes fabrics mildew-resistant

    (C) adds to the weight of fabrics

    (D) is compatible with other finishing treatments

Skim the questions and underscore the words which you consider to be key. The questions should look something like this:

5. It is most accurate to state that the <u>author</u> in the preceding selection <u>presents</u>

6. The one of the following articles for which the <u>XYZ Process</u> would be <u>most suitable</u> is

7. The one of the following <u>aspects</u> of the XYZ Process that is <u>not discussed</u> in the preceding selection is its effect on

8. The <u>main reason for treating</u> a fabric with the XYZ Process is to

9. The one of the following which would be considered a <u>minor drawback</u> of the XYZ Process is that it

Skim the reading selection. Get an idea of the subject matter of the selection and of how it is organized.

Now read the selection carefully and underscore the words which you think are especially important. This fact-filled selection might be underlined like this:

<u>Cotton fabrics treated</u> with the <u>XYZ Process</u> have <u>features</u> that make them <u>far superior</u> to any previously known <u>flame-retardant-treated cotton fabrics</u>. XYZ Process-treated fabrics are durable to <u>repeated laundering</u> and <u>dry cleaning</u>; are <u>glow-resistant</u> as well as <u>flame-resistant</u>; when exposed to flames or intense heat <u>form tough, pliable</u>, and <u>protective chars</u>; are <u>inert physiologically to persons handling</u> or exposed to the fabric; are only <u>slightly heavier than untreated</u> fabrics; and are <u>susceptible to further wet</u> and <u>dry finishing treatments</u>. In addition, the treated fabrics exhibit <u>little</u> or <u>no adverse change in feel</u>, <u>texture</u>, and <u>appearance and are shrink-, rot-, and mildew-resistant. The treatment reduces strength only slightly</u>. Finished fabrics have <u>"easy care"</u> properties in that they are <u>wrinkle resistant</u> and <u>dry rapidly</u>.

Now read each question and all its answer choices, and try to choose the correct answer for each question.

The correct answers are: 5. (**B**), 6. (**D**), 7. (**A**), 8. (**D**), 9. (**C**). How did you do on these? Read the explanations.

5. (**B**) This is a combination main idea and interpretation question. If you cannot answer this question readily, reread the selection. The author clearly thinks that the XYZ Process is terrific and says so in the first sentence. The rest of the selection presents a wealth of facts to support the initial claim.

6. (**D**) At first glance you might think that this is an inference question requiring you to make a judgment based upon the few drawbacks of the process. Closer reading, however, shows you that there is no contact for the correct answer here. This is a simple question of fact. XYZ Process is a treatment for cotton fabrics.

7. (**A**) Your underlinings should help you with this question of fact. Cost is not mentioned; all other aspects of the XYZ Process are. If you are having trouble finding mention of the effect of the XYZ Process on the human body, add to your vocabulary list "inert" and "physiologically."

8. (**D**) This is a main idea question. You must distinguish between the main idea and the supporting and incidental facts.

9. (**C**) Obviously a drawback is a negative feature. The selection mentions only two negative features. The treatment reduces strength slightly, and it makes fabrics slightly heavier than untreated fabrics. Only one of these negative features is offered among the answer choices.

You should be getting better at reading and at answering questions. Try this next selection on your own. Read and underline the questions. Skim the selection. Read and underline the selection. Read questions and answer choices and mark your answers. Then check your answers against the answers and explanations that follow the selection.

Selection for Questions 10 to 12

Language performs an essentially social function: It helps us to get along together, to communicate, and to achieve a great measure of concerted action. Words are signs that have significance by convention, and those people who do not adopt the conventions simply fail to communicate. They do not "get along," and a social force arises that encourages them to achieve the correct associations. By "correct" is meant as used by other members of the social group. Some of the vital points about language are brought home to an English visitor to American, and vice versa, because our vocabularies are nearly the same—but not quite.

10. As defined in the preceding selection, usage of a word is "correct" when it is

   (A) defined in standard dictionaries

   (B) used by the majority of persons throughout the world who speak the same language

   (C) used by the majority of educated persons who speak the same language

   (D) used by other persons with whom we are associating

11. In the preceding selection, the author is concerned primarily with the

   (A) meaning of words

   (B) pronunciation of words

   (C) structure of sentences

   (D) origin and development of language

12. According to the preceding selection, the main language problem of an English visitor to America stems from the fact that an English person

   (A) uses some words that have different meanings for Americans

   (B) has different social values than the Americans

   (C) has had more exposure to non-English speaking persons than Americans have had

   (D) pronounces words differently than Americans do

The correct answers are 10. (**D**), 11. (**A**), 12. (**A**).

10. (**D**) The answer to this question is stated in the next to last sentence of the selection.

11. (**A**) This main idea question is an easy one to answer. You should have readily eliminated all of the wrong choices.

12. (**A**) This is a question of fact. The phrasing of the question is quite different from the phrasing of the last sentence, but the meaning is the same. You may have found this reading selection more difficult to absorb than some of the others, but you should have had no difficulty answering this question by eliminating the wrong answers.

Here is one more reading selection and its questions. Once more explanations follow the correct answers. Follow the procedure you have learned and be sure to read the explanations even if you have a perfect score.

Selection for Questions 13 to 18

Since almost every office has some contact with date-processed records, a Senior Stenographer should have some understanding of the basic operations of data processing. Data processing systems now handle about one-third of all office paperwork. On punched cards, magnetic tape, or on other mediums, data are recorded before being fed into the computer for processing. A machine such as the key punch is used to convert the data written on the source document into the coded symbols on punched cards or tags. After data has been converted, it must be verified to guarantee absolute accuracy of conversion. In this manner, data becomes a permanent record that can be read by electronic computers that compare, store, compute, and otherwise process data at high speeds.

One key person in a computer installation is a programmer, the man or woman who puts business and scientific problems into special symbolic languages that can be read by the computer. Jobs done by the computer range all the way from payroll operations to chemical process control, but most computer applications are directed toward management data. About half of the programmers employed by businesses come to their positions with college degrees; the remaining half are promoted to their positions, without regard to education, from within the organization on the basis of demonstrated ability.

13. Of the following, the best title for the preceding selection is

    (A) "The Stenographer as Data Processor"

    (B) "The Relation of Key Punching to Stenography"

    (C) "Understanding Data Processing"

    (D) "Permanent Office Records"

14. According to the preceding selection, a Senior Stenographer should understand the basic operations of data processing because

    (A) almost every office today has contact with data processed by computer

    (B) any office worker may be asked to verify the accuracy of data

    (C) most offices are involved in the production of permanent records

    (D) data may be converted into computer language by typing on a key punch

15. According to the preceding selection, the data that the computer understands is most often expressed as

    (A) a scientific programming language

    (B) records or symbols punched on tape, cards, or other media

    (C) records on cards

    (D) records on tape

16. According to the preceding selection, computers are used most often to handle

    (A) management data

    (B) problems of higher education

    (C) the control of chemical process

    (D) payroll operations

17. Computer programming is taught in many colleges and business schools. The preceding selection implies that programmers in industry

    (A) must have professional training

    (B) need professional training to advance

    (C) must have at least a college education to do adequate programming tasks

    (D) do not need college education to do programming work

18. According to the preceding selection, data to be processed by computer should be

    (A) recent

    (B) complete

    (C) basic

    (D) verified

The correct answers are: 13. (**C**), 14. (**A**), 15. (**B**), 16. (**A**), 17. (**D**), 18. (**D**).

13. (**C**) Choosing the best title for this selection is not easy. Although the Senior Stenographer is mentioned in the first sentence, the selection is really not concerned with stenographers or with their relationship to key punching. Eliminate choices (A) and (B). Permanent office records are mentioned in the selection, but only along with other equally important uses for data processing. Eliminate choice (D). When in doubt, the most general title is usually correct.

14. (**A**) This is a question of fact. Any one of the answer choices could be correct, but the answer is given almost verbatim in the first sentence. Take advantage of answers that are handed to you in this way.

15. (**B**) This is a question of fact, but it is a tricky one. The program language is a symbolic language, not a scientific one. Reread carefully and eliminate choice (A). (B) includes more of the information in the selection than either (C) or (D), and so is the best answer.

16. (**A**) This is a question of fact. The answer is stated in the next to the last sentence.

17. (**D**) Remember that you are answering the questions on the basis of the information given in the selection. In spite of any information you may have to the contrary, the last sentence of the selection states that half the programmers employed in business achieved their positions by moving up from the ranks without regard to education.

18. (**D**) Judicious underlining proves very helpful to you in finding the correct answer to this question buried in the middle of the selection. Since any one of the answers might be correct, the way to deal with this question is to skim the underlined words in the section, eliminate those that are not mentioned, and choose the appropriate answer.

Before you begin the model exams, review this list of hints for scoring high on reading comprehension tests.

1. Read the questions and underline key words.

2. Skim the selection to get a general idea of the subject matter, the point that is being made, and the organization of the material.

3. Reread the selection giving attention to details and point of view. Underscore key words and phrases.

4. If the author has quoted material from another source, be sure that you understand the purpose of the quote. Does the author agree or disagree?

5. Carefully read each question or incomplete statement. Determine exactly what is being asked. Watch for negatives or all-inclusive words such as *always*, *never*, *all*, *only*, *every*, *absolutely*, *completely*, *none*, *entirely*, *no*.

6. Read all the answer choices. Eliminate those choices that are obviously incorrect. Reread the remaining choices and refer to the selection, if necessary, to determine the best answer.

7. Avoid inserting your own judgments into your answers. Even if you disagree with the author or even if you spot a factual error in the selection, you must answer on the basis of what is stated or implied in the selection.

8. Do not allow yourself to spend too much time on any one question. If looking back at the selection does not help you to find or figure out the answer, choose from among the answers remaining after you eliminate the obviously wrong answers. Mark the question in the text booklet, and go on. If you have time at the end of the exam or exam portion, reread the selection and the question. Often a fresh look provides new insights.

English Usage and Grammar

Questions testing your facility with English usage and grammar are often included in employment examinations in an effort to test your ability to recognize good, clear writing. If you can choose the most effective means of expressing a thought, then, by inference, it is concluded than you are able to express yourself well in writing. This Grammar and Usage Review is meant to serve as a quick refresher course. It should "bring back" the rules, hints, and suggestions supplied by many teachers over the years.

PARTS OF SPEECH

A **noun** is the name of a person, place, thing, or idea: teacher, city, desk, democracy

Pronouns substitute for nouns: he, they, ours, those

An **adjective** describes a noun: warm, quick, tall, blue

A **verb** expresses action or state or being: yell, interpret, fell, are

An **adverb** modifies a verb, an adjective, or another adverb: fast, slowly, friendly, well

Conjunctions join words, sentences, and phrases: and, but, or

A **preposition** shows position in time or space: in, during, after, behind

Nouns

There are different kinds of nouns:

> **Common nouns** are general: house, girl, street, city
>
> **Proper nouns** are specific: White House, Jane, Main Street, New York
>
> **Collective nouns** name groups: team, crowd, organization, Congress

Nouns have cases:

> **Nominative**—the subject, noun of address, or predicate noun
>
> **Objective**—the direct object, indirect object, or object of the preposition
>
> **Possessive**—the form that shows possession

Pronouns

A pronoun must agree with the noun to which it refers in gender, person, and number. There are several kinds of pronouns. (Pronouns also have cases.)

Demonstrative pronouns: this, that, these, those

Indefinite pronouns: all, any, anybody

Interrogative pronouns: who, which, what

Personal Pronouns

		Nominative	Objective	Possessive
Singular	1st person	I	me	mine
	2nd person	you	you	yours
	3rd person	he, she, it	him, her, it	his, hers, its
Plural	1st person	we	us	ours
	2nd person	you	you	yours
	3rd person	they	them	theirs

Adjectives

Adjectives answer the questions "Which one?", "What kind?", and "How many?"
There are three uses of adjectives:

A **noun modifier** is usually placed directly before the noun it describes: He is a *tall* man.

A **predicate adjective** follows an inactive verb and modified the subject: He is *happy*. I feel *terrible*.

An **article** or **noun marker** are other names for these adjectives: the, a, an.

Adverbs

Adverbs answer the questions "Why?", "How?", "Where?", "When?", and "To What degree?"
Adverbs should NOT be used to modify nouns. Adverbs modify:

Verbs	The old man walked <u>slowly</u>.
Adjectives	It was an <u>unusually hot summer</u>.
Other Adverbs	The days passed <u>too quickly</u>.

Verbs

Verbs are the most important part of speech. A verb may stand along, as an imperative sentence such as "Stop!" conversely, no group of words can function as a sentence without a verb.
Attributes of a Verb

Mood	*I laugh. (indicative—factual)*
	If I were laughing . . . (subjective—wishful)
	Laugh! (imperative—forceful)

Voice	*I moved the chair.* (active)
	The chair was moved by me. (passive)
Agreement of Persons and Number	*We don't know.* (1st person plural subject and verb)
	He doesn't know. (3rd person singular subject and verb).
Tense	*I laugh.* (present)
	We had laughed. (past perfect)
	She will be laughing. (future progressive)

Type of Verbs

Transitive	completed by a noun or pronoun
	We invited our friends.
Intransitive	completed in itself or by an adverb
	She fell. She fell down.
Copulative	a form of is or a sensory/seeming verb
	She is pretty. We felt bad. He appeared depressed.

Principal Parts of a Verb

	Present	*Past*	*Present Perfect*
Regular	walk	walked	have walked
	bathe	bathed	have bathed
Irregular	ring	rang	have rung
	eat	ate	have eaten

English Verb Time Lines

Simple Tenses	*Past*	*Present*	*Future*
Simple	I walked	I walk	I will walk
Progressive	I was walking	I am walking	I will be walking
Emphatic	I did walk	I do walk	

Perfect Tenses

Past Perfect	*Present Perfect*	*Future Perfect*
I had walked	I have walked	I will have walked
I had walked three miles by the time you met me.	I have walked three miles to get here.	I will have walked three miles by the time you catch up with me.

Past Perfect	Present Perfect	Future Perfect
activity begun and completed in the past before some other past action.	activity begun in the past, completed in the present.	activity begun at any time and completed in the future.

SELECTED RULES OF GRAMMAR

1. The subject of a verb is in the nominative case even if the verb is understood and not expressed.

     Example: They are as old as we. (As we are)

2. The word *who* is in the nominative case. *Whom* is in the objective case.

     Example: The trapeze artist who ran away with the clown broke the lion tamer's heart. (*Who* is the subject of the verb *ran*.)

     Example: The trapeze artist *whom* he loved ran away with the circus clown. (*Whom* is the object of the verb *loved*.)

3. The word *whoever* is in the nominative case. *Whomever* is in the object case.

     Example: Whoever comes to the door is welcome to join the party (*Whoever* is the subject of the verb *comes*.)

     Example: Invite whomever you wish to accompany you. (*Whomever* is the object of the verb *invite*.)

4. Nouns or pronouns connected by a form of the verb *to be* should always be in the nominative case.

     Example: It is *I*. (Not *me*)

5. A pronoun that is the object of a preposition or of a transitive verb must be in the objective case.

     Example: It would be impossible for *me* to do that job alone. (*Me* is the object of the preposition *for*.)

     Example: The attendant gave *me* the keys to the locker. (*Me* is the indirect object of the verb *gave*.)

6. *Each, either, neither, anyone, anybody, somebody, someone, every, everyone, one, no one,* and *nobody* are singular pronouns. Each of these words takes a singular verb and a singular pronoun.

     Example: *Neither likes* the pets of the other.
     Everyone must wait *his* turn.
     Each of the patients *carries* insurance.
     Neither of the women *has* completed *her* assignment.

7. When the correlative conjunctions *either/or* and *neither/nor* are used, the number of the verb agrees with the number of the last subject.

     Example: Neither John nor *Greg eats* meat.

     Example: Either the cat or the *mice take* charge in the barn.

8. A subject consisting of two or more nouns joined by a coordinating conjunction takes a plural verb.

> *Example:*   Paul *and* Sue *were* the last to arrive.

9. The number of the verb is not affected by the addition to the subject of words introduced by *with, together with, no less than, as well as,* etc.

> *Example:*   The *captain,* together with the rest of the team, *was delighted* by the victory celebration.

10. A verb agrees in number with its subject. A verb should not be made to agree with a noun that is part of a phrase following the subject.

> *Example:*   *Mount Snow,* one of my favorite ski areas, *is* in Vermont.
>
> *Example:*   The *mountains* of Colorado, like those of Switzerland, *offer* excellent skiing.

11. A verb should agree in number with the subject, not with the predicate noun or pronoun

> *Example:*   Poor study *habits are* the leading cause of unsatisfactory achievement in school.
>
> *Example:*   The leading *cause* of unsatisfactory achievement in school *is* poor study habits.

12. A pronoun agrees with its antecedent in person, number, and gender

> *Example:*   Since you were absent on Tuesday, you will have to ask Mary or Beth for her notes on the lecture. (Use *her,* not their, because two singular antecedents joining by *or* take a singular pronoun.)

13. *Hardly, scarcely, barely, only,* and *but* (when it means *only*) are negative words. Do NOT use another negative in conjunction with any of these words.

> *Example:*   He *didn't have but* one hat. (WRONG)
> He had *but* one hat. OR He had *only* one hat.
>
> *Example:*   I *can't hardly* read the small print. (WRONG)
> I *can hardly* read the small print. OR I *can't* read the small print.

14. *As* is a conjunction introducing a subordinate clause, while *like* is a preposition. The object of a preposition is a noun or phrase.

> *Example:*   She did *as* she was told.
>
> *Example:*   He behaves *like* a fool.
>
> *Example:*   The gambler accepts only hard currency *like* gold coins.

15. When modifying the words *kind* and *sort,* the words *this* and *that* always remain in the singular.

> *Example:*   *This kind* of apple makes the best pie.
>
> *Example:*   *That sort* of behavior will result in severe punishment.

16. In sentences beginning with *there is* and *there are,* the verb should agree in number with the noun that follows it.

> *Example:*   There *isn't* an unbroken *bone* in her body. (The singular subject *bone* takes the singular verb *is.*)
>
> *Example:*   There *are* many *choices* to be made. (The plural subject *choices* takes the plural verb *are.*)

17. A noun or pronoun modifying a gerund should be in the possessive case.

> *Example:*   Is there any criticism of Arthur's going? (*Going* is a gerund. It must be modified by *Arthur's* not by Arthur.)

18. DO NOT use the possessive case when referring to an inanimate object.

> *Example:*   He had difficulty with the *store's* management. (WRONG)
> He had difficult with the management of the store.

19. When expressing a condition contrary to fact or a wish, use the subjunctive form *were*.

> *Example:*   I wish I *were* a movie star.

20. Statements equally true in the past and in the present are usually expressed in the present tense. The contents of a book are also expressed in the present tense.

> *Example:*   He said that Venus is a planet. (Even though he made the statement in the past, the fact remains the Venus *is* a planet.)

> *Example:*   In the book *Peter Pan*, Wendy says, "I can fly." (Every time one reads the book, Wendy *says* it again.)

ANTECEDENTS AND MODIFIERS

1. *It,* when used as a relative pronoun, refers to the nearest noun. In your writing, you must be certain that the grammatical antecedent is indeed the intended antecedent.

> *Example:*   Since the mouth of the cave was masked by underbrush, *it* provided an excellent hiding place. (Do you really mean that the underbrush is an excellent hiding place, or do you mean the cave?)

2. *Which* is another pronoun that causes reference problems. In fact, whenever using pronouns, you must ask yourself whether or not the reference of the pronoun is clear.

> *Example:*   The first chapter awakens your interest in cloning, which continues to the end of the book. (What continues, cloning or your interest?)

> *Example:*   Jim told Bill that he was about to be fired. (Who is about to be fired? This sentence can be interpreted to mean that Jim was informing Bill about Bill's impending termination or about his, Jim's, own troubles.)

In your writing, you may find that the most effective way to clear up an ambiguity is to recast the sentence.

> *Example:*   The first chapter awakens your interest in cloning. The following chapters build upon this interest and maintain it throughout the book.

> *Example:*   Jim told Bill, "I am about to be fired." OR Jim told Bill, "You are about to be fired."

3. Adjectives modify only nouns and pronouns. Adverbs modify verbs, adjectives, and other adverbs.

> *Example:*   One can swim in a lake as *easy as* in a pool. (WRONG)
> One can swim in a lake as *easily* as in a pool (The adverb *easily* must modify the verb *can swim.*)

> *Example:*   I was *real* happy. (WRONG)
> I was *really* happy. (The adverb *really* must be used to modify the adjective *happy.*)

Sometimes context determines the use of adjective or adverb.

> *Example:*   The old man looked *angry*. (*Angry* is an adjective describing the old man. [angry old man])
>
> The old man looked *angrily* out of the window. (*Angrily* is an adverb describing the man's manner of looking out the window.)

4. Phrases should be placed near the words they modify.

> *Example:*   The author says that he intends to influence your *life in the first chapter*. (WRONG)
>
> The *author in the first chapter* says . . . OR *In the first chapter*, the author says . . .
>
> *Example:*   He played the part *in Oklahoma* of Jud. (WRONG)
>
> He played the part of Jud *in Oklahoma*.

5. Adverbs should be placed near the words they modify

> *Example:*   The man was *only* willing to sell one horse. (WRONG)
>
> The man was willing to sell *only* one horse

6. Clauses should be placed near the words they modify.

> *Example:*   The man has an appointment *who is waiting in the office*. (WRONG)
>
> The man *who is waiting in the office* has an appointment.

7. A modifier must modify something.

> *Example:*   Having excellent control, a no-hitter was pitched. (WRONG)
>
> (*Having excellent control* does not modify anything.)
>
> Having excellent control, the pitcher pitched a no-hitter. (*Having excellent control* modifies *the pitcher*.)
>
> *Example:*   The day passed quickly, climbing the rugged rocks. (WRONG)
>
> The day passed quickly as we climbed the rugged rocks.
>
> *Example:*   While away on vacation, the pipes burst. (WRONG) (The pipes were not away on vacation.)
>
> While we were away on vacation, the pipes burst.
>
> *Example:*   To run efficiently, the serviceman should oil the lawnmower. (WRONG)
>
> The serviceman should oil the lawnmower to make it run efficiently.

NOTE: The best test for the placement of modifiers is to read the sentence literally. If you read a sentence literally and it is literally ridiculous, it is WRONG. The meaning of a sentence must be clear to any reader. The words of the sentence *must make sense*.

SENTENCE STRUCTURE

1. Every sentence must contain a verb. A group of words, no matter how long, without a verb is a sentence fragment, not a sentence. A verb may consist of one, two, three, or four words.

> *Example:*   The boy *studies* hard.
>
> The boy *will study* hard.
>
> The boy *has been studying* hard.
>
> The boy *should have been studying* hard.

The words that make up the single verb may be separated.

> *Example:*   It *is* not *snowing*.
>
> It *will* almost certainly *snow* tomorrow.

2. Every sentence must have a subject. The subject may be a noun, a pronoun, or a word or group of words functioning as a noun.

> *Example:*   *Fish* swim. (noun)
> *Boats* are sailed. (noun)
> *She* is young. (pronoun)
> *Running* is good exercise. (gerund)
> *To argue* is pointless. (infinitive)
> *That he was tired* was evident. (noun clause)

In commands, the subject is usually not expressed but is understood to be *you.*

> *Example:*   Mind your own business.

3. A phrase cannot stand by itself as a sentence. A phrase is any group of related words which has no subject or predicate and which is used as a single part of speech. Phrases may be built around prepositions, particles, gerunds, or infinitives.

> *Example:*   The boy *with curly hair* is my brother. (Prepositional phrase used as an adjective modifying *boy*)

> *Example:*   My favorite cousin lives *on a farm.* (Prepositional phrase used as an adverb modifying *lives*)

> *Example:*   *Beyond the double white line* is out of bounds. (Prepositional phrase used as a noun, subject of the sentence)

> *Example:*   A thunderstorm *preceding a cold front* is often welcome. (Participial phrase used as an adjective modifying *thunderstorm*)

> *Example:*   We eagerly awaited the pay envelopes *brought by the messenger.* (Participial phrase used as an adjective modifying *envelopes*)

> *Example:*   *Running a day camp* is an exhausting job. (Gerund phrase used as a noun, subject of the sentence)

> *Example*:   The director is paid well for *running the day camp.* (Gerund phrase used as a noun the object of the preposition *for*)

> *Example:*   *To breathe unpolluted air* should be every person's birthright. (Infinitive phrase used as a noun, the subject of the sentence)

> *Example:*   The child began *to unwrap his gift.* (Infinitive phrase used as a noun, the object of the verb *began*)

> *Example:*   The boy ran away from home *to become a marine.* (Infinitive phrase use as an adverb modifying *ran away*)

4. *A main, independent,* or *principal* clause can stand alone as a complete sentence or it may be combined with another clause.

> *Example:*   The sky darkened ominously, and rain began to fall. (Two independent clauses joined by a coordinating conjunction.)

A *subordinate or dependent* clause must never stand along. It is not a complete sentence despite the fact that it has a subject and a verb. A subordinate clause usually is introduced by subordinating conjunction. Subordinate clauses may act as adverbs, adjectives, or nouns.

Subordinate adverbial clauses are generally introduced by the subordinating conjunctions *when, while, because, as soon as, if after, although, as before, since, than, though, until,* and *unless.*

> *Example:*   *While we were waiting for the local,* the express roared past.

> *Example:*   The woman applied for a new job *because she wanted to earn more money.*

Example: *Although a subordinate clause contains both subject and verb*, it cannot stand alone *because it is introduced by a subordinating word.*

Subordinate adjective clauses may be introduced by the pronouns *who, which,* and *that.*

Example: The play *which he liked best* was a mystery.

Example: I have a neighbor *who served in the Peace Corps.*

Subordinate noun clauses may be introduced by *who, what,* or *that.*

Example: The stationmaster says *that the train will be late.*

Example: I asked the waiter *what the stew contained.*

Example: I wish I knew *who backed into my car.*

5. Two independent clauses cannot share one sentence without some form of connective. If they do, they form a run on sentence. Two principal clauses may be joined by a coordinating conjunction, by a comma followed by a coordinating conjunction, or by a semicolon. They may form two distinct sentences. Two main clauses may NEVER be joined by a comma without a coordinating conjunction. This error is called a comma splice.

    Example:

    - A college education has never been more important than it is today it has never cost more. (WRONG—run-on sentence)

    - A college education has never been more important than it is today, it has never cost more. (WRONG—comma splice)

    - A college education has never been more important than it is today and it has never cost more. (WRONG—The two independent clauses are not equally short, so a comma is required before the coordinating conjunction.)

    - A college education has never been more important than it is today, and it has never cost more. (CORRECT)

    - A college education has never been more important than it is today; it has never cost more. (CORRECT)

    - A college education has never been more important than it is today. It has never cost more. (CORRECT)

    - A college education has never been more important than it is today. And it has never cost more. (CORRECT)

    - While a college education has never been more important than it is today, it has never cost more. (CORRECT)

6. Direct quotations are bound by all the rules of sentence formation. Beware of comma splices in divided quotations.

    Example: "Your total is wrong," he said, "add the column again." (WRONG)
    "Your totals is wrong," he said. "Add the column again." (CORRECT—The two independent clauses form two separate sentences.)

    Example: "Are you lost?" she asked, "may I help you?" (WRONG)
    "Are you lost?" she asked. "May I help you" (CORRECT—Two main clauses; two separate sentences.)

7. Comparisons must be logical and complete. Train yourself to concentrate on each sentence so that you can recognize errors.

    Example: Wilmington is larger than any city in Delaware. (WRONG)
    Wilmington is larger than any *other* city in Delaware. (CORRECT)

Example: He is as fat, if not fatter, than his uncle. (WRONG)
He is as fat *as*, if not fatter than, his uncle. (CORRECT)

Example: I hope to find a summer job other than a lifeguard. (WRONG)
I hope to find a summer job other than *that of* lifeguard. (CORRECT)

Example: Law is a better profession than an accountant. (WRONG)
Law is a better profession than *accounting*. (CORRECT)

8. Avoid the "is when" and "is where" construction.

Example: A limerick is when a short poem has a catchy rhyme. (WRONG)
A limerick *is* a short poem with a catchy rhyme. (CORRECT)

Example: To exile is where a person must live in another place. (WRONG)
To exile a person is to force him to live in another place. (CORRECT)

9. Errors in parallelism are often quite subtle, but you should learn to recognize and avoid them.

Example: Skiing and to skate are both winter sports. (WRONG)
Skiing and *skating* are both winter sports. (CORRECT)

Example: She spends all her time eating, asleep, and on her studies. (WRONG)
She spends all her time eating, *sleeping,* and *studying*. (CORRECT)

Example: The work is neither difficult nor do I find it interesting. (WRONG)
The work is neither difficult nor *interesting*. (CORRECT)

Example: His heavy drinking and the fact that he gambles makes him a poor role model. (WRONG)
His heavy *drinking* and *gambling make* him a poor role model. (CORRECT)

10. Avoid needless shifts in point of view. A shift in point of view is a change within the sentence from one tense or mood to another, from one subject or voice to another, or from one person or number to another. Shifts in point of view destroy parallelism within the sentence.

Example: After he *rescued* the kitten, he rushes down the ladder to find its owner. (Shift from past tense.) CHANGE TO: After he *rescued* the kitten, he *rushed* down the ladder to find its owner.

Example: First stand at attention and then you *should salute* the flag. (Shift from imperative to indicative mood.) CHANGE TO: First *stand* at attention and then *salute* the flag.

Example: Mary especially likes math, but history is also enjoyed by her. (The subject shifts from *Mary to history;* the mood shifts from active to passive.) CHANGE TO: *Mary* especially *likes* math, but *she* also *enjoys* history.

Example: George rowed around the island and soon the mainland came in sight. (The subject changes from *George* to the *mainland*.) CHANGE TO: *George rowed* around the island and soon *came in sight* of the mainland.

Example: The captain welcomed *us* aboard, and the crew enjoyed showing *one* around the boat. (The object shifts from first to third person.) CHANGE TO: The captain welcomed *us* aboard, and the crew enjoyed showing *us* around the boat.

Example: *One* should listen to the weather forecast so that *they* may anticipate a hurricane. (The subject shifts from singular to plural.) CHANGE TO: *One* should listen to the weather forecast so that *he* may anticipate a hurricane.

TROUBLESOME WORDS

There are a few groups of words that are often confused. You probably have many of these under control. Others may consistently give you trouble. Your choice of the best version of a sentence may hinge upon your understanding the correct uses of the words in these troublesome groups.

1. **their, they're, there**

   Their is the possessive of *they*.

   > *Example:*   The Martins claimed *their* dog from the pound because it belonged to them.

   They're is the contraction for *they are*.

   > *Example:*   Tom and Marie said that *they're* going skiing in February.

   There means *at that place*.

   > *Example:*   You may park your car over *there*.

   This last form is also used in sentences or clauses where the subject comes after the verb.

   > *Example:*   *There* is no one here by that name.

2. **your, you're**

   Your is the possessive of you.

   > *Example:*   Didn't we just drive past *your* house?

   You're is the contraction for you are.

   > *Example:*   When we finish caroling, *you're* all coming inside for hot chocolate.

3. **whose, who's**

   Whose is the possessive of who.

   > *Example:*   The handwriting is very distinctive, but I cannot remember *whose* it is.

   Who's is the contraction for *who is*.

   > *Example:*   *Who's* calling at this hour of night?

4. **its, it's**

   Its is the possessive of *it*.

   > *Example:*   The injured cat is licking *its* wounds.

   It's is the contraction for *it is*.

   > *Example:*   *It's* much too early to leave for the airport.

5. **which, who, that**

   Which as a relative pronoun refers only to objects.

   > *Example:*   This is the vase *which* the cat knocked over.

   Who and *whom* refer only to people.

   > *Example:*   The boy *who* won the prize is over there.

   That may refer to objects or people. *That* is used only in restrictive clauses.

   > *Example:*   This is the vase *that* the cat knocked over. The boy *that* won the prize is over there.

6. **learn, teach**

   To *learn* is to *acquire* knowledge.
   To *teach* is to *impart* knowledge.

   > *Example:*   My mother *taught* me all that I have *learned*.

7. **between, among**

   Between commonly applies to only two people or things.

   > *Example:*   Let us keep this secret *between you and me*.

   Among always implies that there are more than two.

   > *Example:*   The knowledge is secure *among the members* of our club.

   > *Exception:*   *Between* may be used with more than two objects to show the relationship to each object to each of the others, as in "The teacher explained the difference *between* adjective, adverb, and noun clauses."

8. **beside, besides**

   Beside is a preposition meaning *by the side of it*.

   > *Example:*   He sat *beside* his sick teacher.

   Besides, an adverb means *in addition to*.

   > *Example:*   *Besides* his father, his mother also was ill.

9. **lay, lie**

   The verb *to lay*, except when referring to hens, may be used only if you could replace it with the verb *to put*. At all other times, use a form of the verb *to lie*.

   > *Example:*   You may *lay* the books upon the table.
   > Let sleeping dogs *lie*.

10. **many/much, fewer/less, number/amount**

    The rule of *many/much, fewer/less, number/amount* is governed by a simple rule of thumb. If the object can be counted, use *many, fewer, number*. If the object is though of as a single mass or unit, use *much, less, amount*.

    > *Examples:*   *Many* raindrops make *much* water.
    > If you have *fewer* dollars, you have *less* money.
    > The *amount* of property you own depends upon the *number* of acres in your lot.

11. **I, me**

    The choice of *I* or *me* when the first person pronoun is used with one or more proper names may be tested by eliminating the proper names and reading the sentence with the pronoun alone.

    > *Example:*   John, George, Marylou, and (me *or* I) went to the movies last night (By eliminating the names you can readily choose *I went to the movies*.) It would be very difficult for Mae and (I *or* me) to attend the wedding. (Without *Mae* it is clear that *difficult for me* is correct.)

12. **already, all ready**

    Already means *prior to some specified time*.
    >   *Example:*   It is *already* too late to submit your application.

    All ready means *completely ready*.
    >   *Example:*   The cornfield is *all ready* for the seed to be sown.

13. **altogether, all together**

    Altogether means *entirely*.
    >   *Example:*   It is *altogether* too foggy to drive safely.

    All together means *in sum* or *collectively*.
    >   *Example:*   The family will be *all together* at the Thanksgiving dinner table.

14. **two, to, too**

    Two is the numeral 2
    >   *Example:*   There are *two* sides to every story.

    To means *in the direction of*.
    >   *Example:*   We shall go *to* school.

    Too means *more than* or *also*.
    >   *Example:*   It's *too* cold to go swimming today.
    >   We shall go, *too*.

GRAMMAR FUNDAMENTALS IMPARTED BY THE QUESTION AND ANSWER METHOD

Directions: Mark each of the following sentences as correct or incorrect by writing C or I beside its number. As you make your judgments, try to think of the rule that makes the sentence right or wrong. The 42 sentences are followed by explanations.

1. They are as old as us.
2. She is older than him.
3. Whom do you suppose paid us a visit.
4. Punish whomever is guilty.
5. It is me.
6. Can it be them?
7. Can it be her?
8. It would be impossible for you and I.
9. This is the death knell for we individualists.
10. He had a great deal of trouble with the store's management.
11. I, who's older, know better than you.
12. The man's hair is gray.
13. Is there any criticism of Arthur going?
14. Everybody tried their hardest.
15. I do not like these sort of cakes.
16. The government are unanimously agreed upon this action.
17. The government is unanimously agreed upon this action.
18. She don't like to engage in such activity.
19. The use of liquors are dangerous.
20. The district attorney, as well as many of his aides, have been involved in the investigation.
21. Either the fifth or the seventh of the courses they have laid open are to be accepted.
22. The fighting and wrestling of the two men is excellent.
23. The worst feature of the play were the abominable actors.
24. There is present a child and two dogs.
25. I shall go. You will go. He will go. We shall go. You will go. They will go.
26. I will; I repeat I will. You shall; I say you shall. He shall; I say he shall. We will; we say we will. You shall; I say you shall. They shall; I say they shall.
27. When he saw me he says his prayers.
28. If I only knowed what the results of my action would be I would have restrained myself.
29. He spoke slow and careful.
30. The sun shines bright on my old Kentucky home.
31. She looks beautiful.
32. A Washington street car accident resulted in two deaths.
33. The man gave the wrong reply.
34. The boy answered wrong.
35. He always has and will do it.
36. We hoped that you would have come to the party.
37. I intended to have gone.
38. In the parlor, my cousin kept a collection of animals which he shot.
39. He said that Venus was a planet.
40. If he was here, I should be happy.
41. I wish that I was a man.
42. By giving strict obedience to commands, a soldier learns discipline, and consequently would have steady nerves in time of war.

Explanatory Answers

Most of the 42 statements are grammatically incorrect. The errors are those of CASE, AGREEMENT, NUMBER, or PRINCIPAL PARTS. The proper form for each incorrect statement is given below. Following the proper form is a brief explanation of the grammatical principle underlying the correction.

Statements Involving Case

1. They are as old as we (are).
2. She is older than he (is).

PRINCIPLE: (1, 2) The subject of a verb is in the nominative case, even when the verb is remote, or understood (not expressed).

NOTE: *Than* and *as* are conjunctions, not prepositions. When they are followed by merely a pronoun, this pronoun is not their object, but part of a clause, the rest of which may be understood. The case of this pronoun is determined by its relation to the rest of the unexpressed clause. Sometimes the understood clause calls for the objective: "I like his brother better than (I like) him."

3. Who do you supposed paid us a visit?

PRINCIPLE: Guard against the improper attraction of *who* into the objective case by intervening expressions.

4. Punish whoever is guilty.

PRINCIPLE: Guard against the improper attraction of *who* or *whoever* into the objective case by preceding verbs or prepositions.

5. It is I.
6. Can it be they?
7. Can it be she?

PRINCIPLE: (5, 6, 7) Nouns or pronouns connected by the verb *to be* (in any of its forms: *is, was, were, be, etc.)* agree in case. *To be* never takes an object, because it does not express action.

8. It would be impossible for you and me.
9. This is the death knell for us individualists.

PRINCIPLE: (8, 9) The object of a preposition or a verb is in the objective case.

10. He had a great deal of trouble with the management of the store.

PRINCIPLE: It is usually awkward and slightly illogical to attribute possession to inanimate objects.

11. I, who am older, know better than you.

PRINCIPLE: A pronoun agrees with its antecedent in person, number, and gender, but not in case.

12. The man's hair is gray.

PRINCIPLE: A noun or pronoun used to express possession is in the possessive case. Do not omit the apostrophe from nouns, or from pronouns which require it, such as *one's*.

13. Is there any criticism of Arthur's going?

PRINCIPLE: A noun or pronoun linked with a gerund should be in the possessive case.

Statements Involving Number

14. Everybody tried his hardest.

PRINCIPLE: Each, every, every one, everybody, anybody, either, neither, no one, nobody, and similar words are singular.

15. I do not like this sort of cakes.

PRINCIPLE: Do not let *this* or *that*, when modifying *kind* or *sort*, be attracted into the plural by a following noun.

16. 17. Both statements are correct.

PRINCIPLE: (16, 17) Collective nouns may be regarded as singular or plural, according to the meaning intended.

18. She doesn't like to engage in such activity.

PRINCIPLE: Do not use *don't* in the third person singular. Use *doesn't. Don't* is a contraction of *do not*.

Statements Involving Agreement

19. The use of liquors is dangerous.

    PRINCIPLE: A verb agrees in number with the subject. A verb should not agree with a noun which intervenes between it and the subject.

20. The district attorney, as well as many of his aides, has been involved in the investigation.

    PRINCIPLE: The number of the verb is not affected by the addition to the subject of words introduced by: *with, together with, no less than, as well as,* etc.

21. Either the fifth or the seventh of the courses they have laid open is to be accepted.

    PRINCIPLE: Singular subjects joined by *nor* or *or* take a singular verb.

22. The fighting and wrestling of the two men are excellent.

    PRINCIPLE: A subject consisting of two or more nouns joined by *and* takes a plural verb.

23. The worst feature of the play was the abominable actors.

    PRINCIPLE: A verb should agree in number with the subject, not with a predicate noun.

24. There are present a child and two dogs.

    PRINCIPLE: In "there is" and "there are" sentences, the verb should agree in number with the noun that follows it.

25. The conjugation is correct:

    PRINCIPLE: To express simple futurity or mere expectation, use *shall* with the first person (both singular and plural) and *will* with the second and third.

26. All the sentences are correct.

    PRINCIPLE: To express resolution or emphatic assurance, reverse the usage: that is, use *will* with the first person (both singular and plural) and *shall* with the second and third.

Statements Involving Principal Parts

27. When he saw me he said his prayers.

28. If I only knew what the results of my action would be, I would have restrained myself

    PRINCIPLE: Use the correct form of the past tense and the past participle. Avoid *come, done, bursted, knowed, says,* for the past tense; and *(had) eat, (had) froze, (have) ran, (has) wrote, (are) suppose,* for the past participle.

    Memorize the principle parts of the most common "irregular" verbs. The principle parts are the infinitive *(to play)*, the first person of the past tense *(played)*, and the past participle *(played)*. The sample *(play)* is a "regular" verb; that is, the past tense and the past participle are formed by adding *ed* to the infinitive. This is not the case with "irregular" verbs. One way to recall the principal parts of "irregular" verbs is to repeat as follows: today I choose; yesterday I chose; often in the past I have chosen. Thus, the principal parts of choose are *choose* (infinitive); *chose* (past tense); and *chosen* (past participle).

29. He spoke slowly and carefully.

    PRINCIPLE: Do not use an adjective to modify a verb.

30. The statement is correct because *bright* modifies *sun*.

    PRINCIPLE: In such sentences as "He stood firm," and "The cry rang clear," the modifier should be an adjective if it refers to the subject, an adverb if it refers to the verb.

31. Statement is correct grammatically.

    PRINCIPLE: After a verb pertaining to the senses, an adjective is used to denote a quality pertaining to the subject. (An adverb is used only when the reference is clearly to the verb.)

32. A street car accident in Washington resulted in two deaths.

    PRINCIPLE: Use "made" adjectives with caution. When an adjective phrase that normally follows the noun is condense and placed before the noun as an attributive modifier, the result may be awkward, or even confusing.

33. 34. Both are correct.

PRINCIPLE: Certain adverbs do not differ in form from adjectives. When form does not indicate which of the two parts of speech is intended, the word must be classified according to its use in the sentence.

35. He always has done it, and always will do it.

PRINCIPLE: Do not use a verb, conjunction, preposition, or noun in a double capacity when one of the uses is ungrammatical.

36. We hoped that you would come to the party.

(The principle verb *hoped* indicates a past time. In that past time our hope was that you *would* come, not that you *would have* come.)

37. I intended to go.

(The principle verb *intended* indicates a past time. In that past time I intended to do something. What? Did I intended to *go* or to *have gone*?)

38. In the parlor, my cousin kept a collection of animals which he had shot.

PRINCIPLE: When narration in the past tense is interrupted for reference to preceding occurrence, the past perfect tense is used.

39. He said that Venus is a planet.

PRINCIPLE: General statements equally true in the past and in the present are usually expressed in the present tense.

40. If he were here I should be happy.

41. I wish that I were a man.

PRINCIPLE: The subjunctive mode of the verb *to be* is used to express a condition contrary to fact, or a wish.

42. By giving strict obedience to commands a soldier learns discipline, and consequently *will have* steady nerves in time of war.

PRINCIPLE: Use the correct auxiliary. Make sure that the tense, mode, or aspect of successive verbs is not altered without reason.

English Usage Drill

Directions: Underline the word or phrase that correctly completes each of the following sentences.

1. The reason he retired is (because, that, on account of) he is old.

2. The (number, amount, sum) of dying elm trees is rapidly increasing.

3. Put the book (in, into) this drawer.

4. Miss Smith made (less, fewer) errors than the other typists.

5. (Let us, Leave us) face it—the jury cannot make a determination of the facts.

6. (Due to, Because on account of, Because of) his long absence, he was unable to keep up with his class.

7. The customs in that part of the country are much (different from, different than) what I expected.

8. When she (graduates, will graduate, graduates from) college, she will be twenty-one.

9. I believe that we are (apt, likely, liable) to have good weather tomorrow.

10. I hope to be able to (reciprocate, retaliate) the assistance you have given me.

11. Where is the file (which, who, that) was left on the table?

12. (Regardless, Irregardless) of your decision, I shall have to go.

13. He fidgeted, (like, as) most children do, while the adults were discussing the problem.

14. The clerk who had fainted told me that he felt (alright, all right, okay), and so I didn't make an accident report.

15. What you are doing is (real, mighty, very) important.

16. The storm raged (continually, continuously) for twelve hours.

17. (Can, May) I ask you to double-check the totals?

18. She is taller (then any, than any, than any other) salesperson in the store.

19. Do you have enough (capitol, capital) to make the down payment on a car?

20. Americans should (join, join together) to destroy racial prejudice.

21. She asked the student to (bring, take) the book to the principal.

22. From the tone of the letter, it was easy to (infer, imply) that the writer was grateful.

23. If looks (like, as, as if) they will come.

24. For the sake of expediency, we divided the work (between, among) the four of us.

25. The slayer of Dr. King tried in (every way, every which way) to avoid the death penalty.

26. The reason Frank is going to Arizona is that he (despises, detests) a damp climate.

27. Get in touch with me in a (couple of, few) days.

28. Through a ruse, the prisoners (affected, effected) their escape from the penitentiary.

29. I am (anxious, eager) to hear about your trip to Africa.

30. You always look slender in (that, those) sort of clothes.

31. I (all ready, already) anticipate the good times we shall have on the cruise.

32. Please (loan, lend) me five dollars.

33. I shall try (an, to) attend one meeting.

34. No sooner had he finished his studies (when, then, than) he dashed out to play.

35. Such talk (irritates, aggravates) me.

36. Let's meet (around, about) six o'clock.

37. His father (learned, taught, teached) him how to bait a hook.

38. The scouts hiked a mile (further, farther) than they had intended.

39. There was a great (bunch, crowd) of people waiting for the ticket booth to open.

40. The milk carton sprung a leak, and the milk (spilled out, poured out) all over the refrigerator.

41. The Senator opposed school prayer as a matter of (principal, principle).

42. I think that Report A is (equally, just) as good as Report B.

43. I can read almost anything, but these (childish, childlike) books bore me.

44. She was promoted because she was more (discrete, discreet) than the other secretary.

45. Swimming is a (healthy, healthful) pastime.

46. The boss insisted on no one (but you, else but you) for the assignment.

47. We are quite (enthused, enthusiastic) about this new opportunity.

48. George did (like, as) his mother told him.

49. An excellent grade of synthetic rubber was (discovered, invented) in 1954 by Goodrich-Gulf scientists.

50. (That there, This there, That, This here) statue is one of the many that needs a good scrubbing.

51. The advertisement states, "Let our coffee (compliment, complement) your good cooking."

52. The drug-crazed boy was under the (illusion, delusion) that he could fly.

53. The artist was totally (uninterested, disinterested) in nuclear physics.

54. Several of the players consoled (each other, one another) as they straggled into the dugout.

55. (Enclosed herewith, Enclosed) is a copy of the book you ordered.

Answers to English Usage Drill

1. **that.** The use of *because* is redundant. The word *reason* implies that there is a cause.

2. **number.** The elm trees can be counted.

3. **into.** Motion from one place to another is expressed by *into*.

4. **fewer.** The errors can be counted.

5. **let us.** *Let* is used in conjunction with a verb. Here the verb is *(to) face*.

6. **Because of.** Never start a sentence with *due to*; *because on account of* is redundant.

7. **different from.** The correct idiomatic expression is *different from*.

8. **graduates from.** The college graduates the student; the student graduates *from* the college.

9. **likely.** *Liable* is used for undesirable happenings; *apt* refers to habitual events.

10. **reciprocate.** *Retaliate* has a negative connotation.

11. **that.** *That* is required to introduce the essential clause referring to an object.

12. **regardless.** *Irregardless* is unacceptable.

13. **as.** *Like* is a preposition and cannot act as a subordinate conjunction to introduce a clause.

14. **all right.** There is no such word as *alright; okay* is a colloquialism to be avoided whenever possible.

15. **very.** *Mighty* means *powerful* or *bulky*; *real* means *true*.

16. **continuously.** *Continuously* means without interruption; *continually* means happening often at intervals.

17. **May.** *May* is used for permission; *can* is used for a physical possibility.

18. **than any other.** *Than*, not *then*, is used in comparisons. Since the subject is one of the salespersons herself, she must e taller than any other one.

19. **capital.** *Capitol* is the building.

20. **join.** *Join together* is redundant.

21. **take.** One *takes from* the speaker and *brings to* another location.

22. **infer.** The listener *infers*; the speaker or writer *implies*. In this sentence we are "listening" to the writer.

23. **as if.** *Like* is a preposition and cannot act as a subordinate conjunction to introduce a clause; *as* along in incomplete; *as if* serves as a subordinate conjunction.

24. **among.** *Between* is used for two; *among* for three or more.

25. **every way.** *Every which way* is unnecessarily wordy.

26. **detest.** *Despise* means to *look down upon*; *detest* means to *hate*.

27. **few.** *Couple* is used for two things that are joined.

28. **effected.** *Affected* means *influenced*; *effected* means *brought about*.

29. **eager.** *Anxious* means *worried*.

30. **that.** Since *sort* is a singular noun, its modifier (*that*) must also be singular.

31. **already.** *All ready* means that all persons are ready.

32. **lend.** *Loan* is a noun.

33. **try to.** This is an idiomatic construction.

34. **than.** *No sooner . . . than* is the correct idiom.

35. **irritates.** To *aggravate* is to *make worse*; to *irritate* is to *annoy*.

36. **about.** *Around* is incorrect for the idea of "approximately."

37. **taught.** To *learn* is to *acquire* knowledge; to *teach* is to *give* knowledge. *Teached* is an incorrect past tense.

38. **farther.** *Further* is used for *time* or for *abstract distance*; *farther* is used for *concrete distance*.

39. **crowd.** *Bunch* refers to things.

40. **spilled out.** To *pour* is to send flowing with *direction,* and *control*; to *spill* is to start an *accidental* flow.

41. **principle.** The noun *principal* means *leader*; the adjective *principal* means *chief* or *main*. A *principle* is a fundamental *truth* or *belief*.

42. **just.** *Equally* is redundant; *just*, although correctly used, could be omitted from the sentence without changing its meaning.

43. **childish.** *Childlike* means *innocent*; *childish* means *silly*.

44. **discreet.** *Discrete* means *separate*.

45. **healthful.** *Healthy* means *having health*; *healthful* means *giving health*.

46. **but you.** *Else* is a superfluous word.

47. **enthusiastic.** *Enthused* is unacceptable.

48. **as.** The conjunction *as*, not the preposition *like*, must be used to connect a main clause and its subordinate clause.

49. **invented.** Man *discovers* what has already been there; he *invents* something that had no prior existence.

50. **that.** *This here, that there* and *this there* are all incorrect.

51. **complement.** A *compliment* is an expression of admiration that is unlikely to come from the coffee; a *complement* is a completion.

52. **delusion.** An *illusion* is a wrong idea that will probably not influence action nor do any harm; a *delusion* is a wrong idea that will probably influence action, often with dire consequences.

53. **uninterested.** *Disinterested* means *impartial*.

54. **one another.** *Each other* refers to two; *one another* refers to three or more.

55. **enclosed.** *Enclosed herewith* is redundant.

Answer Sheet for an Actual Previous Exam

1. Ⓐ Ⓑ Ⓒ Ⓓ   2. Ⓐ Ⓑ Ⓒ Ⓓ   3. Ⓐ Ⓑ Ⓒ Ⓓ   4. Ⓐ Ⓑ Ⓒ Ⓓ   5. Ⓐ Ⓑ Ⓒ Ⓓ

6. Ⓐ Ⓑ Ⓒ Ⓓ   7. Ⓐ Ⓑ Ⓒ Ⓓ   8. Ⓐ Ⓑ Ⓒ Ⓓ   9. Ⓐ Ⓑ Ⓒ Ⓓ   10. Ⓐ Ⓑ Ⓒ Ⓓ

11. Ⓐ Ⓑ Ⓒ Ⓓ   12. Ⓐ Ⓑ Ⓒ Ⓓ   13. Ⓐ Ⓑ Ⓒ Ⓓ   14. Ⓐ Ⓑ Ⓒ Ⓓ   15. Ⓐ Ⓑ Ⓒ Ⓓ

16. Ⓐ Ⓑ Ⓒ Ⓓ   17. Ⓐ Ⓑ Ⓒ Ⓓ   18. Ⓐ Ⓑ Ⓒ Ⓓ   19. Ⓐ Ⓑ Ⓒ Ⓓ   20. Ⓐ Ⓑ Ⓒ Ⓓ

21. Ⓐ Ⓑ Ⓒ Ⓓ   22. Ⓐ Ⓑ Ⓒ Ⓓ   23. Ⓐ Ⓑ Ⓒ Ⓓ   24. Ⓐ Ⓑ Ⓒ Ⓓ   25. Ⓐ Ⓑ Ⓒ Ⓓ

26. Ⓐ Ⓑ Ⓒ Ⓓ   27. Ⓐ Ⓑ Ⓒ Ⓓ   28. Ⓐ Ⓑ Ⓒ Ⓓ   29. Ⓐ Ⓑ Ⓒ Ⓓ   30. Ⓐ Ⓑ Ⓒ Ⓓ

31. Ⓐ Ⓑ Ⓒ Ⓓ   32. Ⓐ Ⓑ Ⓒ Ⓓ   33. Ⓐ Ⓑ Ⓒ Ⓓ   34. Ⓐ Ⓑ Ⓒ Ⓓ   35. Ⓐ Ⓑ Ⓒ Ⓓ

36. Ⓐ Ⓑ Ⓒ Ⓓ   37. Ⓐ Ⓑ Ⓒ Ⓓ   38. Ⓐ Ⓑ Ⓒ Ⓓ   39. Ⓐ Ⓑ Ⓒ Ⓓ   40. Ⓐ Ⓑ Ⓒ Ⓓ

41. Ⓐ Ⓑ Ⓒ Ⓓ   42. Ⓐ Ⓑ Ⓒ Ⓓ   43. Ⓐ Ⓑ Ⓒ Ⓓ   44. Ⓐ Ⓑ Ⓒ Ⓓ   45. Ⓐ Ⓑ Ⓒ Ⓓ

46. Ⓐ Ⓑ Ⓒ Ⓓ   47. Ⓐ Ⓑ Ⓒ Ⓓ   48. Ⓐ Ⓑ Ⓒ Ⓓ   49. Ⓐ Ⓑ Ⓒ Ⓓ   50. Ⓐ Ⓑ Ⓒ Ⓓ

51. Ⓐ Ⓑ Ⓒ Ⓓ   52. Ⓐ Ⓑ Ⓒ Ⓓ   53. Ⓐ Ⓑ Ⓒ Ⓓ   54. Ⓐ Ⓑ Ⓒ Ⓓ   55. Ⓐ Ⓑ Ⓒ Ⓓ

56. Ⓐ Ⓑ Ⓒ Ⓓ   57. Ⓐ Ⓑ Ⓒ Ⓓ   58. Ⓐ Ⓑ Ⓒ Ⓓ   59. Ⓐ Ⓑ Ⓒ Ⓓ   60. Ⓐ Ⓑ Ⓒ Ⓓ

61. Ⓐ Ⓑ Ⓒ Ⓓ   62. Ⓐ Ⓑ Ⓒ Ⓓ   63. Ⓐ Ⓑ Ⓒ Ⓓ   64. Ⓐ Ⓑ Ⓒ Ⓓ   65. Ⓐ Ⓑ Ⓒ Ⓓ

66. Ⓐ Ⓑ Ⓒ Ⓓ   67. Ⓐ Ⓑ Ⓒ Ⓓ   68. Ⓐ Ⓑ Ⓒ Ⓓ   69. Ⓐ Ⓑ Ⓒ Ⓓ   70. Ⓐ Ⓑ Ⓒ Ⓓ

71. Ⓐ Ⓑ Ⓒ Ⓓ   72. Ⓐ Ⓑ Ⓒ Ⓓ   73. Ⓐ Ⓑ Ⓒ Ⓓ   74. Ⓐ Ⓑ Ⓒ Ⓓ   75. Ⓐ Ⓑ Ⓒ Ⓓ

76. Ⓐ Ⓑ Ⓒ Ⓓ   77. Ⓐ Ⓑ Ⓒ Ⓓ   78. Ⓐ Ⓑ Ⓒ Ⓓ   79. Ⓐ Ⓑ Ⓒ Ⓓ   80. Ⓐ Ⓑ Ⓒ Ⓓ

81. Ⓐ Ⓑ Ⓒ Ⓓ   82. Ⓐ Ⓑ Ⓒ Ⓓ   83. Ⓐ Ⓑ Ⓒ Ⓓ   84. Ⓐ Ⓑ Ⓒ Ⓓ   85. Ⓐ Ⓑ Ⓒ Ⓓ

86. Ⓐ Ⓑ Ⓒ Ⓓ   87. Ⓐ Ⓑ Ⓒ Ⓓ   88. Ⓐ Ⓑ Ⓒ Ⓓ   89. Ⓐ Ⓑ Ⓒ Ⓓ   90. Ⓐ Ⓑ Ⓒ Ⓓ

91. Ⓐ Ⓑ Ⓒ Ⓓ   92. Ⓐ Ⓑ Ⓒ Ⓓ   93. Ⓐ Ⓑ Ⓒ Ⓓ   94. Ⓐ Ⓑ Ⓒ Ⓓ   95. Ⓐ Ⓑ Ⓒ Ⓓ

96. Ⓐ Ⓑ Ⓒ Ⓓ   97. Ⓐ Ⓑ Ⓒ Ⓓ   98. Ⓐ Ⓑ Ⓒ Ⓓ   99. Ⓐ Ⓑ Ⓒ Ⓓ   100. Ⓐ Ⓑ Ⓒ Ⓓ

An Actual Previous Exam

This is actual examination given to Correction Officer candidates a few years ago.

The Time Allowed for the Entire Examination Is 3¹/₂ Hours.

Directions: Each question has four suggested answers, lettered A, B, C, and D. Decide which one is the best answer. On the sample answer sheet, locate the question number and darken the area which corresponds to the answer that you have selected.

Questions 1 through 25 describe situations which might occur in a correctional institution. The institution houses its inmates in cells divided into groups called cell blocks. In answering the questions, assume that you are a Correction Officer.

1. Correction Officers are often required to search inmates and the various areas of the correctional institution for any items which may be considered dangerous or which are not permitted. In making a routine search, officers should not neglect to examine an item just because it is usually regarded as a permitted item. For instance, some innocent-looking object can be converted into a weapon by sharpening one of its parts or replacing a part with a sharpened or pointed blade. Which of the following objects could most easily be converted into a weapon in this way?

   A. A ballpoint pen.

   B. A pad of paper.

   C. A crayon.

   D. A handkerchief.

2. "Only authorized employees are permitted to handle keys. Under no circumstances should an inmate be permitted to use door keys. When not in use, all keys are to be deposited with the Security Officer." Which one of the following actions does *not* violate these regulations?

   A. A Correction Officer has given a trusted inmate the key to a supply room and sent the inmate to bring back a specific item from that room.

   B. A priest comes to make authorized visits to inmates. The Correction Officer is very busy, so he gives the priest the keys needed to reach certain groups of cells.

   C. An inmate has a pass to go to the library. A Cell block Officer examines the pass, then unlocks the door and lets the inmate through.

   D. At the end of the day, a Correction Officer puts his keys in the pocket of his street clothes and takes them home with him.

3. "Decisions about handcuffing or restraining inmates are often up to the Correction Officers involved. An officer is legally responsible for exercising good judgment and for taking necessary precautions to prevent harm both to the inmate involved and to others." In which one of the following situations is handcuffing or other physical restraint most likely to be needed?

   A. An inmate seems to have lost control of his senses and is banging his fists repeatedly against the bars of his cell.

   B. During the past two weeks, an inmate has deliberately tried to start three fights with other inmates.

   C. An inmate claims to be sick and refuses to leave his cell for a scheduled meal.

   D. During the night an inmate begins to shout and sing, disturbing the sleep of other inmates.

4. "Some utensils that are ordinarily used in a kitchen can also serve as dangerous weapons—for instance, vegetable parers, meat saws, skewers, and ice picks. These should be classified as extremely hazardous." The most sensible way of solving the problem caused by the use of these utensils in a correctional institution is to

   A. try to run the kitchen without using any of these utensils

   B. provide careful supervision of inmates using such utensils in the kitchen

   C. assign only trusted inmates to kitchen duty and let them use the tools without regular supervision

   D. take no special precautions, since inmates are not likely to think of using these common-place utensils as weapons

5. "Inmates may try to conceal objects that can be used as weapons or as escape devices. Therefore routine searches of cells or dormitories are necessary for safety and security." Of the following, it would probably be most effective to schedule routine searches to take place

   A. on regular days and always at the same time of day

   B. on regular days but at different times of day

   C. at frequent but irregular intervals, always at the same time of day

   D. at frequent but irregular intervals and at different times of day

6. "One of the purposes of conducting routine searches for forbidden items is to discourage inmates from acquiring such items in the first place. Inmates should soon come to realize that only possessors of these items have reason to fear or resent such searches." Inmates are most likely to come to this realization if

   A. the searching officer leaves every inmate's possessions in a mess to make it clear that a search has taken place

   B. the searching officer confiscates something from every cell, though he may later return most of the items

   C. other inmates are not told when a forbidden item is found in an inmate's possession

   D. all inmates know that possession of a forbidden item will result in punishment

7. Suppose you are a Correction Officer supervising a work detail of 22 inmates. All 22 checked in at the start of the work period. Making an informal count an hour later, you count only 21 inmates. What is the *first* action to take?

    A. Count again to make absolutely sure how many inmates are present.

    B. Report immediately that an inmate has escaped.

    C. Try to figure out where the missing inmate could be.

    D. Wait until the end of the work period and then make a formal roll call.

8. "The officer who is making a count at night when inmates are in bed must make sure he sees each man. The rule 'See living breathing flesh' must be followed in making accurate counts." Of the following, which is the most likely reason for this rule?

    A. An inmate may be concealing a weapon in the bed.

    B. A bed may be arranged to give the appearance of being occupied even when the inmate is not there.

    C. Waking inmates for the count is a good disciplinary measure because it shows them that they are under constant guard.

    D. It is important for officers on duty at night to have something to do to keep them busy.

9. "When counting a group of inmates on a work assignment, great care should be taken to ensure accuracy. The count method should be adapted to the number of inmates and to the type of location." Suppose that you are supervising 15 inmates working in a kitchen. Most of them are moving about constantly, carrying dishes and equipment from one place to another. In order to make an accurate count, which of the following methods would be most suitable under these circumstances?

    A. Have the inmates "freeze" where they are whenever you call for a count, even though some of them may be carrying hot pans or heavy stacks of dishes.

    B. Have the inmates stop their work and gather in one place whenever it is necessary to make a count.

    C. Circulate among the inmates and make an approximate count while they are working.

    D. Divide the group into sections according to type of work and assign one inmate in each group to give you the number of his section.

10. "Officers on duty at entrances must exercise the greatest care to prevent movement of unauthorized persons. At vehicle entrances, all vehicles must be inspected and a record kept of their arrival and departure." Assume that, as a Correction Officer, you have been assigned to duty at a vehicle entrance. Which of the following is probably the best method of preventing the movement of unauthorized persons in vehicles.

    A. If passenger identifications are checked when vehicle enters, no check is necessary when the vehicle leaves.

    B. Passenger identifications should be checked for all vehicles when vehicle enters and when it leaves.

    C. Passenger identifications need not be checked when vehicle enters, but should always be checked when vehicle leaves.

    D. Except for official vehicles, passenger identifications should be checked when vehicle enters and when it leaves.

11. In making a routine search of an inmate's cell, an officer finds various items. Although there is no immediate danger, he is not sure whether the inmate is permitted to have one of the items. Of the following, the best action for the officer to take is to

    A. confiscate the item immediately

    B. give the inmate the benefit of the doubt, and let him keep the item

    C. consult his rule book or his supervising officer to find out whether the inmate is permitted to have the item

    D. leave the item in the inmate's cell, but plan to report him for an infraction of the rules

12. It is almost certain that there will be occasional escape attempts or an occasional riot or disturbance that requires immediate emergency action. A well-developed emergency plan for dealing with these events includes not only planning for prevention and control, and planning for action during the disturbance, but also planning steps that should be taken when the disturbance is over. When a disturbance is ended, which of the following steps should be taken *first*?

    A. Punish the ringleaders.

    B. Give first aid to inmates or other persons who were injured.

    C. Make an institutional count of all inmates.

    D. Adopt further security rules to make sure such an incident does not occur again.

13. It is often important to make notes about an occurrence that will require a written report or personal testimony. Assume that a Correction Officer has made the following notes for the warden of the institution about a certain occurrence: "10:45 a.m. March 16, 1982. Cell block A. Robert Brown was attacked by another inmate and knocked to the floor. Brown's head hit the floor hard. He was knocked out. I reported a medical emergency. Dr. Thomas Nunez came and examined Brown. The doctor recommended that Brown be transferred to the infirmary for observation. Brown was taken to the infirmary at 11:15 a.m." Which of the following important items of information is missing or is incomplete in these notes?

    A. The time that the incident occurred.

    B. The place where the incident occurred.

    C. The names of both inmates involved in the fight.

    D. The name of the doctor who made the medical recommendation.

14. A Correction Officer has made the following notes for the warden of his institution about an incident involving an infraction of the rules: "March 29, 1982. Cell block B-4. Inmates involved were A. Whitman, T. Brach, M. Purlin, M. Verey. Whitman and Brach started the trouble about 7:30. I called for assistance. Officer Haley and Officer Blair responded. Officer Blair got cut, and blood started running down his face. The bleeding looked very bad. He was taken to the hospital and needed 8 stitches." Which of the following items of information is missing or is incomplete in these notes?

    A. The time and date of the incident.

    B. The place of the incident.

    C. Which inmates took part in the incident.

    D. What the inmates did that broke the rules.

15. Your Supervising Officer has instructed you to follow a new system for handling inmate requests. It seems to you that a new system is not going to work very well and that inmates may resent it. What should you do?

    A. Continue handling requests the old way, but do not let your Supervising Officer know you are doing this.

    B. Continue using the old system until you have a chance to discuss the matter with your Supervising Officer.

    C. Begin using the new system, but plan to discuss the matter with your Supervising Officer if the system really does not work well.

    D. Begin using the new system, but make sure the inmates know that it is not your idea and you do not approve of it.

16. Inmates who are prison-wise may know a good many tricks for putting something over. For instance, it is an officer's duty to stop fights among inmates. Therefore, inmates who want to distract the officer's attention from something that is going on in one place may arrange for a phony fight to take place some distance away. To avoid being taken in by a trick like this, a Correction Officer should

    A. ignore any fights that break out among inmates

    B. always make an inspection tour to see what is going on elsewhere before breaking up a fight

    C. be alert for other suspicious activity when there is any disturbance

    D. refuse to report inmates involved in a fight, if the fight seems to have been phony

17. Copies of the regulations are posted at various locations in the cell block so that inmates can refer to them. Suppose that one of the regulations is changed and the Correction Officers receive revised copies to post in their cell blocks. Of the following, the most effective way of informing the inmates of the revision is to

    A. let the inmates know that you are taking down the old copies and putting up new ones in their place

    B. post the new copies next to the old ones, so that inmates will be able to compare them and learn about the change for themselves

    C. leave the old copies up until you have had a chance to explain the change to each inmate

    D. post the new copies in place of the old ones and also explain the change orally to the inmates

18. A fracture is a broken bone. In a simple fracture, the skin is not broken. In a compound fracture, a broken end of the bone pierces the skin. Whenever a fracture is feared, the first thing to do is to prevent motion of the broken part. Suppose that an inmate has just tripped on a stairway and twisted his ankle. He says it hurts badly, but you cannot tell what is wrong merely by looking at it. Of the following, the best action to take is to

    A. tell the inmate to stand up and see whether he can walk

    B. move the ankle gently to see whether you can feel any broken ends of bones

    C. tell the inmate to rest a few minutes and promise to return later to see whether his condition has improved

    D. tell the inmate not to move his foot and put in a call for medical assistance

19. "It is part of institutional procedure that at specified times during each 24-hour period all inmates in the institution are counted *simultaneously*. Each inmate *must* be counted at a specific time. All movement of inmates ceases from the time the count starts until it is finished and cleared as correct." Assume that, as a Correction Officer, you are making such a count when an inmate in your area suddenly remembers he has an important 9 a.m. clinic appointment. You check his clinic pass and find that this is true. What should you do?

A. Let him go to the clinic even though he may be counted again there.

B. Take him off your count and tell him to be sure he is included in the count being made at the clinic.

C. Keep him in your count and tell him to inform the officer at the clinic that he has already been counted.

D. Ask him to wait a few minutes until the counting period is over and then let him go to the clinic.

20. "Except in the case of a serious illness or injury (when a doctor should see the inmate immediately) emergency sick calls should be kept to a minimum, and inmates should be encouraged to wait for regular sick-call hours." In which of the following cases is an emergency sick call most likely to be justified?

A. An inmate has had very severe stomach pains for several hours.

B. An inmate has cut his hand, and the bleeding has now stopped.

C. An inmate's glasses have been broken, and he is nearly blind without them.

D. A normally healthy inmate has lost his appetite and does not want to eat.

21. "People who have lost their freedom are likely to go through periods of depression, or to become extremely resentful or unpleasant. A Correction Officer can help inmates who are undergoing such periods of depression by respecting their feelings and treating them in a reasonable and tactful manner." Suppose that an inmate reacts violently to a simple request made in a normal, routine manner by a Correction Officer. Of the following, which is likely to be the most effective way of handling the situation?

A. Point out to the inmate that it is his own fault that he is in jail, and he has nobody to blame for his troubles but himself.

B. Tell the inmate that he is acting childishly and that he had better straighten out.

C. Tell the inmate in a friendly way that you can see he is feeling down, but that he should comply with your request.

D. Let the inmate know that you are going to report his behavior unless he changes.

22. An inmate tells you, a Correction Officer, of his concern about the ability of his wife and children to pay for rent and food while he is in the institution. Of the following, which is the best action to take?

A. Assure him that his wife and children are getting along fine, although you do not actually know this.

B. Put him in touch with the social worker or the correction employee who handles such problems.

C. Offer to lend him money yourself if his family is really in need.

D. Advise him to forget about his family and start concentrating on his own problems.

23. "It is particularly important to notice changes in the general pattern of an inmate's behavior. When an inmate who has been generally unpleasant and who has not spoken to an officer unless absolutely necessary, becomes very friendly and cooperative, something has happened, and the officer should take steps to make sure what." Of the following possible explanations for this change in behavior, which one is the *least* likely to be the real cause?

    A. The inmate may be planning some kind of disturbance or escape attempt and is trying to fool the officer.

    B. The inmate may be trying to get on the officer's good side for some reason of his own.

    C. His friendliness and cooperation may indicate a developing mental illness.

    D. He may be overcoming his initial hostile reactions to his imprisonment.

24. As a Correction Officer, you have an idea about a new way for handling a certain procedure. Your method would require a minor change in the regulations, but you are sure it would be a real improvement. The best thing for you to do is to

    A. discuss the idea with your Supervising Officer, explaining why it would work better than the present method

    B. try your idea on your own cell block, telling inmates that it is just an experiment and not official

    C. attempt to get officers on other cell blocks to use your methods on a strictly unofficial basis

    D. forget the whole thing, since it might be too difficult to change the regulations

25. "Correction Officers assigned to visiting areas have a dual supervisory function, since their responsibilities include receiving persons other than inmates as well as handling inmates. Here, of all places, it is important for an officer to realize that he is acting as a representative of his institution and that what he is doing is very much like public relations work." Assume that you are a Correction Officer assigned to duty in a visiting area. Which of the following ways of carrying out this assignment is most likely to result in good public relations?

    A. You should treat inmates and visitors sternly, because this will let them know that the institution does not put up with any nonsense.

    B. You should be friendly to inmates, but suspicious of visitors.

    C. You should be stern with inmates, but polite and tactful with visitors.

    D. You should treat both inmates and visitors in a polite and tactful way.

Answer questions 26 through 30 on the basis of the following passage.

The handling of supplies is an important part of correctional administration. A good deal of planning and organization is involved in purchase, stock control, and issue of bulk supplies to the cell block. This planning is meaningless, however, if the final link in the chain—the Cell block Officer who is in charge of distributing supplies to the inmates—does not do his job in the proper way. First, when supplies are received, the officer himself should immediately check them or should personally supervise the checking, to make sure the count is correct. Nothing but trouble will result if an officer signs for 200 towels and discovers hours later that he is 20 towels short. Did the 20 towels "disappear," or did they never arrive in the first place? Second, all supplies should be locked up until they are actually distributed. Third, the officer must keep accurate records when supplies are issued. Complaints will be kept to a minimum if the officer makes sure that each inmate has received the supplies to which he is entitled, and if the officer can tell from his records when it is time to reorder to prevent a shortage. Fourth, the officer should either issue the supplies himself or else personally supervise the issuing. It is unfair and unwise to put an inmate in charge of supplies without giving him adequate supervision. A small thing like a bar of soap does not mean much to most people, but it means a great deal to the inmate who cannot even shave or wash up unless he receives the soap that is supposed to be issued to him.

26. Which one of the following jobs is *not* mentioned by the passage as the responsibility of a Cell block Officer?

    A. Purchasing supplies.

    B. Issuing supplies.

    C. Counting supplies when they are delivered to the cell block.

    D. Keeping accurate records when supplies are issued.

27. The passage says that supplies should be counted when they are delivered. Of the following, which is the best way of handling this job?

    A. The Cell block Officer can wait until he has some free time and then count them himself.

    B. An inmate can start counting them right away, even if the Cell block Officer cannot supervise his work.

    C. The Cell block Officer can personally supervise an inmate who counts the supplies when they are delivered.

    D. Two inmates can count them when they are delivered, supervising each other's work.

28. The passage gives an example concerning a delivery of 200 towels that turned out to be 20 towels short. The author of the passage uses this example to show that

    A. the missing towels were stolen

    B. the missing towels never arrived in the first place

    C. it is impossible to tell what happened to the missing towels because no count was made when they were delivered

    D. it does not matter that the missing towels were not accounted for because it is never possible to keep track of supplies accurately

29. The main reasons given by the passage for making a record when supplies are issued is that keeping record

    A. will discourage inmates from stealing supplies

    B. is a way of making sure that each inmate receives the supplies to which he is entitled

    C. will show the officer's superiors that he is doing his job in the proper way

    D. will enable the inmates to help themselves to any supplies they need

30. The passage says that it is unfair to put an inmate in charge of supplies without giving him adequate supervision. Which of the following is the most likely explanation of why it would be "unfair" to do this?

    A. A privilege should not be given to one inmate unless it is given to all the other inmates too.

    B. It is wrong to make one inmate work when all the others can sit in their cells and do nothing.

    C. The Cell block Officer should not be able to get out of doing a job by making an inmate do it for him.

    D. The inmate in charge of supplies could be put under pressure by other inmates to do them "special favors."

Answer questions 31 through 35 on the basis of the following passage.

The typical Correction Official must make predictions about the probable future behavior of his charges in order to make judgments affecting those individuals. In learning to predict behavior, the results of scientific studies of inmate behavior can be of some use. Most studies that have been made show that older men tend to obey rules and regulations better than younger men and tend to be more reliable in carrying out assigned jobs. Men who had good employment records on the outside also tend to be more reliable than men whose records show haphazard employment or unemployment. Oddly enough, men convicted of crimes of violence are less likely to be troublemakers than men convicted of burglary or other crimes involving stealth. While it might be expected that first offenders would be much less likely to be troublemakers than men with previous convictions, the difference between the two groups is not very great. It must be emphasized however, that predictions based on a man's background are only likelihoods—they are never certainties. A successful Correction Officer learns to give some weight to a man's background, but he should rely even more heavily on his own personal judgment of the individual in question. A good officer will develop in time a kind of sixth sense about human beings that is more reliable than any statistical prediction.

31. The passage suggests that knowledge of scientific studies of inmate behavior would probably help the Correction Officer to

    A. make judgments that affect the inmates in his charge

    B. write reports on all major infractions of the rules

    C. accurately analyze how an inmate's behavior is determined by his background

    D. change the personalities of the individuals in his charge

32. According to the information in the passage, which one of the following groups of inmates would tend to be most reliable in carrying out assigned jobs?

    A. Older men with haphazard employment records.

    B. Older men with regular employment records.

    C. Younger men with haphazard employment records.

    D. Younger men with regular employment records.

33. According to the information in the passage, which of the following are most likely to be troublemakers?

    A. Older men convicted of crimes of violence.

    B. Younger men convicted of crimes of violence.

    C. Younger men convicted of crimes involving stealth.

    D. First offenders convicted of crimes of violence.

34. The passage indicates that information about a man's background is

    A. a sure way of predicting his future behavior

    B. of no use at all in predicting his future behavior

    C. more useful in predicting behavior than a Correction Officer's expert judgment

    D. less reliable in predicting behavior than a Correction Officer's expert judgment

35. The passage names two groups of inmates whose behavior might be expected to be quite different, but who in fact behave only slightly differently. The two groups are

    A. older men and younger men

    B. first offenders and men with previous convictions

    C. men with good employment records and men with records of haphazard employment or unemployment

    D. men who obey the rules and men who do not

Questions 36 through 42 are based on the following pictures of objects found in cells A, B, C, and D in a correctional institution.

36. Which item can be found in every cell?

    A. cup

    B. money

    C. pencil

    D. toothpaste

37. Which cell has toothpaste but *no* toothbrush?

    A. A

    B. B

    C. C

    D. D

38. If knives and forks are prohibited in cells, how many cells are in violation of this rule?

    A. 1

    B. 2

    C. 3

    D. 4

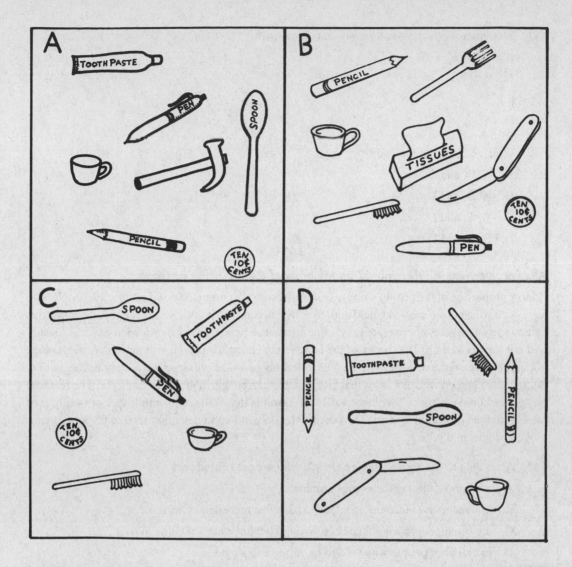

39. One inmate failed to return his tool in the woodworking shop before returning to his cell. That inmate is in cell

    A. A

    B. B

    C. C

    D. D

40. The cell with the greatest number of objects is

    A. A

    B. B

    C. C

    D. D

41. How many cells have at least one eating utensil?

    A. 1

    B. 2

    C. 3

    D. 4

42. Which cells contain money?

    A. A, B, and C

    B. A, B, and D

    C. A, C, and D

    D. B, C, and D

Answer questions 43 through 47 on the basis of the following passage.

A large proportion of the people who are behind bars are not convicted criminals but are people who have been arrested and are being held until their trial in court. Experts have often pointed out that this detention system does not operate fairly. For instance, a person who can afford to pay bail usually will not stay locked up. The theory of the bail system is that the person will make sure to show up in court on time because otherwise he will forfeit his bail—he will lose the money he has put up. Sometimes a person who can show that he is a stable citizen with a job and a family will be released on "personal recognizance" (without bail). The result is that well-to-do, employed, or family men often avoid the detention system. The people who do wind up in detention tend to be poor, unemployed, single, and young.

43. According to the above passage, people who are put behind bars

    A. are almost always dangerous criminals

    B. include many innocent people who have been arrested by mistake

    C. are often people who have been arrested but have not yet come to trial

    D. are all poor people who tend to be young and single

44. The passage says that the detention system works unfairly against people who are

    A. rich

    B. married

    C. old

    D. unemployed

45. The passage uses the expression "forfeit his bail." Even if you had not seen the word *forfeit* before, you could figure out from the way it is used in the passage that *forfeiting* probably means

    A. losing track of something

    B. giving up something

    C. finding something

    D. avoiding something

46. When someone is released on "personal recognizance," this means that

    A. the judge knows that he is innocent

    B. he does not have to show up for a trial

    C. he has a record of previous convictions

    D. he does not have to pay bail

47. Suppose that two men were booked on the same charge at the same time and that the same bail was set for both of them. One man was able to put up bail, and he was released. The second man was not able to put up bail, and he was held in detention. The writer of the passage would most likely feel that this result is

    A. unfair, because it does not have any relation to guilt or innocence

    B. unfair, because the first man deserves severe punishment

    C. fair, because the first man is obviously innocent

    D. fair, because the law should be tougher on poor people than on rich people

Questions 48 through 53 are based on the following list of items permitted in cells.

ITEMS PERMITTED IN CELLS

comb	mop
spoon	towel
cup	letters
envelopes	pen
broom	soap
washcloth	money
writing paper	chair
books	dustpan
toothpaste	brushes
toothbrush	pencil

The questions consist of sets of pictures of four object labeled A, B, C, and D. Choose the one object that is *not* in the above list of items permitted and mark its letter on your answer sheet. Disregard any information you may have about what is or is not permitted in any institution. Base your answers solely on the above list. Mark only one answer for each question.

48.

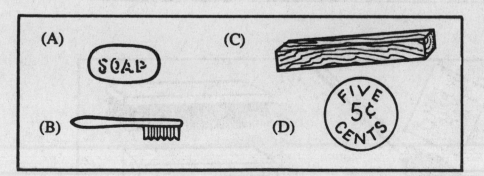

49.

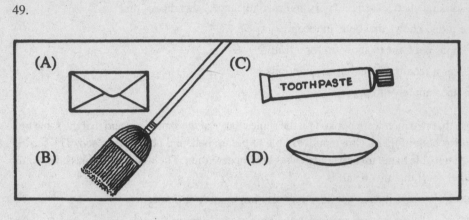

50.

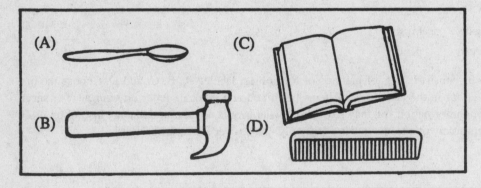

51.

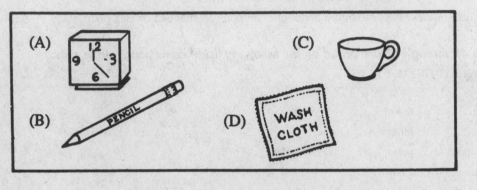

52.

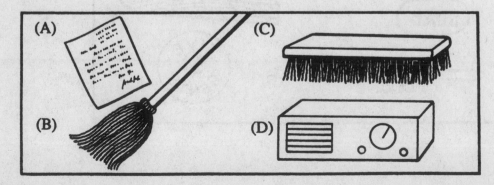

53.

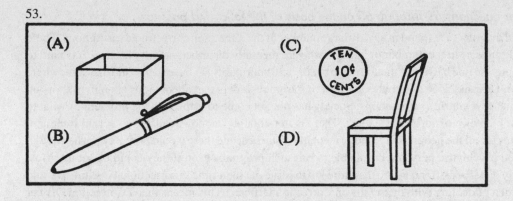

Questions 54 through 58 are based on the following list showing the name and number for each of nine inmates.

1-Johnson	4-Thompson	7-Gordon
2-Smith	5-Frank	8-Porter
3-Edwards	6-Murray	9-Lopez

Each question consists of 3 sets of numbers and letters. Each set should consist of the numbers of three inmates and the first letter of each of their names. The letters should be in the same order as the numbers. In at least two of the three choices, there will be an error. On your answer sheet, mark only that choice in which the letters correspond with the numbers and are in the same order. If all three sets are wrong, make choice D on your answer sheet.

Sample Question: A. 386 EPM
                       B. 542 FST
                       C. 474 LGT

Since 3 corresponds to E for Edwards, 8 corresponds to P for Porter, and 6 corresponds to M for Murray, choice A is correct and should be entered on your answer sheet. Choice B is wrong because letters T and S have been reversed. Choice C is wrong because the first number, which is 4, does *not* correspond with the first letter of choice C, which is L. It should have been T. If choice A were also wrong, then D would be the correct answer.

54. A. 382 EGS
    B. 461 TMJ
    C. 875 PLF

55. A. 549 FLT
    B. 692 MJS
    C. 758 GFP

56. A. 936 LEM
    B. 253 FSE
    C. 147 JTL

57. A. 569 PML
    B. 716 GJP
    C. 842 PTS

58. A. 356 FEM
    B. 198 JPL
    C. 637 MEG

Answer questions 59 through 63 on the basis of the following passage.

"Mental disorders are found in a fairly large number of the inmates in correctional institutions. There are no figures as to the number of inmates who are mentally disturbed—partly because it is hard to draw a precise line between "mental disturbance" and "normality"—but experts find that somewhere between 15% and 25% of inmates are suffering from disorders that are obvious enough to show up in routine psychiatric examinations. Society has not yet come to grips with the problem of what to do with mentally disturbed offenders. There is not enough money available to set up treatment programs for all the people identified as mentally disturbed; and there would probably not be enough qualified psychiatric personnel available to run such programs even if they could be set up. Most mentally disturbed offenders are therefore left to serve out their time in correctional institutions, and the burden of dealing with them falls on Correction Officers. This means that a Correction Officer must be sensitive enough to human behavior to know when he is dealing with a person who is not mentally normal and that the officer must be imaginative enough to be able to sense how an abnormal individual might react under certain circumstances.

59. According to the above passage, mentally disturbed inmates in correctional institutions

    A. are usually transferred to mental hospitals when their condition is noticed

    B. cannot be told from other inmates, because tests cannot distinguish between insane people and normal people

    C. may constitute as much as 25% of the total inmate population

    D. should be regarded as no different from all the other inmates

60. The passage says that today the job of handling mentally disturbed inmates is mainly up to

    A. psychiatric personnel

    B. other inmates

    C. Correction Officers

    D. administrative officials

61. Of the following, which is a reason given in the passage for society's failure to provide adequate treatment programs for mentally disturbed inmates?

    A. Law-abiding citizens should not have to pay for fancy treatment programs for criminals.

    B. A person who breaks the law should not expect society to give him special help.

    C. It is impossible to tell whether an inmate is mentally disturbed.

    D. There are not enough trained people to provide the kind of treatment needed.

62. The expression "abnormal individual" as used in the last sentence of the passage, refers to an individual who is

    A. of average intelligence

    B. of superior intelligence

    C. completely normal

    D. mentally disturbed

63. The author of the passage would most likely agree that

    A. Correction Officers should not expect mentally disturbed persons to behave the same way a normal person would behave

    B. Correction Officers should not report infractions of the rules committed by mentally disturbed persons

    C. mentally disturbed persons who break the law should be treated exactly the same way as anyone else

    D. mentally disturbed persons who have broken the law should not be imprisoned

Questions 64 through 70 are based on the roster of inmates, the instructions, the table, and the sample question given below.

Twelve inmates of a correctional institution are divided into three permanent groups in their workshop. They must be present and accounted for in these groups at the beginning of each workday. During the day, the inmates check out of their groups for various activities. They check back in again when those activities have been completed. Assume that the day is divided into three activity periods.

ROSTER OF INMATES

Group X	Ted	Frank	George	Harry
Group Y	Jack	Ken	Larry	Mel
Group Z	Phil	Bob	Sam	Vic

The following table shows the movements of these inmates from their groups during the day. Assume that all were present and accounted for at the beginning of Period I.

		Group X	**Group Y**	**Group Z**
Period I	Check-outs	Ted, Frank	Ken, Larry	Phil
Period II	Check-ins	Frank	Ken, Larry	Phil
	Check-outs	George	Jack, Mel	Bob, Sam, Vic
Period III	Check-ins	George	Mel, Jack	Sam, Bob, Vic
	Check-outs	Frank, Harry	Ken	Vic

Sample Question:

At the end of Period II, the inmates remaining in Group X were

    A. Ted, Frank, Harry

    B. Frank, Harry

    C. Ted, George

    D. Frank, Harry, George

During Period I, Ted and Frank were checked out from Group X. During Period II, Frank was checked back in and George was checked out. Therefore, the members of the group remaining out are Ted and George. The two other members of the group, Frank and Harry, should be present. The correct answer is B.

64. At the end of Period I, the total number of inmates remaining in their own permanent groups was

    A. 8
    B. 7
    C. 6
    D. 5

65. At the end of Period I, the inmates remaining in Group Z were

    A. George and Harry
    B. Jack and Mel
    C. Bob, Sam, and Vic
    D. Phil

66. At the end of Period II, the inmates remaining in Group Y were

    A. Ken and Larry
    B. Jack, Ken, and Mel
    C. Jack and Ken
    D. Ken, Mel, and Larry

67. At the end of Period II, the total number of inmates remaining in their own permanent groups was

    A. 8
    B. 7
    C. 6
    D. 5

68. At the end of Period II, the inmates who were *not* present in Group Z were

    A. Phil, Bob, and Sam
    B. Sam, Bob, and Vic
    C. Sam, Vic, and Phil
    D. Vic, Phil, and Bob

69. At the end of Period III, the inmates remaining in Group Y were

    A. Ted, Frank, and George
    B. Jack, Mel, and Ken
    C. Jack, Larry, and Mel
    D. Frank and Harry

70. At the end Period III, the total number of inmates *not* present in their own permanent groups was

    A. 4
    B. 5
    C. 6
    D. 7

Answer questions 71 through 75 solely on the basis of the Report of Offense that appears below.

REPORT OF OFFENSE   Report No. _____ 26743_____

                                               Date of Report _____ 10-12_____

Inmate _____ Joseph Brown _____

Age _____ 27 _____   Number _____ 61274 _____

Sentence _____ 90 days _____   Assignment _____ KU-187 _____

Place of offense _____ R.P.W., 4-1 _____   Date of offense _____ Oct. 11 _____

Offense _____ Assaulting inmate _____

Details _____ During 9:00 p.m. cellblock cleanup, inmate John Jones asked for pail being used by Brown. Brown refused. Correction officer requested that Brown comply. Brown then threw pail at Jones with intent to injure him and said he would "get" Jones. Jones not hurt. _____

Force used by officer _____ None _____

Name of reporting officer _____ R. Rodriguez _____ No. _____ C-2056 _____

Name of superior officer _____ P. Ferguson _____

---

71. The person who made out this report is

    A. Joseph Brown

    B. John Jones

    C. R. Rodriquez

    D. P. Ferguson

72. Disregarding the details, the specific offense reported was

    A. insulting a fellow inmate

    B. assaulting a fellow inmate

    C. injuring a fellow inmate

    D. disobeying a Correction Officer

73. The number of the inmate who committed the offense is
    A. 26743
    B. 61274
    C. KU-187
    D. C-2056

74. The offense took place on
    A. October 11
    B. June 12
    C. December
    D. November 13

75. The place where the offense occurred is identified in the report as
    A. Brown's cell
    B. Jones's cell
    C. KU-187
    D. R.P.W., 4-1

76. Add $51.79, $29.39, and $8.98. The correct answer is
    A. $78.97
    B. $88.96
    C. $89.06
    D. $90.16

77. Add $72.07, $31.54, then subtract $25.75. The correct answer is
    A. $77.86
    B. $82.14
    C. $88.96
    D. $129.36

78. Start with $82.47, then subtract $25.50, $4.75, and $0.35. The correct answer is
    A. $30.60
    B. $51.87
    C. $52.22
    D. $65.25

79. Add $19.35 and $37.75, then subtract $9.90 and $19.80. the correct answer is
    A. $27.40   C. $37.30
    B. $37.00   D. $47.20

80. Multiply $38.85 by 2; then subtract $27.90. The correct answer is
    A. $21.90   C. $49.80
    B. $48.70   D. $50.70

81. Add $53.66, $9.27, and $18.75; then divide by 2. The correct answer is
    A. $35.84   C. $40.84
    B. $40.34   D. $41.34

82. Out of 192 inmates in a certain cell block, 96 are to go on a work detail, and another 32 are to report to a vocational class. All the rest are to remain in the cell block. How many inmates should be left on the cell block?
    A. 48   C. 86
    B. 64   D. 128

83. Assume that you, as a Correction Officer, are responsible for seeing that the right number of utensils are counted out for a meal. You need enough utensils for 620 men. One fork and one spoon are needed for each man. In addition, one ladle is needed for each group of 20 men. How many utensils will be needed altogether?
    A. 1,240   C. 1,550
    B. 1,271   D. 1,860

84. Assume that you, as a Correction Officer, are supervising the inmates who are assigned to a dishwashing detail. There is a direct relationship between the amount of time it takes to do all the dishwashing and the number of inmates who are washing dishes. When two inmates are washing dishes, the job takes six hours. If there are four inmates washing dishes, how long should the job take?
    A. 1 hour   C. 3 hours
    B. 2 hours   D. 4 hours

85. Assume that you, as a Correction Officer, are in charge of supervising the laundry sorting and counting. You expect that on a certain day there will be nearly 7,000 items to be sorted and counted. If one inmate can sort and count 500 items in an hour, how many inmates are needed to sort all 7,000 items in one hour?
    A. 2   C. 7
    B. 5   D. 14

86. A carpentry course is being given for inmates who want to learn a skill. The course will be taught in several different groups. Each group should contain at least 12 but no more than 16 men. The smaller the group the better, as long as there are at least 12 men per group. If 66 inmates are going to take the course, they should be divided into

   A. 4 groups of 16 men

   B. 4 groups of 13 men and 1 group of 14 men

   C. 3 groups of 13 men and 2 groups of 14 men

   D. 6 groups of 11 men

87. Of the 100 inmates in a certain cell block, one-half were assigned to cleanup work, and one-fifth were assigned to work in the laundry. How many inmates were *not* assigned for cleanup work or laundry work?

   A. 30   C. 50

   B. 40   D. 60

88. A certain cell block has a maximum capacity of 250 inmates. On March 26, there were 200 inmates housed in the cell block, 12 inmates were added on that day, and 17 inmates were added on the following day. No inmates left on either day. How many more inmates could this cell block have accommodated on the second day?

   A. 11   C. 21

   B. 16   D. 28

89. A certain cell block has 240 inmates. From 8 a.m. to 9 a.m. on March 25, 120 inmates were assigned to cleanup work and 25 inmates were sent for physical examinations. All the other inmates remained in their cells. How many inmates should have been in their cells during this hour?

   A. 65   C. 95

   B. 85   D. 105

90. There were 254 inmates in a certain cell block at the beginning of the day. At 9:30 a.m., 12 inmates were checked out of the dispensary. At 10:00 a.m., 113 inmates were checked out to work details. At 10:30 a.m., 3 inmates were checked out to another cell block. How many inmates were present in this cell block at 10:45 a.m. if none of the inmates who were checked out had returned?

   A. 116   C. 136

   B. 126   D. 226

91. There were 242 inmates in a certain cell block at the beginning of the day. At 9:00 a.m., 116 inmates were checked out to a recreational program. At 9:15, 36 inmates were checked out to an educational program. At 9:30, 78 inmates were checked out on a work detail. By 10:15, the only inmates who had returned were 115 inmates who had been checked back in from the recreational program. A count made at 10:15 should show that the number of inmates present in the cell block is

   A. 127   C. 135

   B. 128   D. 137

Questions 92 through 96 are based on the Fact Situation and the Report of Inmate Injury form below. The questions ask how the report form should be filled in, based on the information given in the Fact Situation.

Fact Situation

Peter Miller is a Correction Officer assigned to duty in cell block A. His superior officer is John Doakes. Miller was on duty at 1:30 p.m. on March 21 when he heard a scream for help from cell 12. He hurried to cell 12 and found inmate Richard Rogers stamping out a flaming book of matches. Inmate John Jones was screaming. It seems that Jones had accidentally set fire to the entire book of matches while lighting a cigarette, and had burned his left hand. Smoking was permitted at this hour. Miller reported the incident by phone, and Jones was escorted to the dispensary, where his hand was treated at 2:00 p.m. by Dr. Albert Lorillo. Dr. Lorillo determined that Jones could return to his cell block, but that he should be released from work for four days. The doctor scheduled a re-examination for March 22. A routine investigation of the incident was made by James Lopez. Jones confirmed to this officer that the above statement of the situation was correct.

REPORT OF INMATE INJURY

(1) Name of inmate _____   (2) Assignment _____

(3) Number _____   (4) Location _____

(5) Nature of injury _____   (6) Date _____

(7) Details (how, when, where injury was incurred) _____
_____

(8) Received medical attention: date _____   time _____

(9) Treatment _____

(10) Disposition (check one or more):

_____ (10-1) Return to housing area   _____ (10-2) Return to duty

_____ (10-3) Work release __ days   _____ (10-4) Re-examine in __ days

(11) Employee reporting injury _____

(12) Employee's supervisor or superior officer _____

(13) Medical officer treating injury _____

(14) Investigating officer _____

(15) Head of institution _____

---

92. Which of the following should be entered in Item 1?

   A. Peter Miller

   B. John Doakes

   C. Richard Rogers

   D. John Jones

93. Which of the following should be entered in Item 11?

   A. Peter Miller

   B. James Lopez

   C. Richard Rogers

   D. John Jones

94. Which of the following should be entered in Item 8?

    A. 2/21, 1:30 p.m.

    B. 2/21, 2:00 p.m.

    C. 3/21, 1:30 p.m.

    D. 3/21, 2:00 p.m.

95. For Item 10, which of the following should be checked?

    A. only 10-4

    B. 10-1 and 10-4

    C. 10-1, 10-3, and 10-4

    D. 10-2, 10-3, and 10-4

96. Of the following items, which one *cannot* be filled in on the basis of the information given in the Fact Situation?

    A. Item 12

    B. Item 13

    C. Item 14

    D. Item 15

Answer questions 97 through 100 based on the following chart, which shows an 8-hour schedule for 4 groups of inmates. The numbers across the top of the chart stand for hours of the day: the hour beginning at 8:00, the hour beginning at 9:00, and so forth. The exact number of men in each group is given at the left-hand side of the chart. An hour when the men in a particular group are scheduled to be out of their cell block is marked with an x.

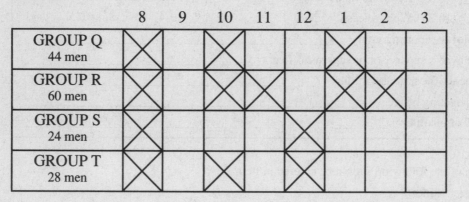

97. How many of the men were in their cell block from 11:00 to 12:00?

    A. 60

    B. 96

    C. 104

    D. 156

98. At 10:45, how many of the men were *not* in their cell block?

    A. 24

    B. 60

    C. 96

    D. 132

99. At 12:30, what proportion of the men were *not* in their cell block?

    A. $\frac{1}{4}$

    B. $\frac{1}{3}$

    C. $\frac{1}{2}$

    D. $\frac{2}{5}$

100. During the period covered in the chart, what percentage of the time did the men in Group S spend in their cell block?

    A. 60%

    B. 65%

    C. 70%

    D. 75%

END OF EXAM

ANSWER KEY FOR ACTUAL PREVIOUS EXAM

1. A	21. C	41. D	61. D	81. C
2. C	22. B	42. A	62. D	82. B
3. A	23. C	43. C	63. A	83. B
4. B	24. A	44. D	64. B	84. C
5. D	25. D	45. B	65. C	85. D
6. D	26. A	46. D	66. A	86. B
7. A	27. C	47. A	67. D	87. A
8. B	28. C	48. C	68. B	88. C
9. B	29. B	49. D	69. C	89. C
10. B	30. D	50. A	70. B	90. B
11. C	31. A	51. B	71. C	91. A
12. B	32. B	52. D	72. B	92. D
13. C	33. C	53. A	73. B	93. A
14. D	34. D	54. B	74. A	94. D
15. C	35. B	55. C	75. D	95. C
16. C	36. A	56. A	76. D	96. D
17. D	37. A	57. C	77. A	97. B
18. D	38. B	58. C	78. B	98. D
19. D	39. A	59. C	79. A	99. B
20. A	40. B	60. C	80. C	100. D

Explanatory Answers for Actual Previous Exam

1. **(A)** While the corner of a pad of paper might serve as a blunt instrument, actual conversion into a weapon is most feasible with a ballpoint pen.

2. **(C)** In choice (A) an inmate is handed a key, clearly a violation. In choice (B), the priest, though not an inmate, is also not an authorized employee, so his being handed a key is in violation. The Correction Officer who takes home the keys in choice (D) is violating the regulation that keys must be deposited with the Security Officer when not in use.

3. **(A)** The inmate who repeatedly bangs his fists against the bars of his cell is in danger of causing himself bodily harm. This inmate *must* be restrained.

4. **(B)** A kitchen cannot be operated without certain utensils which have the potential of use as dangerous weapons. The sensible cautionary procedure is to maintain careful supervision in the kitchen.

5. **(D)** The element of surprise is necessary to effective searches. Any pattern to the searches would serve as warning to inmates to temporarily stash weapons or escape devices in an area not subject to search.

6. **(D)** Choice (A) and (B) would have the reverse effect. Inmates would come to fear searches even if not guilty. Choice (C) does not serve the purpose at all since inmates would not learn of the punishment which follows possession of a forbidden item.

7. **(A)** Don't jump the gun and sound the alarm on the basis of an informal count, but do make the formal count right away; then act on the basis of fact, if indeed an inmate is missing.

8. **(B)** Cover of darkness is best for escape, so the officer must be certain that the blanketed heap in the bed is really the inmate.

9. **(B)** To insure accuracy you must count inmates yourself, and you must count them when they are not in motion. Endangering their safety is not necessary; let the inmates put things down before you count.

10. **(B)** Accomplices may be smuggled into the prison, so vehicles must be checked at entry as well as at exit. Official vehicles are not immune from escapees hiding themselves inside, so they must also be searched.

11. **(C)** A Correction Officer should not act rashly, but should always follow through with research and consultations whenever there is a doubt.

12. **(B)** Health and safety always come first. Tend to the injured.

13. **(C)** The reporting officer has forgotten to name the inmate who attacked Brown.

14. **(D)** The officer has neglected to state the nature of the trouble and what rules were broken.

15. **(C)** You must follow your supervisor's instructions. If you have an opportunity to discuss the new methods before they are to go into effect, by all means raise your questions with your supervisor. If not, go to the new procedures; they may work well. If they do not work well, speak to your supervisor. Professional behavior dictates that you NEVER discuss your misgivings with the inmates.

16. **(C)** The rule is that you must act to stop the fight, but, knowing that the fight might be a diversionary tactic, keep alert.

17. **(D)** Never assume literacy. Always explain changes along with your posting.

18. **(D)** Since there is the possibility of a fracture, and a fracture must not be moved, the best policy is to have the inmate sit still and send for medical assistance.

19. **(D)** This prison rule is stated very clearly. The clinic can wait. Count the prisoner in the proper place at the proper time.

20. **(A)** Sever stomach pains may indicate appendicitis or some other true medical emergency. The other three choices describe problems that can wait until morning.

21. **(C)** Within prison limits, try tact and kindness first.

22. **(B)** The well-being of dependents is a very real concern. The inmate should be introduced to professionals who can contact the family and take necessary steps to assist them.

23. **(C)** Sudden cooperativeness is not a common sign of impending mental illness. Look for other causes.

24. **(A)** Innovation and initiative are fine qualities, but get permission from your supervisor before making changes.

25. **(D)** You should treat everyone in a polite and tactful way.

26. **(A)** The Cell block Officer enters the supplies picture after the purchasing stage.

27. **(C)** The Cell block Officer is responsible, therefore he should count the supplies himself or personally supervise the inmate who does the counting.

28. **(C)** The only way to know how many items were actually delivered is to make a count upon receipt.

29. **(B)** Choice (D) is wrong. Choices (A) and (C) are correct statements, but they are not supported by the passage.

30. **(D)** The unfairness is putting an inmate in a position where other inmates might take advantage of him.

31. **(A)** The scientific studies of inmate behavior may help the officer to understand and broadly predict specific behaviors but will not give deep understanding of individuals nor assist in making significant changes in personalities.

32. **(B)** The passage states that older men and men who had good employment records tend to be the most reliable within a prison setting.

33. **(C)** The passage states that the troublemakers tend to be the younger men convicted of crimes involving stealth.

34. **(D)** The passage states that information about a man's background is helpful but no substitute for the Correction Officer's expert judgment based upon experience.

35. **(B)** Surprisingly, first offenders and men with previous convictions behave similarly in prison.

Questions 36 through 42: If you made any mistakes, look back at the pictures and count again.

43. **(C)** The first sentence tells us that many people behind bars are simply awaiting trial.

44. **(D)** The unemployed tend to have neither bail money nor proof of stability, so they cannot be released on personal recognizance.

45. **(B)** The passage tells you that when the person forfeits his bail he loses the money he put up.

46. **(D)** The person who is released on personal recognizance does not have to pay bail, but he must show up for trial and be judged innocent or guilty.

47. **(A)** The writer clearly feels that the bail system is unfair because it is based on economic status rather than upon guilt or innocence.

Questions 48 to 53. Look at the list and questions again to correct your errors.

54. **(B)** (A) should read 382 EPS; (C) should read 875 PGF.

55. **(C)** (A) should read 549 FTL; (B) should read 692 MLS.

56. **(A)** (B) should read 253 SFE; (C) should read 147 JTG.

57. **(C)** (A) should read 569 FML; (B) should read 716 GJM.

58. **(C)** (A) should ready 356 EFM; (B) should read 198 JLP.

59. **(C)** The passage suggests that 15% to 25% of prison inmates may be mentally disturbed.

60. **(C)** The burden of dealing with mentally disturbed prison inmates falls mainly upon Correction Officers.

61. **(D)** The passage mentions both the costs and the lack of trained personnel as reasons for failure to provide treatment programs.

62. **(D)** In this passage, "abnormal individual" means one who is mentally disturbed.

63. **(A)** The last sentence of the passage means that the Correction Officer must understand that a mentally disturbed person may not behave in the same way that a normal, healthy person behaves.

64. **(B)** There are twelve inmates. Five check out during Period I, leaving seven in their permanent groups.

65. **(C)** Phil checked out, leaving Bob, Sam, and Vic.

66. **(A)** During Period II, Jack and Mel checked out, but Ken and Larry returned.

67. **(D)** In Group X, Ted stayed out, and George checked out; two remained. In group Y, two checked out, but the two who had been out during Period I returned. In Group Z, three checked out while one returned. Group X two plus Group Y two plus Group Z one equals five.

68. **(B)** Bob, Sam, and Vic checked out during Period II.

69. **(C)** Larry returned during Period II and did not leave. Mel and Jack checked back in during Period III. Only Ken checked out.

70. **(B)** In Group X, Ted had never returned after checking out in Period I; Frank and Harry both checked out during Period III. In Group Y, as mentioned in question 69, only Ken was missing. In Group Z, Phil remained since his return in Period II; Sam, Bob, and Vic all returned, but Vic checked out again. So, three were not present in Group X, and one each out in Groups Y and Z for a total of five.

Questions 71 to 75. Look back at the report to see where you made your errors.

76. **(D)** $51.79
     29.39
     + 8.98
     $90.16

77. **(A)** $72.07
     +31.54
     103.61
     −25.75
     $77.86

78. **(B)** $82.47   **OR** $25.50
     −25.50   4.75
     56.97   + 0.35
     − 4.75 $30.60
     52.22
     − 0.35 $82.47
     $51.87   −30.60
                   $51.87

79. **(A)** $19.35   **OR** $ 9.90
     +37.75   + 19.80
     57.10 $29.70
     −9.90
     47.20 $57.10
     −19.80   −29.70
     $27.40 $27.40

80. **(C)** $38.85
     × 2
     77.70
     −27.90
     $49.80

81. **(C)** $53.66
     9.27
     +18.75
   $81.68 ÷ 2 = $40.84

82. **(B)**   192 inmates   **OR**   96 to work detail
       −96 on work detail   +32 to class
        96   128 out of cell block
       −32 to class
       64 remaining   192 total
                        −128 out of cell block
                        64 remaining

83. **(B)** 620 men × 2 utensils per man = 1,240 personal utensils

$$620 \div 20 = 31 \text{ groups of 20 each requiring a ladle}$$

1,240	forks and spoons
+ 31	ladles
1,271	utensils

84. **(C)** Two inmates take six hours to wash the dishes. Four inmates is twice as many as two inmates. Since there is a direct relationship between the time it takes to do the dishes and the number of numbers, twice the inmates should wash the dishes in half the time. Half of six hours is three hours.

85. **(D)** 7,000 items ÷ 500 items per inmate = 4 inmates to do the job.

86. **(B)** Choice (A) does not place all 66 men; choice (C) provides for 67 men; the groups in choice (D) are smaller than regulation.

87. **(A)**
One-half of 100 = 50 assigned to cleanup
One-fifth of 100 = 20 assigned to the laundry
70 inmates assigned; 100 − 70 = 30 not assigned.

88. **(C)** 200 + 12 + 17 = 229 inmates in the cell block
250 − 229 = 21 remaining places

89. **(C)** 240 −120 to cleanup = 120 − 25 for physicals = 95 remaining

90. **(B)** 12 inmates to dispensary + 113 to work + 3 to another cell block = 128 checked out. 254 − 128 = 126 remaining.

91. **(A)** 242 − 116 to recreation = 126 − 36 to education = 90 − 78 to work detail = 12 + 115 returned from recreation = 127 in the cell block.

92. **(D)** The injured inmate is John Jones.

93. **(A)** Peter Miller, the Correction Officer on duty at the time of the injury, reported the injury.

94. **(D)** Jones was treated on March 21 at 2:00 p.m. (The injury occurred at 1:30.)

95. **(C)** Jones was returned to his cell block, released from work for four days and was scheduled for reexamination the next day.

96. **(D)** The name of the head of the institution is not given in the Fact Situation.

97. **(B)** There is a total of 156 men. 44 + 60 + 24 + 28 = 156
156 − 60 out from 11:00 to 12:00 = 96 in the cellblocks.

98. **(D)** From 10:00 to 11:00 only the 24 men of Group S were in their cell block. 156 − 24 = 132 not in their cell blocks.

99. **(B)** At 12:30, 24 + 28 = 52 men were not in their cell block.
$156 \div 3 = 52$, $\frac{1}{3}$ of the men were not in their cell block.

100. **(D)** The men in Group S were in for 6 of the 8 hours or 75% of the time.

Answer Sheet for Model Examination 1

1. Ⓐ Ⓑ Ⓒ Ⓓ   2. Ⓐ Ⓑ Ⓒ Ⓓ   3. Ⓐ Ⓑ Ⓒ Ⓓ   4. Ⓐ Ⓑ Ⓒ Ⓓ   5. Ⓐ Ⓑ Ⓒ Ⓓ

6. Ⓐ Ⓑ Ⓒ Ⓓ   7. Ⓐ Ⓑ Ⓒ Ⓓ   8. Ⓐ Ⓑ Ⓒ Ⓓ   9. Ⓐ Ⓑ Ⓒ Ⓓ   10. Ⓐ Ⓑ Ⓒ Ⓓ

11. Ⓐ Ⓑ Ⓒ Ⓓ   12. Ⓐ Ⓑ Ⓒ Ⓓ   13. Ⓐ Ⓑ Ⓒ Ⓓ   14. Ⓐ Ⓑ Ⓒ Ⓓ   15. Ⓐ Ⓑ Ⓒ Ⓓ

16. Ⓐ Ⓑ Ⓒ Ⓓ   17. Ⓐ Ⓑ Ⓒ Ⓓ   18. Ⓐ Ⓑ Ⓒ Ⓓ   19. Ⓐ Ⓑ Ⓒ Ⓓ   20. Ⓐ Ⓑ Ⓒ Ⓓ

21. Ⓐ Ⓑ Ⓒ Ⓓ   22. Ⓐ Ⓑ Ⓒ Ⓓ   23. Ⓐ Ⓑ Ⓒ Ⓓ   24. Ⓐ Ⓑ Ⓒ Ⓓ   25. Ⓐ Ⓑ Ⓒ Ⓓ

26. Ⓐ Ⓑ Ⓒ Ⓓ   27. Ⓐ Ⓑ Ⓒ Ⓓ   28. Ⓐ Ⓑ Ⓒ Ⓓ   29. Ⓐ Ⓑ Ⓒ Ⓓ   30. Ⓐ Ⓑ Ⓒ Ⓓ

31. Ⓐ Ⓑ Ⓒ Ⓓ   32. Ⓐ Ⓑ Ⓒ Ⓓ   33. Ⓐ Ⓑ Ⓒ Ⓓ   34. Ⓐ Ⓑ Ⓒ Ⓓ   35. Ⓐ Ⓑ Ⓒ Ⓓ

36. Ⓐ Ⓑ Ⓒ Ⓓ   37. Ⓐ Ⓑ Ⓒ Ⓓ   38. Ⓐ Ⓑ Ⓒ Ⓓ   39. Ⓐ Ⓑ Ⓒ Ⓓ   40. Ⓐ Ⓑ Ⓒ Ⓓ

41. Ⓐ Ⓑ Ⓒ Ⓓ   42. Ⓐ Ⓑ Ⓒ Ⓓ   43. Ⓐ Ⓑ Ⓒ Ⓓ   44. Ⓐ Ⓑ Ⓒ Ⓓ   45. Ⓐ Ⓑ Ⓒ Ⓓ

46. Ⓐ Ⓑ Ⓒ Ⓓ   47. Ⓐ Ⓑ Ⓒ Ⓓ   48. Ⓐ Ⓑ Ⓒ Ⓓ   49. Ⓐ Ⓑ Ⓒ Ⓓ   50. Ⓐ Ⓑ Ⓒ Ⓓ

51. Ⓐ Ⓑ Ⓒ Ⓓ   52. Ⓐ Ⓑ Ⓒ Ⓓ   53. Ⓐ Ⓑ Ⓒ Ⓓ   54. Ⓐ Ⓑ Ⓒ Ⓓ   55. Ⓐ Ⓑ Ⓒ Ⓓ

56. Ⓐ Ⓑ Ⓒ Ⓓ   57. Ⓐ Ⓑ Ⓒ Ⓓ   58. Ⓐ Ⓑ Ⓒ Ⓓ   59. Ⓐ Ⓑ Ⓒ Ⓓ   60. Ⓐ Ⓑ Ⓒ Ⓓ

61. Ⓐ Ⓑ Ⓒ Ⓓ   62. Ⓐ Ⓑ Ⓒ Ⓓ   63. Ⓐ Ⓑ Ⓒ Ⓓ   64. Ⓐ Ⓑ Ⓒ Ⓓ   65. Ⓐ Ⓑ Ⓒ Ⓓ

66. Ⓐ Ⓑ Ⓒ Ⓓ   67. Ⓐ Ⓑ Ⓒ Ⓓ   68. Ⓐ Ⓑ Ⓒ Ⓓ   69. Ⓐ Ⓑ Ⓒ Ⓓ   70. Ⓐ Ⓑ Ⓒ Ⓓ

71. Ⓐ Ⓑ Ⓒ Ⓓ   72. Ⓐ Ⓑ Ⓒ Ⓓ   73. Ⓐ Ⓑ Ⓒ Ⓓ   74. Ⓐ Ⓑ Ⓒ Ⓓ   75. Ⓐ Ⓑ Ⓒ Ⓓ

76. Ⓐ Ⓑ Ⓒ Ⓓ   77. Ⓐ Ⓑ Ⓒ Ⓓ   78. Ⓐ Ⓑ Ⓒ Ⓓ   79. Ⓐ Ⓑ Ⓒ Ⓓ   80. Ⓐ Ⓑ Ⓒ Ⓓ

81. Ⓐ Ⓑ Ⓒ Ⓓ   82. Ⓐ Ⓑ Ⓒ Ⓓ   83. Ⓐ Ⓑ Ⓒ Ⓓ   84. Ⓐ Ⓑ Ⓒ Ⓓ   85. Ⓐ Ⓑ Ⓒ Ⓓ

TEAR HERE

The five model exams that follow are closely patterned on actual examinations given to Correction Officer candidates in the past few years. The five exams vary in format, content, difficulty, and timing because each model exam represents an exam given in a different jurisdiction at a different time.

Model Examination 1

MEMORY BOOKLET

Directions: You will be given 10 minutes to study the scene below and to try to notice and remember as many details as you can. You may not take any notes during this time.

TEST QUESTION BOOKLET

Time: 2 hours, 45 minutes — 85 questions

Directions: Now that the Memory Booklets have been collected, you have 2 hours and 45 minutes in which to answer the test questions. The first 14 questions are based on the scene that you just studied. Answer these questions first. Then proceed directly to the remaining 71 questions. Choose the best answer to each question and mark its letter on your answer sheet.

Answer questions 1-14 on the basis of the scene in the memory booklet.

1. The students in this classroom are seated at
   - (A) arm chairs
   - (B) long tables
   - (C) individual desks
   - (D) desks for two persons

2. The teacher is
   - (A) saluting the flag
   - (B) wearing a short-sleeved shirt, vest, and bow tie
   - (C) not wearing glasses
   - (D) wearing a long-sleeved shirt and striped tie

3. The time at which this hostage situation is occurring is
   - (A) 4:10
   - (B) 2:25
   - (C) 4:20
   - (D) 1:35

4. The person who is bald is
   - (A) standing in the doorway
   - (B) requesting information
   - (C) seated in the middle row
   - (D) threatening the teacher

5. The total number of people in this scene is
   - (A) 11
   - (B) 13
   - (C) 14
   - (D) 15

6. The person wearing a headscarf is

(A) volunteering an answer

(B) wearing earrings

(C) wearing a striped shirt

(D) left handed

7. Regardless of what else may be taught in this classroom, the room is specially equipped as

(A) an art room

(B) a chemistry classroom

(C) a computer laboratory

(D) a music studio

8. There is an empty desk

(A) between the student wearing a sleeveless sweater and the person with the long braid

(B) at the left end of the third row

(C) in the front row directly in front of the teacher's outstretched arm

(D) nowhere in this room

9. The person carrying the submachine gun is

(A) looking at her watch

(B) standing beside the teacher

(C) aiming at the students

(D) looking out the window

10. The person with light curly hair and a print blouse is

(A) armed with a knife

(B) volunteering an answer

(C) standing

(D) seated in the front row

11. An accurate statement about this scene is that

(A) the students are inattentive

(B) one of the lights is not in good working order

(C) hats are not permitted in the classroom

(D) all of the chalkboards are clean

12. The four dials behind the teacher

(A) indicate the time in different time zones

(B) all appear to indicate the same thing

(C) are various weather instruments

(D) give different readings which cannot be determined

13. The teacher's left hand is

    (A) resting on the counter in front of him

    (B) raised as if fending off the gunman

    (C) pointing to a student

    (D) resting on a book

14. The person wearing a plaid shirt is

    (A) sleeping

    (B) writing

    (C) looking to his left

    (D) eyeing the gunman

15. Police Officer Ruiz, on patrol in a residential area, arrives at the scene of a fire and, after speaking with a bystander on the street, makes the following notes:

    > Place of occurrence: 1520 Clarendon Road, Brooklyn
    >
    > Time of occurrence: 6:32 A.M.
    >
    > Type of building: two-family frame dwelling
    >
    > Event: fire; suspected arson
    >
    > Suspect: male, white, approx. 6-foot, wearing jeans
    >
    > Witness: Mary Smith of 1523 Clarendon Road, Brooklyn

    Officer Ruiz must now write up a report of the incident. Which of the following expresses the information *most clearly, accurately, and completely*?

    (A) At 6:32 A.M. Mary Smith of 1523 Clarendon Road, Brooklyn, saw a white male wearing approximately 6-foot blue jeans running from the building across the street.

    (B) A white male wearing blue jeans ran from the house at 1520 Clarendon Road at 6:32 A.M. Mary Smith saw him.

    (C) At 6:32 A.M. a 6-foot white male wearing blue jeans ran from a burning two-family frame structure at 1520 Clarendon Road, Brooklyn. He was observed by a neighbor, Mary Smith.

    (D) A two-family frame house is on fire at 1520 Clarendon Road in Brooklyn. A white male in blue jeans probably did it. Mary Smith saw him run.

16. As a student at the police academy, you are handed the following scenario: Police Officer Wu, assigned to the transit division, reports to a token booth and obtains this information from a sobbing woman.

> Time of occurrence: 1:22 A.M.
>
> Place of occurrence: uptown-bound platform, 59th Street Station, 7th Avenue line
>
> Victim: Juana Martinez
>
> Crime: purse snatching
>
> Description of suspect: unknown, fled down steps to lower platform

Officer Wu must now call in an alert to the police dispatcher. Which of the following expresses the information *most clearly, accurately, and completely*?

(A) Juana Martinez had her purse snatched on the subway platform at 59th Street Station. She didn't see him.

(B) A purse was just snatched by a man who ran down the steps from the 7th Avenue token booth at 59th Street Station. Her name is Juana Martinez.

(C) It is 1:22 A.M. The person who snatched Juana Martinez' purse is downstairs at 59th Street Station.

(D) I am at 59th Street Station, uptown-bound 7th Avenue token booth. A Juana Martinez reports that her purse was just snatched by a man who fled down the steps to a lower platform.

17. Police officers assigned to patrol in a radio car are instructed to adhere to the following rules concerning the use of the police radios in patrol cars:

1. The use of the radio is to be restricted to performance of duty only.

2. All conversations should be to the point and as short as possible.

3. Names of people are not to be used.

4. All conversations should begin by identifying the vehicle by number.

5. A message received is to be acknowledged by "ten-four."

Police Officers Abel and Flynn apprehend two men in the act of robbing a jewelry store. They place the men in Patrol Car 14 and radio in a report of the activity. Which one of the following messages would be in conformance with the procedure specified?

(A) "Officers Abel and Flynn, car one-four, proceeding to station house with two prisoners."

(B) "Car one-four, proceeding to station house with two prisoners."

(C) "Car one-four, Officers Abel and Flynn, proceeding to station house with two prisoners."

(D) "Car one-four, proceeding to station house with prisoners Bossey and Warren."

18. Quite often a police officer is required to give assistance to an injured person. Upon responding to a call to assist an injured person, a police officer should be guided by the following procedure:

    1.   Administer first aid.

    2.   Call for medical assistance.

    3.   Call again if the ambulance does not respond within 20 minutes.

    4.   Accompany the injured person to the hospital if he or she is unconscious or unidentified.

    5.   Witness the search of an unconscious or unidentified person.

    6.   Attempt to identify the person who is unconscious or unidentified by a search of his or her property.

Officer Alcorn, while on patrol, observes a man lying in the front yard of a four-family house. Upon questioning, the man reveals that he fell while repairing the roof of his house. He says he is in a great deal of pain and is unable to move. Officer Alcorn summons an ambulance and gives the man first aid. He then requests that the man give him his name, but the man refuses. The ambulance arrives in 15 minutes, and Officer Alcorn resumes patrol. Officer Alcorn failed to fulfill his obligations in this incident because he

(A) did not make a second call for the ambulance when the man was in great pain

(B) failed to accompany the man to the hospital

(C) did not attempt to locate a physician while waiting for the ambulance

(D) failed to relieve the injured man's pain through the administration of proper first aid

Questions 19 and 20 are based on the following situation:

On a hot summer afternoon, three prisoners are missing from the state penitentiary located on the wooded outskirts of a small upstate city. Their means of escape has not yet been established, so search parties are dispatched near and far.

19. Police car 43 leaves the city traveling west on highway 9. After three miles, the car makes a right turn onto route 21. Two miles up route 21, a dirt road forks off in a diagonal right. Car 43 turns onto the dirt road and continues until it reaches a farmhouse on the right hand side of the road. The car turns into the driveway and both officers get out. When the driver gets out, in which direction is she facing?

(A) Northeast

(B) Southwest

(C) East

(D) South

20. Correction Officers English and Miller leave the prison by the south gate, turn right, and run into the woods. They run half way around a large boulder that lies directly in their path, and continue looking to the right and to the left. They stop and peer into a dense clump of bushes on their left. In what direction are they looking?

(A) East

(B) North

(C) South

(D) West

21. Taxes are deducted each pay period from the amount of salaries or wages, including payments for overtime, paid to law enforcement personnel in excess of the withholding exemptions allowed under the Internal Revenue Act. The amount of tax to be withheld from each payment of wages to any employee will be determined from the current official table of pay and withholding exemptions to be found on page 32 of the employee manual.

The paragraph best supports the statement that salaries of law enforcement personnel

(A) do not include overtime

(B) are determined by provisions of the Internal Revenue Act

(C) are paid from tax revenues

(D) are subject to tax deductions

22. A police officer on foot patrol is stopped by a man who shouts that a neighbor's child has just been raped. The officer goes to the scene of the alleged crime and is told by the hysterical mother that her eight-year-old daughter was raped in the apartment while she was in the basement with the laundry. The child is crying and bleeding on the bed. The mother screams that she believes the man is on the roof. The police officer should *first*

(A) call for medical assistance

(B) attempt to calm the hysterical mother

(C) go to the roof to search for the accused man

(D) question the child as to what actually took place

23. At 11 A.M. on Saturday, June 11, Police Officer Szulk on bicycle patrol in Highland Park is approached by a boy walking a dog. The boy tells officer Szulk of a body to which his dog has just led him. Officer Szulk accompanies the boy to the dog's find and notes the following:

> Location: underbrush about 80 yards south of Civil War Monument, Highland Park
>
> Occurrence: discovery of body of fully clothed Hispanic female in early 20s
>
> Reporter: Bill Sawyer, age 12
>
> Identity of victim: unknown

Officer Szulk is about to call his precinct to report this incident and to request assistance. Which of the following conveys all the information *most clearly, accurately, and completely*?

(A) A woman was found by Bill Sawyer in the park near the Civil War Monument. He doesn't know her.

(B) The body of an unknown Hispanic woman was found at 11 A.M. by 12-year-old Bill Sawyer's dog in the Highland Park underbrush south of the Civil War Monument.

(C) There is a body in the underbrush in Highland Park. She is a Hispanic woman and Bill Sawyer, a 12-year-old with a dog, found her.

(D) On Saturday, June 11, Bill Sawyer found a body of a dead woman all dressed up in the park with his dog.

24. Police Officer Rios is investigating a furniture store break-in which evidently had occurred during the previous night. She compiles the following information:

> Location: Berger's Furniture Store, 1509 Orchard Street
>
> Incident: burglary
>
> Date of event: night of Tuesday, May 3 to Wednesday, May 4
>
> Time of event: between 9:40 P.M. and 8:15 A.M.
>
> Reporter: Mo Berger, owner, of 108 West 12th Street
>
> Damage: broken window; empty cash register

Officer Rios must write up a report of this incident for follow-up. Which of the following expresses the information *most clearly, accurately, and completely*?

(A) Mo Berger had a burglary between closing on May 3 and opening May 4. He got a broken window and they emptied the cash register.

(B) Berger's Furniture Store at 1509 West Orchard Street had a burglary at night on May 3rd. They broke a window and took the money.

(C) Mo Berger of 108 West 12th Street reports that his Berger's Furniture Store on 1509 Orchard Street was broken into between 9:40 P.M. May 3 and 8:15 A.M. May 4. Contents of the cash register are missing.

(D) Mo Berger's Furniture Store was burgled through a broken window on 1509 Orchard Street during the night May 3-4. The burglars took everything out of the cash register. Mr. Berger lives at 108 West 12th Street and keeps the store open from 8:15 A.M. to 9:40 P.M.

Answer questions 25 and 26 solely on the basis of the following procedure:

Police officers responding to complaints of loud or violent disagreements between members of a family are directed to follow the procedure below:

1. When knocking on the door of the premises in which the dispute is taking place, do not stand directly in front of it.

2. Separate the parties taking part in the dispute by taking them into different rooms.

3. Attempt to calm the people involved while interviewing them.

4. Stay out of the dispute; do not take sides.

5. If an insult is directed at you, ignore it.

6. Advise the parties in the argument where they may go for counseling.

7. Do not say anything that will direct the people's anger at you.

8. Make no arrests unless one of the participants is hurt.

25. Officers Claymore and Peron, arriving at the scene of a family dispute, separate a screaming couple into different rooms. The wife shouts that her husband is having an affair with his secretary and that she is going to file for divorce. The wife picks up the ringing telephone, listens briefly, and then slams it down. She shouts to her husband, "Your secretary just called, but she didn't leave a message." At his point, it would be proper for one of the police officers to advise that the

(A) husband end this affair at once

(B) wife go ahead with her divorce plans

(C) wife trust her husband

(D) couple seek the help of local marriage counselors

26. Two officers respond to a complaint of gunshots and loud arguing taking place in an apartment. They approach the apartment and hear a television set playing. They stand in front of the door, knock on it, and are told to enter. A man and a woman are sitting on a couch watching a murder mystery on television. The couple states that they have been watching the program for almost two hours. The officers evaluate the situation and decide that a mistake has been made. They apologize and leave. One of the actions taken by the officers does not conform to the procedure for dealing with this type of situation. This occurred when they

(A) determined that a mistake had been made and then apologized and left the premises

(B) interviewed both people in the same room

(C) investigated the complaint even though they could her no argument

(D) stood in front of the door while knocking on it

27. The term *homicide* means

(A) manslaughter

(B) murder

(C) killing of one person by another person

(D) death caused by a felony

Answer questions 28 and 29 on the basis of the following definitions:

Assault is committed when a person intentionally causes physical injury to another person or when a person acting recklessly causes physical injury to another person.

Harassment is committed when an individual, with intent to annoy or frighten another individual, does strike, shove, kick, or subject that individual to physical contact or attempts or threatens to do the same, or uses abusive or obscene language, or makes an obscene gesture in a public place, or follows a person in a public place, or repeatedly engages in conduct which serves no legitimate purpose but which results in alarming or seriously annoying another person.

Reckless Endangerment is committed when a person, failing to exercise caution, engages in conduct which creates a substantial risk of serious injury to another person.

28. As a result of a dispute over a parking space, Anne Blount and Bea Wallace engage in an argument during which Blount pushes Wallace in an attempt to scare her. Wallace is not hurt, but she makes an obscene gesture in the direction of Blount. Referring to the definitions given, which one of the following best describes the incident?

(A) Blount committed assault, and Wallace committed harassment.

(B) Blount and Wallace both committed harassment.

(C) Neither Blount nor Wallace committed harassment.

(D) Wallace committed assault, and Blount committed harassment.

29. William Hammer, fully intending to scare James Bates, drives his car at high speed in the direction of Bates who quickly jumps out of the path of the vehicle. In turning in the direction of Bates, Hammer narrowly misses Fred Collins, a bystander. Neither Bates nor Collins is injured. According to the definitions, Hammer

(A) did not commit an assault against Bates or Collins

(B) did not commit a crime

(C) committed an assault against Bates and Collins

(D) committed an assault against Collins only

30. Police Officer Polara answers a motorist's request for directions by telling the motorist to: "Proceed south, as you are now headed, for two blocks; turn right at the traffic light and, at the next intersection, turn right again. Immediately after you see a gas station on your right, make a left turn and go one block. You will see the store you are seeking on your left." In what direction will the car be traveling when the motorist reaches his destination?

(A) North

(B) South

(C) East

(D) West

31. A police officer attempting to extract information from a witness should not ask questions that can be answered by a "yes" or "no." A police officer is interviewing a witness to a car accident that resulted in serious injury to two people. The officer has reason to believe that the car involved went through an intersection against the light. Of the following, the proper question for the officer to ask the witness would be:

(A) Did you see the car go through a red light?

(B) Can you recall if the light turned red before the car went through the intersection?

(C) What color was the light at the time the car went through the intersection?

(D) Was the light red when the car went through the intersection?

32. Police Officer Dobbo is alerted by radio to go to an apartment in which there is a child in distress. The information is:

> Location: 97 West 98th Street, Apt. 2-B
>
> Time of call: 1:32 P.M.
>
> Name of caller: Martha Ho
>
> Child: Barney Ho, 21 months
>
> Event: head caught between spokes of chair back

Now that she has dealt with this emergency, Officer Dobbo must make a record for her activity log. Which of the following expresses the information *most clearly, accurately, and completely*?

(A) At 1:32 P.M. Martha Ho of 97 West 98th Street, Apt. 2-B, requested assistance for Barney Ho, aged 21 months, who was caught in a chair. I removed a spoke from the chair back and released the child.

(B) Barney Ho, 21 months, got his head stuck in a chair. His mother called at 1:32 P.M., and I went and got his head out. This was in Apt. 2-B.

(C) Martha Ho, mother of Barney Ho, a 21-month old little boy, of 98 West 97th Street called at 1:32 P.M. because Barney had his head stuck in a chair. I got him out of the chair by removing a spoke from the back.

(D) When Barney Ho got his head stuck at 1:32 P.M., his mother called from 97 West 98th Street and asked for someone to come and help him in Apt. 2-B. The chair should be thrown out.

33. Police Officer Neilly is approached by a woman along his post. The woman tells him that she would like to file a complaint against the husband of her employer. This is the information that Office Neilly takes down:

> Date: March 30
>
> Complainant: Janina Klinski, age 34
>
> Address of complainant: 5630 Grand Concourse, Apt. 3-W
>
> Accused: Joseph Johns, mid-50s
>
> Address of accused: 120 Palisades Heights, Apt. 19-A
>
> Complaint: sexual abuse

Officer Neilly informs the woman of the proper legal procedures for filing this complaint. Then he records his conversation with Ms. Klinski in his log book. Which of the following expresses the information *most clearly, accurately, and completely*?

(A) Janina Klinski who lives at 5630 Grand Concourse, Apt. 3-W, says that she was sexually abused on March 30 by an older man, Joseph Johns.

(B) On March 30, Janina Klinski, 34, of 5630 Grand Concourse, Apt. 3-W, complained that she had been sexually abused by Joseph Johns of 120 Palisades Heights, Apt. 19-A, the husband of her employer.

(C) Joseph Johns, who is in his 50s, sexually abused Janina Klinski on March 30, she said. Janina Klinski works for Joseph Johns' wife at 5630 Grand Concourse, Apt. 3-W.

(D) Janina Klinski said that Joseph Johns sexually abused her at 120 Palisades Heights, Apt. 19-A, where she worked for Mrs. Johns on March 30. Janina Klinski is 34 years old, and Joseph Johns is in his mid-50s.

34. Beverly Bowers, who has been convicted of aggravated assault and who has exhausted all appeals, surrenders herself at the Women's Correctional Facility to serve her sentence. Ms. Bowers hands over her purse, and the contents of her wallet are inventoried thus:

>5 $20 bills
>
>7 $10 bills
>
>13 $5 bills
>
>2 $1 bills
>
>9 quarters
>
>21 dimes
>
>17 nickels
>
>8 pennies

How much money was in Ms. Bowers' purse?

(A) $237.88

(B) $242.28

(C) $243.06

(D) $244.68

Answer questions 35 and 36 on the basis of the following procedure:

1. When a prisoner requests medical attention or is in apparent need of it, the police officer should arrange for the prisoner to be promptly examined by a doctor.

2. In the event that a prisoner is in need of medical treatment, the police officer should notify a supervisor immediately so that an ambulance can be summoned. Prisoners who are drug addicts and who are in need of treatment for their addiction should be taken to a hospital by a radio car.

3. Under no circumstances should a police officer prescribe any medication for a prisoner.

4. A police officer should not attempt to diagnose a prisoner's illness or injury and should not attempt to treat the prisoner except in a situation where first aid is required. First aid should be administered promptly.

5. A doctor is the only one authorized to administer medicine to a prisoner. When a doctor is not available, the police officer in charge of the prisoner should then give him or her the medicine and watch him or her take it.

35. Alan Fox, a prisoner well known to police because of his long record, is in custody when he claims that he has a severe headache as a result of being badly beaten. There are no apparent signs of a physical injury, but the prisoner is demanding medical attention. The police officer in charge of Alan Fox should

(A) consider the prisoner's long record before deciding to call a doctor

(B) give the prisoner two aspirins

(C) ignore the prisoner's request for medical attention since there are no apparent physical injuries

(D) see that Alan Fox is promptly examined by a doctor

36. It is a hot summer day, and Officer Stone has in his custody a prisoner who is a drug addict. The prisoner opens his shirt to reveal a large unhealed wound which is obviously infected. Officer Stone suggests to the prisoner that he call a doctor in to examine him, but the prisoner refuses, saying the wound is of no consequence. In this instance, Officer Stone should

   (A) request that his supervisor call an ambulance

   (B) closely examine the wound in order to evaluate its severity

   (C) adhere to the prisoner's wishes and do nothing about the matter

   (D) take the prisoner at once to a hospital in a radio car

37. Detectives assigned to investigate violent crimes with no obvious motive and no apparent witnesses must direct their whole effort toward success in their work. If they wish to succeed in such investigations, their work will be by no means easy, smooth, or peaceful; on the contrary, they will have to devote themselves completely and continuously to a task that requires all their ability.

   The paragraph best supports the statement that an investigator's success depends most upon

   (A) ambition to advance rapidly in rank

   (B) persistence in the face of difficulty

   (C) training and experience

   (D) superior ability

38. A police officer should not ask leading questions, that is, questions which suggest the answer that the officer desires. A police officer is called to the scene of an accident that involved a red and a green car. It would be proper for the officer to ask a witness to the accident,

   (A) "You observed the red car hit the green car, didn't you?"

   (B) "Did you see the green car hit the red car?"

   (C) "The red car caused the accident, didn't it?"

   (D) "Just what caused the accident between the red car and the green car?"

39. As part of an exercise at the police academy, a recruit is given the following information to organize into a short report:

> Location: northwest corner of Smith Street and Tenth Avenue
>
> Date: August 2
>
> Time: 3:35 P.M.
>
> Event: fire hydrant fully opened without sprinkler cap
>
> Suspect: unidentified white male, approximately 20 years old, 5 ft. 10 in., 160 lb., wearing blue jeans and torn white sneakers.
>
> Witnesses: neighborhood children

Which of the following expresses this information *most clearly, accurately, and completely*?

(A) On August 2 at 3:35 P.M., the fire hydrant at the northwest corner of Smith Street and Tenth Avenue was fully opened with water gushing from it without a water-saving sprinkler cap. Neighborhood children reported that an unfamiliar white teenager wearing blue jeans and torn white sneakers had probably opened the hydrant.

(B) The fire hydrant at the corner of Smith and Tenth was opened by a 20-year old, average height and weight man in blue jeans and torn sneakers this hot and sticky afternoon around 3:30 the children said.

(C) Some neighborhood children said that the fire hydrant had been opened by a white man they didn't know who was about standard size with blue jeans and torn sneakers. The date is August 2; the time 3:35 P.M.

(D) The northwest fire hydrant at Smith Street and Tenth Avenue was opened on August 2 at 3:35 P.M. The children playing in the water do not know who did it.

40. In another police academy exercise, a recruit is handed the following information collected by a police officer arriving at the scene of a robbery immediately after it had occurred:

> Time: 5:28 P.M.
>
> Place: Aneke's Bridal Fashions, 280 Second Avenue
>
> Reporter: Aneke Blau, owner
>
> Event: knife-point robbery; $200 taken
>
> Suspect: white woman, red hair, blue jeans, white T-shirt

The police officer is calling in a report so that cars in the vicinity can search for the suspect. Which of the following expresses this information *most clearly, accurately, and completely*?

(A) Aneke Blau reported at 5:28 P.M. her store Aneke's Bridal Fashions was robbed at knifepoint at 280 Second Avenue. A white woman with red hair took $200 from her wearing blue jeans and white T-shirt.

(B) At 5:28 P.M. a red-haired woman took $200 from 280 Second Avenue at Aneke's Bridal Fashions owned by Aneke Blau who was robbed by a white woman. She was wearing blue jeans and a white T-shirt and used a knife.

(C) In a robbery that occurred at knifepoint, a red-haired white woman robbed the owner of Aneke's Bridal Fashions. Aneke Blau, the owner of the 280 Second Avenue store was robbed of $200. She said she was wearing blue jeans and white T-shirt at 5:28 P.M.

(D) Just before 5:28 P.M., Aneke Blau, owner of Aneke's Bridal Fashions located at 280 Second Avenue was robbed of $200 at knifepoint. The suspect is a white female with red hair, wearing blue jeans and white T-shirt.

41. In taking a report of a missing person, a police officer must request the following information in the following order:

1. Sex of missing person
2. Age of missing person
3. Name of missing person
4. Name and relationship of person making the report
5. Place and time missing person was last seen
6. Physical description of person and clothing
7. Other special identifying features

Police Officer Manning is practically bowled over by a hysterical, tearful woman who is wailing, "My baby she missing." Officer Manning's first question should be:

(A) Where did you lose the baby?

(B) How old is the baby?

(C) Is the baby a boy or a girl?

(D) Are you the baby's mother?

42. Police Officer Klein leaves the police garage by the western gate, makes a left turn and begins to cover her assigned area. After four blocks, Officer Klein turns west. When Officer Klein has driven five more blocks, she is passed by a speeding car going in the opposite direction. She makes a quick U-turn and follows the speeding car. After eight blocks, the speeding car turns left, loses control, and crashes into a telephone pole. The location of the crash is

(A) in front of the police garage

(B) due south of the police garage

(C) southeast of the police garage

(D) northeast of the police garage

Answer questions 43 and 44 on the basis of the following definitions:

Burglary is committed when an individual, without authorization, enters or remains in a building with the intent of committing a crime.

Criminal mischief is committed when a person intentionally damages the property of another person, having no right to do so nor any reasonable ground to believe that he has the right to do so.

Larceny is committed when a person intentionally deprives another of property or wrongfully takes, obtains, or withholds property from the owner of that property without the use of force, violence, or threat of injury. Larceny is committed, for example, when property is obtained under false pretenses, finding and not returning lost property, or the intentional issuance of a bad check.

Robbery is committed when a person, against another person's will, takes property from that person.

43. Jane Wills finds a diamond ring on the sidewalk of a busy street. She keeps it. According to the definitions, Wills committed

    (A) the crime of larceny

    (B) the crime of burglary

    (C) the crime of robbery

    (D) none of the listed crimes

44. Elwood Tompkins is waiting at a bus station to hand over a package of expensive jewelry to a representative of the XYZ Transfer Company. Phil Shore learns of the shipment and decides to steal the package. He goes to the bus station, presents himself to Tompkins, and says he is from XYZ. Tompkins gives Shore the package believing he is from XYZ. Shore is not armed. The definitions indicate that Shore committed the crime of

    (A) robbery

    (B) burglary

    (C) criminal mischief

    (D) larceny

Answer questions 45 through 47 on the basis of the following procedure:

A police officer responding to a situation that involves a person or persons who seem to be dead should take the following steps:

1. The officer should assume that the person is alive unless the officer is absolutely sure that he or she is dead.

2. If the officer is absolutely sure that the person is dead, and if the body is in public view, the body should be covered with a waterproof covering.

3. The officer should summon a sergeant to the scene.

4. The officer should immediately call the homicide detectives if the death is suspicious.

5. The body should be searched for identification if the death took place in a public area. In the event that the death took place in the home of a person who lived alone, both the body and the home are to be searched. All searches must be witnessed by a sergeant.

6. Property of a dead person may be released only to a relative who lived with the deceased.

7. Do not notify relatives or family of a death over the telephone. However, if you receive a call from a relative concerning the person's condition, you may inform the relative of the death.

45. A police officer is summoned to the scene of an accident. The victim, a young woman, is lying on the street, apparently dead. She is surrounded by bystanders. In this situation, the officer should first

(A) cover the body with a waterproof covering

(B) notify the homicide detectives

(C) search the body to determine its identity

(D) check to see if the woman is alive

46. A police officer is sent to the apartment of an elderly man who obviously has been dead for a few days. The officer closes the door to the apartment is now alone with the body. His first act should be to

(A) summon a sergeant

(B) search the apartment

(C) search the body

(D) cover the body

47. A police officer, while searching the home of a dead man who had lived alone, is approached by the man's sister who requests permission to remove a few family albums from the apartment. The officer, in this instance, should

(A) give her the albums since she is the dead man's sister

(B) not give her the albums since she did not live with the dead man

(C) give her the albums since they contain only family pictures

(D) not give her the albums until she proves that she is the deceased's sister

48. Police Officer Ling reports to her precinct from a corner police call box six blocks north of the precinct house along her assigned patrol route. She turns left at that corner, walks one block, and turns left again. After walking three more blocks, Officer Ling turns right, walks two full blocks, and checks in from another corner call box. The call box from which Officer Ling is now calling is located

(A) 4 blocks north and 2 blocks east of the precinct house

(B) 3 blocks north and 3 blocks east of the precinct house

(C) 3 blocks north and 3 blocks west of the precinct house

(D) 2 blocks north and 4 blocks west of the precinct house

49. As Officer Ling stands at the call box, she witnesses a car sideswiping a parked car almost directly in front of her and continuing on its way at a high speed. This is the information that Officer Ling rapidly takes note of:

> Location: in front of 158 Broome Street, just south of Potter Avenue
>
> Incident: sideswipe of parked car by speeding car; hit and run
>
> Damage: removed right side mirror and badly smashed right front fender
>
> Description of speeding car: red two-door Honda Accord, approximately 1994; no occupants besides male driver; New Jersey license plate beginning 7T4, traveling west
>
> Description of damaged car: black four-door Saturn SL-1, 1993, license plate Connecticut XYZ-123

Officer Ling is on foot and cannot pursue the speeding car, but she can transmit the information directly to the sergeant with whom she is checking in. Which of the following expresses the needed information *most clearly, accurately and completely*?

(A) A speeding red car and driver from New Jersey and going west just hit a black four-door 1993 Saturn, Connecticut license plate XYZ-123 on Broome Street.

(B) A red two-door Honda Accord, New Jersey license plate beginning 7T4, with only male driver, last seen traveling west on Broome Street near Potter at high speed after hitting black Saturn on right side.

(C) A black 1993 four-door Saturn SL-1 parked in front of 158 Broome Street just south of Potter Avenue was just hit and damaged by a red two-door Honda Accord from New Jersey that was speeding and didn't stop. It is speeding west.

(D) A speeding car, a red two-door Honda Accord from Connecticut, license plate beginning 7T4, just sideswiped a black Saturn in front of 158 Broome Street. Its only occupant is the male driver, and the car is speeding west.

50. Police Officer Jonas assigned to the housing division is patrolling a large city housing project in his car when he notices an elderly gentleman wandering aimlessly in circles. The man tells Officer Jonas that thinks that his name is Bob and that he once lived here but was kidnapped by aliens in a flying saucer and just escaped. Officer Jonas puts the man in his car and radios the following information to his sergeant:

> Incident: lost, disoriented adult
>
> Location: Orchard Houses, southeast sector, in front of Building 3
>
> Description: white male, about 80, 5 ft. 7 in., weight 150, thin gray hair, blue eyes, wearing gray pants, white shirt, and green windbreaker, "Bob"

Which of the following expresses the information *most clearly, accurately, and completely*?

(A) An old man who might be Bob says that he was left in front of Building 3 by aliens who kidnapped him. He is about 5 ft. 7 in, weighs about 150 lbs. and has thin gray hair and blue eyes. He is wearing gray pants, white shirt, and a windbreaker.

(B) Bob is an old man who was kidnapped by aliens and returned to Orchard Houses where he lives in Building 3. He is confused wearing gray pants, a white shirt, and a green windbreaker. He has gray hair and blue eyes and is average size.

(C) A confused white man, about 80, was found in front of Building 3, southeast sector, Orchard Houses. The man is about 5 ft. 7 in, weighs about 150 lbs. And has thin gray hair and blue eyes. He is wearing gray pants, white shirt, and a windbreaker and is uncertain of his name and his residence.

(D) A man with thin gray hair and blue eyes wearing gray pants, a white shirt, and a green windbreaker says he is Bob who was left by aliens in front of Orchard Houses where he used to live before they kidnapped him. He is 5 ft. 7 in. and weighs 150 lbs.

Answer questions 51 and 52 on the basis of the following Employee Leave Regulations:

As a full-time permanent city employee under the Career and Salary Plan, Officer Peter Smith earns an "annual leave allowance." This consists of a certain number of days off a year with pay and may be used for vacation, for personal business, or for observing religious holidays. During his first 8 years of city service, he will earn an "annual leave allowance" of 20 days off a year (an average of $1\frac{2}{3}$ days off a month). After he has finished 8 full years of working for the city, he will begin earning an additional 5 days off a year. His "annual leave allowance" will then be 25 days a year and will remain at this amount for 7 full years. He will begin earning an additional 2 days off a year after he has completed a total of 15 years of city employment.

A "sick leave allowance" of 1 day a month is also given to Officer Smith, but it can be used only in case of actual illness. When Smith returns to work after using "sick leave allowance," he must have a doctor's note if the absence is for a total of more than 3 days, but he may also be required to show a doctor's note for absences of 1, 2, or 3 days.

51. According to the preceding passage, Mr. Smith's "annual leave allowance" consists of a certain number of days off a year that he

    (A) does not get paid for

    (B) gets paid for at time and a half

    (C) may use for personal business

    (D) may not use for observing religious holidays

52. According to the preceding passage, when he uses "sick leave allowance," Mr. Smith may be required to show a doctor's note

    (A) even if his absence is for only 1 day

    (B) only if his absence is for more than 2 days

    (C) only if his absence is for more than 3 days

    (D) only if his absence is for 3 days or more

Answer questions 53 and 54 on the basis of the drawing below. This drawing shows some vital interior parts of a police revolver and the order in which they fit together.

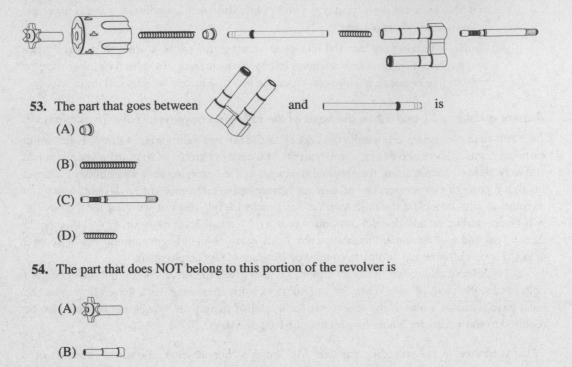

53. The part that goes between and ⬡▭▭▭ is

   (A) 𝕆)

   (B) ⟨⟨⟨⟨⟨⟨⟨⟨⟨⟩

   (C) ▭▬▬

   (D) ⟨⟨⟨⟨⟨⟨⟨

54. The part that does NOT belong to this portion of the revolver is

   (A) 𝕏▭

   (B) ▭▭▭

   (C) ◐

   (D)

55. Police officers are often assigned to the scene of a fire to control traffic and, at times, to close off a street to all traffic except emergency vehicles. Two officers assigned to this duty arrive in a radio car which they park across one end of a street, blocking traffic. After locking their radio car, they then proceed to the other end of the street on foot to block off traffic at that end. The action taken by these police officers should be considered

   (A) improper, because they should have remained in their car in order to be able to move quickly if they were needed

   (B) proper, since a person who may have started the fire would be effectively trapped

   (C) improper, because their car was left unattended and therefore could not be moved to permit emergency vehicles to enter

   (D) proper, because the street is now closed to all but emergency vehicles

56. While on routine patrol, Police Officer Kalb is approached by a furious citizen who complains about nighttime activity in the church parking lot next door to his home. These are the facts collected by Officer Kalb:

> Date: July 21
>
> Time: 10:30 A.M.
>
> Complainant: Peter Lynch of 168 Carman Road
>
> Complaint: nighttime noise, rowdiness, drinking, drag racing, and sex in parking lot of St. Mary's Church at 170 Carman Road

Officer Kalb is writing up a report of this complaint. Which of the following expresses the information *most clearly, accurately, and completely*?

(A) Peter Lynch of St. Mary's on 170 Carman Road says the parking lot should be locked at 10:30 A.M. People drink there at night, and he doesn't like it.

(B) Peter Lynch of 168 Carman Road complains of nighttime noise and rowdiness in the parking lot of St. Mary's at 170 Carman. He demands police action, perhaps padlocking of the lot at night.

(C) There is drinking and sex in the St. Mary's parking lot at night at 170 Carman Road. Peter Lynch says the police should do something on July 21st.

(D) Padlocking the parking lot of St. Mary's might be the solution to nightly disturbances at 170 Carman Road according to Peter Lynch of 168 Carman Road at 10:30 A.M. on July 21st.

57. It is mid-January, and many members of the precinct house staff are out with the flu. Officer Seguaro is covering the dispatcher's desk on an emergency basis. Officer Seguaro receives a call reporting alleged child abuse and consults the following rules for the procedure to be followed in prescribed order:

1. Ask for the name, address, and telephone number of the caller.
2. Ask for the name and address of the person being abused.
3. Ask the nature of the abuse.
4. Ask for the name of the abuser.
5. Dispatch police to the scene of the alleged abuse.
6. If the reporter is at a location not proximate to the scene of the abuse and abused, dispatch police to interview caller.
7. Ask caller his or her relationship to abused and abuser.
8. Assure caller that all information will be kept confidential.

Officer Seguaro asks the caller his name, address, and telephone number, then asks for the name and address of the person being abused. She learns that the caller lives in the apartment directly across the hall from the little girl who is being beaten by a shouting male, unidentified since the beating is taking place behind closed doors. Officer Seguaro immediately dispatches a patrol car to the scene. The next thing for Officer Seguaro to do is

(A) dispatch another patrol car to interview the caller

(B) ask the caller his relationship to the abused

(C) ask the names of likely suspects

(D) assure the caller that all information will be kept confidential

58. As part of a police academy exercise, you are handed the following set of facts:

>Date of event: February 26 or February 27
>
>Time of event: between 10 P.M. and 8 A.M.
>
>Event: stolen car
>
>Location: in front of 10-15 Moss Place between Harlan Blvd. and Montrose Pike
>
>Description: red 4-door 1989 Mazda 626, NY plate PYD 123
>
>Owner: Donald Tramp

Which of the following expresses this information *most clearly, accurately and completely*?

(A) Donald Tramp's car was stolen in front of Harlan Boulevard and Moss Place at 10-15 on February 26 or 27. It is a red 4-door Mazda

(B) A red 4-door 1989 Mazda 26 was stolen by Donald Tramp on February 26 or 27 between 10 P.M. and 8 A.M. Its plate is PYD 123.

(C) From the front of 10-15 Moss Place between Harlan Blvd. And Montrose Pike overnight between February 26 and 27 was stolen the red Mazda of Donald Tramp.

(D) Donald Tramp reports that his red 4-door 1989 Mazda 626, bearing NY plates PYD 123 was stolen from the front of 10-15 Moss Place between Harlan Boulevard and Montrose Pike during the night of February 26-27.

59. Part of the training at the police academy involves preparing reports that are useful to various divisions within the police department. Crimes and criminals are often pursued and investigated from more than one angle, yet all investigators begin with the same report. Officer Monroe has taken these details from a woman who has just been raped:

>Location: 583 Cooper Terrace, elevator
>
>Time: 2:25 P.M.
>
>Occurrence: rape and robbery
>
>Weapon: knife
>
>Perpetrator: white male, approx. 25 yrs., slight build, medium height, wearing blue jeans and red T-shirt
>
>Items stolen: pocketbook, pearl ring, cameo brooch
>
>Victim: Bella Luciano, age 67, of 583 Cooper Terrace

Officer Monroe must prepare a report to be used in apprehending the criminal, recovering the property, and securing the premises. Which of the following expresses the information *most clearly, accurately, and completely*?

(A) A 25-year-old white male raped 67-year-old Bella Luciano with a knife in the elevator. He robbed her too.

(B) At 2:15 P.M. a man raped Bella Luciano in the elevator of 583 Cooper Terrace and robbed her of her pocketbook, pearl ring, and cameo brooch.

(C) A white male, approximately 25 years of age, slightly built and of medium height, wearing blue jeans and a red T-shirt robbed and raped at knifepoint Bella Luciano, age 67, in the elevator of 583 Cooper Terrace at 2:15 P.M. Items stolen were: pocketbook, pearl ring, and cameo brooch.

(D) A pocketbook, pearl ring, and cameo brooch were stolen at knifepoint from Bella Luciano when a man raped her in the elevator. He was 67 years old, medium sized, and wearing blue jeans and a red T-shirt.

60. A fire truck with lights flashing and siren wailing pulled out of the firehouse and headed north towards the site of a fire. After one block, the fire truck turned right. At the next corner it turned right again, proceeding for two blocks before turning left. At successive corners, the fire truck then turned right and right again. At the next intersection, an impatient motorist crossed the path of the fire truck, and the fire truck hit the car on its right side. In which direction was the car traveling?

    (A) North

    (B) South

    (C) East

    (D) West

61. Police Officer D'Onofrio is the first to arrive at the scene of a one-car accident in which a motorist has wrapped his car around a tree. Gasoline is pouring from the ruptured tank and smoke is escaping from the popped hood. The motorist is bleeding profusely from a bad gash on his neck, is slumped unconscious in a contorted position, and has a visibly broken arm. The *first* thing Officer D'Onofrio should do is

    (A) apply pressure on the wound to stop the bleeding

    (B) pull the man from the car

    (C) splint and bandage the broken arm

    (D) administer mouth-to-mouth artificial respiration to restore the man to consciousness

62. A police officer who becomes aware of an unsafe condition with regard to sidewalks or streets along his or her patrol must promptly notify the city department that is responsible for repairing the unsafe condition. The procedure for making this notification is as follows:

    1. Note the nature of the unsafe condition in the memo book.

    2. Enter the exact location of the unsafe condition in the memo book.

    3. Phone or radio the desk officer at the precinct house with information about the unsafe condition and its location.

    4. If the unsafe condition is a malfunctioning traffic signal, notify the Traffic Department.

    Police Officer Mardikian sits four full minutes in his patrol car at the intersection of Broadway and West 128th Street waiting for a red light that refuses to turn green. He pulls up at the curb and writes in his memo book that a traffic signal located at Broadway and West 128th Street is out of order and will not change. From his car he radios to his precinct house and tells the desk officer of this unsafe condition. The next action Officer Mardikian must take is to

    (A) notify the Traffic Department

    (B) jump out and direct traffic

    (C) note in his memo book the time that he notified the precinct house

    (D) continue to cover his assigned patrol route

Answer questions 63 and 64 on the basis of the following procedure:

Preservation of life is a police officer's highest responsibility. Safeguarding members of the public is the officer's first duty, but then self-preservation takes precedence over guaranteeing all civil rights to all people. The Stop and Frisk procedure was instituted to protect police officers along with protecting the public and protecting property. The procedure is:

1. Follow the person and observe to determine if there is cause to suspect that the person has committed, is committing, or is about to commit a crime.

2. If there is cause for suspicion, stop the person, request identification and an explanation for his or her behavior.

3. Frisk if the explanation or nature of suspicious behavior leads the officer to believe that he or she may be physically injured or killed.

4. Search if the frisk leads to suspicion that the individual is concealing a weapon.

5. Confiscate the weapon unless the individual produces a permit.

6. Arrest the person for illegal possession of a weapon.

63. Just after 11 P.M., Police Officer Poplis patrolling a commercial district that has recently been the target of night time break-ins finds herself following a man who is walking slowly, peering into darkened windows, and trying doorknobs. Officer Poplis should now

   (A) stop and frisk the man so that he does not injure or kill her

   (B) continue following the man to see if he will break into a store

   (C) stop the man and ask him to identify himself and to explain his conduct

   (D) ignore the man and cover the remainder of her post to discourage break-ins

64. At 3:30 A.M., Police Officer Moro turns a corner and comes upon two men in their twenties who are alternately shouting at each other and caressing one another. Some of the words that pass between them are threats of bodily harm. Officer Moro approaches the two men, asks for identification and for an explanation of what is going on. The young men assure Officer Moro that this is simply a lovers' quarrel and that their threats are merely words. Officer Moro should now

   (A) ask the men why they are quarreling

   (B) frisk the men to be certain they will not harm each other or him

   (C) search for concealed weapons

   (D) leave the men alone and move on

Answer question 65 on the basis of the following definitions:

Felony murder is committed when a person, acting alone or with others, commits or attempts to commit the crimes of robbery, burglary, kidnapping, arson, or rape, and in the course and furtherance of such crime, or immediate flight therefrom, he, or another participant, if there be any, causes the death of a person other than one of the participants.

Murder is committed when a person, following a period of lengthy planning, intentionally causes the death of another person.

65. The difference between murder and felony murder is that

   (A) in murder someone is killed; in felony murder the crime may be attempted

   (B) in the case of felony murder some other crime must be committed along with the murder

(C) murder is planned; felony murder may be incidental to another crime

(D) felony murder is part of a calculated crime; murder may be impulsive upon extreme provocation or emotional stress

Answer questions 66 and 67 on the basis of the following paragraph:

Proper firearms training is one phase of law enforcement that cannot be ignored. No part of the training of a law officer is more important or more valuable. The officer's life, and often the lives of his or her fellow officers, depend directly upon skill with the weapon he or she is carrying. Proficiency with the revolver is not attained exclusively by the volume of ammunition used and the number of hours spent on the firing line. Supervised practice and the use of training aids and techniques help make the shooter. It is essential to have a good firing range where new officers are trained and older personnel practice in scheduled firearms sessions. The fundamental points to be stressed are grip, stance, breathing, sight alignment, and trigger squeeze. Coordination of thought, vision, and motion must be achieved before the officer gains confidence in shooting ability. Attaining this ability will make the student a better officer and enhance his or her value to the force.

66. The paragraph best supports the statement that

    (A) skill with weapons is a phase of law enforcement training that is too often ignored

    (B) the most useful and essential single factor in the training of a law officer is proper firearms training

    (C) the value of an officer to the force is enhanced by the officer's self-confidence and coordination

    (D) the lives of law enforcement officers always depend directly upon the skill with weapons displayed by fellow officers

67. The word *stance* as used in this paragraph means

    (A) attitude

    (B) opinion

    (C) angle of head

    (D) placement of feet

68. An off-duty police officer visiting a friend in another city stops to fill his tank with gasoline and discovers a holdup in progress at the gas station. When he identifies himself as a law officer, the robber takes off at high speed and the officer gives chase. They proceed west on the highway for three miles. Then they make a right turn off the highway onto a secondary road for another mile and a half, and then a left turn onto a dirt road. Driving at high speed on the dirt road, the holdup man's car develops a flat tire. The man jumps out of the driver's seat and runs directly into the woods. The police officer follows on foot, but loses sight of his suspect. The officer then turns around to walk back to his car. In what direction is he walking?

    (A) North

    (B) South

    (C) East

    (D) West

69. As a student at the police academy you are handed the following scenario: Police Officer Hakim on routine nighttime patrol in a commercial area discovers that the front door of the dark liquor store is not locked. She carefully opens the door a crack and hears sounds inside. Prudently she steps away from the door and radios for backup. Three fellow officers promptly arrive to reinforce her. They open the door and surprise the burglars into surrender without firing a shot. Here are the details:

> Location: Sam's Spirits, 250 Main Street
>
> Date: Tuesday, May 9
>
> Time: 1:20 A.M.
>
> Event: break-in; attempted theft
>
> Officers involved: Peter Nwazota, Amy Zadrozny, and Frank O'Kun
>
> Suspects: Seth Dowling and Tim Farr

Officer Hakim must file a report about this incident. Which of the following expresses the information *most clearly, accurately, and completely*?

(A) Seth Dowling and Tim Farr broke into the liquor store at 1:20 on Tuesday, May 9. Peter Nwazota, Amy Zadrozny, Frank O'Kun, and I captured them.

(B) At 1:20 A.M. on Tuesday, May 9 a break-in was discovered at Sam's Spirits, 250 Main Street. With backup assistance of Peter Nwazota, Amy Zadrozny, and Frank O'Kun, the suspects Seth Dowling and Tim Farr were peacefully arrested.

(C) Peter Nwazota, Amy Zadrozny, and Frank O'Kun helped me take Seth Dowling and Tim Farr into custody when they broke in to Sam's Spirits on Tuesday night at 1:20 A.M.

(D) Theft of the liquor store at 250 Main Street was averted on May 9 at 1:20 A.M. when the suspects were surprised and didn't shoot at Peter Nwazota, Amy Zadrozny, Tim Farr, and me.

70. When summoned to a location at which there is a street fight in which the participants are armed with knives and a large crowd is watching, a police officer must follow this procedure in precise order:

1. Call for reinforcements.

2. Await arrival of reinforcements.

3. Firmly demand that the participants stop fighting at once.

4. Ask spectators to step back.

5. Restrain spectators.

6. With assistance of other officers, grab fighters from behind and forcibly separate them.

7. Confiscate weapons.

Police Officer Fisher has reported to the scene of a street fight. He has sent for reinforcements who have just arrived. He has demanded that the participants stop fighting, but they are still wielding their knives at one another. Officer Fisher should now

(A) draw his gun and fire into the air

(B) grab spectators from behind and restrain them

(C) ask the spectators politely to step out of the way

(D) confiscate the weapons

71. The objective of prison education, in its broadest sense, should be the socialization of the inmates through varied impressional and expressional activities, with emphasis on individual inmate needs. The objective of this program shall be the return of these inmates to society with a more wholesome attitude toward living, with a desire to conduct themselves as good citizens, and with the skill and knowledge which will give them a reasonable chance to maintain themselves and their dependents through honest labor. To this end, each prisoner shall be given a program of education which, on the basis of available data, seems most likely to further the process of socialization and rehabilitation.

On the basis of the preceding paragraph, which is the *most* accurate statement?

(A) Machine shop work is a good example of an expressional activity.

(B) The educational program advocated for prisoners is designed for their rehabilitation but not their socialization.

(C) Group needs, as distinguished from individual needs, should be given the greater consideration in the socialization of prison inmates.

(D) The socialization process includes the acquisition of skills and knowledge on the part of prison inmates.

72. Prison inmates are known to be extremely ingenious in crafting weapons and escape implements from items in ordinary use in the prison. For this reason objects must be counted and accounted for in the same manner as are prisoners. The mess hall procedure is:

1. As inmates bus their trays to the kitchen window, count the cutlery.

2. Have inmates stand in single line against the south wall.

3. Separately count all spoons and all forks.

4. If there is any discrepancy, have count repeated by another officer.

5. Thoroughly search each prisoner, one by one.

6. Confiscate cutlery found.

7. Return prisoners to their cells.

Lunch period is over in the medium security wing of the state penitentiary, and Officer Karski has accepted all the trays and has counted a spoon and a fork from each one. The inmates are all standing against the south wall. The next thing that Officer Karski should do is

(A) return the prisoners to their cells

(B) separately count all the spoons and forks

(C) ask another officer to repeat the count

(D) thoroughly search each prisoner

73. Keeping track of tools in the woodworking shop, Officer Firkin discovers an inmate attempting to return to her cell with a scrap of emery cloth tucked into her sleeve. Officer Firkin must write a report of this incident. The facts are:

> Incident: stealing of emery cloth, 3 x 5 inches
>
> Location: woodworking shop, ground level, west wing
>
> Inmate: Pearl Pratt, #45698
>
> Date: Wednesday, June 4
>
> Time: 3:52 P.M.

Which of the following expresses this information *most clearly, accurately, and completely*?

(A) Pearl Pratt tried to steal a piece of emery cloth from the west wing woodworking shop on Wednesday, June 4, at 3:52 P.M.

(B) At 3:52 P.M. on Wednesday, June 4, Pearl Pratt #45689 tried to steal a 3 x 5 piece of emery cloth from the ground level shop in the west wing.

(C) On Wednesday, June 4, at 3:52 P.M., Pearl Pratt, #45698, was caught trying to steal a 3 x 5 piece of emery cloth from the west wing woodworking shop.

(D) Pearl Pratt, #45698, tried to steal a piece of emery cloth from the woodworking shop in her sleeve in the west wing woodworking shop at 3:52 on Wednesday. She got caught.

74. Prison inmate Alex Bey has managed to slip out of the line returning from exercise and is searching for a place to hide until he can escape. Bey turns into a corridor and runs west to a staircase on his right. He then goes up those stairs to the first landing. He goes through a door on the right side of the landing, runs down the hall and through the second door on his left. The door takes him into a stairwell with stairs up to the right and down to the left. Bey chooses to go down. In what direction is he going?

(A) North

(B) South

(C) East

(D) West

75. Officer Witkowsky standing guard in the southwest tower of the outer gate notices suspicious activity in a clump of bushes beyond the road. She promptly alerts Officer Penzoil who is on patrol along the periphery of the wall with his dog Braveheart. Officer Witkowsky jots down these notes to help with the report she must file at the end of her tour:

> Incident: unexplained activity in bushes beyond road
>
> Location: southwest tower, outer gate
>
> Date: Saturday, April 23
>
> Time: 7:52 A.M.
>
> Action taken: alerted Officer Penzoil on foot patrol with dog Braveheart

Which of the following expresses this information *most clearly, accurately, and completely*?

(A) Suspicious activity in bushes beyond the road was noted from southwest tower, outer gate on Saturday, April 23 at 7:52 A.M. Officer Penzoil and his dog Braveheart went to investigate.

(B) Officer Penzoil and Braveheart the dog checked the bushes of the outer gate of the southwest tower across the road at 7:52 on Saturday, April 23.

(C) Activity by Officer Penzoil and Braveheart was checked out in the bushes on the other side of the road of the southwest tower outside the gate. It was in the morning on Saturday, April 23, at 7:52.

(D) Officer Penzoil and his dog Braveheart got involved in suspicious activity at 7:52 A.M. on April 23 in the southwest tower bushes across the road.

76. The Commissioner of Correction and the superintendents of all penitentiaries in the state shall, so far as practicable, cause all the prisoners in the state correctional institutions who are physically capable thereof to be employed at hard labor for not to exceed eight hours of each day other than Sundays and public holidays. Such hard labor shall be either for the purpose of production of supplies for said institutions, or for the state, or for any political division thereof, or for any public institutions owned or managed and controlled by the state, or for the purpose of industrial training, or partly for one and partly for the other of such purposes.

On the basis of the preceding paragraph, which is the *most* accurate statement?

(A) State convict labor may be used to supply products for any institution controlled by the state.

(B) Supplies manufactured by prisoners in a state prison must be utilized within the said institution.

(C) A prisoner in good physical condition may generally be employed beyond eight hours at hard labor in a state prison.

(D) The chief aim in forcing prison inmates to work is to provide them with industrial training.

Answer questions 77 and 78 on the basis of the following diagram of part of a prison complex.

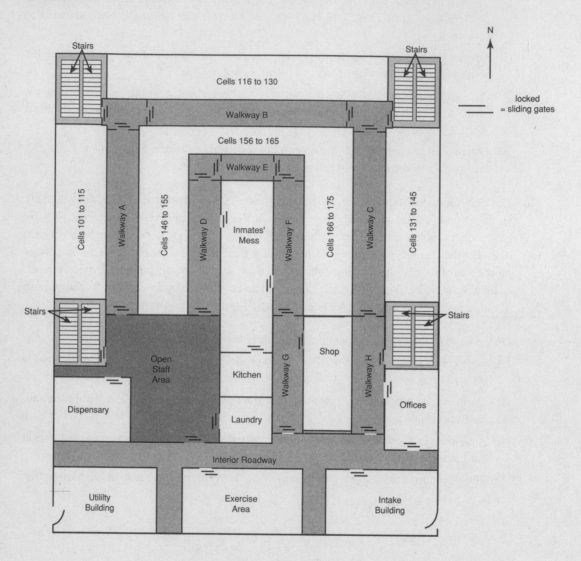

77. An inmate working in the kitchen has scalded himself badly in lifting the lid from a large pot of boiling water. The quickest way to get him to the dispensary is to

(A) go through the laundry, then through the open staff area and into the dispensary

(B) go diagonally across the inmates' mess, exiting to walkway D, down walkway D into and across the open staff area to the dispensary

(C) go through a portion of the inmates' mess, exiting to walkway F, then through walkway G to the interior roadway, then west on the roadway and take a right turn into the open staff area and around the corner to the dispensary

(D) exit the kitchen into walkway G and proceed in order through walkways F, E, and D through the open staff area and into the dispensary

78. It is time for the inmates in cells 328 and 329 (third tier cells directly above 128 and 129 which are in the first tier) to take their auto repair training in the shop. The correction officer escorting these inmates should take them

    (A) into walkway B and down the northeast stairway to walkway C, then from walkway C to walkway H and into the shop

    (B) across walkway B to the northwest stairs, down the stairs to walkway A, then through the open staff area and left into walkway D, following around from walkway D into walkway E and then walkway F, entering walkway G from walkway F and into the shop

    (C) down the nearest stairs and into walkway C, then across to walkway F, from walkway F to walkway G and into the shop

    (D) into walkway B and down the northwest stairs to walkway C, from walkway C through walkway H and into the interior roadway, turn right into the interior roadway and right again into walkway G and north on walkway G to the shop entrance

79. In some jurisdictions, smoking by prison inmates is entirely prohibited. Where smoking is permitted, it is restricted to outside recreation areas and is strictly controlled. The correction officer supervising smokers must follow these rules:

    1. Confine the inmate who asks permission to smoke to the southwest quadrant of the exercise yard.
    2. Personally light the cigarette with your cigarette lighter.
    3. Immediately return the lighter to your shirt pocket.
    4. Constantly observe the smokers to make certain that there is no lighting from one cigarette to another.
    5. Immediately confiscate all cigarettes if there is any violation of regulations.
    6. Collect butts and account for all smoked cigarettes before returning prisoners to their cells.

    Correction Officer Tomassi is approached by inmate Grant who requests permission to smoke a cigarette. Officer Tomassi walks with Grant to the southwest corner of the exercise yard, lights Grant's cigarette with his lighter, and puts the lighter back in his pocket. As he watches the smokers, Officer Tomassi observes Grant handing his cigarette to inmate Wylie so that Wylie may light his own cigarette. Officer Tomassi must now

    (A) take out his cigarette lighter and light Wylie's cigarette

    (B) send Wylie to the southwest corner of the exercise yard

    (C) confiscate all cigarettes

    (D) count all the smoked butts

80. Choose which one of the following sentences contains a grammatical error.

    (A) Without good leadership, the basic changes desired in the inmates of a correctional institution cannot be brought about.

    (B) Formerly nothing was as important than custody in prison management.

    (C) In their daily work, Correction Officers should not allow their personal problems to affect their relations with the inmates.

    (D) A repressive atmosphere in a prison is not suitable for the development of a sense of responsibility consistent with freedom.

81. Read the two sentences that follow and mark your answer: (A) if only the first sentence contains an error; (B) if only the second sentence contains an error; (C) if both sentences contain errors; (D) if neither sentence contains an error.

    I.   When a prison system produces no change in prisoners and the period of imprisonment is short, the period during which society is protected is also short.

    II.   Public attitudes of hostility toward and rejection of an ex-prisoner can undo the beneficial effects of even an ideal correctional system.

82. Correction Officer Martinson is assigned to watch duty in the tower at the northeast corner of the outer wall of a large penitentiary. Officer Martinson begins by looking due north. Seeing nothing unusual, she slowly turns to her left scanning the horizon and then bringing her gaze in towards the prison walls. When Officer Martinson has made a half-circle turn, she is startled by a loud noise on her left. Officer Martinson wheels toward the noise and is looking

(A) north

(B) south

(C) east

(D) west

Use the following tables to choose the answers to questions 83 and 84.

Codes

Age	Borough	County	Charge	Location
A 13-14	Br=Bronx	BX=Bronx	1 Arson	I on own recognizance Ia out on bail
B 15-16	Bn=Brooklyn	KI=Kings	2 Assault	II Children's Shelter IIa Juvenile Detention
C 17-18	Mn=Manhattan	NY=New York	3 Burglary	III Women's Shelter
D 19-20	Qn=Queens	QU=Queens	4 Larceny	
	SI=Staten Island	RI=Richmond	5 Rape 5A Statutory rape 5C Prostitution 6 Robbery	V Rikers Island

Roster of Cases

Name	Sex	Age	Address	Charge	Current Location
Franklin	M	18	123 W. 231 St., Bronx	robbery	Rikers Island
Arthur	M	15	7210 Rockaway Pkwy., Queens	burglary	Juvenile Detention
Mason	F	20	1556 E. 14 St., Brooklyn	assault	on own recognizance

Name	Sex	Age	Address	Charge	Current Location
Carmack	M	16	5005 Grand Concourse, Bronx	assault	Juvenile Detention
Sanders	F	14	1020 Avenue A, Manhattan	prostitution	Juvenile Detention
Tench	F	17	12 Hinkley Place, Brooklyn	robbery	Women's Shelter
Dithers	M	13	56 Jane St., Manhattan	burglary	Children's Shelter
Lathrop	M	18	286 Clove Lake Rd., Staten Island	statutory rape	out on bail

83. Each of the following three sets of codes describes one of the individuals mentioned above:

    B Br BX 2 IIa

    B Qn QU 3 IIa

    C Br BX 6 V

Which of the following names the three individuals described in the correct order?

(A) Carmack, Tench, Franklin

(B) Carmack, Arthur, Franklin

(C) Arthur, Mason, Franklin

(D) Carmack, Mason, Arthur

84. Which of the following correctly describes three individuals on the roster of cases?

(A) A Mn NY 5C II

    C Qn QU 3 IIa

    B Br BX 5 V

(B) C Bn KI 6 III

    C Br BX 6 V

    A Qn QU 4 I

(C) A Mn NY 5C IIa

    D Bn KI 2 I

    C Bn KI 6 III

(D) B Qn QU 3 IIa

    A Mn NY 1 II

    A Br BX 4 V

85. A prison inmate is entitled to meet with his or her attorney on any day of the week between the hours of 10:00 A.M. and 4:00 P.M. on one hour's notice to the superintendent's office. All other visitors are subject to the following rules:

    1. Spouses, children, and parents may visit no more than two at a time on Sundays only between the hours of 10:30 A.M. and 12 noon and between the hours of 1:30 P.M. and 4:30 P.M.

    2. An unlimited number of children under the age of 14 may accompany one adult visitor to a prison inmate provided that they are the children of that inmate.

    3. Visitors other than spouses, children, and parents may visit one at a time and only between the hours of 2:00 P.M. and 4:00 P.M. on Sundays.

    4. All visitors, regardless of age or relationship and including attorneys, must pass through a metal detector upon entry to the visiting hall and must be subject to pat down search.

    5. Visitors arriving in groups larger than those permitted may not enter the visiting hall but must wait in the outer lobby of the administration building, entering the visiting hall by turns in the prescribed numbers.

On Sunday afternoon at 1:45 P.M. Sandor Yates, common law husband of inmate Barbara Welsh, arrives at the prison with 7-month-old Thelma, 3-year-old Thomas, 6-year-old Matilda, 11-year-old Brian, and 13-year old Jeanine. Correction Officer Hopkins asks Mr. Yates if all of these children are the children of Barbara Welsh, and Mr. Yates assures Officer Hopkins that this is indeed the case. Officer Hopkins should now

(A) walk the family through the metal detectors and pat down each member

(B) ask the family to wait in the outer lobby until group visiting hours begin at 2:00

(C) pat down Mr. Yates, Jeanine and Brian and send Matilda and Thomas through the metal detector

(D) send the family home because they did not give one hour's notice of their arrival.

END OF EXAM

ANSWER KEY FOR MODEL EXAMINATION 1

1. C	12. D	23. B	34. B	45. D	56. B	67. D	78. D
2. D	13. A	24. C	35. D	46. A	57. B	68. A	79. C
3. A	14. C	25. D	36. A	47. B	58. D	69. B	80. B
4. D	15. C	26. D	37. B	48. C	59. C	70. C	81. D
5. C	16. D	27. C	38. D	49. B	60. A	71. D	82. C
6. B	17. B	28. B	39. A	50. C	61. B	72. B	83. B
7. B	18. B	29. A	40. D	51. C	62. A	73. C	84. C
8. A	19. A	30. D	41. C	52. A	63. C	74. D	85. A
9. C	20. C	31. C	42. C	53. D	64. D	75. A	
10. D	21. D	32. A	43. A	54. B	65. C	76. A	
11. B	22. A	33. B	44. D	55. C	66. B	77. B	

Explanatory Answers for Model Examination 1

1. **(C)** As far as we can see, each student is seated at individual desk.

2. **(D)** The teacher is wearing round frame glasses, a long-sleeved white shirt, vest, and striped tie. He is gesturing with his right hand, not saluting the flag.

3. **(A)** The time indicated on the clock is 4:10. If there is a clock, expect a time question.

4. **(D)** The bald black man has his handgun aimed directly at the teacher.

5. **(C)** There are 14 people in the scene. Always count people in a memory picture.

6. **(B)** The woman wearing a headscarf is sitting at the far left in the third row and is wearing earrings.

7. **(B)** The long counter at the front of the room, where the teacher is standing, has a sink with two faucets at one end and two gas jets as well. Clearly, the room is equipped as a chemistry classroom.

8. **(A)** The empty desk is in the second row between the student in the sleeveless sweater and the student with the long braid.

9. **(C)** The woman in the doorway wearing a camouflage design jumpsuit is aiming her submachine gun at the roomful of students.

10. **(D)** The woman in the second seat from the left in the front row has light-colored curly hair and is wearing a print blouse.

11. **(B)** The students are either taking notes or watching the teacher; one person is wearing a baseball cap; writing can be seen on the chalkboard. However, the dark area on the ceiling indicates that a light is not in good working order.

12. **(D)** The dial faces are illegible, but each has a single pointer pointing in a different direction, so we know that they are not clocks.

13. **(A)** The teacher's left hand is on the counter in front of him. His right hand is raised, but not towards the gunman.

14. **(C)** The student in the far left seat in the front row is wearing a plaid shirt and is looking off to his left.

15. **(C)** Choices (A) and (B) neglect to mention the fire. (D) leaves out the time and expresses an opinion. A report should be factual, not conjectural.

16. **(D)** Only this statement gives all relevant information in logical order. Choice (A) does not give adequate location information; the other choices are garbled.

17. **(B)** Rule 3 prohibits use of names over the radio.

18. **(B)** Rule 4 of the procedure indicates that Officer Alcorn should have accompanied the man to the hospital since the man refused to identify himself.

19. **(A)**

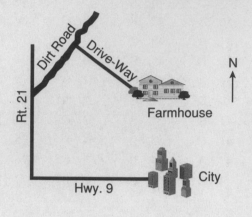

20. **(C)**

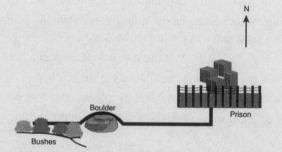

21. **(D)** The paragraph tells us that the payroll department complies with IRS regulations in withholding taxes from salaries and wages. The IRS determines the tax, not the salaries.

22. **(A)** The most important thing is to get medical help for the child.

23. **(B)** Officer Szulk wants assistance. He must be specific about his location.

24. **(C)** Choice (D) includes all the information, but (C) is clearer.

25. **(D)** Rule 4 explains why the other choices are wrong. Choice (D) conforms with rule 6.

26. **(D)** The officers violated rule 1. The officers had no way of knowing that there was no gun and no argument. If there were, a knock at the door might easily provoke a shot at the door.

27. **(C)** The dictionary definition of *homicide* is "the killing of one person by another."

28. **(B)** Both committed harassment: Blount because she pushed Wallace in an attempt to scare her and Wallace because she made an obscene gesture at Blount.

29. **(A)** Hammer did not injure either Bates or Collins so he is not guilty of assault. Without a full list of definitions of all crimes, you cannot state that he committed no crime. In fact, Hammer was intentionally reckless.

30. **(D)**

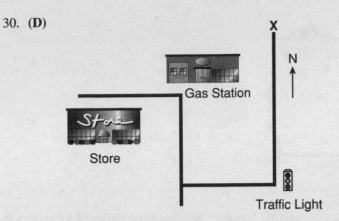

31. **(C)** All other choices can be answered by "yes" or "no."

32. **(A)** Choices (B) and (D) are incomplete. (C) has the address wrong.

33. **(B)** All other choices leave out some of the information.

34. **(B)**

$20	×	5	=	$100.00
$10	×	7	=	70.00
$5	×	13	=	65.00
$1	×	2	=	2.00
$.25	×	9	=	2.25
$.10	×	21	=	2.10
$.05	×	17	=	.85
$.01	×	8	=	.08
				$242.28

35. **(D)** Rule 1. An officer should never assume the responsibility of deciding whether or not a prisoner requires the services of a doctor.

36. **(A)** Rule 2 governs. It is apparent that the prisoner requires medical attention even though there is no emergency. Medical attention is required for the prisoner's wound, not for his drug addition, therefore an ambulance should be called.

37. **(B)** In saying that investigators must devote themselves completely though the work may not be easy, smooth, or peaceful, the paragraph is saying that they must be persistent in the face of difficulty.

38. **(D)** All other choices are leading questions.

39. **(A)** This is the only choice that gives time, date, location, and description of a suspect.

40. **(D)** Who was robbed and by whom? Who was wearing what? When and where did it happen? Choice (D) tells it best.

41. **(C)** The rule states that the first question must relate to the sex of the missing person. The fact that the woman referred to the baby as "she" is no guarantee that the baby is a girl. Confusion of pronouns is very common among people for whom English is not the primary language, especially in time of stress.

42. **(C)**

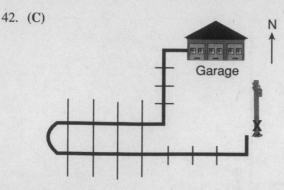

43. **(A)** According to the definition of *larceny*, one may be considered guilty of this crime if found property is not returned to its owner. Since the question makes no reference to a search for the rightful owner, one must assume intent to keep the ring.

44. **(D)** *Larceny* also involves obtaining property under false pretenses, the situation here.

45. **(D)** In compliance with Rule 1, the first thing the officer must do is ascertain that the woman is indeed dead.

46. **(A)** The officer is certain that the man is dead, and the body is in the apartment not in public view. Rule 3 requires that the officer now summon a sergeant to the scene.

47. **(B)** The sister did not live with the dead man so, according to Rule 6, the albums may not be released to her.

48. **(C)**

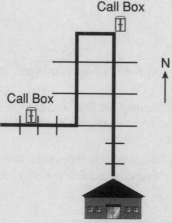

49. **(B)** At this moment police cars in the area would need as much information as possible about the offending car. Details about the car that was hit, aside from color, are not relevant to pursuit. Choices (A) and (C) give incomplete descriptions; choice (D) has the state of registration wrong.

50. **(C)** Since the man is clearly confused, the information he has given about his residence or former residence, how he arrived at this location, and possibly even his name should not be reported as fact. Physical description of the man is very important for purposes of establishing his identity and of finding a responsible person to claim him.

51. **(C)** The second sentence lists the permissible uses of annual leave allowance.

52. **(A)** According to the last sentence of the paragraph, he *may* be required to show a doctor's note for absences of 1, 2, or 3 days.

53. **(D)**

54. **(B)**

55. **(C)** The officers were assigned to close off the street to all traffic except emergency vehicles. They have used poor judgment. Their unattended parked police car cannot be moved easily to permit arriving emergency vehicles to enter the street.

56. **(B)** Choices (A) and (C) are both garbled and incomplete. (D) is accurate, but (B) is far clearer.

57. **(B)** Officer Seguaro has followed the procedure properly through step 5. Since the caller is just across the hall from the location of the child abuse, there is no reason to send a second car. The caller has already said that he does not know the identity of the abuser, so there is no point to asking his relationship to the abuser. But, the caller might be related to the child being beaten. Officer Seguaro must ask.

58. **(D)** This is an all-inclusive description. (B) is wrong; (A) is garbled; (C) neglects to describe the car.

59. **(C)** This report is correct and very complete. (A) gives neither description nor address; (B) neglects to describe the perpetrator; and (C) describes the man wrong and omits the location.

60. **(A)**

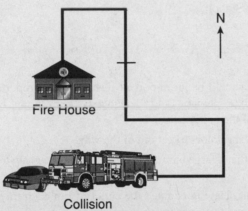

61. **(B)** The car is hot and is leaking gasoline. An explosion is a very real and imminent danger. Officer D'Onofrio must get the victim and himself away from the car as quickly as possible, even at the risk of causing the victim some harm by moving him. Officer D'Onofrio's second act should be to apply pressure to stop the bleeding. Artificial respiration restores breathing, not consciousness. The arm can wait.

62. **(A)** According to the rules as stated, Officer Mardikian is now responsible for notifying the Traffic Department to repair the signal light. You might expect that the desk officer could notify the Traffic Department and that the officer would be better utilized directing traffic, but you must answer exam questions on the basis of the rules as printed. Actual procedures may, of course, be different.

63. **(C)** Officer Poplis has already followed the man. His walking slowly and peering into windows might just be a way of killing time, but his trying doorknobs is clear reason to suspect that he intends to commit a crime. Asking for identification and explanation for the behavior is the proper next step.

64. **(D)** Officer Moro should be satisfied that a crime has not been committed, is not being committed, and will not be committed. The reason for the quarrel is none of his business. It is time for Police Officer Moro to move on.

65. **(C)** The definitions make it quite clear that murder is planned and intentional, while felony murder refers to accidental death that occurs during commission or *attempted commission*—which is why (B) is wrong—of another crime.

66. **(B)** If no part of the training of a law officer is more important or more valuable (sentence 2), then clearly the most useful and essential single factor in the training of a law officer is proper firearms training. Choice (A) is incorrect because the first sentence says only that firearms training *cannot* be ignored not that it *is* ignored. Choice (D) is an overstatement; lives often depend directly upon weapons skills, but not always.

67. **(D)** In describing standing posture, *stance* refers specifically to placement of feet.

68. **(A)**

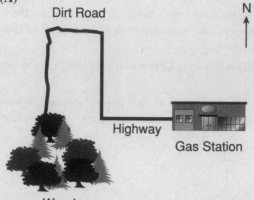

69. **(B)** The fact that no shots were fired should be an important feature of this report. Neither (A) nor (C) mentions it. In addition these choices fail to adequately identify and locate the liquor store. (D) confuses the names of the participants.

70. **(C)** The next step, step 4, is to ask the spectators to get out of the way.

71. **(D)** The second sentence makes clear that a large part of socialization is fortifying the person with a means to earn a living.

72. **(B)** Check and double-check is the rule. Having counted the cutlery from each tray, Officer Karski must now count all the spoons and forks separately.

73. **(C)** Choice (A) is incomplete because it omits the prisoner's number; (B) is inaccurate because it gets the number wrong; (D) is unclear—surely the woodworking shop was not in her sleeve.

74. **(D)**

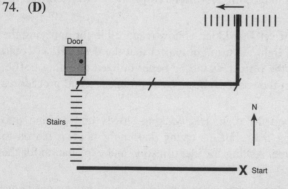

75. **(A)** Choice (B) omits the reason for the investigation; (C) and (D) manage to turn the officer and his dog into suspects rather than investigators.

76. **(A)** The paragraph clearly prohibits hard labor for more than eight hours a day. The supplies produced may be used in any institution controlled by the state, their use is not restricted to the prison in which they are produced. The work may provide industrial training to the prisoners involved, but that is not a requirement of the work component.

77. **(B)** There is no door from the kitchen to the laundry nor does the kitchen open onto walkway
G, so both (A) and (D) are impossible; (C) represents the long way round.

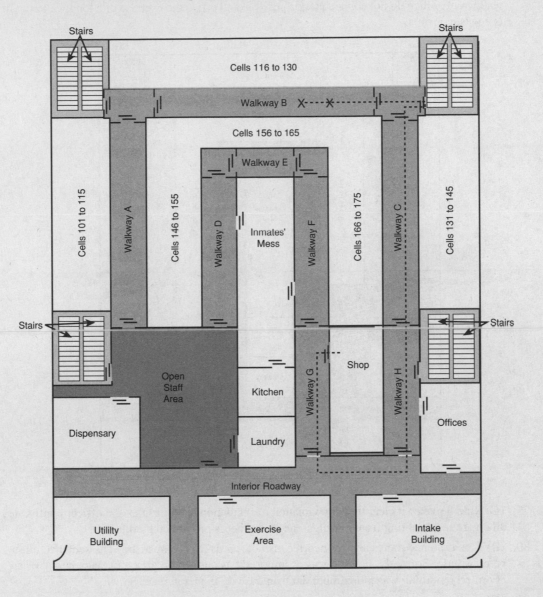

78. **(D)** There is no entry from walkway H to the shop, so (A) is impossible; choice (C) doesn't tell how the inmates get to the nearest stairway nor how they get from walkway C to walkway F which do not connect; (B) is possible and offers the exercise of a long walk, but it is a waste of time.

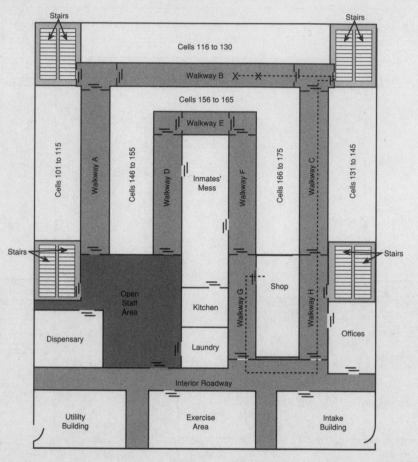

79. **(C)** Rule 5 makes it clear that any violation of regulations requires that the officer confiscate all cigarettes. Lighting from one cigarette to another is prohibited by rule 4.

80. **(B)** This sentence represents an incorrect use of words in a comparison. The sentence might be recast as, "Formerly, nothing was as important as custody in prison management," or as, "Formerly, nothing was more important than custody in prison management."

81. **(D)** Both sentences are correctly written.

82. **(C)**

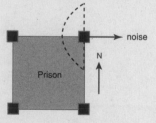

83. **(B)** Choosing the correct answer to this type of question is tedious but not difficult. Go through the tables methodically, eliminating one choice at a time. Only five inmates are named among the choices. Do not waste time trying to match any other individuals to the codes.

84. **(C)** These codes correctly describe Sanders, Mason and Tench. Choosing the answer to this question is not as difficult as it first appears. Looking at choice (A): the first code seems to describe Sanders, but places her in the wrong facility. Since the first code does not describe one of the eight individuals, you can eliminate (A) altogether. The question requires that all three codes describe individuals on the roster. Eliminating (B) takes a bit more work. The first code describes Tench and the second Franklin, but the only person from Queens is 15 years old, code B. Once you have verified (C) as the answer, there is no point to checking out (D). (D) is easy to eliminate because both A-coded individuals are from Manhattan.

85. **(A)** This is a big crowd, but it conforms to the rules for admitting as a group spouse and children under 14. Everyone must go through the metal detectors and be patted down, as required by rule 4.

Answer Sheet for Model Examination 2

1. Ⓐ Ⓑ Ⓒ Ⓓ
2. Ⓐ Ⓑ Ⓒ Ⓓ
3. Ⓐ Ⓑ Ⓒ Ⓓ
4. Ⓐ Ⓑ Ⓒ Ⓓ
5. Ⓐ Ⓑ Ⓒ Ⓓ
6. Ⓐ Ⓑ Ⓒ Ⓓ
7. Ⓐ Ⓑ Ⓒ Ⓓ
8. Ⓐ Ⓑ Ⓒ Ⓓ
9. Ⓐ Ⓑ Ⓒ Ⓓ
10. Ⓐ Ⓑ Ⓒ Ⓓ
11. Ⓐ Ⓑ Ⓒ Ⓓ
12. Ⓐ Ⓑ Ⓒ Ⓓ
13. Ⓐ Ⓑ Ⓒ Ⓓ
14. Ⓐ Ⓑ Ⓒ Ⓓ
15. Ⓐ Ⓑ Ⓒ Ⓓ
16. Ⓐ Ⓑ Ⓒ Ⓓ
17. Ⓐ Ⓑ Ⓒ Ⓓ
18. Ⓐ Ⓑ Ⓒ Ⓓ
19. Ⓐ Ⓑ Ⓒ Ⓓ

20. Ⓐ Ⓑ Ⓒ Ⓓ
21. Ⓐ Ⓑ Ⓒ Ⓓ
22. Ⓐ Ⓑ Ⓒ Ⓓ
23. Ⓐ Ⓑ Ⓒ Ⓓ
24. Ⓐ Ⓑ Ⓒ Ⓓ
25. Ⓐ Ⓑ Ⓒ Ⓓ
26. Ⓐ Ⓑ Ⓒ Ⓓ
27. Ⓐ Ⓑ Ⓒ Ⓓ
28. Ⓐ Ⓑ Ⓒ Ⓓ
29. Ⓐ Ⓑ Ⓒ Ⓓ
30. Ⓐ Ⓑ Ⓒ Ⓓ
31. Ⓐ Ⓑ Ⓒ Ⓓ
32. Ⓐ Ⓑ Ⓒ Ⓓ
33. Ⓐ Ⓑ Ⓒ Ⓓ
34. Ⓐ Ⓑ Ⓒ Ⓓ
35. Ⓐ Ⓑ Ⓒ Ⓓ
36. Ⓐ Ⓑ Ⓒ Ⓓ
37. Ⓐ Ⓑ Ⓒ Ⓓ
38. Ⓐ Ⓑ Ⓒ Ⓓ

39. Ⓐ Ⓑ Ⓒ Ⓓ
40. Ⓐ Ⓑ Ⓒ Ⓓ
41. Ⓐ Ⓑ Ⓒ Ⓓ
42. Ⓐ Ⓑ Ⓒ Ⓓ
43. Ⓐ Ⓑ Ⓒ Ⓓ
44. Ⓐ Ⓑ Ⓒ Ⓓ
45. Ⓐ Ⓑ Ⓒ Ⓓ
46. Ⓐ Ⓑ Ⓒ Ⓓ
47. Ⓐ Ⓑ Ⓒ Ⓓ
48. Ⓐ Ⓑ Ⓒ Ⓓ
49. Ⓐ Ⓑ Ⓒ Ⓓ
50. Ⓐ Ⓑ Ⓒ Ⓓ
51. Ⓐ Ⓑ Ⓒ Ⓓ
52. Ⓐ Ⓑ Ⓒ Ⓓ
53. Ⓐ Ⓑ Ⓒ Ⓓ
54. Ⓐ Ⓑ Ⓒ Ⓓ
55. Ⓐ Ⓑ Ⓒ Ⓓ
56. Ⓐ Ⓑ Ⓒ Ⓓ
57. Ⓐ Ⓑ Ⓒ Ⓓ

58. Ⓐ Ⓑ Ⓒ Ⓓ
59. Ⓐ Ⓑ Ⓒ Ⓓ
60. Ⓐ Ⓑ Ⓒ Ⓓ
61. Ⓐ Ⓑ Ⓒ Ⓓ
62. Ⓐ Ⓑ Ⓒ Ⓓ
63. Ⓐ Ⓑ Ⓒ Ⓓ
64. Ⓐ Ⓑ Ⓒ Ⓓ
65. Ⓐ Ⓑ Ⓒ Ⓓ
66. Ⓐ Ⓑ Ⓒ Ⓓ
67. Ⓐ Ⓑ Ⓒ Ⓓ
68. Ⓐ Ⓑ Ⓒ Ⓓ
69. Ⓐ Ⓑ Ⓒ Ⓓ
70. Ⓐ Ⓑ Ⓒ Ⓓ
71. Ⓐ Ⓑ Ⓒ Ⓓ
72. Ⓐ Ⓑ Ⓒ Ⓓ
73. Ⓐ Ⓑ Ⓒ Ⓓ
74. Ⓐ Ⓑ Ⓒ Ⓓ
75. Ⓐ Ⓑ Ⓒ Ⓓ

TEAR HERE

Model Examination 2

MEMORY BOOKLET

Directions: You will be given 10 minutes to study the five photographs in this memory booklet. Concentrate on each and try to notice and remember as many details as you can. You may not take any notes.

A courtroom scene.

A portion of a cell block.

A car being ticketed.

Civilian employees in the office.

A staff training session.

TEST QUESTION BOOKLET

Time: 3 hours — 75 questions

Directions: Questions 1 to 30 are based on the five photographs you just studied. Answer these questions first, while your memory is still fresh. On your answer sheet darken the letter of the multiple-choice answer you select. Answer true or false questions by darkening **A** for true and **B** for false. These questions are worth $\frac{1}{2}$ point each.

Questions 1 to 6 are based on the photograph of a courtroom.

1. The judge is
   - (A) addressing the witness
   - (B) conferring with the attorney
   - (C) looking over some papers
   - (D) handing documents to a court officer

2. The person standing is
   - (A) waving papers at the judge
   - (B) curly haired
   - (C) wearing a dark suit
   - (D) looking at the witness

3. The man in the light suit is wearing dark socks.
   - (A) true
   - (B) false

4. Two people can be seen seated in the jury box.
   - (A) true
   - (B) false

5. The stenographer is not wearing glasses.
   - (A) true
   - (B) false

6. An American flag is to the left of the judge.
   - (A) true
   - (B) false

Questions 7 to 12 are based on the photograph of a portion of a prison cell block.

7. The lighting in the cell block is provided by
   (A) skylights
   (B) fluorescent tubes
   (C) spotlights which are not visible in the picture
   (D) incandescent ceiling fixtures

8. The cells in the two middle tiers appear to be designed for
   (A) one inmate only
   (B) at least two inmates
   (C) four inmates
   (D) there is no way to tell

9. Hanging of laundry is a permitted use for the walkway in front of the cells.
   (A) true
   (B) false

10. Two people are seated at a table on the floor level of the cell block.
    (A) true
    (B) false

11. This photograph was taken with many cell doors open.
    (A) true
    (B) false

12. Someone has hung a message on the grate of a cell.
    (A) true
    (B) false

Questions 13 to 18 are based on the photograph of the car being ticketed.

13. The car is best described as a
    (A) four-door sedan
    (B) two-door convertible
    (C) three-door hatchback
    (D) two-door sedan

14. The automobile is getting a ticket because it
    (A) is facing the wrong way on a one-way street
    (B) is parked on the wrong side of the street
    (C) is parked beside a fire hydrant
    (D) has overstayed its meter

15. The car has whitewall tires.

    (A) true

    (B) false

16. The person giving the ticket is wearing a tie.

    (A) true

    (B) false

17. This ticketing is occurring on a sunny day.

    (A) true

    (B) false

18. There is heavy traffic on the street.

    (A) true

    (B) false

Questions 19 to 24 are based on the photograph of civilian employees in the office.

19. The man with glasses is

    (A) pointing at his paper with his finger

    (B) reading a magazine

    (C) taking notes

    (D) studying a graph

20. Behind the man and woman can be seen

    (A) a row of notebooks

    (B) an open box

    (C) a telephone

    (D) a window

21. The man who is wearing a tie is wearing glasses.

    (A) true

    (B) false

22. There is an empty chair in the room.

    (A) true

    (B) false

23. There is a Styrofoam cup on one desk.

    (A) true

    (B) false

24. The woman is wearing boots.

    (A) true

    (B) false

Questions 25 to 30 are based on the photograph of the staff training session.

25. The person wearing a white jacket is
    (A) looking at the instructor
    (B) wearing glasses
    (C) holding a pen
    (D) sitting in a wooden chair

26. The man with the mustache is
    (A) left-handed
    (B) African-American
    (C) wearing a turtleneck shirt
    (D) taking notes

27. The instructor is pointing to the figures on a chart.
    (A) true
    (B) false

28. The person to the right of the instructor is speaking or is about to speak.
    (A) true
    (B) false

29. There are two open books on the table.
    (A) true
    (B) false

30. The person in the plaid jacket is wearing earrings.
    (A) true
    (B) false

> **Directions:** Questions 31 to 45 are based on prison rules. The rules printed here may or may not be accurate or current, but you must base your answer strictly on the rules as stated on this exam. Each question based on prison rules is worth one point.

Questions 31 to 33 are based on the following rules:

Transport of prisoners from one institution to another constitutes a risky maneuver which must be accomplished strictly according to established procedure. Strip-search all prisoners prior to loading them on the bus. If transporting an even number of prisoners, handcuff the prisoners in pairs. If transporting only one prisoner and in the case of the final prisoner in an odd count, cuff together the hands of that prisoner behind his or her back. Apply leg irons to the outer leg of each prisoner cuffed to another prisoner, that is, shackle the leg opposite the hand that is cuffed to the bracket in the floor of the bus at the end of the bench on which that prisoner is seated. Shackle prisoners who are cuffed with their hands behind their backs by their left legs. At boarding, verify identities of prisoners and double-check all restraints. Seat prisoners on the bus in alternate rows so that there is an empty bench between rows of prisoners.

Correction Officers accompanying prisoners being transported are assigned to the bus in the ratio of one officer, not including the driver, for each group of four prisoners, but in no instance may fewer than two officers accompany prisoners being transferred between prisons. At least one officer must be stationed in front of the prisoners and facing them. At least one officer must be stationed to the rear of all prisoners where activity may be observed from behind. Officers must maintain easy clearance so as to be able to move within the bus as needed. Under no circumstances may any officer, with the exception of the driver, be so positioned as to present his or her back to any prisoner.

31. Cooper, Johns, Lorant, Frusciante, Chavez, Sweeny, and Hammer have all been sentenced to prison terms of longer than one year and must now be transferred from the county jail, where they had been held pending sentencing, to the upstate penitentiary.

    Correction Officer Krupka has strip-searched each of these prisoners and has handcuffed the right hand of Cooper to the left hand of Johns, the left hand of Lorant to the right hand of Chavez, the right hand of Frusciante to the left hand of Hammer, and the two hands of Sweeny behind Sweeny's back. Officer Fielding is attaching leg irons to the prisoners. Which of the following actions should Fielding take?

    (A) Attach a leg iron to Lorant's left leg

    (B) Attach a leg iron to Sweeny's right leg

    (C) Attach a leg iron to Cooper's left leg

    (D) Attach leg irons to both of Sweeny's legs

32. The maximum security Lakeside Penitentiary has become dangerously overcrowded, so the superintendent has selected nine inmates who have proven to be untroublesome for transfer to a medium security institution in another county. The inmates have been strip-searched, handcuffed, and placed in leg irons according to procedure and have been seated on the bus. Officer Tolbert, the driver, gets into the driver's seat. Officer Graves stands at the front of the bus facing the seated prisoners. Officer Schlesinger stands at the back of the bus to observe the prisoners from behind. Officer Cronin should

(A) sit in the empty seat beside the ninth prisoner

(B) get off the bus because he is not needed

(C) sit on an empty bench between rows of prisoners

(D) station himself at an empty corner of the bus

33. Officer Yeager is standing outside the bus at the foot of the steps checking on prisoners as they board. Officer Yeager verifies names and serial numbers of prisoners being transported and notes date and time on the official list. She tests handcuffs to be certain that they are securely locked and makes sure that leg irons are in place. Then Officer Yeager pats down each prisoner before allowing them to board the bus. Officer Yeager is taking a nonstandard action by

(A) patting down the prisoners

(B) checking off names and serial numbers on a list

(C) standing outside the bus at the foot of the steps

(D) testing handcuffs

Questions 34 and 35 are based on the following rules:

Religious observance by prison inmates may not be infringed unless a religious practice is in conflict with prison safety or security rules. The faith of an inmate must not be questioned or ridiculed. Wherever possible encourage religious practice. Officers should take steps to accommodate specific reasonable requests.

34. Father Flaherty, a Roman Catholic priest, comes every Saturday afternoon to hear confession from inmates. One Saturday, inmate Mohammed ibnIman requests permission to go to confession. Officer Trotsky knows that ibnIman turns toward Mecca and prays five times every day. Officer Trotsky should

(A) ask ibnIman why he, a devout Moslem, wants to confess to a Catholic priest

(B) turn down the request as totally out of order

(C) grant permission while laughingly saying, "Sure, if you think that will help save your Moslem soul."

(D) schedule a time for ibnIman to go to confession

35. Inmate Ratner approaches Officer Hill and tells Hill that Wednesday night is the anniversary of his father's death. Ratner would like to light a 24-hour memorial candle for his father on that night. Officer Hill should

(A) tell Ratner that lighting a candle is impossible because prisoners are not permitted to use matches or lighters

(B) permit Ratner to light a candle in his cell under supervision because this observance is very meaningful to the prisoner

(C) arrange for Ratner to observe an officer's lighting of a candle in the supervisor's office and for Ratner to say a prayer while there

(D) tell Ratner that he, Officer Hill, will light a candle for him at his home and will be certain that it burns for 24 hours

Answer question 36 on the basis of the following rules:

A prisoner held under minimum security who has served more than two-thirds of his or her sentence with no rules violations may be awarded a weekend pass for a visit to the home of his or her parents or spouse. The prisoner must register the telephone number of the home he or she will be visiting and must call the prison's toll-free monitoring number at noon and at 9:00 P.M. of the first day of the visit and at 8:00 A.M. and 2:00 P.M. of the second day of the visit. The monitoring telephone has a display which indicates the phone number from which the call is originating. A call originating from any number other than that registered is cause for immediate revocation of the pass and retrieval of the prisoner.

36. Inmate Zakris has served 18 months of a 21-month sentence and requests a weekend pass to the home she shares with her husband and 5-year-old son. She registers her home telephone number and is granted the pass which begins at 9:00 A.M. Saturday. Promptly at 8:00 A.M. on Sunday, Zakris telephones the prison, but the number displayed on the monitor is not the number she had registered. Zakris tells Officer Right, who takes the call, that she has taken her son to visit with her parents at their home. Officer Right should

    (A) ask for the phone number at her parents' home

    (B) revoke her pass and send a Correction Officer to bring Zakris back to prison immediately

    (C) tell Zakris to return to her own home at once and to call in as soon as she gets there

    (D) accept the call and explanation

Answer questions 37 and 38 on the basis of the following rules:

Considering the number of prison inmates and the violent character of many of these inmates, prison riots are a very rare occurrence. However, even a minor disturbance in a prison tends to have a contagious effect and must be instantly contained before it expands into a major riot. An incipient riot is broadcast throughout the prison by an alarm signal of one long and two short blasts. Alarm signal buttons are placed along all prison walls at 35 foot intervals and are activated by insertion of a special key carried by all Correction Officers.

At the first sign of unrest, all prisoners throughout the prison must immediately be returned to and confined in their cells. Classes, work assignments, and recreation are all canceled. Meals are to be delivered to the cells. Routine sick call is suspended, but inmates who are under treatment or who become visibly ill or injured must receive treatment. Where feasible, prison doctors will attend to prisoners in their cells. Where facilities of the infirmary are imperative for treatment, prisoners may be individually escorted to the infirmary one at a time. Such prisoners must be handcuffed with both hands behind their backs. The only exception to this rule is such instance when the prisoner's injury is such as to make handcuffing behind the back hazardous to the condition being treated. If a prisoner cannot be handcuffed from behind, an attempt should be made to handcuff the hands in front. The escorting officer must be armed, alert, and positioned behind the prisoner for rapid response.

37. The prisoners from cell block 3, Tier 2, north wing of the prison have been shooting baskets in the gym. Suddenly inmate Lyons wheels around and throws a basketball with great force directly at Correction Officer Bryant. Immediately other inmates begin pelting Officer Bryant with basketballs. Officer Glidden, observing this activity, turns his key in the nearest alarm signal device. On hearing the alarm, Officer Ring, overseeing preparation of lunch by prisoners in the south wing kitchen, should

    (A) begin assigning delivery of meals to the cells

    (B) organize the prompt return of all inmate kitchen workers to their cells

(C) handcuff all inmates in the kitchen with their hands behind their backs preparatory to return to their cells

(D) continue to supervise the preparation of lunch

38. In response to an alarm that has sounded signaling a disturbance in a remote section of the penitentiary, all prisoners have been returned to their cells. Officer Umeh, patrolling a walkway in cell block D, comes upon inmates Hughes and Mazza fighting in the cell they share. Hughes is bleeding from a gash in his scalp and his right arm, also bleeding, is awkwardly distorted with the hand in front of Hughes' waist and with bone protruding. Officer Umeh has good reason to suspect that the arm is broken. Officer Umeh should

(A) send for a doctor

(B) cuff Hughes' hands behind his back and march him to the infirmary

(C) cuff Hughes' hands in front of him and march him to the infirmary

(D) cuff his own right hand to Hughes' left hand and march him to the infirmary

Answer questions 39 to 41 on the basis of the following rules:

Except in the instance of prisoners under sentence of death or sentence of life imprisonment with no opportunity for parole, preparation for parole should begin upon admittance to the prison and must be ongoing throughout the duration of incarceration. Preparation for parole should consist of, but not be limited to, literacy education, courses preparatory to the GED, college courses by correspondence or television, industrial training, health and family life education, socialization, and psychological assistance with personal adjustment difficulties. While all of these measures in preparation for parole are mandated to be available to prospective parolees, they may not be denied to any prisoner.

At the intake interview the admitting officer must advise each new inmate of the various services and opportunities available to him or her. During the evaluation period, administer to each new inmate batteries of aptitude, achievement, and interest tests. If appropriate, supplement psychological tests and diagnostic interviews with projective techniques in order to complete a profile of each inmate and to plan a comprehensive program of preparation for release to parole. Refusal of a prospective parolee to accept the program of preparation will weigh negatively among factors being considered by the parole board. Any prisoner who declines parole preparation must be advised that such refusal may lead to delay or denial of parole.

The intake officer should briefly describe work and volunteer activities that are available to prisoners who exhibit good behavior and attitudes after their first six months in the prison.

39. Upon entering the Women's Correctional Facility, new inmate Joan Harrison learns that she may enroll for two academic courses and one industrial course, each meeting five days a week for 45 minutes. In addition, she may take her choice among recreational arts and crafts and sports and fitness offerings and a facilitated group-therapy session that meets twice weekly. Harrison, an educated woman, eagerly signs up for two college courses and joins the softball team. However, she still protests her innocence and bitterly declines any counseling or group therapy of a rehabilitative nature. Officer Gladstone, who is in charge of tailoring a program for Ms. Harrison, should

(A) tell Ms. Harrison that she will never be paroled if she doesn't go for rehabilitation

(B) suggest that Ms. Harrison add a handicraft, such as quilting, to her program

(C) accept Ms. Harrison's choices without comment for the moment, but note the need for follow up on getting Ms. Harrison into some form of therapy later on

(D) urge Ms. Harrison to volunteer to help out in the prison library

40. Logan Chambers, who raped and murdered five women, has been sentenced to death. At his intake interview, Chambers tells admitting Officer Ben Simon that he would like to earn a GED diploma in prison and is eager to learn typesetting and printing. Chambers would also like to be a member of a group that meets twice weekly to learn budgeting and household management. Officer Ben Simon should tell Chambers that

(A) his positive attitude is sure to win him early parole

(B) his requests are ridiculous since he will soon be dead and will have no use for the knowledge and skills he develops

(C) he may learn typesetting and printing because these skills may be useful within the prison community but that he may not take up valuable space in the GED classroom nor in any group developing skills useful only to free individuals

(D) he has made solid choices and will be enrolled as he wishes

41. Bram Byrd dropped out of school at the age of 16 after having completed slightly fewer than eight years of school. He has been in and out of jail and prison over the last six years and is now serving time for drug sales. Testing indicates that Byrd is not very intelligent, but that he certainly can accept and profit from education and training. Byrd is not ambitious, submits lethargically through testing and interviews answering in monosyllables, and makes no inquiries of what training or activities are open to him. At the end of the evaluation period, Officer Selicki should

(A) assign Byrd to a cell block and tell him to stay out of trouble

(B) describe the options open to Byrd and urge him to get education and training so that he does not need to run drugs for a living

(C) send Byrd for drug detox and rehabilitation

(D) tell Byrd that he will not get out of prison until he has a high school education and a skill

Answer questions 42 and 43 on the basis of the following rules:

No matter how carefully the inmates are supervised, contraband still manages to find its way into the hands of prison inmates. Some contraband items, most notably drugs and escape plans, enter on the persons of visitors. Other contraband items, especially ingeniously crafted escape implements, are created or stolen within the prison itself. Frequent, periodic searches of the cells must be carried out according to specified procedures.

Searches should be unannounced and should occur at irregularly spaced intervals and at varying times of day. Officers should take advantage of times that large groups of inmates are out of their cells at meals, recreation, work detail, or classes.

In searching a cell, methodically start with the bed, lifting and turning mattress and pillow, squeezing and shaking all bedding. Lift and turn all books and papers and carefully flip between all pages of all books. Inspect clothing for signs of seams that may have been opened to conceal objects slipped into linings or folds, along with the obvious search of pockets. Inspect all fixtures in the cell by inserting a gloved hand into faucets and drains. Finally, tap gently on all surfaces—walls, floors, and ceilings—to listen for hollowed out areas. Follow any hollow sound at once by cutting out a portion of that surface.

If you discover contraband or any sign of prohibited activity, immediately place the inmate or inmates assigned to that cell into solitary confinement cells with restricted activity. If the hollow sound produces no evidence, assign the inmate or inmates who had been occupying that cell to an empty cell with all surfaces intact pending replastering and total integrity of all surfaces of the disturbed cell.

42. It is 10:00 A.M. on Thursday and the inmates of cell block G are all out of their cells and accounted for at various assigned activities. Officers Zingler and Rhee are on routine cell inspection. They enter cell G-5-e, occupied by inmate Whistler, and lift, squeeze, punch, and shake the mattress and pillow. Officer Zingler lifts and turns papers and books while Officer Rhee turns his attention to Whistler's clothing. Rhee feels an unusual stiffness in the lining behind a pocket of Whistler's jacket and tears open the lining. There he finds an envelope of crack cocaine. The next action Officers Zingler and Rhee should take is to

(A) search the sink and toilet drains

(B) tap the wall, ceiling, and floor surfaces for hollowed out areas that might contain more crack

(C) collect Whistler from his activity and place him in solitary confinement

(D) send for Whistler and ask him where he got the crack

43. In a search of the cell occupied by inmate Flak, Officers Broward and Lee check bedding, books and papers, and clothing and find nothing suspicious. Then Officer Broward pokes her finger into the faucet and down the sink drain. Officer Broward does not feel any foreign object in either faucet or drain, but she sees a discolored spot on the wall just beside the sink and becomes suspicious. Officer Lee taps the area and hears nothing unusual, but agrees that the discolored spot must be investigated. Officer Lee uses a small saw to cut out the discolored area. She discovers that the water pipe behind the cutout area is leaking very slightly. Officer Broward notes on the inspection report that this cell has a leaky pipe and that a plumber should be summoned and returns to the office to file her report. Officer Lee should

(A) immediately have Flak placed into solitary confinement as punishment for damaging her cell

(B) take steps to reassign Flak to another cell with an intact wall

(C) move on to inspect the next cell

(D) find another officer to join her on cell inspection

Answer questions 44 and 45 on the basis of the following rules:

Even the best-run prisons suffer from occasional escapes. Escaped prisoners present a real danger to the public. Generally prisoners who escape are among the most desperate of criminals facing very long or capital sentences and having nothing to lose if they are recaptured. Usually they have managed to arm themselves and will not hesitate to use those arms. Often they are charming as well to get cooperation from unsuspecting members of the public.

At the instant that any prisoner or prisoners cannot be accounted for, prison officials must consider that the prisoner or prisoners have escaped and must act to protect the public. Various measures must be taken simultaneously.

In the prison: Return all prisoners to their cells. Count. Search all possible hiding places within the prison buildings and grounds. Consider all possible points of exit from the prison and inspect carefully. Interview all personnel who might be aware of means of exit.

Outside the prison: Search the periphery of the prison walls. Deploy search teams, each accompanied by a dog, in all directions fanning out from the prison.

In the community: Request that local radio stations broadcast a warning to the public and supply the radio station with full physical descriptions of all escapees. Broadcast warnings should also include useful background information about each escapee along with mention of personal habits and unique identifying characteristics. Submit the same descriptions to television stations and police departments along with faxes of prison photos of the escapees. Request assistance of community and state police.

44. Correction Officers Djilas and Melikian are accompanying ten inmates back to their cells following a data input class in the computer classroom. As they approach a turn in the walkway, inmate Shaw produces a homemade shill and slashes Officer Djilas across the face and neck. As Djilas is momentarily stunned, Shaw grabs his key ring and runs, followed by inmate Pettit. Officer Melikian sounds an alarm and, with the assistance of responding officers, returns the remaining eight inmates to their cells. Correction Officers then make a systematic count of all prisoners throughout the prison. The prison superintendent notifies local media of this event and supplies them with detailed descriptions and photos of the escapees. He requests assistance from community, county, and state police. He orders search teams and dogs to circle the area directly outside the prison walls and then to go into woods, fields, and towns. Then he interviews Officer Djilas to learn how this event was able to occur so as to take steps to avoid future similar incidents. The superintendent has neglected to

(A) give a proper description of the wounded officer to the press

(B) broadcast a warning that the dogs might be dangerous

(C) notify the FBI

(D) search for the missing inmates inside the prison

45. Doing a routine bed-check at 2:00 A.M., Correction Officer Towson senses that the mound in inmate Nilson's bed is not breathing. Officer Towson reaches for the gate to the cell and discovers that it is not locked. Indeed, the mound is a mere jumble of bedding and clothing. Officer Towson sounds an alarm. The superintendent alerts the press and surrounding police forces of the circumstances of the escape and supplies a description of inmate Nilson. Search teams get to work looking for Nilson inside and outside the prison. What other step should be taken?

(A) Rouse all the inmates and count them while they are awake

(B) Cancel classes and recreation

(C) Interview other prisoners to learn if they knew of Nilson's plans

(D) No additional steps are needed at this time

Questions 46 to 60 are worth two points each. Follow the directions before each group of questions.

Directions: Questions 46 to 55 consist of short statements giving information about events. Choose the paragraph that conveys the information most clearly and accurately.

46. Details of an incident in the prison kitchen:

Date: Monday, June 16

Time: 11:10 A.M.

Location: Kitchen, A building, west wing

Event: Inmate Cotton, #458390, spit into soup kettle

Reporter: Inmate Woolsey, #856411

Witness: Inmate Heath, #768503

Action taken: Inmate Cotton put in punishment cell, no privileges, short rations

(A) On Monday, June 16, at 11:10 A.M., inmate Woolsey, #856411, said that inmate Cotton, #458390, spit into his soup. Inmate Heath, #768503, saw him do it. He is in a punishment cell.

(B) In the kitchen of A building, west wing, on Monday, June 16, inmate Woolsey, #856411, reported that he saw inmate Cotton, #458390, spit into the soup kettle. Inmate Heath, #768503, corroborated this report. Cotton has been placed in a punishment cell.

(C) Inmate Cotton, #438390, spit into the soup on Monday, June 16, at 11:10 A.M. according to inmate Woolsey, #856411, and inmate Heath, #768503. He is being punished in kitchen A with no privileges.

(D) It happened at 11:10 A.M. in the kitchen of west wing A building that inmate Cotton, #458390, spit into the soup on Monday, June 16, said inmate Heath, #768503. Inmate Woolsey, #856411, put him in a punishment cell.

47. Description of a rash of burglaries and their outcome:

> Time span: August 1 through August 17
>
> Activity: six burglaries reported
>
> Method: daytime burglar cut telephone wires, entered, stole only money
>
> Location: town of Mason, area bounded by First Street, Lee Road, Wesson Way, and Highland Boulevard
>
> Special feature: none of the affected homes had dogs
>
> Suspect: Tom Smith, 47, of 630 Main Street, former telephone lineman and current garbage collector in the affected area

(A) 47-year-old Tom Smith of 630 Main Street who used to be a telephone man so he knows where the wires come in, and is now a garbage man so he knows who doesn't have a dog, has been cutting telephone wires and stealing money from six people in Mason on August 1 and August 17.

(B) Sometime in the daytime on August 1 and August 17, Tom Smith who is 47 years old and lives at 630 Main Street cut the telephone wires and stole money from six people who don't have dogs on Highland Boulevard and First Street and Lee Road and Wesson Way.

(C) Tom Smith, 47, of 630 Main Street, a garbage collector with experience as a telephone lineman, is suspected of cutting telephone wires and taking money from six homes, none with dogs, in the area bounded by First Street, Lee Road, Wesson Way and Highland Boulevard between August 1 and August 17.

(D) The suspect in the Mason burglaries of August 1 to August 17 is Tom Smith of 630 Main Street. He is a garbage man who cut the wires where there were no dogs in six houses and took the money.

48. A complaint of prison brutality:

> Complainant: Pedro Perez, #754098
>
> Accused: Correction Officer Brophy
>
> Date of Complaint: January 4
>
> Date of alleged brutality: December 25
>
> Location: County Correctional Institute
>
> Alleged action: rough handling, ethnic slurs and obscene language, pistol whipping, and denial of access to Christmas services and festivities
>
> Complainant's representative: John VanDam, Attorney-at-Law

(A) In a complaint filed January 4 by Attorney John VanDam, Pedro Perez, #754098, alleges that Correction Officer Brophy beat him up and called him names and refused to let him celebrate Christmas.

(B) Pedro Perez complains that Correction Officer Brophy is a racist because he beat him up and called him names and wouldn't let him have Christmas at the County Correctional Institution says John VanDam.

(C) John VanDam, a lawyer, says that on January 4 Pedro Perez says that Officer Brophy hit him and cursed at him on Christmas. His number is #754098.

(D) Attorney VanDam has filed a complaint for Pedro Perez, #745098, in which Perez says he had a fight with Officer Brophy on Christmas in the County Correctional Institution. He didn't let him go to church.

49. An urban tragedy:

> Date: Sunday, April 10
>
> Time: 11:20 P.M.
>
> Location: automobile in front of 87 Clark Street
>
> Event: child killed in crossfire
>
> Victim: Katie Josephs, age 3
>
> Suspects: Yolanda Ghari and Rodolfo Marques, known drug dealers, and Gennaro Tocci, #423113, recently paroled from Lakeside Penitentiary

(A) Katie Josephs, a three-year-old, was killed by Yolanda Ghari, Rodolfo Marques, and Gennaro Tocci in the car when they shot her in front of 87 Clark Street at 11:20 P.M. on Sunday, April 10.

(B) Yolanda Ghari, Rodolfo Marques, and Gennaro Tocci, #432113, from Lakeside Penitentiary had a drug dispute and shot Katie Josephs in the car at 87 Clark Street on Sunday, April 10, at 11:20 P.M.

(C) In a shooting about drugs, Katie Josephs was three years old in the car at 87 Clark Street on Sunday, April 10, at 11:20 P.M. The suspects are Gennaro Tocci, #432113, of Lakeside Penitentiary, Yolanda Ghari, and Rodolfo Marques. They deal drugs.

(D) Three-year-old Katie Josephs was caught in crossfire and fatally shot while in a car at 87 Clark Street at 11:20 P.M. on Sunday April 10. Suspects are known drug dealers Yolanda Ghari and Rodolfo Marques and recent parolee Gennaro Tocci, #432113.

50. Raid on a pawn shop suspected of fencing stolen goods:

> Date of complaint: May 9
>
> Premises: Ready Cash Pawn Shop, 526 West 16th Street
>
> Owner: Randy vonGraf of 726 West 19th Street
>
> Complainant: Marina Bodganian of 145 Avenue C, Apt. 1-W
>
> Item of contention: diamond ring
>
> Corroboration: other items in pawn shop with etched social security numbers of items reported stolen

(A) Marina Bodganian of 145 Avenue C, Apt. 1-W, complained that her diamond ring was stolen on May 9 by Randy vonGraf in the Ready Cash Pawn Shop on West 16th Street at #526. There were other serial numbers there.

(B) On May 9 Marina Bodganian of 145 Avenue C, Apt. 1-W, saw her stolen diamond ring in Randy vonGraf's 726 West 19th Street Ready Cash Pawn Shop with other items and stolen serial numbers.

(C) On May 9 Marina Bodganian of 145 Avenue C, Apt. 1-W, reported seeing her stolen diamond ring in Ready Cash Pawn Shop at 526 West 16th Street. A number of items in the shop were identified as stolen items by the social security numbers etched on them. The owner of the pawn shop is Randy vonGraf of 726 West 19th Street.

(D) Marina Bodganian of 145 Avenue C charged that Randy vonGraf of 726 West 19th Street stole her diamond ring and social security number on May 9 at Ready Cash Pawn Shop at 526 West 16th Street.

51. A jailhouse suicide:

> Institution: Women's House of Detention
>
> Location: cell block A, tier 1, cell #45
>
> Date: July 23
>
> Time of discovery: 4:42 A.M.
>
> Inmate: Jennifer Mohan, #8603
>
> Reporter: Correction Officer Francois

(A) Correction Officer Francois found Jennifer Mohan, #8603, hanging in her cell on July 23 at the Women's House of Detention at 4:42 A.M.

(B) Jennifer Mohan, #8603, killed herself by hanging at 4:42 A.M. in cell block A, tier 1, cell #45 in the Women's House of Detention by Correction Officer Francois.

(C) On July 23 at 4:42 A.M. Correction Officer Francois discovered Jennifer Mohan, #8603, hanging in cell #45, cell block A, tier 1 of the Women's House of Detention.

(D) Correction Officer Francois reported at 4:42 A.M. in the Women's House of Detention that Jennifer Mohan was dead in cell #45, cell block A, tier 1. She was hanging.

52. Report of a routine event:

> Date: Sunday, September 3
>
> Time: 11:00 A.M. to 4:00 P.M.
>
> Organization: neighborhood association
>
> Place: 800 block of River Road
>
> Event: legal closing of street for block party

(A) On Sunday, September 3, there was a block party from 11:00 A.M. to 4:00 P.M. on River Road. They closed the street and they had permission.

(B) The neighborhood association received permission to close the street at the 800 block of River Road from 11:00 A.M. to 4:00 P.M. on Sunday, September 3, for a block party.

(C) There was a block party at the neighborhood association of 800 River Road at 11:00 A.M. and 4:00 P.M. on Sunday, September 3. It was legal to close the street.

(D) The block party of the 800 block of River Road got permission and the neighborhood association closed the street from 11:00 A.M. to 4:00 P.M.

53. A highway accident:

> Location: Intersection of Route 9W and Route 303 northbound
>
> Date: Saturday, February 13
>
> Time: 1:15 P.M.
>
> Weather conditions: icy roadway, heavy snow, poor visibility
>
> Vehicles: 1993 Honda Civic, NY 846 YTR, driven by owner Indira Gupti of Milltown, NY, and 1994 Toyota Camry, NJ PTS 533, driven by Chuck Bocock son of owner, Carla Lytle of Westview, NJ
>
> Event: traveling at low speed, front end of Honda Civic skidded into left front door of Toyota Camry
>
> Damage 1: front end of Honda telescoped; air bag deployed; heavily clothed driver sustained no discernible injury
>
> Damage 2: left side of Toyota badly damaged; driver sustained broken ribs and broken left arm with multiple contusions of left leg; driver transported by police ambulance #4 to Good Samaritan Hospital

(A) On Saturday, February 13, at 1:15 P.M. under heavy winter conditions, 1993 Honda Civic, license NY 846 YTR and driven by its owner Indira Gupti of Milltown, NY, skidded into the 1994 Toyota Camry, license NJ PTS 533 registered to Carla Lytle of Westview, NJ, being driven by her son Chuck Bocock. The accident occurred at the intersection of Routes 9W and 303 northbound. The Honda suffered front end damage; its driver was not seriously injured. The Toyota suffered severe damage to its left side, and the driver was removed by police ambulance #4 to Good Samaritan Hospital with fractures of left arm and ribs and injury to left leg.

(B) Chuck Bocock of Milltown, NY, driving his mother's 1993 Honda Civic, skidded into Indira Gupti who was driving a 1994 Toyota Camry in an icy snowstorm on Route 9W and Route 303 northbound at 1:15 P.M. on Saturday, February 13. Both cars were damaged, but only Bocock was badly injured and went by ambulance to the hospital. Indira Gupti used her airbag.

(C) It was snowing on Saturday, February 13, at 1:15 P.M. when, at the intersection of 9W and 303 northbound, Indira Gupti of Milltown, NY, driving a 1993 Honda Civic, New York plate PTS 533, skidded into the driver's side of Carla Lytle's 1994 Toyota Camry, New Jersey plate 846 YTR, being driven by her son, Chuck Bocock. Bocock was injured on his left side and went to Good Samaritan Hospital in police ambulance #4.

(D) The drivers were careful and not drunk, but it was snowing and icy and they couldn't see when they skidded on Route 9W and Route 303 northbound on Saturday, February 13 at 1:15 P.M. Chuck Bocock, the driver of a 1994 Toyota Camry from New Jersey, was damaged and was taken by police ambulance #4 to Good Samaritan Hospital. The other driver, a Honda Civic, was injured in the front end by an air bag.

54. Off-duty Correction Officer McKenzie notices an apparently unsupervised small boy wandering aimlessly on White Road between Locust Lane and Sprague Avenue. He asks the child his name and is told "Bobby." The child, who appears to be no more than three years old, has curly blond hair and is wearing striped pants and a white T-shirt with Mickey Mouse on the front. The youngster cannot tell his last name or where he lives. Officer McKenzie calls the police dispatcher from the nearest call box and asks the dispatcher to check with the local precinct, and possibly other precincts as well, to see if a child matching this description has been reported missing. Which of the following statements empresses this information most clearly and accurately?

(A) Bobby is all alone on White Road between Locust Lane and Sprague Avenue. Has anyone missed him?

(B) A small blond boy wearing striped pants and a Mickey Mouse T-shirt and identifying himself as "Bobby" is wandering on White Road between Locust Lane and Sprague Avenue. Has he been reported missing?

(C) Correction Officer McKenzie who is not on duty has little Bobby on White Road between Locust Lane and Sprague Avenue in striped pants. He is blond and missing.

(D) An off-duty little boy named Bobby is with Correction Officer McKenzie at a call box on White Road between Locust Lane and Sprague Avenue. He likes Mickey Mouse and wears striped pants.

55. Dorothy Hultz of 17-12 Highland Way stops in at the precinct house and complains to the desk officer, Sergeant Tortino, that she has been receiving obscene telephone calls. She tells the officer that the calls come in to her telephone—824-6686—between 7 and 9 P.M., and that the caller, an unknown male with a husky voice and no particular accent, breathes heavily, asks obscene questions, and makes obscene suggestions to any female answering the phone. Sergeant Tortino instructs Ms. Hultz that all household members should hang up promptly when receiving such calls. By which of the following reports will Sergeant Tortino convey the information to the telephone company most clearly and accurately?

(A) An unidentified male with a husky voice has been making obscene phone calls to 824-6686, the home of Dorothy Hultz at 17-12 Highland Way between 7 and 9 P.M.

(B) Dorothy Hultz gets obscene calls from a husky man at 824-6686 at 17-12 Highland Way between 7 and 9 P.M.

(C) A husky voice breathes hard and is obscene between 7 and 9 P.M., says Dorothy Hultz over the telephone of 824-6686 at 17-12 Highland Way.

(D) Between 7 and 9 P.M., any female receives a husky obscene voice at 824-6686 from 17-12 Highland Way by Dorothy Hultz.

Directions: Questions 56 to 60 consist of five sentences, numbered 1 to 5, which may be out of order. Select the most reasonable order of the sentences so as to form a logical, cohesive story.

56. 1. Cartons of cigarettes, some burst open, were scattered all over the highway.

2. One of the trucks overturned.

3. One police officer called for an ambulance for the driver of the overturned truck, who appeared to be seriously injured.

4. Another police officer noticed that the federal tax stamps on the cigarettes were counterfeit.

5. There was a turnpike crash between two trucks.

(A) 5 - 2 - 3 - 4 - 1

(B) 5 - 1 - 2 - 3 - 4

(C) 5 - 2 - 1 - 3 - 4

(D) 1 - 5 - 2 - 3 - 4

57. 1. Everyone entering the elevators for the upper floors of the municipal building must pass through a metal detector.

2. A sign in the lobby read, "All applicants for the Correction Officer exam must check their weapons."

3. As the man approached the elevator, the alarm began to sound.

4. The Correction Officer exam was being given on the seventh floor.

5. The man was not permitted to take the exam.

(A) 4 - 2 - 3 - 1 - 5

(B) 2 - 4 - 1 - 3 - 5

(C) 1 - 2 - 3 - 4 - 5

(D) 2 - 1 - 4 - 5 - 3

58. 1. An off-duty Correction Officer was seated in a restaurant.

    2. Two men entered, drew guns, and robbed the cashier.

    3. The officer made no attempt to stop the robbery.

    4. He justified his conduct by claiming that an officer, when off duty, is a private citizen.

    5. He finished his meal and walked out of the restaurant.

    (A) 1 - 2 - 5 - 3 - 4

    (B) 2 - 1 - 5 - 4 - 3

    (C) 1 - 2 - 3 - 4 - 5

    (D) 1 - 2 - 3 - 5 - 4

59. 1. Upon their arrival at the scene, the officers could not find evidence of a break-in.

    2. The officers climbed over the fence and observed two people running into an alleyway.

    3. Two people disappeared into the darkness.

    4. However, as the officers continued their investigation, they heard noises coming from the rear of the building.

    5. As the officers raced to the rear of the building, they saw four people alighting from the roof by way of a ladder.

    (A) 1 - 4 - 5 - 2 - 3

    (B) 5 1 4 2 3

    (C) 1 - 2 - 3 - 4 - 5

    (D) 5 - 1 - 2 - 3 - 4

60. 1. The Correction Officer noticed a ticking suitcase under a workbench in the boiler room.

    2. The suitcase was clean of any dust.

    3. The boiler room was hot and dusty.

    4. The Correction Officer opened the suitcase and found pajamas and an alarm clock inside.

    5. The Correction Officer was searching the prison in response to a bomb threat.

    (A) 1 - 2 - 3 - 4 - 5

    (B) 5 - 4 - 3 - 2 - 1

    (C) 5 - 1 - 3 - 2 - 4

    (D) 1 - 5 - 3 - 2 - 4

Directions: Questions 61 to 75 are based on reading passages. Read each paragraph and answer the question that follows it according to what was stated or implied in the paragraph. Each of these questions is worth one point.

61. Unfortunately, specialization in industry creates workers who lack versatility. When a laborer is trained to perform only one task, she is almost entirely dependent for employment on the demand for that particular skill. If anything happens to interrupt that demand, she is unemployed.

    The paragraph best supports the statement that
    (A) the demand for labor of a particular type is constantly changing
    (B) the average laborer is not capable of learning more than one task at a time
    (C) some cases of unemployment are due to laborers' lack of versatility
    (D) too much specialization is as dangerous as too little

62. The indiscriminate or continual use of any drug without medical supervision is dangerous. Even drugs considered harmless may result in chronic poisoning if used for a period of years. Pharmacists should not renew prescriptions without consulting the doctor. The doctor prescribed a given amount because he or she wished to limit use of the drug to a certain time. Never use a drug prescribed for someone else just because your symptoms appear similar. There may be differences, apparent to an expert but hidden from you, that indicate an entirely different ailment requiring different medication.

    The paragraph best supports the statement that
    (A) the use of drugs is very dangerous
    (B) once a physician has prescribed a drug, it is safe to renew the prescription
    (C) people with similar symptoms are usually suffering from the ailment
    (D) a drug considered harmless may be dangerous if taken over a long period of time without supervision

63. The storage battery is a lead-acid, electrochemical device used for storing energy in its chemical form. The battery does not actually store electricity, but converts an electrical charge into chemical energy that is stored until the battery terminals are connected to a closed external circuit. When the circuit is closed, the chemical energy inside the battery is transformed back into electrical energy through a chemical action, and, as a result, current flows through the circuit.

    The paragraph best supports the statement that a lead-acid battery stores
    (A) current
    (B) electricity
    (C) atomic energy
    (D) chemical energy

64. The term "custody," as used in the criminal-treatment system, means control, under law, over an individual who has committed a criminal act. Probation, imprisonment, and parole are types of custody. Historically, imprisonment was viewed as punishment, and parole developed as a means of relieving the punishment of prison.

The paragraph best supports the statement that

(A) parole is generally unrelated to the punishment process

(B) probation and parole do not involve custody of the individual

(C) violent inmates are rarely under control

(D) probation developed as an alternative to punishment

65. I consider that man's brain originally is like a little empty attic, and you have to stock it with such furniture as you choose. A fool takes in all the lumber of every sort that he comes across. The knowledge that might be useful to him gets crowded out or is jumbled up with a lot of other things so that he has difficulty laying his hands on it. It is a mistake to think that the little room has elastic walls and can distend to any size. Depend upon it, there comes a time when for every addition of knowledge you forget something that you knew before.

The best supports the statement that knowledge

(A) should be sought for its own sake

(B) should be avoided

(C) should be acquired only if it is necessary

(D) may be acquired without limitation

66. It's dangerous to change the weather and the climate. We do not know enough about how such changes will affect the earth. What may seem good for one area may be bad for another. If you change a grassland into a vegetable farm, where will the cattle in the area graze? Before we tinker with our natural environment, we should be very sure of what we are doing.

The paragraph best supports the statement that the writer believes that

(A) changes in climate and weather may be harmful

(B) changing climate and weather will improve the earth's surface

(C) man should never meddle with the natural environment

(D) it's easy to figure out what will happen when you change the weather

67. In many states, criminal responsibility extends to persons sixteen years of age or more who are not, by reason of mental disease or defect, deprived of substantial capacity to know or appreciate either the nature and consequences of their conduct or that such conduct is wrong.

The most reasonable implication of this statement is that

(A) a person fifteen years and eleven months old who stabs a seventeen-year-old is not criminally responsible

(B) when a person who is sixteen years of age commits a robbery, he is rarely considered criminally responsible

(C) a fifteen-year-old who is considered a danger to society may not be placed in official custody

(D) a fifteen-year-old cannot be placed under parole supervision

68. During the last century and a half the economic life of the western world has been transformed by a series of remarkable inventions and the general application of science to the productive process. A revolution more profound in its effects than any armed revolt that ever shook the foundations of a political state has been achieved in the three realms of manufacturing, agriculture, and communication.

The paragraph best supports the statement that science

(A) has shaken the foundations of manufacturing, agriculture, and communication

(B) has revolutionized the productive process

(C) is the tool of the inventor

(D) has been an important factor in the founding of the agricultural process

69. Since duplicating machines are being changed constantly, the person who is in the market for such a machine should not purchase offhand the kind with which he or she is most familiar or the one recommended by the first salesperson who calls. Instead, the purchaser should analyze the particular equipment situation and then investigate all the possibilities.

The paragraph best supports the statement that when duplicating equipment is being purchased

(A) the purchaser should choose equipment that can be used with the least extra training

(B) the needs of the purchaser's office should determine the selection

(C) the buyer should have his or her needs analyzed by an office equipment salesperson

(D) the recommendations of salespeople should usually be ignored

70. Those correction theorists who are in agreement with severe and rigid controls as a normal part of the correctional process are confronted with a contradiction: this is so because a responsibility which is consistent with freedom cannot be developed in a repressive atmosphere. They do not recognize this contradiction when they carry out their programs with dictatorial force and expect convicted criminals exposed to such programs to be reformed into free and responsible citizens.

The paragraph best supports the statement that a repressive atmosphere in a prison

(A) does not conform to present day ideas of freedom of the individual

(B) is admitted by correction theorists to be in conflict with the basic principles of the normal correctional process

(C) is advocated as the best method of maintaining discipline when rehabilitation is of secondary importance

(D) is not suitable for the development of a sense of responsibility consistent with freedom

71. For the United States, Canada has become the most important country in the world, yet there are few countries about which Americans know less. Canada is the third largest country in the world; only Russia and China are larger. The area of Canada is more than a quarter of the whole British Empire.

    The paragraph best supports the statement that

    (A) the British Empire is smaller than Russia or China

    (B) the territory of China is greater than that of Canada

    (C) Americans know more about Canada than about China or Russia

    (D) the United States is the most important nation in the world as far as Canada is concerned

72. There has been a slump in first-aid training in the industries, and yet one should not fall into the error of thinking there is less interest in first aid in industry. The falling off has been in the number of new employees needing such training. It appears that in industries interested in first-aid training, there is now actually a higher percentage of people so trained than there ever were before.

    The paragraph best supports the statement that first-aid training is

    (A) a means of avoiding the most serious effects of accidents

    (B) being abandoned because of expense

    (C) sometimes given to new workers in industry

    (D) of great importance to employees

73. A recently published article states: "Weight for height and age is, as many have previously held, an inadequate index of the 'nutritional status' of a child. It is unscientific and unfair to set average weight as a goal for all children or for an individual child. Weighing and measuring, however, should be continued as a record of the trend of individual growth that is of value to the physician in relation to other findings and as valuable devices to interest the child in his or her growth."

    The paragraph implies that weighing and measuring the height of children

    (A) are useful to the physician

    (B) are of no value and should be stopped

    (C) are of no value but give interesting information

    (D) indicate the nutritional status of the child

74. Neither immediate protection for the community nor long-range reformation of the prisoner can be achieved by prison personnel who express toward the offender whatever feelings of frustration, fear, jealousy, or hunger for power they may have.

    The significance of this statement for Correction Officers is that they should

    (A) be on the constant lookout for opportunities to prove their courage to inmates

    (B) not allow deeply personal problems to affect their relations with the inmates

    (C) not try to advance themselves on the job because of personal motives

    (D) spend a good part of their time examining their own feelings in order to understand better those of the inmates.

75. Since ninety-five percent of prison inmates are released, and a great majority of these within two to three years, a prison that does nothing more than separate the criminal from society offer little promise of real protection to society.

The paragraph best supports the inference that

(A) once it has been definitely established that a person has criminal tendencies, that person should be separated for the rest of his life from ordinary society

(B) prison sentences in general are much too short and should be lengthened to afford greater protection to society

(C) punishment, rather than separation of the criminal from society, should be the major objective of a correctional system

(D) when a prison system produces no change in prisoners and the period of imprisonment is short, the period during which society is protected is also short

END OF EXAM

ANSWER KEY FOR MODEL EXAMINATION 2

1. C	16. A	31. C	46. B	61. C
2. C	17. A	32. D	47. C	62. D
3. A	18. B	33. A	48. A	63. D
4. B	19. D	34. D	49. D	64. D
5. A	20. A	35. C	50. C	65. C
6. B	21. B	36. B	51. C	66. A
7. D	22. B	37. B	52. B	67. A
8. B	23. A	38. C	53. A	68. B
9. A	24. B	39. C	54. B	69. B
10. B	25. C	40. D	55. A	70. D
11. B	26. D	41. B	56. C	71. B
12. A	27. B	42. C	57. B	72. C
13. D	28. A	43. B	58. D	73. A
14. C	29. A	44. D	59. A	74. B
15. A	30. B	45. A	60. C	75. D

Explanatory Answers for Model Examination 2

1. **(C)** The judge is studying some papers before him.

2. **(C)** The person standing, presumably an attorney, is wearing a dark suit. He has straight hair and seems to be waiting to proceed.

3. **(A)** The stenographer, who is wearing a light suit, is wearing dark socks.

4. **(B)** Only one person, a woman, can be seen in a corner of the jury box (to the left of the attorney's head).

5. **(A)** The stenographer is not wearing glasses. The judge is wearing glasses, and the witness is wearing dark glasses.

6. **(B)** Whatever flag there is in the courtroom is to the right of the judge.

7. **(D)** Incandescent ceiling fixtures can be seen above the walkways.

8. **(B)** A careful look into the cells indicates that they contain bunk beds. There is no way to tell if there is more than one bunk bed per cell.

9. **(A)** Clothes are hanging along the walkway of the lowest tier.

10. **(B)** There is only one person seated at a table on the floor level.

11. **(B)** The doors to a few cells in the lowest tier appear to be open but most are closed.

12. **(A)** Some message is hanging on the outside of a third-tier cell.

13. **(D)** The car is a full-size two-door hardtop.

14. **(C)** The car is parked beside a fire hydrant.

15. **(A)** The left rear tire has a narrow whitewall strip.

16. **(A)** The ticketing officer is wearing a tie.

17. **(A)** Bright sunshine is reflecting from the car's rear window, and objects are casting heavy shadows.

18. **(B)** There is no traffic at all.

19. **(D)** The man at the right is wearing glasses and is studying a graph.

20. **(A)** There is a row of loose-leaf notebooks on the shelf behind the man and woman seated at the same desk. The open box is behind the other man.

21. **(B)** The man in the suit and tie is not wearing glasses.

22. **(B)** There are no empty chairs in the room.

23. **(A)** The Styrofoam cup is next to the pen in a pen-stand in front of the man in the suit.

24. **(B)** The woman is wearing white low-heeled shoes.

25. **(C)** The woman in the white jacket, with pen in hand, is looking at someone across the table. She is seated in an upholstered chair and is not wearing glasses.

26. **(D)** The man with the mustache is taking notes with his right hand. He is wearing a shirt and tie and is not African-American.

27. **(B)** The instructor has her back to the writing on the chart or board.

28. **(A)** The instructor is intently waiting to hear what he has to say.

29. **(A)** Each of the women seated at the table has a large book open before her.

30. **(B)** If the woman in the plaid suit is wearing earrings, we cannot see them because her hair covers her ears. The other women are wearing earrings.

31. **(C)** Cooper's right hand is cuffed, so he must be shackled by the left leg.

32 **(D)** Officer Cronin must stay on the bus because nine prisoners require three guards not counting the driver. Cronin must position himself where he can observe all prisoners, with his back to none, and ready to move quickly if needed.

33. **(A)** The prisoners should have been strip searched before cuffing. The pat down at boarding is not specified in the boarding procedure.

34. **(D)** The rules are clear. Officer Trotsky must not question or ridicule the request and must take steps to accommodate ibnIman.

35. **(C)** The request is reasonable, but prison safety must remain paramount. The creative solution offered by choice (C) allows the prisoner maximum participation in this observance while maintaining strict adherence to the prison fire regulations.

36. **(B)** The rules are clear. Zakris has violated the conditions of her pass and must be returned at once to the prison.

37. **(B)** Safety and discipline are the first concern. The inmates will not starve if lunch is served late. According to the rules, Officer Ring must get the inmates back to their cells.

38. **(C)** The nature of the injury suggests that the doctor will need X-ray and other infirmary-based equipment. Since the injured hand is in front of the prisoner's waist, cuffing the hands at the front is feasible.

39. **(C)** Harrison has just entered the facility. Counseling and therapy can be added when she has become more reconciled. Choice (A) is incorrect because the word *never* is much too strong; (D) is incorrect because volunteer activities are open only to inmates who have exhibited good behavior and attitudes in their first six months.

40. **(D)** The rule is clear: " . . . these measures in preparation for parole . . . may not be denied to any prisoner."

41. **(B)** The rules require that the new prisoner must be advised of the options open to him whether or not he requests this information. Choice (D) is an overstatement. Lack of cooperation may negatively affect parole, but the prisoner will surely be released when he has completed his full sentence. Further, the prisoner should accept training, but there is no requirement that he profit from it.

42. **(C)** Further search and questioning can be done later. The rules require that the inmate be immediately placed into solitary confinement.

43. **(B)** Flak has done nothing wrong and should not be punished. However she is entitled to undamaged quarters. She should be assigned to another cell.

44. **(D)** There is no certainty that the escapees have made their way outside the prison. The prison compound itself must undergo a thorough search.

45. **(A)** The count is very important and must be done swiftly and accurately. This is the best way to avoid being duped by dummies in the beds.

46. **(B)** Choice (A) raises the question, "Who is in a punishment cell?" (C) and (D) are both garbled.

47. **(C)** Aside from being incomplete and somewhat inaccurate in detailing dates and location, both (A) and (B) make positive statements accusing the suspect. He is only a suspect. (D) neglects to define the area in which burglaries occurred.

48. **(A)** (B) is a childish statement omitting all details. Both (C) and (D) lead to confusions: Whose number is 754098? Who didn't let whom go to church?

49. **(D)** (A) is inadequate; (B) has Tocci's number wrong; (C) is a garbled statement.

50. **(C)** Both (A) and (D) accuse the pawn shop owner of the theft and make other garbled statements. (B) confuses the address of the pawn shop with its owner's residence.

51. **(C)** (A) and (D) leave out important identifying details. (B) is not incorrect but is poorly stated.

52. **(B)** All other choices make unclear statements.

53. **(A)** Choice (B) attributes the skid to the wrong driver; (C) switches the license plates; (D) is too chatty for a report and is garbled as well.

54. **(B)** (A) is an inadequate description of the child; (C) and (D) are garbled.

55. **(A)** In (B) the man is husky rather than his voice; (C) and (D) are garbled.

56. **(C)** 5 - 2 - 1 - 3 - 4

57. **(B)** 2 - 4 - 1 - 3 - 5

58. **(D)** 1 - 2 - 3 - 5 - 4

59. **(A)** 1 - 4 - 5 - 2 - 3

60. **(C)** 5 - 1 - 3 - 2 - 4

61. **(C)** Worker's with limited, specialized skills are limited to employment where the specific skills are needed. The paragraph does not address the problems of workers whose skills are not sufficiently specialized.

62. **(D)** This is stated in the first two sentences. The paragraph states that persons with similar symptoms *may* have different ailments, not that they necessarily *do*.

63. **(D)** So stated in the second sentence.

64. **(D)** This is the meaning of the last sentence.

65. **(C)** The paragraph advocates selective learning. The author suggests that unnecessary learning leads to forgetting of more important information.

66. **(A)** See the first sentence. On the other hand, choice (C) is too emphatic. The paragraph does not say *never;* it just says to be careful.

67. **(A)** A person fifteen years and eleven months old is under the age of sixteen and thus is not criminally responsible even though he or she commits a criminal act.

68. **(B)** Read carefully. The answer is stated in the first sentence. The second sentence is commentary.

69. **(B)** The last sentence gives this answer. The paragraph specifically cautions against choosing equipment on the sole basis of familiarity with its operation.

70. **(D)** This is a restatement of the theme of the paragraph.

71. **(B)** The paragraph is very short, but it requires careful reading. The only statement supported by the paragraph is that China is larger than Canada.

72. **(C)** If fewer new employees need such training now, clearly the training is being given to some new workers.

73. **(A)** The last sentence says that weighing and measuring are of value to the physician.

74. **(B)** Frustrations, fears, jealousies, and hunger for power fall into the category of deeply personal problems. Correction Officers must not allow such problems to affect their relations with prison inmates nor to distract them from their responsibilities.

75. **(D)** A short period of incarceration protects society for only a short time. If rehabilitation occurs during the imprisonment, the protection of society is extended into the time that the rehabilitated prisoner is released.

Answer Sheet for Model Examination 3

1. Ⓐ Ⓑ Ⓒ Ⓓ   2. Ⓐ Ⓑ Ⓒ Ⓓ   3. Ⓐ Ⓑ Ⓒ Ⓓ   4. Ⓐ Ⓑ Ⓒ Ⓓ   5. Ⓐ Ⓑ Ⓒ Ⓓ

6. Ⓐ Ⓑ Ⓒ Ⓓ   7. Ⓐ Ⓑ Ⓒ Ⓓ   8. Ⓐ Ⓑ Ⓒ Ⓓ   9. Ⓐ Ⓑ Ⓒ Ⓓ   10. Ⓐ Ⓑ Ⓒ Ⓓ

11. Ⓐ Ⓑ Ⓒ Ⓓ   12. Ⓐ Ⓑ Ⓒ Ⓓ   13. Ⓐ Ⓑ Ⓒ Ⓓ   14. Ⓐ Ⓑ Ⓒ Ⓓ   15. Ⓐ Ⓑ Ⓒ Ⓓ

16. Ⓐ Ⓑ Ⓒ Ⓓ   17. Ⓐ Ⓑ Ⓒ Ⓓ   18. Ⓐ Ⓑ Ⓒ Ⓓ   19. Ⓐ Ⓑ Ⓒ Ⓓ   20. Ⓐ Ⓑ Ⓒ Ⓓ

21. Ⓐ Ⓑ Ⓒ Ⓓ   22. Ⓐ Ⓑ Ⓒ Ⓓ   23. Ⓐ Ⓑ Ⓒ Ⓓ   24. Ⓐ Ⓑ Ⓒ Ⓓ   25. Ⓐ Ⓑ Ⓒ Ⓓ

26. Ⓐ Ⓑ Ⓒ Ⓓ   27. Ⓐ Ⓑ Ⓒ Ⓓ   28. Ⓐ Ⓑ Ⓒ Ⓓ   29. Ⓐ Ⓑ Ⓒ Ⓓ   30. Ⓐ Ⓑ Ⓒ Ⓓ

31. Ⓐ Ⓑ Ⓒ Ⓓ   32. Ⓐ Ⓑ Ⓒ Ⓓ   33. Ⓐ Ⓑ Ⓒ Ⓓ   34. Ⓐ Ⓑ Ⓒ Ⓓ   35. Ⓐ Ⓑ Ⓒ Ⓓ

36. Ⓐ Ⓑ Ⓒ Ⓓ   37. Ⓐ Ⓑ Ⓒ Ⓓ   38. Ⓐ Ⓑ Ⓒ Ⓓ   39. Ⓐ Ⓑ Ⓒ Ⓓ   40. Ⓐ Ⓑ Ⓒ Ⓓ

41. Ⓐ Ⓑ Ⓒ Ⓓ   42. Ⓐ Ⓑ Ⓒ Ⓓ   43. Ⓐ Ⓑ Ⓒ Ⓓ   44. Ⓐ Ⓑ Ⓒ Ⓓ   45. Ⓐ Ⓑ Ⓒ Ⓓ

46. Ⓐ Ⓑ Ⓒ Ⓓ   47. Ⓐ Ⓑ Ⓒ Ⓓ   48. Ⓐ Ⓑ Ⓒ Ⓓ   49. Ⓐ Ⓑ Ⓒ Ⓓ   50. Ⓐ Ⓑ Ⓒ Ⓓ

51. Ⓐ Ⓑ Ⓒ Ⓓ   52. Ⓐ Ⓑ Ⓒ Ⓓ   53. Ⓐ Ⓑ Ⓒ Ⓓ   54. Ⓐ Ⓑ Ⓒ Ⓓ   55. Ⓐ Ⓑ Ⓒ Ⓓ

56. Ⓐ Ⓑ Ⓒ Ⓓ   57. Ⓐ Ⓑ Ⓒ Ⓓ   58. Ⓐ Ⓑ Ⓒ Ⓓ   59. Ⓐ Ⓑ Ⓒ Ⓓ   60. Ⓐ Ⓑ Ⓒ Ⓓ

TEAR HERE

Model Examination 3

Trainees Going to Class
(Photograph courtesy of the Federal Law Enforcement Training Center Annual Report)

Security Control Post

Hospital Ward
(Photograph courtesy of Naval Photographic Center)

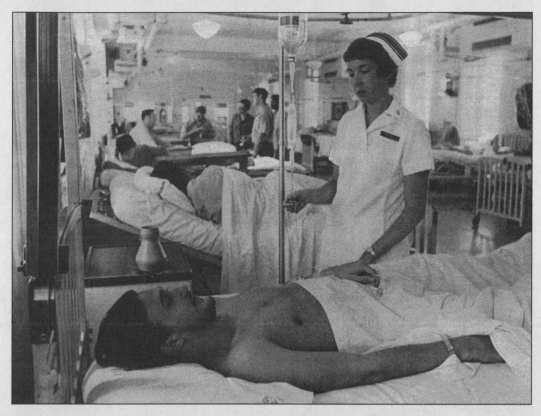

A View Outside the Prison

MODEL EXAMINATION 3

180 Minutes—60 Questions

Questions 1 through 3 are based upon the photograph of trainees going to class.

1. The people in the photograph are
   (A) three men and three women
   (B) four men and two women
   (C) four women and two men
   (D) five men and one woman

2. What can be seen behind the people?
   (A) athletic fields
   (B) an airport
   (C) trees
   (D) trees and traffic

3. The uniforms consist of
   (A) dark slacks and dark long-sleeved shirts
   (B) dark slacks and light short-sleeved shirts
   (C) dark slacks and light long-sleeved shirts
   (D) dark slacks and dark short-sleeved shirts

Questions 4 and 5 are based upon the photograph of the security control post.

4. The number of active TV monitors visible in the photograph is
   (A) 8
   (B) 10
   (C) 11
   (D) 13

5. Choose which of the following statements is NOT correct.
   (A) There are three telephones on the table.
   (B) The black man is holding a pen.
   (C) The white man is not wearing a watch.
   (D) The woman has one hand on the table

Questions 6 to 8 are based upon the photograph of the hospital ward.

6. The expression on the nurse's face is
   (A) happy
   (B) caring
   (C) sad
   (D) angry

7. The patient with visitors is
   (A) in the fifth bed
   (B) out of bed
   (C) being fed intravenously
   (D) sitting up

8. The patient in the second bed
   (A) is watching the nurse intently
   (B) is wearing no pajama top
   (C) is being fed intravenously
   (D) has his back to the camera

Questions 9 and 10 are based upon the photograph of the view outside the prison.

9. The number of vehicles visible outside is
   (A) 0
   (B) 1
   (C) 2
   (D) 3

10. Choose which of the following statements is correct.
   (A) A mountain range can be seen in the distance.
   (B) The photograph was taken on a bright, sunny day.
   (C) The people in the picture are ignoring each other.
   (D) The guard tower is visible on the left.

11. You, a Correction Officer, notice something unusual in the cell block under your care. You should immediately

    (A) report the matter in writing to your superior officer

    (B) investigate the matter

    (C) wait for a time to see whether anything happens

    (D) blow your whistle and sound a general alarm

12. A prison inmate asks you to recommend a good lawyer to him. You should

    (A) comply with his request

    (B) tell him you wish to consult your superior officer before making your suggestion

    (C) tell him that it would be undesirable for you as a Correction Officer to make such recommendation

    (D) suggest that he study the law himself since he has plenty of time

13. An inmate under your care is epileptic. You should

    (A) pay no attention to him

    (B) take special care that he does not work in such a place as to make it easy for him to hurt himself

    (C) endeavor to make him comfortable at all times

    (D) take special care that he does not escape

14. Of the following, you, a Correction Officer, will most likely find it necessary to be able to

    (A) shoot accurately to halt a prisoner's escape

    (B) subdue prisoners with physical strength

    (C) keep your temper when insulted by a prisoner

    (D) speak the vernacular commonly used by prison inmates

15. You receive instructions from your supervisor which you do not fully understand. For you to ask for a further explanation would be

    (A) good; chiefly because your supervisor will be impressed by your interest in your work

    (B) poor; chiefly because the time of your supervisor will be needlessly wasted

    (C) good; chiefly because proper performance depends on full understanding of the work to be done

    (D) poor; chiefly because officers should be able to think for themselves

16. An inmate tells you that the prisoner in the cell next to hers has stolen her pocket radio. Of the following, the best action for you to take *first* is to

    (A) ask the inmate on what she bases her accusation

    (B) ask the inmate to put her complaint in writing, including a description of the stolen article

    (C) search the cell of the accused

    (D) report the accusation to your supervisor

17. Prison Rule: A Correction Officer must be in control of all of his or her keys at all times. Prison Rules: Under no circumstances may a prisoner be unsupervised. You are escorting a prisoner to a dental appointment in another part of the prison. As you pass through a gate from one section to another, your key breaks in the lock. You are unable to remove the portion of the key from the lock. You should

    (A) continue with the prisoner, since the key is stuck and useless

    (B) stay with the key and send the prisoner along to the dental appointment

    (C) send the prisoner back to get another Correction Officer as escort

    (D) remain with the prisoner beside the gate until another Correction Officer appears to escort the prisoner and to send for the locksmith, even though it will make the prisoner late for the dentist

18. As a Correction Officer, the *best* action for you to take with respect to complaints made by inmates is to

    (A) ignore these complaints since it is only natural for prison inmates to complain

    (B) investigate all complaints thoroughly

    (C) tell the inmates to submit all complaints to your superior officer whose responsibility it is to handle such matters

    (D) weigh the merit of each complaint before you take further action

19. At times you, in your capacity as a Correction Officer, may be expected to testify in court about a prisoner. In preparation for such testimony, the *most* important of the following actions for you to take is to

    (A) wear your newest uniform so as to create a good impression

    (B) refresh your memory about the facts of the case before going to court

    (C) discuss what you are going to say with the head of the organization representing Correction Officers

    (D) talk to the prisoner about the testimony he or she is going to give

20. As a Correction Officer supervising a prisoner who operates a piece of dangerous machinery, you should *not*

    (A) keep an account of the amount of work the prisoner turns out

    (B) tell the prisoner about problems that might arise in operating the machine

    (C) answer the prisoner's questions about written operational instructions which the prisoner should have read

    (D) allow the prisoner to make mistakes for a day or two before correcting the mistakes

21. You observe that George and Henry, who previously had been rather cool towards one another, suddenly seem to have a lot to say to each other. They spend a great deal of time talking, whispering and laughing together. You should

    (A) ask them to share their joke with you

    (B) tell them that whispering is prohibited and all communication must be made in a normal voice

    (C) report their unusual behavior to your supervisor

    (D) watch them carefully to be certain that nothing more than friendship is developing

22. The Department of Correction has a regulation that prohibits socializing between Correction Officers and prison inmates. The *best* reason for this rule is that

    (A) a Correction Officer who socializes with inmates may be tempted to help them escape

    (B) socializing with prisoners leads them to the mistaken impression that the Correction Officer is "on their side"

    (C) the Correction Officer may become lax in his duties of guarding the prisoners

    (D) prisoners who socialize with the Correction Officers will be beaten by the other prisoners

23. A prisoner goes berserk in the dining room of a prison. He begins to complain loudly and profanely about the quality of the food. Of the following, the Correction Officer in charge of the dining room should *immediately*

    (A) tell the prisoner to calm down and to be happy he is eating a meal

    (B) get the inmate to stop by asking the other prisoners to ignore him

    (C) have the prisoner removed from the dining hall

    (D) inspect the food to find out whether anything is wrong with it

24. Giving the prisoners job training in their assigned tasks is one of the duties of the Correction Officer. When giving this training, the Officer should be sensitive to the fact that

    (A) a prisoner who learns quickly will become a model prisoner

    (B) a prisoner who learns slowly has no interest in learning

    (C) one prisioner can learn a job just as fast as any other prisoner

    (D) a prisoner may lack confidence in his or her ability to learn the job

25. A prison regulation prohibits a Correction Officers from individually punishing a prisoner, even though the prisoner is caught breaking the rule, and requires instead that the infraction be reported to a superior officer. The *most* likely reason for such a rule is that

    (A) Correction Officers cannot judge the effects of punishment

    (B) most Correction Officers would give punishment which is too severe

    (C) if punishment is given, it should be administered by the institution itself in line with correctional policy

    (D) additional punishment is bad policy in a rehabilitation setting

26. One inmate, Helen, has attracted your attention because she reminds you so much of your own younger sister. The *best* way for you to deal with your feelings toward Helen is to

    (A) grant her little favors and explain to the other inmates how Helen resembles your sister

    (B) suppress your feelings and treat Helen like everyone else

    (C) ask that Helen be transferred to the care of another Correction Officer

    (D) treat Helen a bit more harshly than other prisoners because you are so disappointed in her

27. A prisoner regulation requires that a doctor prescribing medicine for a prisoner must personally observe the prisoner taking the medicine in his or her presence. The most fundamental reason for this rule in a prison is to

    (A) enable the doctor to give prompt treatment if the prisoner has an unexpected reaction to the medication

    (B) keep prisoners from saving up the medicine and from using it for improper purposes

    (C) be certain that the medicine is taken so that the prisoner will soon get well

    (D) discourage prisoners from pretending illnesses in order to avoid work assignments

28. A prisoner who has a reputation as a liar comes to you with a story that an escape is being planned by several other inmates. He names the inmates and gives details of their plans. The *best* action for you to take is to

    (A) take him to your superior officer

    (B) tell him that you know of his reputation and that there is no use to his trying to win favor with you

    (C) ask some other prisoners, not the named, if there is any truth to his story

    (D) alert your fellow Correction Officers to keep a special eye on the named inmates

29. Alicia, a new prisoner in your care, is especially lethargic and unresponsive. She refuses to participate or to follow instructions. The *first* thing you should do in your management of Alicia is

    (A) lock her in her cell

    (B) request a suicide watch

    (C) ask another officer who is fluent in Spanish to try to reason with her

    (D) check her records to see if there is any notation about physical or language limitations or about her mental state

30. A Correction Officer, alone on duty, sees two of several prisoners in a work detail under his supervision suddenly begin to beat each other with their fists. The Officer immediately wades in and attempts to forcibly separate the two enraged prisoners. In most instances, an action like this by a Correction Officer would be

    (A) desirable; such prompt movement by the Officer will prevent the fight from spreading

    (B) undesirable; since other prisoners would be unsupervised while the Officer acts, the two should be allowed to fight it out

    (C) desirable; seeing an Officer act so quickly, other prisoners will be hesitant to start fights in the future

    (D) undesirable; an immediate call for help should be made before the Officer takes personal action

31. In recreation yard conversation, José learns that Bill, who committed essentially the same crime that José committed, is serving a much shorter sentence. José becomes sullen and hostile and complains bitterly to you about injustices and prejudice in the criminal justice system. The *best* way to calm José is to

(A) suggest that he ask Bill what defense tactics he used in order to draw a lighter sentence

(B) tell José that since criminals have committed crimes there is no requirement that they be treated fairly

(C) assure José that he had a wise judge and got what he deserved

(D) explain to José that sentencing is based not only upon the nature of the crime but also on previous records and special circumstances surrounding the crime at the time

32. It is absolutely forbidden for Correction Officers to accept any gifts from prisoners or their families. The most important reason for this rule is that

(A) favors would be expected in return

(B) the gifts may have been stolen

(C) prison populations and their families generally cannot afford gifts

(D) prisoners who had not given gifts might turn against the gift givers

33. You are in charge of a group of inmates who work in a shop where they use several tools. The most practical method for making sure that no tools are smuggled out at the end of the work day is to

(A) assign a special place to each tool and check to see that each tool is in its assigned place before you and the inmates leave

(B) chain each tool to the work bench with a long chain

(C) search the inmates before they leave the shop

(D) have each inmate give you a receipt for each tool he uses and return the receipt to the inmate when the tool is returned

34. While walking through a prison corridor, you come upon an unfamiliar inmate lying on the floor unconscious with blood on his face. The *first* action for you to take is to

(A) examine the inmate to see what first aid assistance you can give

(B) go through the inmate's pockets to see what identification he has on his person

(C) go to the warden's office to get assistance

(D) ask the prisoners in the area what happened

35. It is prison regulation that a Correction Officer who is escorting a group of prisoners must always walk at the back of the group. The *best* reason for this regulation is that

(A) the Officer can keep the stragglers from falling behind

(B) no fights can develop behind the officer

(C) there is no opportunity for the Officer to be attacked from behind

(D) the Officer can see in which direction escapees run

36. A Correction Officer should shoot if

(A) he observes an inmate in the act of stealing from another inmate

(B) he observes one inmate about to strike another

(C) an inmate armed with a pick attacks another Officer

(D) never

37. Every Monday the prison office issues a bulletin telling of changes in rules and regulations, new educational and social programs which are being offered, and special events for the week. Your *best* action with respect to this bulletin is to

    (A) post it on the bulletin board and tell prisoners that the bulletin is there for all to read

    (B) read the bulletin aloud to the prisoners and then post it

    (C) have the same prisoner, the one with the commanding voice, read the bulletin aloud each week then post it

    (D) choose a different prisoner each week to read the bulletin aloud before posting

38. A large group of prisoners, larger than usual, is congregated in the center of the exercise area talking quietly but with great animation. A couple of prisoners keep looking furtively over their shoulders at you. The *first* thing you should do is

    (A) summon some other Correction Officers to join you in observing these prisoners

    (B) call aside one of the prisoners whom you know by experience to be cooperative and forthright and ask him what is going on

    (C) notify the warden of this unusual congregation

    (D) step up to the group and tell the prisoners to disperse and get back to their exercise and recreation

39. A new prisoner, a Sikh, insists upon wearing a tightly wound turban on his head at all times, in defiance of prison regulations but in accordance with his religion. Your *best* action would be

    (A) confiscate the turban; rules are rules

    (B) ask a couple of other prisoners to jump the Sikh and snatch the turban and bring it to you

    (C) send the Sikh to solitary confinement

    (D) privately ask the Sikh to unwind his turban for you so that you may be satisfied that no weapon is involved; then consult the warden

40. Frank and Nick, two prisoners who have never distinguished themselves in any way, approach you and tell you that they have information about a gambling ring in their cell block. They offer to amass details for you and to name names, asking for nothing in return. You should

    (A) thank them and tell them that you eagerly await their full report

    (B) thank them for alerting you to the situation but assure them that you and your fellow officers will pick up the surveillance from there

    (C) reprimand them for carrying tales

    (D) report them to the warden as participants in a gambling ring

Directions: For questions 41 through 50, choose the answer which best combines the three short sentences. Your choice should convey all the information in a clean, succinct, and grammatical manner.

41. Zirconium is considered to be a rare metal.
    Copper, tin, and lead are mined from the earth's crust.
    There is more zirconium than copper, tin and lead in the earth's crust.

(A) Zirconium is a metal rarely found in the earth's crust, with copper, tin and lead.

(B) Copper, tin, and lead are abundant in the earth's crust, as is zirconium.

(C) Copper, tin, and lead are metals found in the earth's crust, unlike zirconium.

(D) Although zirconium is classified as a rare metal, it is more abundant in the earth's crust than copper, tin or lead.

42. Male mosquitos feed on vegetable juice.
    Female mosquitos drink animal blood.
    Only female mosquitos are equipped to draw blood.

    (A) Mosquitos cause distress to humans because of their feeding habits which are painful and blood-thirsty.

    (B) Mosquitos have a liquid diet.

    (C) Male mosquitos are incapable of drawing blood. Only female mosquitos drink animal blood.

    (D) People are bitten by female mosquitos that drink their blood and have ability to draw it and are not bitten by male mosquitos that don't have the ability to draw blood but drink vegetable juice.

43. A police dog must accept food only from its trainer.
    Poisoned meat causes painful death.
    Strict discipline is part of a police dog's training.

    (A) Part of the discipline in a police dog's training is learning to accept food only from its master. Thus the police dog is not lured to a painful death from eating poisoned meat.

    (B) A disciplined police dog eats poisoned meat only when it is served by its trainer.

    (C) A police dog is disciplined to eat only food given by their trainer. This way they don't die from eating poisoned meat.

    (D) The police dog is disciplined to know what is poisoned meat and eats only food that is not poisoned by its trainer.

44. Before World War II, Dutch elm disease was controlled and limited.
    During the war, quarantines and tree sanitation measures were relaxed.
    Dutch elm disease is a fatal fungus infection.

    (A) Dutch elm disease, which is a fatal fungus infection, used to be controlled by quarantines and tree sanitation measures and was curtailed during World War II.

    (B) Before World War II, Dutch elm disease, a fatal fungus infection, was controlled by quarantines and tree sanitation.

    (C) Relaxation of quarantines and tree sanitation during World War II caused Dutch elm disease to be fatal fungus infection.

    (D) The fatal fungus infection, Dutch elm disease, relaxed quarantines and tree sanitation during World War II.

45. John has a bag of marbles.
Mary and I have no marbles.
John is willing to share equally.

   (A) Mary and I want John's marbles, but John won't give them to us.

   (B) Mary and me will each get some of John's marbles.

   (C) John will divide his marbles between Mary and I.

   (D) When the marbles are shared, John, Mary and I will each have one-third.

46. There are three salespersons in the store.
Lois, one of the salespersons, is 5'9" tall.
Neither Bob nor Alice, both of whom sell in the store, is as tall as 5'9".

   (A) Of all the salespersons in the store, Lois is taller.

   (B) Lois is taller than any salesperson in the store.

   (C) Lois is taller than any other salesperson in the store.

   (D) Of all the salespersons, neither Bob nor Alice are as tall as Lois.

47. Backgammon is a complex game.
You must be able to change strategies often to play it well.
It is easy to learn.

   (A) Backgammon is a complex game, and you must change strategies often to learn it well.

   (B) Though backgammon is easy to learn, it is a complex game which requires frequent shifts of strategy when played well.

   (C) To learn to play backgammon you must shift complex strategies easily.

   (D) You must easily learn to shift strategies to play the complex game of backgammon well.

48. Fish in tropical waters are colorful.
They swim among coral reefs.
You can see them from glass-bottomed boats.

   (A) You can swim in tropical waters and see glass-bottomed boats, colorful fish, and coral reefs.

   (B) You can see glass-bottomed fish swimming among coral reefs and colorful boats in tropical waters.

   (C) In tropical waters, you can see glass-bottomed boats, colorful fish, and coral reefs swimming.

   (D) From glass-bottom boats, you can see colorful fish swimming in tropical waters among coral reefs.

49. The hiker was lost.
A St. Bernard rescued him.
It happened in the Alps.

   (A) The hiker was rescued by a St. Bernard lost in the Alps.

   (B) The lost Alpine hiker was rescued by a St. Bernard.

   (C) The hiker in the lost Alps was rescued by a St. Bernard.

   (D) In the Alps the hiker was rescued by a lost St. Bernard.

50. Taxes are deducted from all wages.
Workers who must work at night are paid overtime.
The rate of tax to be withheld is fixed by law.

(A) The law requires that people who are paid overtime must pay taxes.

(B) According to the law, people who work at night must be paid overtime and deduct taxes.

(C) The tax rate on overtime pay is deducted from wages by law and is paid at night.

(D) By law a fixed rate of taxes is deducted from all wages, including those paid as overtime for night work.

Directions: For questions 51 to 60, read each passage, the question which follows it, and the four answer choices. Choose the answer which best conveys the meaning of the passage.

51. At times it has been suggested that it is incongruous for the government to employ one lawyer to prosecute and another to defend the same prisoner. This is a superficial point of view, for it overlooks the principle that the government should be as anxious to shield the innocent as it is to punish the guilty.

The paragraph best supports the statement that

(A) it is not properly within the scope of the government to provide criminals with both prosecuting and defending lawyers

(B) a person held for a crime, if he be poor, need never fear that he will not be adequately defended, because the government makes provision for competent lawyers to aid him in his defense

(C) although sometimes criticized, it is governmental policy to shield the innocent by providing legal defense for indigent persons accused of crime

(D) it is an incongruous point of view that the government should concurrently shield the innocent and punish the guilty

52. The capacity of banks to grant loans depends, in the long run, on the amount of money deposited with them by the public. In the short run, however, it is a well known fact that banks not only can, but do lend more than is deposited with them. If such lending is carried to excess, it leads to inflation.

The paragraph best supports the statements that

(A) banks often indulge in the vicious practice of lending more than is deposited with them.

(B) in the long run, a sound banking policy operates for the mutual advantage of the bankers and the public

(C) inflation is sometimes the result of excess lending by the banks

(D) bank lending is always in direct ratio with bank deposits

53. There exists a false but popular idea that a clue is a mysterious fact that most people overlook but which some very keen investigator easily discovers and recognizes as having, in itself, a remarkable meaning. The clue is most often an ordinary fact that an observant person picks up—something that gains its significance when, after a long series of careful investigations, it is connected with a network of other clues.

   To be of value clues must be
   (A) discovered by skilled investigators
   (B) found under mysterious circumstances
   (C) connected with other facts
   (D) discovered soon after the crime

54. Certain chemical changes, such as fermentation, are due to the action of innumerable living microorganisms known as bacteria. Bacteria also cause the decomposition of sewage.

   Certain chemical changes are due to
   (A) bacteria
   (B) oxidation
   (C) fermentation
   (D) decomposition

55. Any business not provided with capable substitutes to fill all important positions is a weak business. Therefore, a foreman should train each man not only to perform his own particular duties but also to do those of two or three positions.

   The paragraph best supports the statement that
   (A) dependence on substitutes is a sign of a weak organization
   (B) training will improve the strongest organization
   (C) the foreman should be the most expert at any particular job under him
   (D) vacancies in vital positions should be provided for in advance

56. The coloration of textile fabrics composed of cotton and wool generally requires two processes, as the process used in dyeing wool is seldom capable of fixing the color upon cotton. The usual method is to immerse the fabric in the requisite baths to dye the wool and then to treat the partially dyed material in the manner found suitable for cotton.

   The dyeing of textile fabrics composed of cotton and wool
   (A) is more successful when the material contains more cotton than wool
   (B) is not satisfactory when solid colors are desired
   (C) is restricted to two colors for any one fabric
   (D) is based upon the methods required for dyeing the different materials

57. The increasing size of business organizations has resulted in less personal contact between superior and subordinate. Consequently, business executives today depend more upon records and reports to secure information and exercise control over the operations of various departments.

The increasing size of business organizations

(A) has caused a complete cleavage between employer and employee

(B) has resulted in less personal contact between superior and subordinate

(C) has tended toward class distinctions in large organizations

(D) has resulted in a better means of controlling the operations of various departments

58. Most solids, like most liquids, expand when heated and contract when cooled. To allow for this, roads, sidewalks, and railroad tracks are constructed with spacings between sections so that they can expand during the hot weather.

If roads, sidewalks, and railroad tracks were not constructed with spacings between sections

(A) nothing would happen to them when the weather changed

(B) they could not be constructed as easily as they are now

(C) they would crack or break when the weather changed

(D) they would not appear to be even

59. In a lightning-like military advance, similar to that used by the Germans, the use of persistent chemicals is unnecessary. It might even be a considerable detriment to a force advancing over a broad front.

The paragraph best supports the statement that

(A) chemicals should not be used by a defending army

(B) the Germans advanced in a narrow area

(C) an advancing army may harm itself through the use of chemicals

(D) chemical welfare is only effective if used by an advancing army

60. It is probably safe to assume that for most people mental growth ceases somewhere between fourteen and a half and sixteen. After that, any increase in ability to meet novel situations is gained from experience. Intellectual growth is likewise ascribed to wider experience and more information, rather than to an increase in mental capacity.

Most individuals somewhere between fourteen and a half and sixteen

(A) make demands on mere experience rather than on native ability

(B) show an increase rather than a decrease in general mental capacity

(C) have achieved their total mental growth

(D) cease to show increased capacity to meet novel situations

END OF EXAM

ANSWER KEY FOR MODEL EXAMINATION 3

1. B	13. B	25. C	37. B	49. B
2. C	14. C	26. B	38. C	50. D
3. D	15. C	27. B	39. D	51. C
4. C	16. A	28. A	40. B	52. C
5. C	17. D	29. D	41. D	53. C
6. B	18. D	30. D	42. C	54. A
7. D	19. B	31. D	43. A	55. D
8. D	20. D	32. A	44. B	56. D
9. D	21. D	33. A	45. D	57. B
10. B	22. C	34. A	46. C	58. C
11. B	23. C	35. C	47. B	59. C
12. C	24. D	36. C	48. D	60. C

Explanatory Answers for Model Examination 3

Questions 1 through 10: If you missed any of these questions, look back at the pictures and observe more closely.

11. **(B)** Something that appears to be unusual may or may not have any great significance. Certainly, you should not just ignore it and wait for further developments. On the other hand, do not be an alarmist and do not jump to conclusions. Go ahead and investigate; then act on the basis of real knowledge or justified suspicions.

12. **(C)** You must keep your distance from the prisoners. It is not your place to recommend a lawyer or even a choice of lawyers. You might recommend the prison library and its directories of attorneys.

13. **(B)** During an epileptic attack, the epileptic loses consciousness falls to the floor and may flail his or her arms and legs. The epileptic should not work in a place where an epileptic attack might present real danger to him or her. In all other respects, the epileptic should be treated like everyone else.

14. **(C)** You will often find prisoners to be insolent and insulting, and you will have to control your temper under such verbal attack. Having to subdue prisoners with physical strength or having to shoot to thwart an escape are rare occurrences. The Correction Officer should not stoop to the language of the prisoners, but should speak clearly and correctly at all times.

15. **(C)** Obviously, you must fully understand instructions to do a good job. The time spent getting the instructions straight is time well spent.

16. **(A)** Since the inmate has accused a specific other inmate, there should be some basis to the accusation. You must find the basis for the specific accusation before proceeding with any action.

17. **(D)** You are obliged to follow all rules exactly. A dental appointment is not a life or death matter, so you have no room to make your own judgment as to the inaccessibility of the key or the reliability of the prisoner.

18. **(D)** As a Correction Officer, you will hear many complaints from inmates. You listen to each complaint before deciding which ones merit thorough investigation and referral to your superior.

19. **(B)** You should know the whole picture, be aware of the background of the prisoner, the nature of the crime and the individual's prison behavior before attempting to answer questions.

20. **(D)** You are in charge of the prisoner's safety. You must instruct, observe, and correct to assure safe operation of dangerous machinery.

21. **(D)** Prisoners are permitted to make new friends. Correction Officers are permitted to take note and monitor the direction of new friendships.

22. **(C)** It is important that lines of authority be maintained at all times. If the Correction Officer becomes "one of the boys," he is likely to let down his guard and become lax in his duties.

23. **(C)** Any bizarre behavior disrupts routine and may lead to disorder or worse. The disruptive prisoner must be removed quickly and quietly.

24. **(D)** Many factors contribute to criminal behavior, and there are many individual differences among criminals. One known contributing factor to criminal behavior is a feeling or inferiority and lack of self-confidence. You must consider this possibility when giving training.

25. **(C)** Prisoners can easily sense capricious behavior on the part of Correction Officers, so it is best for all punishment to be a matter of policy, not judgment on the part of any Officer.

26. **(B)** You are an adult and must behave as an adult. Suppress your feelings and treat Helen like any other inmate.

27. **(B)** Many medicines which are highly effective in proper doses have very different qualities and effects when given in massive doses. It is therefore important that prisoners take the prescribed medications at the prescribed times for maximum effectiveness and to preclude their hoarding them for abusive purposes.

28. **(A)** A prospective escape is not a matter to be trifled with. You cannot delay and observe. Since the inmate has names and details, he should be thoroughly interviewed by your superior officer. Under no circumstances should you discuss this information with other prisoners.

29. **(D)** It is possible that Alicia is deaf, physically disabled, ill or depressed, or that English is unintelligible to her. Check the records; then proceed on the basis of the problem. Punishment is called for only if there are no other reasons for her noncompliance.

30. **(D)** There is no way of knowing how a fight will develop. An inmate may have a homemade weapon; other prisoners might join in. The Officer must summon reinforcements before placing himself into the fight.

31. **(D)** Calm reasoning and logical explanation may not work, but this certainly is the avenue to take.

32. **(A)** All the answer choices may be true, but the most important reason for the Correction Officer to not accept gifts is so that he or she avoids being in a position of obligation to the prisoner.

33. **(A)** All the choices would work, but the most practical and orderly method is that described in choice (A). This is also the most dignified method and the least demeaning to the prisoners.

34. **(A)** Health and safety come first.

35. **(C)** Protect yourself. You must be able to see all of the inmates at all times.

36. **(C)** Shooting is justified when the life of a fellow officer is clearly in danger.

37. **(B)** You must not assume literacy among all the prisoners. The bulletin must be read aloud. Choosing the same prisoner each week smacks of favoritism and would put that prisoner into a difficult position among his peers. In choosing a different prisoner each week, you run the risk of choosing a prisoner who will be embarrassed by poor reading skills.

38. **(C)** When behavior is alarmingly out of the ordinary and gives the appearance of leading to a dangerous situation within a short period, it is best to let the warden know about it right away. The warden will undoubtedly send other Correction Officers to back you up.

39. **(D)** Choice (B) is clearly the worst option. You must balance the rules themselves with the reasons for the rules and for your obligation to respect the religious practices of inmates. By privately checking for weapons, you are satisfying the reason for this particular rule. The problem of religious privileges is a sticky one and best relegated to the warden.

40. **(B)** You are not in the position of employing inmates, and you do not want to put yourself into a position of obligation to Frank and Nick. You should most certainly avail yourself of the information they have given and follow through with your own observation.

41. **(D)** Choice (A) inserts an extra dimension, that of the metals being found together. Choice (B) assumes an unstated abundance of the metals and contradicts the rarity of zirconium. Choice (C) denies that zirconium exists in the earth's crust.

42. **(C)** Choice (A) leaves out the sex distinctions entirely. Choice (B) is true but inadequate. Choice (D) is factually correct but is an unwieldy run-on sentence.

43. **(A)** Choice (B) is true but ridiculous. Choice (D) is only ridiculous. Choice (C) is grammatically incorrect. "A police dog" is singular, so all pronouns referring to the dog must also be singular.

44. **(B)** Choice (A), when extricated from the run-on sentence, states that Dutch elm disease was curtailed during Word War II. Choice (C) states that relaxation of quarantines caused the disease to become a fatal fungus infection. The disease always was fatal. Choice (D) makes no sense at all.

45. **(D)** Choice (A) is false. In choice (B) the subject should read "Mary and I." In Choice (C) "Mary and me" is the object of the preposition *between*.

46. **(C)** In choice (A), since the comparison is among three persons, "Lois is tallest." choice (B) is impossible. Lois cannot be taller than any salesperson in the store because she is one of the salespersons and cannot be taller than herself. Choice (D) must read, "neither Bob nor Alice *is*."

47. **(B)** Read carefully. Each of the wrong choices misses the full meaning of the three sentences.

48. **(D)** Choice (A) is correct, but the point is that one should observe the scene from glass-bottomed boats. Choice (B) is ridiculous. As for choice (C), coral reefs are stationary.

49. **(B)** The modifier must be carefully placed so as to leave no doubt as to who or what was lot.

50. **(D)** Choice (A) is true but inadequate in covering the message. Choice (B) incorrectly suggests that workers deduct their own taxes. Choice (C) is ridiculous.

51. **(C)** The paragraph states the principle that the government must shield the innocent. Ordinarily this is done through the establishment of trial machinery whereby the accused may present his case to a jury of his peers. Since, under this principle, every accused is entitled to trial, the government provides counsel for indigent defendants. Choice (B) is incorrect because the government does not guarantee the competence of the lawyers it provides. Choice (D) contradicts the paragraph. Choice (A) is incorrect, for the government provides prosecuting lawyers for its own benefits, not for the benefit of the accused.

52. **(C)** This is the best interpretation of the paragraph. While the paragraph is cautionary, it is not judgmental, so choice (A) is incorrect. Choice (D) is directly contradicted by the paragraph.

53. **(C)** The paragraph tells us that the value of the clue lies in its relationship to all the other clues.

54. **(A)** Fermentation and decomposition are chemical changes brought about by the action of bacteria.

55. **(D)** The point of this paragraph is that a business should be prepared to fill unexpected vacancies with pretrained staff members.

56. **(D)** The paragraph tells us that the dyeing of wool requires a process quite different from that for dyeing cotton. Fabric which contains both wool and cotton fibers must go through both processes, one after the other.

57. **(B)** See the first sentence.

58. **(C)** The spaces allow roads, sidewalks, and railroad tracks to expand in summer and contract in winter without cracking or breaking.

59. **(C)** In stating that the use of chemicals might be a detriment to an advancing force, the paragraph means that an advancing army might cause harm to itself with its own chemicals.

60. **(C)** The first sentence states that for most people mental growth ceases between the ages of fourteen and a half and sixteen. The remainder of the paragraph explains that what may later appear to be increased capacity must be ascribed to greater experience and information.

Answer Sheet for Model Examination 4

1. Ⓐ Ⓑ Ⓒ Ⓓ   2. Ⓐ Ⓑ Ⓒ Ⓓ   3. Ⓐ Ⓑ Ⓒ Ⓓ   4. Ⓐ Ⓑ Ⓒ Ⓓ   5. Ⓐ Ⓑ Ⓒ Ⓓ

6. Ⓐ Ⓑ Ⓒ Ⓓ   7. Ⓐ Ⓑ Ⓒ Ⓓ   8. Ⓐ Ⓑ Ⓒ Ⓓ   9. Ⓐ Ⓑ Ⓒ Ⓓ   10. Ⓐ Ⓑ Ⓒ Ⓓ

11. Ⓐ Ⓑ Ⓒ Ⓓ   12. Ⓐ Ⓑ Ⓒ Ⓓ   13. Ⓐ Ⓑ Ⓒ Ⓓ   14. Ⓐ Ⓑ Ⓒ Ⓓ   15. Ⓐ Ⓑ Ⓒ Ⓓ

16. Ⓐ Ⓑ Ⓒ Ⓓ   17. Ⓐ Ⓑ Ⓒ Ⓓ   18. Ⓐ Ⓑ Ⓒ Ⓓ   19. Ⓐ Ⓑ Ⓒ Ⓓ   20. Ⓐ Ⓑ Ⓒ Ⓓ

21. Ⓐ Ⓑ Ⓒ Ⓓ   22. Ⓐ Ⓑ Ⓒ Ⓓ   23. Ⓐ Ⓑ Ⓒ Ⓓ   24. Ⓐ Ⓑ Ⓒ Ⓓ   25. Ⓐ Ⓑ Ⓒ Ⓓ

26. Ⓐ Ⓑ Ⓒ Ⓓ   27. Ⓐ Ⓑ Ⓒ Ⓓ   28. Ⓐ Ⓑ Ⓒ Ⓓ   29. Ⓐ Ⓑ Ⓒ Ⓓ   30. Ⓐ Ⓑ Ⓒ Ⓓ

31. Ⓐ Ⓑ Ⓒ Ⓓ   32. Ⓐ Ⓑ Ⓒ Ⓓ   33. Ⓐ Ⓑ Ⓒ Ⓓ   34. Ⓐ Ⓑ Ⓒ Ⓓ   35. Ⓐ Ⓑ Ⓒ Ⓓ

36. Ⓐ Ⓑ Ⓒ Ⓓ   37. Ⓐ Ⓑ Ⓒ Ⓓ   38. Ⓐ Ⓑ Ⓒ Ⓓ   39. Ⓐ Ⓑ Ⓒ Ⓓ   40. Ⓐ Ⓑ Ⓒ Ⓓ

41. Ⓐ Ⓑ Ⓒ Ⓓ   42. Ⓐ Ⓑ Ⓒ Ⓓ   43. Ⓐ Ⓑ Ⓒ Ⓓ   44. Ⓐ Ⓑ Ⓒ Ⓓ   45. Ⓐ Ⓑ Ⓒ Ⓓ

46. Ⓐ Ⓑ Ⓒ Ⓓ   47. Ⓐ Ⓑ Ⓒ Ⓓ   48. Ⓐ Ⓑ Ⓒ Ⓓ   49. Ⓐ Ⓑ Ⓒ Ⓓ   50. Ⓐ Ⓑ Ⓒ Ⓓ

51. Ⓐ Ⓑ Ⓒ Ⓓ   52. Ⓐ Ⓑ Ⓒ Ⓓ   53. Ⓐ Ⓑ Ⓒ Ⓓ   54. Ⓐ Ⓑ Ⓒ Ⓓ   55. Ⓐ Ⓑ Ⓒ Ⓓ

56. Ⓐ Ⓑ Ⓒ Ⓓ   57. Ⓐ Ⓑ Ⓒ Ⓓ   58. Ⓐ Ⓑ Ⓒ Ⓓ   59. Ⓐ Ⓑ Ⓒ Ⓓ   60. Ⓐ Ⓑ Ⓒ Ⓓ

61. Ⓐ Ⓑ Ⓒ Ⓓ   62. Ⓐ Ⓑ Ⓒ Ⓓ   63. Ⓐ Ⓑ Ⓒ Ⓓ   64. Ⓐ Ⓑ Ⓒ Ⓓ   65. Ⓐ Ⓑ Ⓒ Ⓓ

66. Ⓐ Ⓑ Ⓒ Ⓓ   67. Ⓐ Ⓑ Ⓒ Ⓓ   68. Ⓐ Ⓑ Ⓒ Ⓓ   69. Ⓐ Ⓑ Ⓒ Ⓓ   70. Ⓐ Ⓑ Ⓒ Ⓓ

71. Ⓐ Ⓑ Ⓒ Ⓓ   72. Ⓐ Ⓑ Ⓒ Ⓓ   73. Ⓐ Ⓑ Ⓒ Ⓓ   74. Ⓐ Ⓑ Ⓒ Ⓓ   75. Ⓐ Ⓑ Ⓒ Ⓓ

76. Ⓐ Ⓑ Ⓒ Ⓓ   77. Ⓐ Ⓑ Ⓒ Ⓓ   78. Ⓐ Ⓑ Ⓒ Ⓓ   79. Ⓐ Ⓑ Ⓒ Ⓓ   80. Ⓐ Ⓑ Ⓒ Ⓓ

81. Ⓐ Ⓑ Ⓒ Ⓓ   82. Ⓐ Ⓑ Ⓒ Ⓓ   83. Ⓐ Ⓑ Ⓒ Ⓓ   84. Ⓐ Ⓑ Ⓒ Ⓓ   85. Ⓐ Ⓑ Ⓒ Ⓓ

86. Ⓐ Ⓑ Ⓒ Ⓓ   87. Ⓐ Ⓑ Ⓒ Ⓓ   88. Ⓐ Ⓑ Ⓒ Ⓓ   89. Ⓐ Ⓑ Ⓒ Ⓓ   90. Ⓐ Ⓑ Ⓒ Ⓓ

91. Ⓐ Ⓑ Ⓒ Ⓓ   92. Ⓐ Ⓑ Ⓒ Ⓓ   93. Ⓐ Ⓑ Ⓒ Ⓓ   94. Ⓐ Ⓑ Ⓒ Ⓓ   95. Ⓐ Ⓑ Ⓒ Ⓓ

96. Ⓐ Ⓑ Ⓒ Ⓓ   97. Ⓐ Ⓑ Ⓒ Ⓓ   98. Ⓐ Ⓑ Ⓒ Ⓓ   99. Ⓐ Ⓑ Ⓒ Ⓓ   100. Ⓐ Ⓑ Ⓒ Ⓓ

Model Examination 4

Time: 3½ Hours—100 Questions

Directions: Each question has four suggested answers, lettered A, B, C, and D. Decide which one is the best answer, and, on your answer sheet, darken the space for that letter.

1. "Certain inmate types are generally found in prisons. These types are called gorillas, toughs, hipsters, and merchants. Gorillas deliberately use violence to intimidate fearful inmates into providing favors. Toughs are swift to explode into violence against prisoners because of real or imagined insult. Exploitation of others is not their major goal. Hipsters are bullies who choose victims with caution in order to win acceptance among inmates by demonstrating physical bravery. Their bravery, however, is false. Merchants exploit other inmates through manipulation in sharp trading of goods stolen from prison supplies or in trickery in gambling." Based on the above information, the inmate who beats other inmates so that they provide him with extra cigarettes and coffee is, most likely, a

   (A) tough
   (B) gorilla
   (C) merchant
   (D) hipster

Base your answer to question 2 solely on the information below:

A Correction Officer may not smoke while on duty or in any non-smoking areas of the correctional facility at any time. The Receiving Room is a non-smoking area.

2. Officer Jomes arrives at the facility 15 minutes before his shift is to begin. He visits the officer on duty in the Receiving Room and, while there, smokes two cigarettes. Officer Jomes's conduct is

   (A) proper, because no one in the Receiving Room objects to the cigarette smoke
   (B) improper, because there is no smoking allowed in the Receiving Room at any time
   (C) proper, because Officer Jomes is not yet on duty
   (D) improper, because Officer Jomes should be more concerned about his health

Base your answer to question 3 solely on the information below:

A Correction Officer's badge is a proud possession. It identifies him or her as a trained professional on the prison staff. The badge is issued to the Correction Officer but remains the property of the Correction Department. The department requires that the Correction Officer wear the badge over the left pocket whenever in uniform and that the Correction Officer keep it within his or her possession at all times.

3. Correction Officer Berkey is at home on his day off and is trying to get some well-deserved rest. His four-year-old son Billy is whining and begging his daddy to take him to the zoo. Finally, Correction Officer Berkey hands his badge to Billy saying, "Go out and play Correction Officer with your friends and leave me alone." Correction Officer Berkey's action is

(A) proper; he needs his rest

(B) improper; Billy is not wearing a uniform

(C) proper; Billy is his own child and is under his control

(D) improper; regulations require a Correction Officer to physically possess the badge even when not wearing it

Base your answer to question 4 solely on the information below:

The constitutionally guaranteed attorney-client privilege provides that the information a client gives to an attorney be kept in confidence. The attorney may advise the client and may prepare a defense based on this private information but must not disclose any of it to the court or to the public.

4. Attorney Kleiner has come to see Inmate Greene, who is awaiting trial in a matter alleging racial bias. Kleiner has a reputation of being a fiery defense attorney; some would even suggest that he engages in unethical tactics. As Kleiner and Greene converse, Correction Officer Torto listens intently. When the attorney's visit is over, Torto prepares notes about Greene's admissions to Kleiner and Kleiner's defense strategies. Torto sends these notes to the prosecutor. Correction Officer Torto's action is

(A) appropriate; justice is best served if the prosecution has all the facts

(B) inappropriate; the attorney-client privilege guarantees privacy

(C) appropriate; Kleiner may thereby be prevented from performing unethical acts

(D) inappropriate; this information should be reserved for the judge and not passed to the prosecutor

Base your answer to question 5 solely on the information below:

Any person over 18 may visit an inmate with the inmate's consent during normal visiting hours. Any person under 18 must be accompanied to the Visiting Room by an adult visitor. An inmate's lawyer may visit an inmate at certain times other than normal visiting hours.

5. The following visitors each come separately and at different times during normal visiting hours to see Inmate Blank: Mrs. Blank, the inmate's grandmother; Ms. Kelly, the inmate's lawyer; David Blank, the inmate's 16-year-old brother; and John Gallo, a 25-year-old former inmate. Inmate Blank consents to see each of them. Which should not be allowed into the Visiting Room?

   (A) Mrs. Blank

   (B) Ms. Kelly

   (C) David Blank

   (D) John Gallo

Base your answers to questions 6 and 7 solely on the information below:

   A Correction Officer may be assigned to distribute packages and letters to inmates. The officer must inspect each package and, if the contents are acceptable, must deliver the package to the inmate within 48 hours after it has arrived at the facility. Letters may not be opened by the officer, and they must be delivered to the addressee within 24 hours after arrival. There is no limit to the number of letters an inmate may receive.

6. Six letters arrive for Inmate Randall on Monday afternoon. Officer Suarez gives three of the letters to Inmate Randall on Tuesday and gives the other three letters to Inmate Randall on Wednesday. The officer's action is

   (A) appropriate because other inmates would become jealous if they saw Inmate Randall receive so many letters on the same day

   (B) inappropriate because the officer should have waited 48 hours before delivering any of the letters

   (C) appropriate because Officer Suarez needed time to open and review the contents of the letters to make sure they were acceptable

   (D) inappropriate because all six of the letters should have been delivered to the inmate within 24 hours after their arrival

7. On Saturday a package arrives addressed to Inmate Shibutani. Correction Officer Park opens the package and discovers that it contains socks, photos of the inmate's children, and a box of homemade fudge. On Sunday morning, Correction Officer Park delivers the package to Inmate Shibutani. This action by the officer is

   (A) correct; there is no reason to withhold this acceptable package from the inmate

   (B) incorrect; packages should be held for 48 hours

   (C) correct; the fudge will melt if held in the mailroom

   (D) incorrect; there should be no mail delivery on Sunday

Answer question 8 solely on the basis of the information below:

Under the Penal Law, a Correction Officer is a peace officer. A peace officer is charged with keeping the peace whether officially on duty or not and whether in uniform or not. A peace officer must attempt to prevent crime from occurring, must attempt to stop crime in progress, and must attempt to assist crime victims.

8. Correction Officer Rice, who has completed his day's tour at the prison where he is employed, is on his way home. About 10 blocks from his home, he comes upon a woman screaming that her purse has just been snatched. Correction Officer Rice begins to chase the perpetrator, who is still visible running up the street. The purse snatcher suddenly turns, shoots, and kills Officer Rice. Correction Officer Rice's widow files to collect "death-in-the-line-of-duty" benefits. Mrs. Rice's request is

   (A) proper; Correction Officer Rice was murdered in cold blood

   (B) improper; Rice was off duty when he was killed

   (C) proper; it is the duty of peace officers to assist victims of crimes in progress

   (D) improper; Rice deliberately put himself in unnecessary danger

Answer question 9 solely on the basis of the information below:

A Correction Officer may be required to accept sums of money for bail and to issue receipts for money received. The Correction Officer must be both honest and extremely careful because very large sums of money may be involved. A Correction Officer who mishandles bail money may be subject to criminal charges and penalties.

9. Correction Officer Pulaski has been in charge of bail monies at the correctional center for the past five years. During this time, Pulaski has received money and has issued receipts with no oversight. An audit has recently revealed a discrepancy of nearly a half million dollars. The superintendent of the facility has suspended Pulaski and has ordered a grand jury investigation. This action by the superintendent is

   (A) proper; criminal behavior must be punished

   (B) improper; accidents can happen and carelessness is not a crime

   (C) proper; Pulaski is a likely suspect and a full investigation is called for

   (D) improper; since Pulaski issued receipts he cannot be held responsible for the missing money

Answer question 10 solely on the information below:

"The Commissioner of Correction may permit any prisoner confined in a state prison, excepting one awaiting the sentence of death, to attend the funeral of his or her father, mother, child, brother, sister, husband, or wife, within the state, or to visit such relative during his or her illness if death is imminent. Any expenses incurred under these provisions, with respect to any prisoner, shall be deemed an expense of maintenance of the prison and be paid from monies available therefore; but the warden, if the rules and regulations of the Commissioner of Correction shall so provide, may allow the prisoner or anyone in his behalf to reimburse the state for such expense."

10. Martha, who is serving a sentence for armed robbery, receives word that her mother, who has been undergoing treatment for cancer, has taken a sudden turn for the worse and is not expected to survive.

    (A) Martha may visit her mother in the hospital.

    (B) Martha may not visit her mother but may attend her funeral.

    (C) Martha may visit her mother but may attend her mother's funeral only if she pays her own expenses.

    (D) Martha may not visit her mother nor go to the funeral unless she can arrange to have her family pay her way.

Answer question 11 solely on the basis of the information below:

The nature of correction work is such that security of the facility may be in jeopardy if even one post is not covered at all times. There can be no exceptions to this rule.

11. Correction Officer Macmillan is scheduled to work a 7 a.m.-to-3 p.m. shift. Macmillan arrived at her post promptly at 7 this morning. She is in the middle of root canal work and scheduled a dental appointment at 4 p.m. today. Her dentist's office is a 30-minute drive from the facility at which she works. Macmillan expects to be relieved at 3 p.m., but her relief does not appear, and she remains on her post until 3:30 p.m. At 3:30, when the relief still has not arrived, Macmillan leaves for her dental appointment. Officer Macmillan's action is

    (A) correct; it is important for her health that she meet her dental appointment and not leave the root canal unfinished

    (B) incorrect; there are to be no exceptions to the full coverage rule

    (C) correct; a half hour of voluntary overtime is already beyond the call of duty

    (D) incorrect; Macmillan should have told her supervisor why she was leaving

Answer question 12 solely on the basis of the information below:

Prison inmates who often have histories of short tempers have few avenues for venting frustrations and hostilities in prison. Since physical violence and destruction of property are not permitted, inmates tend to become verbally abusive. Correction Officers are ready targets of verbal abuse. They must be somewhat thick-skinned and must not overreact to angry words.

12. Correction Officer Fulco is escorting a group of inmates from the exercise yard back to their cellblock on a glorious spring day. The inmates are reluctant to come inside and begin to stray from the line and to cajole Officer Fulco to extend their exercise time. Officer Fulco sharply demands their obedience, and a black inmate turns, spits at her, and regales her with choice profanity about "you dumb guineas." Correction Officer Fulco retorts, "Shut up you dirty nigger and do as you're told." Officer Fulco's reaction is

    (A) appropriate; one insult deserves another, and the inmates expect this type of behavior

    (B) inappropriate; Officer Fulco should recognize anger and frustration and not take the words personally

    (C) appropriate; Fulco's job is to get the inmates back to their cellblock, and this method will be effective

    (D) inappropriate; inmates shower regularly, and to call them "dirty" is inaccurate

Answer question 13 solely on the basis of the information below:

Discipline must be maintained at all times, even when maintenance of order entails infringement of some prisoners' rights and entitlement.

13. One noontime in the dining hall, Inmate Vulgaris leans over and crumbles potato chips into Inmate Topekian's Coca-Cola. Topekian promptly tosses the contents of the cup into Vulgaris's face. Inmate Davis joins the fray by throwing a chicken leg at Topekian. Then many inmates begin throwing food and pandemonium breaks loose. Correction Officers Lynch and DaSilva promptly close the cafeteria line, send for assistance, and herd all the inmates back to their cells. This action by Correction Officers Lynch and DaSilva is

    (A) proper; if inmates were throwing food, they had obviously already had enough to eat

    (B) improper; prisoners must be fed three full meals a day

    (C) proper; this is a reasonable way to restore order

    (D) improper; the inmates still in line will later have it in for the officers for making them miss lunch

Use the information in the paragraph below to answer questions 14 through 16.

"A person who intends to effect or facilitate the escape of a prisoner, whether the escape is effected or attempted or not, and who enters a prison, or conveys to a prisoner any information, or sends into a prison any disguise, instrument, weapon, or other thing, is guilty of felony if the prisoner is held upon a charge, arrest, commitment, or conviction for a felony. The person is guilty of a misdemeanor if the prisoner is held upon a charge, arrest, commitment, or conviction of a misdemeanor."

14. Johnny O. is serving time after conviction for the felony crime of armed robbery. Johnny's friend, Frank, devises an escape scheme and writes a letter to Johnny detailing the plans. Frank, without telling of the contents of the letter, asks Mary P. to deliver the letter to Johnny when she visits the prison to see her husband, Bob. The letter is intercepted by a Correction Officer.

    (A) Frank and Mary are both guilty of felonies.

    (B) Frank is guilty of a felony; Mary is guilty of a misdemeanor.

    (C) Frank is guilty of a felony; Mary is not guilty.

    (D) Frank is guilty of a misdemeanor; Mary is not guilty.

15. On a visit to her boyfriend, Bill, who is awaiting trial in the county jail on a felony charge of grand larceny, Joan orally transmits to Bill instructions for fashioning a cutting tool from objects available to him in the jail. Bill follows these instructions, which had been the invention of Joan's brother Tom, creates the tool, and escapes.

    (A) Joan and Tom are both guilty of felonies.

    (B) Joan is guilty of a felony; Tom is guilty of a misdemeanor.

    (C) Joan is guilty of a felony; Tom is not guilty.

    (D) Neither Joan nor Tom is guilty.

16. While charming little Debbie, age four, distracts a guard, Barbara manages to smuggle a gun to Jim, who is completing a sentence on a misdemeanor conviction. In the course of his escape, Jim shoots and severely injures a Correction Officer.

    (A) Barbara is guilty of a felony; Debbie is guilty of a misdemeanor.

    (B) Barbara is guilty of a felony; Debbie is not guilty.

    (C) Barbara and Debbie are both guilty of misdemeanors.

    (D) Barbara is guilty of a misdemeanor; Debbie is not guilty.

Answer question 17 solely on the basis of the information below:

A Correction Officer is responsible for the health and welfare of the prisoners in his or her charge. Since the Correction Officer is familiar with these inmates and their habits, it is his or her duty to notice changes in behavior that may indicate something is wrong.

17. Inmate Mashke has always been an enthusiastic basketball player. At every opportunity, Mashke could be seen shooting for the net. For three days now Mashke has been sitting out of basketball scrimmage and has not practiced his set shots. Correction Officer Garcia, who is regularly assigned to Mashke's group, asks Mashke why he is not playing. Mashke responds, "I just don't feel like it." On the fourth morning, Garcia summons Mashke and insists that he accompany Garcia to sick call to consult with the doctor. Officer Garcia's action is

    (A) proper; Mashke is developing a mental illness and should be treated at once

    (B) improper; malingering prisoners should not be mollycoddled

    (C) proper; a sudden change of energy level and interests should be investigated by a professional

    (D) improper; the prison budget is limited, and medical attention should not be wasted on a prisoner who is not ill

Base your answer to question 18 solely on the following information:

Regulation: Use the minimum necessary force to maintain order, but do not hesitate to use force to protect life.

18. Correction Officer Braun comes upon a fight in progress in the kitchen. Two prisoners are grappling on the floor, pummeling each other with their fists, ringed by a group of cheering, goading fellow inmates. Officer Braun strides through the group and says, "Come on, break it up." The inmates continue fighting. Correction Officer Braun then says, " If you don't stop, I'll have to shoot." When the fighting does not stop, Braun aims carefully at one prisoner's foot, fires, and wounds him. Correction Officer Braun's action is

    (A) proper; the fight had to be broken up

    (B) improper; life was not in danger, and less force could have stopped the fight

    (C) proper; a kitchen with its available knives and fire is a very dangerous location for a fight

    (D) improper; in such a dangerous situation, a Correction Officer should shoot to kill

Answer questions 19 and 20 solely on the basis of the information below:

Upon admission to a facility, all prisoners, regardless of status—awaiting trial, convicted and awaiting sentence, or awaiting transfer—must surrender wallets, belts, neckties, and shoe-laces. The intake officer must record all items, including itemized contents of purses and wallets, on the daily manifest and must issue a receipt to the prisoner, keeping a duplicate receipt for the prisoner's file. All new prisoners must be given a towel, a bar of soap, a toothbrush, toothpaste, and one blanket.

19. Correction Officer Wong is admitting Mary Adams, who is awaiting arraignment after having been picked up as a suspected burglar. Officer Wong asks Adams for her handbag. Adams replies, "I'll only be here for a couple of hours. My family will have me out in no time. Why go through all that paperwork?" Officer Wong agrees that the effort is unwarranted, takes no possessions from Adams, and does not bother to issue toilet supplies and bedding. Officer Wong's action is

    (A) correct; it is not worthwhile to spend time taking inventory of possessions, nor is it cost effective to hand out supplies to an inmate who will not be there long enough to use them

    (B) incorrect; the prisoner might want to wash or take a nap while awaiting release

    (C) correct; Mary Adams has not been proven guilty so should not have her possessions impounded as if she were

    (D) incorrect; the prison rules apply to all prisoners

20. Correction Officer Sohan has just received Vincent Wyler, who was today convicted of a felonious crime and who will be sentenced in three weeks. Wyler was unable to post bond and has been imprisoned for some time. He has lost a good deal of weight while in prison and is in danger of losing his trousers without a belt. Wyler demonstrates his problem to Officer Sohan and asks if he may keep his belt to hold up his pants. Correction Officer Sohan replies, "I'm sorry, but prison rules do not permit it." Officer Sohan's action is

    (A) appropriate; the rule does not specify any exceptions

    (B) inappropriate; prison decorum requires that all male prisoners wear trousers

    (C) appropriate; a prison who has lost weight in prison is a prime candidate for suicide

    (D) inappropriate; a little kindness is never out of order

Answer questions 21 through 27 on the basis of the information contained in the chart below:

Schedule of Prisoners' Court Appearances

Inmate	Date	Docket #	Charge	County	Court	Judge
Brock	4/12	612392	armed robbery	Kings	Criminal	Gabriel
Whinston	4/15	528789	embezzlement	Queens	Appeals	Cook
Sowders	4/15	139190	grand larceny	Prince	Supreme	Herndon
Torak	4/15	797591	vehicular homicide	Kings	Criminal	Gabriel
Laduca	4/26	427388	manslaughter 2	Pawn	Superior	Molina
Persaud	5/2	437792	burglary	Prince	County	Schwartz
Crofton	5/3	821692	armed robbery	Rook	Criminal	Reilly
Hughes	5/7	668190	burglary	Queens	Appeals	Cook

21. The inmate who is scheduled to be in court on the busiest day is
    (A) Herndon
    (B) Persuad
    (C) Sowders
    (D) Laduca

22. The docket number for the case coming up in Superior Court is
    (A) 437792
    (B) 472388
    (C) 139190
    (D) 427388

23. Two prisoners who will be tried before the same judge are
    (A) Torak and Whinston
    (B) Whinston and Hughes
    (C) Gabriel and Reilly
    (D) Brock and Hughes

24. The prison is located in Rook County. Which inmate will not need to be transported across a county line for her scheduled court appearance?
    (A) Reilly
    (B) Rook
    (C) Laduca
    (D) Crofton

25. The judges who will sit on cases in which people were killed are
    (A) Molina and Gabriel
    (B) Gabriel and Reilly
    (C) Laduca and Torak
    (D) Pawn and Rook

26. The docket number of the burglary not yet up for appeal is
    (A) 668190
    (B) 437729
    (C) 437792
    (D) 528789

27. Which statement is most accurate with reference to the cases being tried on April 15?
    (A) The docket numbers all end with the same two digits
    (B) Two of the crimes are strictly "money crimes."
    (C) The trial of Inmate Sowders will be in the Prince Court of Appeals.
    (D) Judge Schwartz will hear the case of Inmate Torak in Kings Criminal Court.

Answer question 28 solely on the basis of the information below:

Arrest may be a frightening and humiliating experience, especially for young first offenders. Correction Officers must be alert to signs of depression, such as withdrawal and lethargy, as well as to verbal threats of suicide.

28. A 47-year-old suspect is brought in on a charge of exposing himself to little girls. He sits motionless on the bench, glassily staring ahead or at the floor, and responds in nearly whispered monosyllables when questioned. Correction Officer Cheskis gets the suspect into a holding pen as quickly as possible, thinking, "This is a nice quiet one who will give me no trouble." Correction Officer Cheskis then ignores the prisoner. Officer Cheskis's action is
    (A) correct; the suspect is not young
    (B) incorrect; depressed suspects, especially those who are deeply embarrassed by their own behavior, should be watched for suicide
    (C) correct; the suspect did not say that he was considering suicide
    (D) incorrect; sex offenders always attempt suicide

Answer question 29 solely on the basis of the information below:

A Correction Officer escorting a group of inmates from one location to another within the prison must always walk behind the last inmate. At no time should an inmate be permitted to be behind the escorting Correction Officer.

29. Correction Officer Uyeda is escorting a group of inmates from their cellblock to the recreation yard. As the group marches two by two down the corridor, Inmate Daley turns to Uyeda and says, "I forgot my Frisbee. May I please go back for it?" Correction Officer Uyeda replies, "I'm sorry. You'll have to play with something else today and remember your Frisbee tomorrow." Officer Uyeda's response is

    (A) appropriate; a prisoner going back to his cell would break up the neat double-file line

    (B) inappropriate; Frisbee is an approved activity and should not be forbidden

    (C) appropriate; upon returning to the group, Daley would be behind Correction Officer Uyeda

    (D) inappropriate; a Correction Officer should not refuse a reasonable request when it is so politely made

Answer question 30 solely on the basis of the information below:

All visitors to inmates must be checked electronically and visually before being admitted to the visiting area. This rule means that every visitor must pass through metal detectors, open all handbags and packages, and submit to a pat down.

30. On a bitterly cold day, Mrs. Ramirez comes with her baby, Luisa, to visit her husband, Inmate Ramirez. Mrs. Ramirez carries the baby through the metal detectors and permits Correction Officer Perry to search her handbag and the gift parcel she is bringing. Correction Officer Perry also pats Mrs. Ramirez down, but when he asks her to unwrap the baby from the blankets in which it is swaddled, she complains that it is too cold and the baby will get sick. Correction Officer Perry waves Mrs. Ramirez into the visiting area. Correction Officer Perry's action is

    (A) proper, a duty of a peace officer is to protect the health of the public

    (B) improper; babies are notorious smugglers

    (C) proper; Mrs. Ramirez was otherwise so cooperative that surely her concern for her baby's health is genuine

    (D) improper; the rule applies to all visitors, and the baby is a visitor

Base your answers to questions 31 and 32 solely on the information below:

Subject to the availability of an escort, any prisoner may go to the prison library during an unscheduled period to research precedents to his or her own case and to prepare a defense. The Correction Officer assigned as librarian may assist prisoners in locating appropriate materials and may instruct inmates in the use of the books and microfilm. The librarian/Correction Officer may not suggest an actual defense, nor may the Correction Officer assist in preparation of papers.

31. Inmate Lisa feels that her court-appointed attorney did not represent her case adequately and is planning to prepare her own appeal. She approaches the librarian, Correction Officer Stavrou, and asks which volumes to consult with reference to illegal search and seizure and

inadmissible evidence. Officer Stavrou replies, "I am not permitted to choose books for you."
Correction Officer Stavrou's response is

(A) correct; choosing books would be helping with the defense

(B) incorrect; choosing books is assisting in locating appropriate materials

(C) correct; if Correction Officer Stavrou does not know which books would be most helpful, he should not make any recommendation

(D) incorrect; Officer Stavrou should have suggested sources that deal with inadequate representation

32. Correction Officer Ford, who has been assigned to the prison library, notices that Inmate Eiss is struggling to prepare an appeal after conviction for state tax fraud. Officer Ford recognizes that Inmate Eiss firmly understands the law involved and the concepts necessary to his own defense, but Eiss is expressing himself poorly. Officer Ford sits down with Eiss and proceeds to rewrite large portions of a lengthy document supporting Eiss's position. Officer Ford's action is

(A) appropriate; Eiss knows exactly what he wants to say but needs help getting it on paper

(B) inappropriate; a Correction Officer is not permitted to assist in the preparation of appeal papers

(C) appropriate; Eiss understands the law so well it is obvious he is innocent

(D) inappropriate; other inmates will realize that Correction Officer Ford is a good writer and will make too many demands on her time

Use the information in the paragraph below to answer 33 through 35

"A male between the ages of 16 and 30, convicted of a felony, who has not heretofore been convicted of a crime punishable by imprisonment in a state prison, may, in the discretion of the trial court, be sentenced to imprisonment in the state reformatory. Where a male person between the ages of 16 and 21 is convicted of a felony, or where the term of imprisonment of a male convict for a felony is fixed by the trial court at one year or less, the court may direct the convict to be imprisoned in a county penitentiary, instead of a state prison, or in the county jail located in the county where sentence is imposed."

33. Harry, age 32, has been convicted of a felony and has been sentenced to a term of 11 months.

(A) Harry must serve his term in a state prison.

(B) The court may sentence Harry to the state reformatory.

(C) Harry must serve his term in either the county penitentiary or the county jail.

(D) The court may direct that Harry serve at a state prison, the county penitentiary, or the county jail.

34. Mark, age 20, recently released from state prison after serving time for a felony committed when he was 16, has just been convicted of another felony.

(A) Mark must serve his new term in a state prison.

(B) Mark may not serve his term at the state reformatory.

(C) Mark must serve his term at the county penitentiary.

(D) Mark may serve his term in any one of the following: state penitentiary, county penitentiary, state reformatory, or county jail.

35. George, age 27, has just been convicted for his first crime and has been sentenced to a term of four to seven years.

    (A) George must serve his term in a state prison.

    (B) George may be sentenced to either state prison or the state reformatory.

    (C) George may serve his time in a state prison or in the county penitentiary but not in the state reformatory.

    (D) George may serve his sentence at a state prison or at the county jail of the county in which he is sentenced.

Base your answer to question 36 solely on the information below:

Inmates' families often travel great distances at personal expense and under conditions of physical hardship in order to visit with inmates. Correction Officers should, therefore, try to insure that visits are satisfying and productive for both inmate and visitor, while maintaining all prison rules and regulations.

36. Inmate Thompkins' husband has traveled six hours by bus to visit with his wife at the women's prison. Mr. Thompkins enters the visiting area, which is posted with "No Smoking" signs, and lights up a cigarette. Correction Officer Bradley approaches Mr. Thompkins and says, "Smoking is not permitted here. Please put out your cigarette or I will have to ask you to leave." Correction Officer Bradley's action is

    (A) appropriate; only people with legitimate business at the prison are permitted to smoke there

    (B) inappropriate; Mr. Thompkins is disobeying the rule and should be ejected at once

    (C) appropriate; Officer Bradley is doing his best to permit the visit to proceed and yet to have the rules obeyed

    (D) inappropriate; after Mr. Thompkins' long trip, the cigarette will relax him and will make the visit more productive and satisfying

Answer questions 37 and 38 solely on the basis of the information below:

Between the hours of 9 p.m. and 6 a.m. all prisoners must be securely locked into their cells. Life-threatening emergencies such as sudden acute illness of an inmate or fire in the facility constitute legitimate reasons for suspension of this rule.

37. At 9:25 p.m. Correction Officer Mohan receives a telephone call from Veronica Lake, attorney for Inmate Robert Kim. Ms. Lake has an important matter that she would like to discuss with her client before his court appearance, which is scheduled for 10 a.m. tomorrow, and asks that he be brought to the telephone. Correction Officer Mohan tells Ms. Lake that it is past lockup time and Inmate Kim must remain in his cell. Officer Mohan's action is

    (A) correct; need for attorney-client communication is not a life-threatening situation

    (B) incorrect; Inmate Kim may be facing the death penalty if his attorney does not have the information to represent him properly

    (C) correct; all requests for attorney-client contact outside of visiting hours must be made in writing

    (D) incorrect; the attorney-client privilege, since it is constitutionally guaranteed, overrides prison rules

38. At 1:15 a.m. a small fire, probably electrical in origin, breaks out in the guard tower at the southwest corner of the prison yard. Upon learning of this fire, the Correction Officers on duty in cell block B in the northeast wing of the prison rouse all the inmates and march them two by two into the recreation yard. This action by the Correction Officers is

    (A) appropriate; fire is a life-threatening situation

    (B) inappropriate; the inmates will be in the way of the firefighters if they are in the yard

    (C) appropriate; two by two is an orderly manner by which to move inmates and prevent panic

    (D) inappropriate; a small fire in the southwest guard tower does not threaten the lives of inmates in a northeast cellblock

Answer question 39 solely on the basis of the information below:

Correction Officers must scrupulously avoid favoritism or even the appearance of favoritism among inmates.

39. Inmate Zenkel has thick, waist-length, flaming red hair. Zenkel requests Correction Officer Plunkett to issue him an extra towel for drying his hair. Correction Officer Plunkett denies this request. Officer Plunkett's refusal is

    (A) proper; men in prison should not have long hair

    (B) improper; if Zenkel's hair is not dried properly, he may catch cold and in turn infect other inmates

    (C) proper; giving an extra towel to Zenkel might be interpreted as favoritism by other inmates

    (D) improper; Zenkel is likely to lodge a discrimination complaint

Base your answer to question 40 solely on the information below:

Inmates are entitled to prompt, appropriate medical care for all legitimate illnesses or injuries. A Correction Officer is responsible for securing medical care for inmates who require it but may deny care to an inmate who is obviously faking it. A Correction Officer must be wary of denying care without just cause.

40. Inmate Torbert approaches Correction Officer Popovich and complains of a severe toothache. Torbert demands to be taken to the dentist at once. Officer Popovich knows that Torbert has a full set of dentures. Nevertheless, Popovich arranges for a visit to the dentist within the hour. Officer Popovich's action is

    (A) appropriate; Popovich is not a dentist, and the mouth pain could come from a source other than teeth

    (B) inappropriate; it is impossible to have a toothache with no teeth

    (C) appropriate; inmates may be tempted to withhold reporting illnesses if they expect to be ridiculed

    (D) inappropriate; clearly Torbert is trying to get out of the day's assignments

Wednesday Morning Prisoner Movement

Location	# of inmates at 7 a.m.	movement	8 a.m.	9 a.m.	10 a.m.	11 a.m.	noon
Cellblock A	52	in	7	24	46	22	13
		out	28	31	20	37	23
Cellblock B	60	in	5	15	35	25	21
		out	32	40	21	39	35
Cellblock C	74	in	4	28	28	36	30
		out	30	52	47	28	40
Receiving Room	12	in	21	17	8	10	4
		out	12	15	9	21	9
In Court or In Transit	0	leave	20	0	0	0	13
		return	0	0	0	0	7
Sick Call	0	in	21	3	1	7	2
		out	0	16	2	7	5
Hospital (off premises)	9	in	0	3	0	2	0
		out	4	1	0	1	0
Recreation Yard	0	in	0	80	80	80	0
		out	0	0	80	80	80
Wood Shop	0	in	28	30	34	34	0
		out	0	28	30	34	34
Kitchen	0	in	16	48	48	62	0
		out	0	16	48	48	62
Released or Transferred	0	out only	5	3	12	8	0

Note: Prisoners do not necessarily return to their cells between activities.

Base your answers to questions 41 through 48 solely on the information in the chart detailing prisoner movement. "In" refers to movement into the named location; "out" refers to movement out of that location.

41. At which hour could the greatest number of inmates be found in their cells?

(A) 7

(B) 9

(C) 11

(D) 12

42. How many new inmates entered the prison this morning?

(A) 44

(B) 60

(C) 72

(D) 77

43. How many inmates were off the premises at noon?

    (A) 26
    (B) 34
    (C) 54
    (D) 62

44. At which hour were the fewest inmates working in the kitchen?

    (A) 9
    (B) 10
    (C) 11
    (D) 12

45. How many prisoners could be found in Cellblock A at 10 a.m.?

    (A) 50
    (B) 65
    (C) 77
    (D) 129

46. How many prisoners spent more than one-half day in court?

    (A) 6
    (B) 13
    (C) 20
    (D) 27

47. Approximately what percent of the on-premises inmates participated in recreational activities this morning?

    (A) 65%
    (B) 75%
    (C) 82%
    (D) 100%

48. How many prisoners were moved out of their cells at the hour at which the greatest number were moved from their cells?

    (A) 98
    (B) 104
    (C) 123
    (D) 132

Answer question 49 solely on the basis of the information below:

The parole board carefully looks over a prisoner's file when considering that prisoner for parole. Since the file is crucial to the board's decision, it is very important that all notations in the file be clear and complete.

49. At 3:12 p.m. on Thursday, June 11, correction Officer Bodenheim observes Inmate Carlucci taking a swift kick at Inmate Otten's left shin. Bodenheim then observes Inmate Otten giving Inmate Carlucci a hard punch to the right jaw that sends Carlucci heavily to the ground. Correction Officer Bodenheim writes in Carlucci's file: "Thursday, June 11, 3:12 p.m.: Carlucci kicked Inmate Otten." He writes in Otten's file: "Thursday, June 11, 3:12 p.m.: Otten punched Inmate Carlucci in the jaw and knocked him down." These notations are

    (A) appropriate; they tell what each inmate did

    (B) inappropriate; Otten's file should include the provocation for his behavior

    (C) appropriate; the notations carefully detail date and time

    (D) inappropriate; the notation in Carlucci's file should specify that Carlucci kicked Otten's left shin

Base your answer to question 50 solely on the information below:

1 p.m. and 1 a.m. are official inmate-counting times. At the 1 p.m. count, each inmate must stand inside his or her cell at the front gate and must respond with his or her name when addressed by the Correction Officer. At the 1 a.m. count, the Correction Officer must be satisfied that the inmate is in the cell. If the Correction Officer cannot see the inmate's face or if the Correction Officer cannot visibly see that the inmate is breathing or cannot hear sleep sounds from the inmate, the officer must enter the cell to be certain that the inmate is in the bed.

50. Correction Officer Holter is making the 1 p.m. inmate count. She arrives at the cell of Inmate Petroski and finds the inmate lying face down on the cot. Holter says, "Petroski, stand up and be counted." The inmate replies, "Go away, I'm too tired to get up." Officer Holter sharply repeats, "Get up right now," and remains in front of Inmate Petroski's cell. Officer Holter's action is

   (A) correct; the rules require inmates to stand at the 1 p.m. check

   (B) incorrect; there is no question as to the presence or the identity of the inmate

   (C) correct; punishment of inmates requires that they not be allowed to lie down when tired

   (D) incorrect; Holter should go into the cell to check on Petroski's breathing

Base your answers to questions 51 and 52 solely on the information below:

Sick call is a favorite diversion of inmates. If permitted, some inmates would demand daily medical care. A Correction Officer must use some personal judgment in weeding out chronic complainers from the truly ill. Medical care must not be denied when justified.

51. While making a routine cell check, Correction Officer Djerf smells vomit and sees Inmate Constantine doubled over the lavatory. Constantine appears to be very pale and shaky. Djerf says, "Come on Constantine, let's go see the nurse." Inmate Constantine replies, "No, no, I'll be okay. I just have an upset stomach." Djerf persists and forcibly escorts Constantine to sick call. Djerf's action is

   (A) proper; the smell will soon make other inmates ill

   (B) improper; the inmate has not asked to go to sick call

   (C) proper; all apparently ill inmates should receive medical evaluation and care

   (D) improper; Constantine probably forced himself to vomit to get attention

52. Inmate Wright was received on the cellblock only yesterday. At the medical check upon intake, Wright received a clean bill of health. This morning Wright is refusing to go to his first scheduled activity, claiming he has a migraine headache. Correction Officer Paik says, "The doctor said you were healthy just yesterday. We don't allow stayabeds here. Up and out." Officer Paik's action is

   (A) correct; Wright is not sick

   (B) incorrect; Wright has not been in the prison long enough to establish a reputation for begging off work detail

   (C) correct; Wright's medical report says nothing about migraines

   (D) incorrect; Wright has a headache and should be allowed to lie down

Base your answer to question 53 solely on the information below:

All packages addressed to inmates must be opened and inspected for contraband before delivery to the inmates. If a Correction Officer discovers an item of contraband in a package, the entire contents of the package must be withheld. The contents of the package must be itemized on an inventory list in triplicate, and copies of the inventory must be delivered to the inmate, placed in the inmate's file, and kept with the prison records.

53. A package arrives at the prison addressed to Inmate Eberle. Correction Officer Ficklen opens the package and shakes each item enclosed. As Ficklen flips through the pages of a crossword puzzle book, a small note containing details of an escape plan falls out. Officer Ficklen makes out a list in triplicate of the contents of the package, including on the list the crossword puzzle book and the escape plan. Ficklen gives a copy of the list and the items of clothing from the package to Inmate Eberle, withholding the escape plan and the crossword puzzle book. Correction Officer Ficklen's action is

   (A) appropriate; Ficklen made a complete inventory list in triplicate and gave a copy to the inmate

   (B) inappropriate; the crossword puzzle book was harmless and should have been given to the inmate

   (C) appropriate; the clothing in the package was badly needed and was totally unrelated to the contraband

   (D) inappropriate; Ficklen should have confiscated all of the contents of the package

The four paragraphs below are descriptions of four personality types often attributed to youthful offenders. Use these descriptions to answer questions 54 through 59.

"Personality W"	These offenders are lazy and show a general lack of interest in most things around them. Their actions are childish, and often we would consider them as helpless. They are weak and, although they lose their tempers, they are not violent. Frequently they seem preoccupied and may give the impression of being "out of it."
"Personality X"	Offenders in this class feel very guilty and genuinely sorry for their actions, but they are quite likely to repeat the same thing tomorrow. Despite being very selective about their friendships, they usually are willing to talk about their problems. These individuals frequently have nervous or anxious ways. They may impress you as feeling sad or unhappy much of the time.
"Personality Y"	This type of offender is very hostile and aggressive, showing little, if any, concern for the welfare of others. These people have a strong need to create excitement since for them things quickly get too boring. Attempts to control them verbally are not very effective. They are frequently both verbally and physically aggressive. Without qualms, they will lie and manipulate others for their own gain.
"Personality Z"	These individuals have usually been involved in gang activities and demonstrate a high degree of loyalty to that peer group. They are relatively unconcerned about adults because their pleasure is obtained by going along with their friends. Except for their delinquent acts, these people appear quite normal. They are able to get along reasonably well in correctional institutions but generally revert to their prior behavior after release.

54. A counselor described a young offender, Jack K., as follows: "Was nervous during our talk, bit his nails, looked sad and worried, although attentive. Last week he told me he felt 'real bad' about handing in his work report late, and I could see that he did. But the very next day, he was late again with his report." These comments best fit the description of Personality

(A) W

(B) X

(C) Y

(D) Z

55. A counselor described a young offender, Edward F., as follows: "Prefers the company of his former gang members. This is his second time at the institution. He probably won't be able to steer clear of involvement when he gets out again. Gets along with fellow offenders, appears normal, but won't talk about his problems." These comments most nearly fit the description of Personality

(A) W

(B) X

(C) Y

(D) Z

56. A counselor described a young offender, Arthur B., as follows: "Seems to be melancholy for long periods of time. Regrets deeply that he hurt another youngster rather badly in a gang fight before being sentenced. Has only one or two friends." These comments most nearly fit the description of Personality

(A) W

(B) X

(C) Y

(D) Z

57. A counselor described a young offender, George H., as follows: "Didn't seem to care when I suggested that he didn't show enough interest in our activities. When in the shops he tends to stand off on one side, thinking instead of actively working. He's got a temper but doesn't start fights." These comments most nearly fit the description of Personality

(A) W

(B) X

(C) Y

(D) Z

58. A counselor described a young offender, Charles D., as follows: "He is ready to argue at the slightest provocation. Once when he beat another youth he said he was not sorry for what he did, and he did exactly the same thing the next day, watching almost maliciously for my reaction. He seems to really want only his own way." These comments most nearly fit the description of Personality

(A) W

(B) X

(C) Y

(D) Z

59. A counselor described a young offender, Larry M., as follows: "Admitted that he had been bullying some younger residents for 'kicks,' then told me to mind my own business. Kept interrupting me and continued to do so even when I asked him to stop." These comments most nearly fit the description of Personality

(A) W

(B) X

(C) Y

(D) Z

Base your answer to question 60 solely on the information below:

If a prisoner has committed a serious infraction of prison rules, the prisoner may be disciplined by being placed in solitary confinement. A prisoner in solitary confinement receives two meals a day taken alone in the cell, is permitted one-half hour of daily exercise alone in a small yard, may receive two letters a week, and is denied visitors. However, a prisoner in solitary may consult with his or her attorney between the hours of 2 p.m. and 4 p.m. each day.

60. Inmate Sawyer has served one week of a two-week confinement in solitary. Sawyer's wife and two small children arrive at the prison to visit Inmate Sawyer. Correction Officer Finn informs Mrs. Sawyer that Inmate Sawyer is in solitary and cannot have visitors. Correction Officer Finn then informs Sawyer that his family has come to visit but that he cannot see them. Sawyer requests an emergency meeting with his attorney. Attorney Thatcher arrives at 2:15 p.m. and asks to take Inmate Sawyer's wife and children in with him to see Sawyer. Correction Officer Finn permits Attorney Thatcher to bring the children but bars Mrs. Sawyer. Officer Finn's action is

    (A) correct; children are not considered prohibited visitors

    (B) incorrect; attorneys and visitors are not permitted at the same time

    (C) correct; the attorney-client privilege allows attorneys to bring to prisoners whatever or whomever they please

    (D) incorrect; solitary confinement is a punishment, and part of that punishment is denial of visitors except for the attorney

Answer questions 61 and 62 solely on the basis of the information below:

Physical restraint of prisoners' bodies should be held to a minimum. However, physical restraints in the form of handcuffs and leg irons are required whenever prisoners are being transferred from an institution to any other place. Physical restraints should also be used when a prisoner's behavior threatens the life or safety of any human being.

61. Inmates Tinker and Evers are both scheduled to appear for trial in the same courthouse on the same day. Correction Officer Chance handcuffs both Tinker and Evers and clamps a set of leg irons onto Tinker's right leg and Evers' left. This action by Chance is

    (A) appropriate; the prisoners cannot run away when shackled together

    (B) inappropriate; prisoners are no threat to life or safety when riding the bus

    (C) appropriate; handcuffs constitute good weapons for beating each other over the head

    (D) inappropriate; the rule requires a minimum of restraint, which implies that either handcuffs or leg irons should be adequate

62. Correction Officer Kaplan, on routine patrol in the cellblock, comes upon Inmate Serran thrashing wildly on the floor of his two-inmate cell, banging his head and flailing his arms and legs. Kaplan immediately calls for assistance, and Officer Buffamonte joins her with a straitjacket. Together they restrain Serran and transport him to the infirmary. This action by Correction Officer Kaplan is

    (A) correct; the inmate might have seriously injured Kaplan

    (B) incorrect; the inmate was in no way a threat to the life or safety of his cellmate

    (C) correct; the inmate might have hurt himself badly if allowed to continue

    (D) incorrect; the inmate should have been handcuffed at once

Answer question 63 solely on the basis of the information below:

A Correction Officer being called to a disciplinary hearing on any charges is entitled to request the personnel office to produce all documents that the Correction Officer feels could bolster his or her defense.

63. Correction Officer Blakelee's new supervisor has placed charges alleging that Blakelee has reported late on two occasions within the supervisor's three-week tenure. Blakelee's attorney requests Blakelee's attendance records for all seven years of her employment at this prison and copies of all performance reviews. Correction Officer Arthur of the prison personnel office readily produces the attendance records for all seven years but releases only two years' performance reviews. This action by Correction Officer Arthur is

    (A) appropriate; performance reviews are irrelevant to a charge of lateness
    (B) inappropriate; Blakelee is entitled to any documents that she feels will be helpful
    (C) appropriate; if Blakelee persists on being late, she should be disciplined
    (D) inappropriate; two years' worth of attendance records would be adequate

Answer question 64 solely on the basis of the information below:

Prisoners facing the death penalty are entitled to a last meal of their choice. The request for the last meal is to be honored, no matter how bizarre.

64. Inmate O'Day has been convicted of the sex murder of a child and has received the death penalty. All appeals have been exhausted, and execution has been scheduled for midnight. The priest has come for O'Day's final confession, and O'Day has requested that his last meal be strictly Kosher. Correction Officer Assatly laughs at this request and suggests that O'Day would be better off with corned beef and cabbage. Officer Assatly's action is

    (A) appropriate; O'Day is Catholic, and there is no reason for the prison to go to the trouble of bringing in a Kosher meal
    (B) inappropriate; O'Day should be permitted to try every possible way to save his soul
    (C) appropriate; an Irishman should be sent off with an Irish dinner
    (D) inappropriate; for the last meal, the prisoner has free choice

Answer question 65 solely on the basis of the information below:

A men's prison is a very macho environment. Any appearance of effeminate behavior on the part of an inmate is likely to subject that inmate to harassment. Overt homosexual behavior may pose a real danger to the safety of homosexual inmates. Correction Officers must be alert to the possibility of antagonism toward homosexuals and must defuse dangerous encounters.

65. Inmate White is a slightly built individual who tends to swing his hips when he walks and who avoids groups of inmates who brag about their sexual prowess. For the most part, other inmates have ignored White in the three months he has been in the cellblock. Last week Inmate Ford was transferred into the cellblock. Ford has no effeminate mannerisms, but he has clearly been attracted to White, and the feeling seems to be mutual. Of course the other inmates have noticed, and all Corrections Officers are on edge. In the exercise yard, Ford sidles up to White and puts his arm around him. Correction Officer Collins bellows, "Hey, you two, stop smooching." Officer Collins' action is

(A) appropriate; homosexual acts are permitted only in private

(B) inappropriate; the officer is calling all the inmates' attention to the couple

(C) appropriate; Collins is warning them to stop before they get hurt

(D) inappropriate; a Correction Officer should not interfere in inmates' private lives

For questions 66 through 70, read both sentences carefully and mark:

(A) if only the first sentence is grammatically correct

(B) if only the second sentence is grammatically correct

(C) if both sentences are grammatically correct

(D) if neither sentence is grammatically correct

66. (1) Once the count has begun, there were no interruptions.

(2) Some things must be decided between the Correction Officers of the institution themselves.

67. (1) There appears to be conditions that encourage accidents in this prison.

(2) When the inmate first come up to the institution, he was in an emotionally disturbed state and required constant supervision.

68. (1) It is a good rule for we Correction Officers to follow.

(2) The change in the rules had a good effect on the morale of the inmates.

69. (1) There are a bed and a washstand in every cell.

(2) I feel bad because Inmate Scott never has visitors.

70. (1) Good morale in a prison is when there are no fights taking place.

(2) By 8 a.m. every inmate must straighten up his cell.

Base your answer to question 71 solely on the information below:

Needless to say, prison inmates are not permitted to possess weapons at any time. To be certain that there are no concealed weapons in the cells, Correction Officers must periodically inspect all cells.

71. At 9 a.m. on Monday, Correction Officer Blumner announces to the inmates of Cellblock D, "We will be doing a weapons check in the cells Tuesday at noon." This action is

(A) proper; inmates will take the weapons out of the cells

(B) improper; the search should not be limited to the cells

(C) proper; inmates should be warned when their privacy will be invaded

(D) improper; more weapons will be confiscated if inmates are not warned to hide them

Base your answer to question 72 solely on the information below:

Prison inmates can be ingenious at fashioning weapons from eating utensils. At the end of the meal, the inmates bus their trays one at a time, and the Correction Officer who receives the trays counts all items on each one. When all the trays have been bused, the Correction Officer counts all cutlery before inmates are dismissed from the dining hall.

72. At the end of breakfast, Correction Officer Vorperian counts the cutlery and finds she is one spoon short. She counts all the inmates in the room, then recounts the spoons. One spoon still appears to be missing. Vorperian announces that no one will leave the room until all the spoons are accounted for. Correction Officers then approach the inmates one by one in an attempt to secure the spoon. The action taken by Officer Vorperian is

    (A) appropriate; no cutlery may leave the dining hall

    (B) inappropriate; a spoon is not a dangerous weapon

    (C) appropriate; the spoon is government property and appears to have been stolen

    (D) inappropriate; Vorperian should have trusted the other Correction Officers to have collected all of the cutlery from the trays

Base your answer to question 73 solely on the information below:

Rehabilitation of offenders is a major function of the prison system. Rehabilitation involves changing attitudes, training in vocational skills, and basic education. Rehabilitation programs tend to be expensive, but they keep inmates productively occupied and may save the public money in the long run.

73. Inmate Mullins, who is facing the death penalty, asks to enroll in a GED preparatory course in order to earn a high school equivalency diploma. Correction Officer Milowe grants this request and assigns Inmate Mullins to a regularly scheduled class. This action by Officer Milowe is

    (A) appropriate; Mullins will never make anything of himself without a high school diploma

    (B) inappropriate; Mullins is about to die and will have no use for a high school diploma

    (C) appropriate; Mullins may learn something useful and will keep busy

    (D) inappropriate; limited funds should not be wasted in educating inmates who have no use for rehabilitation

Use the information in the paragraph below to answer questions 74 and 75.

"Criminal acts are classified according to several standards. One is whether the crime is major or minor. A major offense, such as murder, would be labeled a felony whereas a minor offense, such as reckless driving, would be considered a misdemeanor. Another standard of classification is the specific kind of crime committed. Examples are burglary and robbery, which are terms often used incorrectly by individuals who are not aware of the actual difference as defined by law. A person who breaks into a building to commit a theft or other major crime is guilty of burglary, while robbery is the felonious taking of an individual's property from his person or in his immediate presence by the use of violence or threat. Other common criminal acts with distinct legal definitions are larceny and assault. The unlawful taking of another's property without his consent and with the intent of depriving him belongs to the first classification while a violent attack on someone or an unlawful threat or attempt to do physical harm belongs to the second category."

74. A young woman was threatened at knife point by a criminal who demanded that she give him her pocketbook and gold watch. The woman screamed and the criminal, frightened, ran off without taking anything. According to the information in the above paragraph, the crime committed was

   (A) assault
   (B) robbery
   (C) larceny
   (D) burglary

75. A man who has been asleep on a bus awakes to find that $350 in cash has been taken from him. According to the above passage, he was subjected to

   (A) robbery
   (B) burglary
   (C) larceny
   (D) assault

Base your answer to question 76 solely on the information below:

On a regularly scheduled basis, all inmates are required to attend lectures presented by outside speakers. These lectures are intended to assist with transition back to society and to address such diverse subjects as planning and sticking to a budget, job hunting, and landlord-tenant relations.

76. This week's lecture presented by a public health physician is to be on AIDS prevention and will include a slide presentation of clinical diagrams. Inmate Osborne approaches Correction Officer Nunno and asks to be excused from the AIDS lecture because, "I have a queasy stomach, and besides, my religion doesn't allow me to look at dirty pictures." Correction Officer Nunno denies the request and requires Inmate Osborne to attend the lecture. Officer Nunno's action is

   (A) proper; this sounds like a lame excuse

   (B) improper; freedom of religion is not suspended in prison

   (C) proper; this is a required lecture on an important health topic

   (D) improper; pornography has no place in prison

Base your answer to question 77 solely on the information below:

In order to maintain discipline, a Correction Officer must make it clear that he or she is in charge at all times. Correction Officers must not permit inmates to order them around in any way. On the other hand, a Correction Officer's effectiveness is enhanced by firm, polite leadership.

77. It is 2 a.m. and Correction Officer Karsky is on a catwalk doing regular rounds, keys jangling loudly as he walks. Inmate Connolly shouts from his cell, "Hey, cut the noise and let a guy sleep." Officer Karsky says, "Sorry," and pockets the keys. Officer Karsky's action is

   (A) appropriate; common courtesy is never out of order

   (B) inappropriate; inmates will lose respect if they find that they can get their way so easily

   (C) appropriate; if the Correction Officer is noisy he may miss the sounds of a prison break in progress

   (D) inappropriate: inmates should be kept aware of the officer's presence at all times, and jangling keys make a good reminder

Answer questions 78 through 80 solely on the basis of the information below:

A large proportion of the people who are behind bars are not convicted criminals but people who have been arrested and are being held until their trial in court. Experts have often pointed out that this detention system does not operate fairly. For instance, a person who can afford to pay bail usually will not get locked up. The theory of the bail system is that the person will make sure to show up in court when he is supposed to since he knows that otherwise he will forfeit his bail—he will lose the money he put up. Sometimes a person who can show that he or she is a stable citizen with a job and a family will be released on "personal recognizance" (without bail). The result is that the well-to-do, the employed, and the family man or woman can often avoid the detention system. The people who do wind up in detention tend to be the poor, the unemployed, the single, and the young.

78. Bartels and Murillo are picked up as they run from a bank carrying sacks of money, and both are charged with armed robbery. Bail is set. Bartels is able to raise bail and is released. Murillo is unable to raise bail and is held in detention. This result is

   (A) fair; a person who is able to raise bail obviously must be innocent

   (B) unfair; it has no relation to guilt or innocence

   (C) fair; the law should be tougher on poor people than on the rich

   (D) unfair; the robbers deserve equal punishment

79. Marlene Rogers, a divorcee with two sons aged eight and ten, is charged with prostitution. Rogers is a homeowner and is regularly employed as a bookkeeper at a business in the community. Rogers is released on "personal recognizance." This means that

   (A) the judge knows Rogers well

   (B) Rogers does not have to show up for trial

   (C) Rogers has no record of previous convictions

   (D) Rogers does not need to put up bail

80. Barney Tripp, an unemployed, single, homeless 19-year-old, is in detention awaiting trial on a misdemeanor charge. He complains bitterly to Correction Officer Lucas that he is an innocent victim of the system and is being treated as a common criminal. Correction Officer Lucas responds, "If you are in jail, then jail is where you belong." Officer Lucas' statement is

   (A) correct; the American system of justice means justice for all

   (B) incorrect; there are some innocent people who are in jail awaiting trial

   (C) correct; everyone who cannot raise bail must belong in jail

   (D) incorrect; Tripp should have been released on personal recognizance

Base your answers to questions 81 through 87 solely on the information in the paragraph and the table below:

Coordination of operations within the entire prison system entails encoding each prison inmate along a number of dimensions and entering the code into the mainframe computer at central corrections headquarters. Each inmate on intake is assigned a 10-digit number. The first four identify the inmate by name. Digits five and six refer to the county of jurisdiction. Digits seven and eight designate the offense for which the inmate was convicted. The last two digits identify the institution in which the inmate is first incarcerated. Subsequent institutional transfers are indicated by adding a hyphen and additional digits after the tenth digit.

Identification Codes

County		Conviction		Institution	
Ames	20	Armed Robbery	07	Allenby Prison	38
Cork	41	Burglary	76	Bates Hospital	13
Kent	62	Grand Larceny	43	Crofton Prison	29
Lime	03	Manslaughter One	92	Harrod Juvenile Facility	66
Tara	55	Murder Three	25	Prouse Prison	74
Wall	18	Rape	11	Tarton Correctional Institute	81

Inmates Currently Being Tracked

Burns	4273034381
Chen	6842180738
Diorio	8256627666
Fenton	7311181129-13-74
Flood	6100209238
Greenberg	3987624329
Herrmann	2361182523-38
Howe	8663551138-29-74
Jones	0307417681
O'Malley	9805201138
Rivera	5683181166
Williams	5386037681-29

81. The county is which the greatest number of violent criminals was convicted is

(A) Wall (C) Tara

(B) Ames (D) Lime

82. The inmate who is serving a sentence on conviction for murder is

(A) Jones (C) Herrmann

(B) Burns (D) Greenberg

83. The inmate who was convicted for armed robbery was sent to

(A) Bates Hospital (C) Croften Prison

(B) Allenby Prison (D) Tarton Correctional Institute

84. Inmate 8663

(A) is under age 18 (C) is serving a sentence for armed robbery

(B) has spent time in the hospital (D) began his prison career in Allenby Prison

85. Of the following inmates, the youngest is probably
    (A) 5386
    (C) 9805
    (B) 5683
    (D) 0307

86. If upon appeal Inmate Chen's conviction is overturned, but Chen is tried and convicted on a new charge so that her new number is 6842187638, the new conviction will be on a charge of
    (A) grand larceny
    (B) armed robbery
    (C) burglary
    (D) manslaughter one

87. The facility to which violent criminals do not seem to be assigned is
    (A) Tarton Correctional Institute
    (B) Bates Hospital
    (C) Crofton Prison
    (D) Harrod Juvenile Facility

Base your answer to question 88 solely on the information below:

Correction Officers are required to uphold the Constitution. The Constitution provides that convicted felons be deprived of the right to vote in federal elections.

88. Inmate Rushneck, who is currently undergoing trial on a charge of homicide, has sent for an absentee ballot for the presidential election. Correction Officer Semmes refuses to deliver the ballot to Rushneck. Officer Semmes' action is
    (A) appropriate; Rushneck is being tried on a felony charge
    (B) inappropriate; Rushneck has not been convicted of anything
    (C) appropriate; Rushneck's voting might interfere with the trial
    (D) inappropriate; Rushneck might be innocent

Base your answer to question 89 solely on the information below:

The privacy of the confessional extends to clergy-inmate communications within the prison walls. While a clergyman should counsel and encourage an inmate to tell the whole story to the authorities, the clergyman is under no obligation to divulge any information.

89. Paul Jernigan, in detention pending trial, asks to see a priest. Jernigan gives the priest information which could affect the outcome of the trial, and the priest urges Jernigan to volunteer this information to the prosecutor. Jernigan tells the priest that he will have to think about it. As the priest leaves, Correction Officer Potamkin asks, "Did he confess? What did he tell you?" The priest declines to give any information to Potamkin. Potamkin angrily tells the priest, "You are obstructing justice. Because of you a guilty person may go free and an innocent person may be punished. It is your duty as a priest to protect the innocent and to see that justice is done." This action by Correction Officer Potamkin is

(A) appropriate; the suspect should not be permitted to protect someone else by taking the rap himself

(B) inappropriate; the Correction Officer has no proof that the suspect gave incriminating information

(C) appropriate; much taxpayer money will be saved if the suspect pleads guilty and thereby avoids a costly trial

(D) inappropriate; the priest has a right to remain silent

Answer question 90 solely on the basis of the information below:

Inmates assigned to maximum security facilities are considered the most desperate individuals and are deemed extremely dangerous to each other, to prison personnel, and to society at large. These prisoners must be controlled with extra surveillance. Any reasonable means must be used to prevent these prisoners from escaping.

90. Correction Officer Urinyi, standing guard at 4 a.m. in a watch tower at the corner of the prison compound, senses activity below. Looking down, Officer Urinyi sees that two inmates have tunneled beneath the wall and are inching their way on their bellies towards the woods beyond the open space. Urinyi recognizes the inmates as Hammer and Gruber. Officer Urinyi takes careful aim and shoots first the forward escapee and then the one closer to the prison walls. Urinyi then sounds a general alarm. This action by Correction Officer Urinyi is

(A) correct; she has effectively foiled the escape

(B) incorrect; the escapees are flat on their bellies and pose no danger to anyone

(C) correct; Urinyi recognizes the prisoners and know that they are dangerous criminals

(D) incorrect; the alarm will alert other inmates to the existence of the escape tunnel

Answer question 91 solely on the basis of the information below:

Under no circumstances may drugs be used in the prison. If an inmate is found with drugs in his or her possession, the drugs must be confiscated and the inmate must be disciplined. Any person attempting to bring drugs into a prison is guilty of a misdemeanor, even if the quantity of drugs is within the legal limit for individual possession.

91. Betsy Barker has come to the prison to visit her best friend, Inmate Troy. At the entry to the prison, Correction Officer Fagoo searches Barker's pocketbook. In the pocketbook Officer Fagoo sees an open package of cigarettes. Fagoo takes the package of cigarettes from the pocketbook and sniffs them, detecting an odor of marijuana. Fagoo confiscates the cigarettes and arrests Betsy Barker. This action by Correction Officer Fagoo is

(A) proper; Barker is smuggling drugs into the prison

(B) improper; the cigarettes are Barker's personal property

(C) proper; anyone bringing drugs into the prison is guilty of a crime

(D) improper; the officer should have held the cigarettes for Barker while Barker visited her friend

Use the information in the paragraph below to answer questions 92 through 95.

"The success or failure of a criminal prosecution usually depends upon the evidence presented to the court. Evidence may be divided into three major classifications: direct evidence, circumstantial evidence, and real evidence. Evidence must also be admissible, that is, material and relevant. An eyewitness account of a criminal act is direct evidence. Where an eyewitness does not have immediate experience, but reasonably infers what happened, circumstantial evidence is offered. Real evidence comprises objects introduced at a trial to prove or disprove a fact. For example, a gun, fingerprints, or bloodstains are real evidence. Real evidence may be direct or circumstantial. Evidence is immaterial if it is unimportant to the trial. For example, if someone is being tried for larceny of a crate of oranges, it is immaterial that the oranges were yellow in color. Evidence is irrelevant or immaterial if it does not prove the truth of a fact at issue. For example, if a murder had been committed with a bow and arrow, it is irrelevant to show that the defendant was well-acquainted with firearms."

92. Jones and Smith go into a room together and close the door. Richards stands outside the door and sees Jones and Smith go in. A shot is heard and Smith rushes out with a smoking gun in his hand. Richards rushes into the room and finds Jones lying on the floor, dead. Richards did not see Smith fire the shot. At Smith's trial for murdering Jones, Richards tells the court what he saw and heard. Richard's story is

(A) inadmissible evidence   (C) irrelevant evidence

(B) real evidence   (D) circumstantial evidence

93. In Smith's trial for murdering Jones, in the above case, Smith's attorney could prove that Smith was an excellent student of history in high school. Such evidence would most likely be classified as

(A) real and material   (C) immaterial and irrelevant

(B) direct and relevant   (D) circumstantial and admissible

94. A Smith's trial for murdering Jones proceeds, the prosecutor proves that Smith owned the gun that killed Jones. Of the following, such evidence is most likely

(A) direct   (C) irrelevant

(B) inadmissible   (D) material

95. As Smith's trial for murdering Jones continues, the prosecutor introduces a surprise witness, Rogers. Rogers says that from an apartment across the street he looked into the window of the room where Jones and Smith were and actually saw Smith point a gun at Jones and shoot him, after which Jones fell to the floor and Smith rushed out of the room. Rogers' story is best described as

(A) real and circumstantial evidence   (C) circumstantial and admissible evidence

(B) direct and relevant evidence   (D) relevant and real evidence

Answer question 96 solely on the basis of the information below:

The goal of imprisonment is to release a rehabilitated individual to society. Rehabilitation includes modification of attitudes and behavior and preparation for earning a livelihood. The educational programs in the prison include academic and vocational programs. Inmates who are considered unsuited to the programs they have chosen may be denied access.

96. Inmate Sarahn is serving a six-year sentence for assault with a deadly weapon. Two years remain to his term. Sarahn's service in this prison has been marked by his short temper and his frequent involvement in fights. Sarahn has expressed a desire to learn to be a barber and would like to join the class that is taught in the prison. Correction Officer Teplitski refuses to admit Sarahn to the class. Officer Teplitski's action is

    (A) appropriate; a violent individual should not be offered easy access to scissors and razors

    (B) inappropriate; the classroom is the ideal place to teach proper use of tools and instruments

    (C) appropriate; not enough time remains in Sarahn's term for proper training

    (D) in appropriate; Sarahn should be permitted to learn a trade so that he need not resort to crime to earn a living

Answer question 97 solely on the basis of the information below:

Correction Officers must maintain complete and accurate files on all inmates. Recordkeeping includes entering all noticeable behavior by an inmate, both exceptionally good behavior and violations of rules. The record should include the date and nature of the behavior, circumstances under which the behavior was observed, and the action taken—whether praise or discipline was offered.

97. Inmate Gallagher, who has generally been an unremarkable prisoner, approaches Correction Officer Crown with a request to make telephone calls beyond the permitted number. When Correction Officer Crown hesitates to grant this favor, Gallagher holds out two $10 bills to Crown. Crown refuses to take the money and denies Gallagher permission to make the excess phone calls. Gallagher returns to assigned activities, and Crown ignores the incident. This action by Crown is

    (A) proper; a Correction Officer should never accept bribes

    (B) improper; the phone calls must have been very important to Gallagher

    (C) proper; permitting an inmate to make calls in excess of the rules is worth more than $20

    (D) improper; Crown should have recorded the attempted bribe in Gallagher's file

Base your answer to question 98 solely on the information below:

Correction Officers are subject to stress and danger in their daily work and so develop a strong sense of internal loyalty and camaraderie with one another. Correction Officers will readily spring to the defense of their colleagues and, of course, expect the same in return. At the same time, Correction Officers are peace officers and are sworn to uphold the law.

98. Correction Officer Floyd has become aware that a cook and three Correction Officers have been smuggling cocaine into the prison and selling it to inmates at great profit to themselves. Two of the Correction Officers involved are very good friends of Floyd. Floyd observes the smuggling operation and is certain that his assessment of what is going on is correct. Correction Officer Floyd then reports this activity to his supervisor. This action by Officer Floyd is

    (A) appropriate; if his friends had any loyalty to Floyd, they would have cut him in

    (B) inappropriate; Floyd should have reported only the cook and not his fellow officers

    (C) appropriate; illegal activity must be stopped by the authorities

    (D) inappropriate; other Correction Officers in the prison will lose respect for Floyd if he betrays the wrongdoers

Answer question 99 solely on the basis of the information below:

Once convicted and imprisoned, an inmate forfeits a variety of rights and privileges, chief among them his or her personal liberty. However, all inmates retain certain basic human and civil rights that may be suspended only when safety demands.

99. Inmates Ng and Ie are both serving long terms in a maximum security facility. The prison service of both inmates has been unremarkable; neither has been involved in any incident worthy of notice or discipline. Both inmates happen to be conversant in the same foreign language and spend a great deal of time speaking to one another in this language that is unintelligible to everyone on the prison staff. Correction Officer Perry orders Ng and Ie to speak only English. When they continue to communicate in their own tongue, Perry punishes each with four days in solitary confinement. This action by Officer Perry is

(A) appropriate; the inmates could have been plotting an uprising

(B) inappropriate; the inmates gave no indication that they were endangering anyone's safety

(C) appropriate; the inmates were denying the Correction Officer's civil rights

(D) inappropriate; freedom of speech must never be curtailed in any way

Answer question 100 solely on the basis of the information below:

Every prisoner has the right to participate in preparation of his or her own appeal. The prison library is well stocked with law books appropriate for prisoners' use, and the Correction Officer who serves as librarian is familiar with various sources. The library space is small, so that supervision does not require assignment of too many Correction Officers. Because of space restrictions, only prisoners actively pursuing appeal are permitted use of the library.

100. Inmate Mariani requests permission to use the prison library during a period in which he was scheduled to be in the gym. In the library Mariani chooses a book at random, opens it on the table before him, and proceeds to write personal letters. The librarian, Correction Officer Kane, looks over Mariani's shoulder, sends for an escort, and ejects Mariani from the library. This action by Officer Kane is

(A) appropriate; the purpose of the library is to serve as a quiet haven

(B) inappropriate; Mariani was not using books needed by anyone else

(C) appropriate; inmates are not permitted to use the library to shirk their other assignments

(D) inappropriate; Officer Kane should have helped Mariani find the best books to prepare his appeal

END OF EXAM

ANSWER KEY FOR MODEL EXAMINATION 4

1. B	21. C	41. A	61. A	81. A
2. B	22. D	42. C	62. C	82. C
3. D	23. B	43. D	63. B	83. B
4. B	24. D	44. D	64. D	84. D
5. C	25. A	45. A	65. B	85. B
6. D	26. C	46. B	66. A	86. C
7. A	27. B	47. D	67. D	87. A
8. C	28. B	48. C	68. B	88. B
9. C	29. C	49. B	69. C	89. D
10. A	30. D	50. A	70. B	90. A
11. B	31. B	51. C	71. D	91. C
12. B	32. B	52. B	72. A	92. D
13. C	33. D	53. D	73. C	93. C
14. C	34. B	54. B	74. A	94. D
15. A	35. B	55. D	75. C	95. B
16. D	36. C	56. B	76. C	96. A
17. C	37. A	57. A	77. A	97. D
18. B	38. D	58. C	78. B	98. C
19. D	39. C	59. C	79. D	99. B
20. A	40. A	60. D	80. B	100. A

Explanatory Answers for Model Examination 4

1. **(B)** Beating other inmates so as to extract cigarettes and coffee from them is using violence to intimidate and to gain favors, behavior typical of the gorilla.

2. **(B)** The Receiving Room is a non-smoking area. The fact that Jomes is not on duty is irrelevant.

3. **(D)** The rule clearly says, "Hold on to the badge." The badge is the property of the Correction Department, and Berkey does not have the discretion to let his child play with and possibly lose or break it.

4. **(B)** The attorney-client privilege is inviolate. Anything one says to the other is strictly between the two. The Correction Officer has no right to listen in. If the officer inadvertently overhears anything, he or she has no right to pass it on.

5. **(C)** David Blank is under age 18 and may be admitted as a visitor only if accompanied by an adult.

6. **(D)** The regulation is that all letters must be delivered within 24 hours and that letters should not be opened by Correction Officers. There is no limit to the number of letters that may be delivered.

7. **(A)** The contents of the package are harmless. The regulation permits that packages may be held 48 hours if necessary; it does not require the delay. Sunday is just another workday in the prison; prisoners may have their mail.

8. **(C)** Under the Penal Law, a peace officer is on duty at all times, even when not officially on duty at his or her regular job. Rice was acting properly as a peace officer and so was killed in the line of duty. (Remember that even if you personally disagree you must answer solely on the basis of the information given.)

9. **(C)** There certainly is reason to suspect Pulaski, and investigation is the proper route to take. He cannot be charged and punished simply on the basis of suspicion.

10. **(A)** Death appears to be imminent for Martha's mother, and Martha may visit her in the hospital. It appears from the quotation that Martha may go to the funeral as well and that the state will incur the costs, though family reimbursement is welcome.

11. **(B)** There can be no exceptions to the full-coverage rule. This is a matter of safety for Correction Officers and inmates.

12. **(B)** A Correction Officer should never stoop to the behavior or the language of the inmates. The Correction Officer is a professional and must serve as a role model. A Correction Officer who cannot stand insults should not be in this business.

13. **(C)** The action seems destined to restore order by eliminating opportunity for further food fights. No one will suffer from missing one meal.

14. **(C)** Frank was attempting to help a convicted felon to escape, so Frank is guilty of a felony. Mary was an innocent courier; she did not intend to help Johnny to escape, so, within the scope of the quoted paragraph, she is not guilty.

15. **(A)** The prisoner being assisted to escape is being held on a felony charge; therefore those who assist in his escape are guilty of felonies. Although all of the assistance is given orally, it is obviously useful. Both Joan and Tom are parties to Bill's escape.

16. **(D)** Debbie is a very young child, far too young to be charged with criminal intent; she is innocent. Since Jim was serving a sentence on a misdemeanor conviction, Barbara is guilty only of a misdemeanor. Jim, on the other hand, is now in serious trouble. The next person who tries to help Jim escape will be guilty of a felony.

17. **(C)** Garcia is alert and sensitive but is not qualified to diagnose Mashke's problem. Insisting on taking the inmate for medical evaluation is a very appropriate action.

18. **(B)** A fist fight on the floor does not represent a life-threatening situation. The officer used excessive force.

19. **(D)** The prison rules apply equally to all prisoners, whether convicted or not.

20. **(A)** The rule lists the items that must be confiscated, and belts are clearly among the items. The reason that inmates may not keep their belts is clearly suicide related, but considering Wyler a suicide candidate is assuming too much. The answer to the question is directly tied to the stated rule. The intake officer could solve the inmate's problem by issuing him trousers in a smaller size.

21. **(C)** The busiest day, with three prisoners scheduled to appear in court, is April 15. Sowders is scheduled for that date.

22. **(D)** This case is that of Laduca, who is up for manslaughter 2.

23. **(B)** Whinston and Hughes will both be tried before Judge Cook.

24. **(D)** Crofton will be tried in Criminal Court in Rook County.

25. **(A)** Judge Molina will sit on the case of Laduca, who is charged with manslaughter 2; Judge Gabriel will sit on the case of Torah, who is charged with vehicular homicide.

26. **(C)** The burglary trial of Persuade is docketed as 437792 in Prince County Court. The other burglary trial, that of Hughes and docketed as 668190, will be in Queens Appeals Court.

27. **(B)** Embezzlement and grand larceny both involve stealing money from unsuspecting victims. The other choices are all incorrect because the docket numbers of the three cases on April 15 end with different digits. Sowders will be tried in Prince Supreme Court; and Judge Gabriel will sit on the trial of Torak.

28. **(B)** The suspect's behavior is consistent with depression, especially in light of the charge against him. While young offenders may be more prone to suicide, suicide watch must not be limited to them.

29. **(C)** A Correction Officer cannot observe in front and behind at the same time. The rule is clear. The officer's response, "I'm sorry," is a recognition of the polite "May I please. . ."

30. **(D)** The reason for this rule is obvious. Babies themselves are not smugglers, but their wrappings provide an excellent hiding place for contraband being smuggled by adults.

31. **(B)** Helping to choose books to support the inmate's own plan of defense is precisely the function of the librarian. Choice (D), suggesting an alternate defense, would be out of order.

32. **(B)** The rule clearly states that the officer may not help with the preparation of papers—even if making no suggestions.

33. **(D)** Harry is too old to be sent to the state reformatory, but since his term is for only 11 months, he may be sent to county penitentiary, to county jail, or to state prison.

34. **(B)** Mark, as a second offender, cannot serve his term in the state reformatory. Even though Mark's sentence is for a term well in excess of one year, he may serve his time at the county penitentiary or at the county jail because he is between the ages of 16 and 21. Mark may, of course, be sent to a state prison.

35. **(B)** As a first offender between the ages of 16 and 30, George may be sent to the state reformatory. State prison is also an option. George's term is too long for a man his age to serve at the county penitentiary or the county jail.

36. **(C)** Never assume literacy. The visitor may not be aware of the smoking prohibition or may have just lit up unconsciously. The officer is correct in informing the visitor of the rule and in requesting compliance. After that long trip, the visitor is unlikely to risk ejection.

37. **(A)** Choice (B) makes assumptions far beyond the given facts. The facts present no legitimate reason for suspension of the prison rules. The conference can wait until morning.

38. **(D)** Common sense in light of the facts.

39. **(C)** Even if the request seems quite reasonable, complying with it would give the appearance of favoritism.

40. **(A)** While this may well be a case of malingering, the officer has no way of knowing for sure. Let the dentist decide.

41. **(A)** You do not need to do any calculations to answer this questions. At the start of the day all inmates except the few in the Receiving Room or at the hospital are in their cells.

42. **(C)** Add up all the inmates who passed through the Receiving Room this morning: 12 + 21 + 17 + 8 + 10 + 4 = 72.

43. **(D)** Prisoners who are off premises are at court, in the hospital, or have been released or transferred elsewhere. In turn: 33 prisoners went to court in two groups and only 7 have returned, so there are 33 − 7 = 26 prisoners at court. There were 9 prisoners in the hospital at the start of the day, and 5 more have gone there; meanwhile, 6 have returned, so, (9 + 5) − 6 = 14 − 6 = 8 are in the hospital at noon.

    Add up the releases: 5 + 3 + 12 + 8 = 28.

    26 + 8 + 28 = 62 prisoners off premises at noon.

44. **(D)** At noon 62 inmates left the kitchen and none entered; therefore no inmates were working in the kitchen at 12.

45. **(A)** Add those inmates moved in at 8, 9, and 10 to the number of inmates already in Cellblock A at the start of the day. Subtract from that total the number moved out in the same hours: (52 + 7 + 24 + 46) − (28 + 31 + 20) =129 − 79 = 50.

46. **(B)** Of the 20 inmates who left for court at 8 a.m., only 7 returned at noon. 13 remained for more than a half day.

47. **(D)** $80 \times 3 = 240$ inmates who participated in recreation. The total prison population was roughly 258 prisoners: 52 in cell block A + 60 in cell block B + 74 in cell block C + 72 new inmates admitted during the day = 258. The number of inmates off premises varied during the morning, but clearly almost all of the inmates who were on premises took recreation, in other words, just about 100%.

48. **(C)** At 9 a.m., 31 inmates were moved from cell block A, 40 were moved from cell block B, and 52 were moved out of cell block C for a total of 123 inmates moved. To be certain that this is the greatest number of inmates moved out of their cell blocks at any hour, you must do the arithmetic for each hour. Thus the movement out of cells at 8 a.m. was $28 + 32 + 30 = 90$; at 10 a.m. it was $20 + 21 + 47 = 88$; at 11 a.m. it was $37 + 39 + 28 = 104$; and at noon it was $23 + 35 + 40 = 98$.

49. **(B)** Carlucci's kicking was the provocation and the punch by Otten was retaliatory. The incomplete entry might lead the parole board to conclude that Otten was aggressive and thereby dangerous. Otten may have overreacted, but the record should clearly describe the known reasons for actions.

50. **(A)** This is prison and rules must be obeyed. This is the 1 p.m. check, not the 1 a.m. check, so the officer does not need to enter the cell. The inmate's identity is not in question, but the inmate must obey the rules.

51. **(C)** The inmate certainly appears to be ill, and the officer is correctly insisting that he receive medical care.

52. **(B)** Migraine headaches come on suddenly. A person who did not have a migraine headache yesterday could certainly have one today. If the inmate had a long history of feigning illness in prison, the officer might be justified in discounting the claim. However, this is a new inmate, so the Correction Officer should take the inmate's word and let him go to sick call.

53. **(D)** The rule says that all contents of a package containing contraband must be held, regardless of the nature of the non-contraband contents that are present.

54. **(B)** Jack K. is a typical "X," nervous and truly sorry for his shortcoming but unable to change his habits.

55. **(D)** Edward F. is a "Z." He gets along in prison and gets along with other inmates, but he keeps coming back.

56. **(B)** Arthur B., another "X," seems unhappy much of the time and, because he is selective, has few friends.

57. **(A)** George H. shows the lack of interest in activities or events that is typical of the "W."

58. **(C)** "Y" is hostile and aggressive and gets pleasure from having others notice these aspects of his behavior. Charles D. fits this pattern.

59. **(C)** Larry M. is another hostile and aggressive "Y."

60. **(D)** Part of a prisoner's punishment in solitary is denial of visitors. Of course children are visitors; choice (A) is ridiculous. The attorney's privilege applies to the right to consult and the right to confidentiality of communication. The attorney does not have the right to contravene prison rules.

61. **(A)** The rule says ". . . handcuffs *and* leg irons . . . whenever being transferred."

62. **(C)** The inmate is a human being and must be restrained from doing damage to himself. The Correction Officer correctly considers the welfare of the inmate as well as that of other inmates and Correction Officers.

63. **(B)** If the officer or the officer's attorney feels that the documents would be helpful to the defense, the documents should be provided.

64. **(D)** The request may seem strange, but the prisoner is entitled to the last meal of his choice.

65. **(B)** More than inappropriate, this behavior is foolhardy. Rather than defusing a problem, the officer is needlessly drawing attention to it. This situation must be handled very quietly and delicately, attracting as little inmate attention as possible.

66. **(A)** Sentence (2) is incorrect because *between* should be used only when there are two; undoubtedly there are far more than two Correction Officers at the institution, so the proper word is *among*.

67. **(D)** Sentence (1) is incorrect because subject and verb do not agree in number. *Conditions*, the subject of the sentence, is plural, so the verb *appear* must also be plural. Sentence (2) is incorrect because the verb must be in the past tense, *came*.

68. **(B)** Sentence (1) is incorrect because the preposition *for* must take the objective case *us*. If you leave the Correction Officers out of the sentence, you can see that "It is a good rule for us to follow."

69. **(C)** Both of these sentences are correct. In (1), *bed and washstand* constitutes a plural subject that takes the plural verb *are*. In (2) it is correct to feel bad when you are sorry. To feel badly refers to the sense of touch.

70. **(B)** Sentence (1) is incorrect because a *when* clause cannot serve to define a noun. The sentence would be better recast, "Good morale *exists* in a prison when there are no fights taking place."

71. **(D)** The element of surprise is very important in a weapons search. Giving the inmates the opportunity to hide their weapons outside the cells, is, in effect, allowing them to keep the weapons.

72. **(A)** Vorperian is in charge, and she is correct in not allowing any cutlery to leave the dining hall. Desperate prisoners might very well modify a spoon to be used as a weapon or use it for digging.

73. **(C)** Laws change and sentences can be reversed. Rehabilitation is a worthwhile goal. Even if Mullins never has use for the high school diploma, the time spent studying is time that he is not creating any problems in the institution.

74. **(A)** An unlawful threat or attempt to do physical harm, even if unsuccessful, constitutes assault.

75. **(C)** Larceny is the taking of another's property. It differs from robbery because violence is not involved.

76. **(C)** Attendance at the lecture is required and is intended as a benefit to the inmates. Clinical diagrams are not "dirty pictures," so dictates of the inmate's religion have no bearing on lecture attendance.

77. **(A)** Requesting quiet at 2 a.m. is not an unreasonable demand. There is no harm in the officer's compliance. In fact, the inmates are more likely to respect him for his humanity.

78. **(B)** The law is not always fair. Sometimes expediency must rule. Presumably Murillo does not qualify for release on his own recognizance, so, in the absence of bail (which he could not afford to forfeit), he must be held to assure his appearance at trial. Choice (D) is the wrong answer because detention pending trial does not constitute punishment. Neither suspect deserves any punishment until trial and conviction.

79. **(D)** It is assumed that Rogers, with her roots in the community, will appear on schedule for trial. The court feels it does not need to hold bail to guarantee her appearance.

80. **(B)** Some of the people being held in jail pending trial will be acquitted of the crimes of which they are accused. Tripp may, indeed, be innocent, However, Tripp does not qualify for release on personal recognizance.

81. **(A)** Inmates from Wall County were convicted for an armed robbery, a murder, and two rapes. From Ames County there were one rape and one manslaughter. In Tara County there was one rape conviction. The convictions from Lime County were for nonviolent crimes, grand larceny and burglary.

82. **(C)** Herrmann, 2361182513-38, with the code 25, is serving a sentence for murder third degree.

83. **(B)** Chen, 6842180738, who is serving a sentence for armed robbery, code 07, is serving at Allenby Prison, code 38.

84. **(D)** Howe, 8663551138-29-74, was first assigned to Allenby Prison, code 38. Howe was subsequently moved first to Crofton Prison, code 29, and finally to Prouse Prison, code 74. Howe is unlikely to be under age 18 since he was never assigned to the juvenile facility; his service is for rape, code 11; and he has not been in the hospital.

85. **(B)** Of the inmates listed, only Rivera, 5683181166, has been assigned to Harrod Juvenile Facility, code 66.

86. **(C)** If Chen's number were to change to 6842187638, she would be serving on conviction for burglary, code 76. Her current number, 8642180738, indicates that the original conviction was on a charge of armed robbery, code 07.

87. **(A)** Of the facilities listed, only Tarton Correctional Institute, code 81, has received no prisoners convicted of violent crimes. Prisoners sent to Tarton have been convicted of grand larceny and burglary. The other facilities appear to receive prisoners convicted of both violent and nonviolent crimes.

88. **(B)** Only convicted felons are to be deprived of the franchise. Since the trial is still in progress, Rushneck has not been convicted and is entitled to vote. Choice (D) is not the right answer because innocence or guilt is irrelevant to the loss of the vote; conviction is what governs.

89. **(D)** As a clergyman the priest has the right to maintain the suspect's information in confidence. Choice (B) may be making a correct statement, but it is not based solely on the information presented.

90. **(A)** Absolutely, the prisoners must not be allowed to escape. Prompt action is essential; an alarm might present an opportunity to escape.

91. **(C)** This is good work by Fagoo. Barker is bringing marijuana into the prison, a prohibited act. Even if Baker was simply carrying her own supply for later use outside the prison, by carrying it in she became a lawbreaker.

92. **(D)** Richards was not an actual eyewitness to the shooting so his testimony cannot be considered direct evidence, but what he did hear and see before and after the shooting constitutes circumstantial evidence.

93. **(C)** Smith's academic record has absolutely nothing to do with his guilt or innocence in this murder case.

94. **(D)** Smith's ownership of the murder weapon is very important evidence in this trial.

95. **(B)** The testimony of an eyewitness is direct evidence; if Rogers actually witnessed the murder his testimony is certainly relevant.

96. **(A)** Safety considerations within the prison take precedence over the inmate's desire to learn a trade. If the inmate is still violent after four years in prison, his behavior has not been modified. It would be most inappropriate to put potentially deadly weapons into his hands.

97. **(D)** To the extent that the officer refused to accept the bribe and denied the favor to the inmate, the action was correct. Had there been only the request (without the attempted bribe), the incident could have gone unrecorded. However attempted bribery is clearly outside of acceptable behavior by inmates. As such, the Correction Officer should have recorded the behavior in the inmate's file.

98. **(C)** Illegal drugs, smuggling, and profiteering by prison staff are all not permitted. Officer Floyd is absolutely correct in reporting this activity to the supervisor. In fact the duty to report illegal activity transcends duty of loyalty to one's fellow officers.

99. **(B)** Officer Perry may feel uncomfortable when the inmates converse and he cannot understand a word, but the inmates have a right to talk to one another. In the absence of any behavior that might lead to suspicion of illegal planning, the Correction Officer cannot prohibit free conversation nor punish the inmates.

100. **(A)** The inmate is using his free time, not avoiding assigned tasks; but he is not using the library for its intended purpose. His actions show that Mariani has come to write letters, not to research an appeal. Thus, the Correction Officer is appropriately ejecting Mariani so as to leave space for inmates who have legitimate library business.

Answer Sheet for Model Examination 5

1. Ⓐ Ⓑ Ⓒ Ⓓ
2. Ⓐ Ⓑ Ⓒ Ⓓ
3. Ⓐ Ⓑ Ⓒ Ⓓ
4. Ⓐ Ⓑ Ⓒ Ⓓ
5. Ⓐ Ⓑ Ⓒ Ⓓ
6. Ⓐ Ⓑ Ⓒ Ⓓ
7. Ⓐ Ⓑ Ⓒ Ⓓ
8. Ⓐ Ⓑ Ⓒ Ⓓ
9. Ⓐ Ⓑ Ⓒ Ⓓ
10. Ⓐ Ⓑ Ⓒ Ⓓ
11. Ⓐ Ⓑ Ⓒ Ⓓ
12. Ⓐ Ⓑ Ⓒ Ⓓ
13. Ⓐ Ⓑ Ⓒ Ⓓ
14. Ⓐ Ⓑ Ⓒ Ⓓ
15. Ⓐ Ⓑ Ⓒ Ⓓ
16. Ⓐ Ⓑ Ⓒ Ⓓ
17. Ⓐ Ⓑ Ⓒ Ⓓ

18. Ⓐ Ⓑ Ⓒ Ⓓ
19. Ⓐ Ⓑ Ⓒ Ⓓ
20. Ⓐ Ⓑ Ⓒ Ⓓ
21. Ⓐ Ⓑ Ⓒ Ⓓ
22. Ⓐ Ⓑ Ⓒ Ⓓ
23. Ⓐ Ⓑ Ⓒ Ⓓ
24. Ⓐ Ⓑ Ⓒ Ⓓ
25. Ⓐ Ⓑ Ⓒ Ⓓ
26. Ⓐ Ⓑ Ⓒ Ⓓ
27. Ⓐ Ⓑ Ⓒ Ⓓ
28. Ⓐ Ⓑ Ⓒ Ⓓ
29. Ⓐ Ⓑ Ⓒ Ⓓ
30. Ⓐ Ⓑ Ⓒ Ⓓ
31. Ⓐ Ⓑ Ⓒ Ⓓ
32. Ⓐ Ⓑ Ⓒ Ⓓ
33. Ⓐ Ⓑ Ⓒ Ⓓ
34. Ⓐ Ⓑ Ⓒ Ⓓ

35. Ⓐ Ⓑ Ⓒ Ⓓ
36. Ⓐ Ⓑ Ⓒ Ⓓ
37. Ⓐ Ⓑ Ⓒ Ⓓ
38. Ⓐ Ⓑ Ⓒ Ⓓ
39. Ⓐ Ⓑ Ⓒ Ⓓ
40. Ⓐ Ⓑ Ⓒ Ⓓ
41. Ⓐ Ⓑ Ⓒ Ⓓ
42. Ⓐ Ⓑ Ⓒ Ⓓ
43. Ⓐ Ⓑ Ⓒ Ⓓ
44. Ⓐ Ⓑ Ⓒ Ⓓ
45. Ⓐ Ⓑ Ⓒ Ⓓ
46. Ⓐ Ⓑ Ⓒ Ⓓ
47. Ⓐ Ⓑ Ⓒ Ⓓ
48. Ⓐ Ⓑ Ⓒ Ⓓ
49. Ⓐ Ⓑ Ⓒ Ⓓ
50. Ⓐ Ⓑ Ⓒ Ⓓ
51. Ⓐ Ⓑ Ⓒ Ⓓ

52. Ⓐ Ⓑ Ⓒ Ⓓ
53. Ⓐ Ⓑ Ⓒ Ⓓ
54. Ⓐ Ⓑ Ⓒ Ⓓ
55. Ⓐ Ⓑ Ⓒ Ⓓ
56. Ⓐ Ⓑ Ⓒ Ⓓ
57. Ⓐ Ⓑ Ⓒ Ⓓ
58. Ⓐ Ⓑ Ⓒ Ⓓ
59. Ⓐ Ⓑ Ⓒ Ⓓ
60. Ⓐ Ⓑ Ⓒ Ⓓ
61. Ⓐ Ⓑ Ⓒ Ⓓ
62. Ⓐ Ⓑ Ⓒ Ⓓ
63. Ⓐ Ⓑ Ⓒ Ⓓ
64. Ⓐ Ⓑ Ⓒ Ⓓ
65. Ⓐ Ⓑ Ⓒ Ⓓ
66. Ⓐ Ⓑ Ⓒ Ⓓ
67. Ⓐ Ⓑ Ⓒ Ⓓ
68. Ⓐ Ⓑ Ⓒ Ⓓ

69. Ⓐ Ⓑ Ⓒ Ⓓ
70. Ⓐ Ⓑ Ⓒ Ⓓ
71. Ⓐ Ⓑ Ⓒ Ⓓ
72. Ⓐ Ⓑ Ⓒ Ⓓ
73. Ⓐ Ⓑ Ⓒ Ⓓ
74. Ⓐ Ⓑ Ⓒ Ⓓ
75. Ⓐ Ⓑ Ⓒ Ⓓ
76. Ⓐ Ⓑ Ⓒ Ⓓ
77. Ⓐ Ⓑ Ⓒ Ⓓ
78. Ⓐ Ⓑ Ⓒ Ⓓ
79. Ⓐ Ⓑ Ⓒ Ⓓ
80. Ⓐ Ⓑ Ⓒ Ⓓ
81. Ⓐ Ⓑ Ⓒ Ⓓ
82. Ⓐ Ⓑ Ⓒ Ⓓ
83. Ⓐ Ⓑ Ⓒ Ⓓ
84. Ⓐ Ⓑ Ⓒ Ⓓ
85. Ⓐ Ⓑ Ⓒ Ⓓ

TEAR HERE

Model Examination 5

Part One—Time: 90 Minutes—45 Questions

Directions: Study the three pictures which follow, noticing as many details as possible—kinds and locations of objects, numbers of items, dates and places. Make no written notes but use ten (10) minutes to commit to memory as many of the details as possible. Later in the exam, you will be asked questions about these pictures.

Picture for questions 1 through 6
Contents of a Woman's Handbag

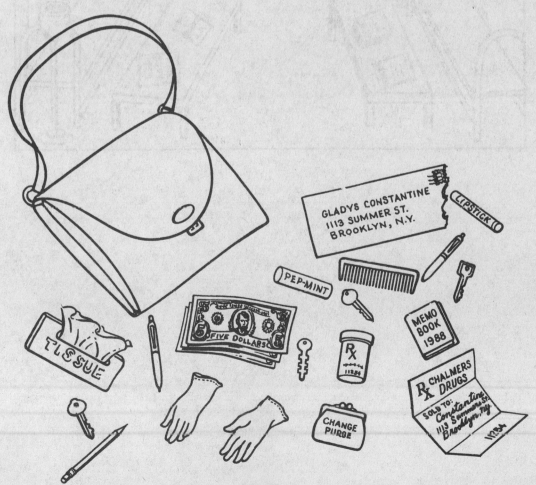

Picture for questions 13 through 18.
The Waiting Room

Picture for questions 25 though 30.
Contents of a Male Suspect's Pockets

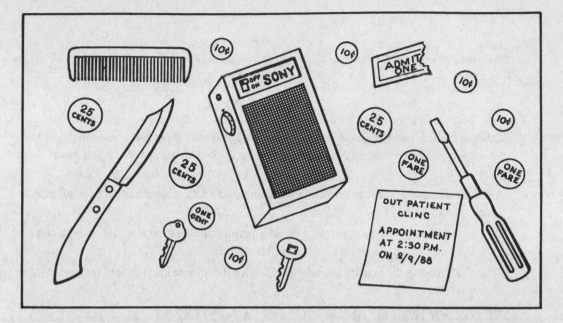

Directions: Questions 1 to 6 are based upon the picture of the contents of a woman's handbag. Do **NOT** look back at the picture when answering these questions. Rely on your memory and mark the answer sheet with the letter of your choice.

1. Where does Gladys Constantine live?

   (A) Chalmers Street in Manhattan   (C) Summer Street in Brooklyn

   (B) Summer Street in Manhattan   (D) Chalmers Street in Brooklyn

2. How many keys were in the handbag?

   (A) two   (C) four

   (B) three   (D) five

3. How much money was in the handbag?

   (A) Exactly five dollars   (C) Exactly ten dollars

   (B) More than five dollars   (D) Less than one dollar

4. The sales slip found in the handbag shows the purchase of which of the following?

   (A) the handbag   (C) tissues

   (B) lipstick   (D) prescription medicine

5. Among the items in the handbag were

   (A) a pair of gloves   (C) two left gloves

   (B) two right gloves   (D) three gloves

6. Which of the following items was **NOT** in the handbag?

(A) a comb

(B) a mirror

(C) a packet of tissues

(D) a pencil

Directions: Read the paragraph carefully. On the basis of the information in the paragraph, choose the best answer to the question and darken its letter on the answer sheet.

7. "Full completion of the sentence means that the final limit of the penalty imposed by the court has been reached and there is no longer any legal authority over the offender in connection with that particular offense." According to the preceding quotation, where there is full completion of the sentence

(A) no further punishment or restraint can be imposed by the government for the offense in question

(B) the court has given the maximum penalty permitted under the law and society can no longer impose any legal restrictions on the offender

(C) the full limit of the penalty permitted by law for the offense has not been imposed by the court

(D) there is no longer any legal authority over the former offender.

8. "Under the state-use system of prison labor, the state conducts a business of manufacture but the use or sale of the goods is limited to the institution where manufactured or to other state institutions and agencies." According to the preceding quotation, under the state-use system of prison labor the

(A) goods manufactured can be used only by state prisons

(B) products of inmate labor cannot be sold on the open market

(C) state competes with private industry in the manufacture of all those articles which are needed to operate a penal institution

(D) variety of articles manufactured is limited to those which can be used in the institution where they are made.

9. "The distinction in the criminal law of the United States between a misdemeanant and a felon was that the former received a sentence of a year or over." Of the following, the most accurate conclusion based on the preceding quotation is that under the criminal law of the United States

(A) a felony was considered a more serious crime than a misdemeanor

(B) all crimes were classified as misdemeanors or felonies

(C) all persons accused of felonies received sentences of more than a year

(D) some misdemeanants received the same prison sentence as some felons.

10. "Paroles may be granted by the board of managers at any time, and prisoners are referred to the board for parole consideration whenever the warden and the classification committee believe they have received the maximum benefit from institutional treatment and training and the conditions in the community are relatively favorable." Of the following, the most accurate conclusion based on the preceding quotation is that

(A) a parole, to be valid, must be approved by the classification committee and the board of managers

(B) during periods of economic depression very few paroles are granted because employment conditions in the community are not favorable

(C) prisoners become eligible for parole upon completion of the required minimum part of their sentence provided their conduct in prison has been satisfactory

(D) prisoners who have not yet benefited from the institutional treatment program are not likely to be referred for parole consideration.

11. "No other apex of prison life has invaded the public interest as frequently as the matter of punishment." According to the preceding quotation, it is most reasonable to assume that the

(A) extent of public interest in all prison matters is very great

(B) punishment is not the only aspect of prison life that the public has been interested in

(C) punishment of any prison inmate will be criticized by the public whenever it is brought to light

(D) study of the punishment of prison inmates is not any easy task.

12. "The old prison is gradually being changed into something that might diagnose and treat the prisoners rather than punish them." According to the preceding quotation

(A) diagnosis and treatment will succeed whenever punishment fails

(B) the objectives and methods of the prison are being modified

(C) the old prison and the new have very little in common

(D) where diagnosis and treatment fail, punishment must be tried.

Directions: Questions 13 to 18 are based upon the picture of the waiting room. Do **NOT** look back at the picture when answering these questions. Rely on your memory and mark the answer sheet with the letter of the answer of your choice.

13. A desk is shown in the drawing. Which of the following is on the desk?

(A) a plant

(B) a telephone

(C) an In-Out file

(D) an "information" sign

14. On which floor is the waiting area?

(A) basement

(B) main floor

(C) second floor

(D) third floor

15. The door immediately to the right of the desk as you see it is the door to

(A) the Personnel Office

(B) the elevator

(C) another corridor

(D) the stairs

16. Among the magazines on the tables in the waiting area are

(A) *Time* and *Newsweek*

(B) *Reader's Digest* and *T.V. Guide*

(C) *New York* and *Reader's Digest*

(D) *Time* and *T.V. Guide*

17. One door is partly open. This is the door to

    (A) the Director's office

    (B) the Personnel Manager's office

    (C) the stairs

    (D) an unmarked office

18. Which of the following statements about the picture is **NOT** correct?

    (A) There is an ashtray on one table.

    (B) There are no people in the room.

    (C) There is an **EXIT** sign above the door to the stairs.

    (D) The Director is in Room 2B.

Directions: Read the paragraph carefully. On the basis of the information in the paragraph, choose the best answer to the question and darken its letter on the answer sheet.

19. "Physical and mental health are essential to the peace officer." According to this statement, the peace officer must be

    (A) as wise as he is strong

    (B) smarter than most people

    (C) sound in mind and body

    (D) stronger than the average criminal.

20. "Teamwork is the basis of successful law enforcement." The factor stressed by this statement is

    (A) co-operation

    (B) determination

    (C) initiative

    (D) pride.

21. "Legal procedure is a means, not an end. Its function is merely to accomplish the enforcement of legal rights. A litigant has no vested interest in the observance of the rules of procedure as such. All that he should be entitled to demand is that he be given an opportunity for a fair and impartial trial of this case. He should not be permitted to invoke the aid of technical rules merely to embarrass his adversary." According to this paragraph, it is most correct to state that

    (A) observance of the rules of procedure guarantees a fair trial

    (B) embarrassment of an adversary through technical rules does not make for a fair trial

    (C) a litigant is not interested in the observance of rules of procedure

    (D) technical rules must not be used in a trial.

22. "One theory states that all criminal behavior is taught by a process of communication within small intimate groups. An individual engages in criminal behavior if the number of criminal patterns which he has acquired exceeds the number of non-criminal patterns." This statement indicates that criminal behavior is

    (A) learned

    (B) instinctive

    (C) hereditary

    (D) reprehensible.

23. "The law enforcement staff of today requires training and mental qualities of a high order. The poorly or partially-prepared staff member lowers the standard of work, retards his own earning power, and fails in a career meant to provide a livelihood and social improvement." According to this statement,

    (A) an inefficient member of a law enforcement staff will still earn a good livelihood

    (B) law enforcement officers move in good social circles

    (C) many people fail in law enforcement careers

    (D) persons of training and ability are essential to a law enforcement staff.

24. "In this state, no crime can occur unless there is a written law forbidding the act or the omission in question, and even though an act may not be exactly in harmony with public policy, such act is not a crime unless it is expressly forbidden by legislative enactment." According to the above statement,

    (A) a crime is committed with reference to a particular law

    (B) acts not in harmony with public policy should be forbidden by law

    (C) non-criminal activity will promote public welfare

    (D) legislative enactments frequently forbid actions in harmony with public policy.

Directions: Questions 25 to 30 are based upon the picture of the contents of a male suspect's pockets. Do **NOT** look back at the picture when answering these questions. Rely on your memory and mark the answer sheet with the letter of your choice.

25. The suspect had a slip in his pockets showing an appointment at an outpatient clinic on

    (A) February 9, 1988

    (B) September 2, 1988

    (C) February 19, 1988

    (D) September 12, 1988

26. The transistor radio that was found on the suspect was made by

    (A) RCA

    (B) GE

    (C) Sony

    (D) Zenith

27. The coins found in the suspect's pockets have a total value of

    (A) 56¢

    (B) 77¢

    (C) $1.05

    (D) $1.26

28. All except one of the following were found in the suspect's pockets. Which was not found?

    (A) a ticket stub

    (B) a comb

    (C) a subway token

    (D) a pen

29. Which statement about the contents of the suspect's pockets is correct?

    (A) There are three dollar bills.

    (B) There are two keys.

    (C) The subway tokens have holes in their centers.

    (D) There is an earpiece for listening to the radio.

30. The pockets of the suspect contained more of one kind of coin than of any other denomination. The most frequently occurring coin is

    (A) penny

    (B) nickel

    (C) dime

    (D) quarter

Directions: Read the passage carefully. On the basis of the information in the paragraph, choose the best answer to the question and darken its letter on the answer sheet.

31. "The unrestricted sale of firearms is one of the main causes of our shameful crime record." According to this statement, one of the causes of our crime record is the

    (A) development of firepower

    (B) ease of securing weapons

    (C) increased skill in using guns

    (D) scientific perfection of firearms.

32. "Every person must be informed of the reason for his arrest unless he is arrested in the actual commission of a crime. Sufficient force to effect the arrest may be used, but the courts frown on brutal methods." According to this statement, a person does not have to be informed of the reason for his arrest if

    (A) brutal force was not used in effecting it

    (B) the courts will later turn the defendant loose

    (C) the person arrested knows force will be used if necessary

    (D) the reason for it is clearly evident from the circumstances.

33. "An important duty of a court attendant is to keep order in the court." On the basis of this statement it probably is true that

    (A) it is more important for a court attendant to be strong than it is for him to be smart

    (B) people involved in court trials are noisy if not kept in check

    (C) not every duty of a court attendant is important

    (D) the maintenance of order is important for the proper conduct of court business.

34. "Ideally, a correctional system should include several types of institution to provide different degrees of custody." On the basis of this statement, one could most reasonably say that

    (A) as the number of institutions in a correctional system increases the efficiency of the system increases

    (B) the difference in degree of custody for the inmate depends on the types of institution in a correctional system

    (C) the greater the variety of institutions, the stricter the degree of custody that can be maintained

    (D) the same type of correctional institution is not desirable for the custody of all prisoners.

35. "The enforced idleness of a large percentage of adult men and women in our prisons is one of the direct causes of the tensions which burst forth in riot and disorder." On the basis of this statement, a good reason why inmates should perform daily work of some kind is that

    (A) better morale and discipline can be maintained when inmates are kept busy

    (B) daily work is an effective way of punishing inmates for the crimes they have committed

    (C) law-abiding citizens must work; therefore, labor should also be required of inmates

    (D) products of inmate's labor will in part pay the cost of their maintenance.

36. "With industry invading rural areas, the use of the automobile, and the speed of modern communications and transportation, the problems of neglect and delinquency are no longer peculiar to cities but are an established feature of everyday life." This statement implies most directly that

    (A) delinquents are moving from cities to rural area

    (B) delinquency and neglect are found in rural areas

    (C) delinquency is not as much of a problem in rural areas as in cities

    (D) rural areas now surpass cities in industry.

37. "Young men from minority groups, if unable to find employment, become discouraged and feel that life is hopeless because of their economic position and may finally resort to any means of supplying their wants." The most reasonable of the following conclusions that may be drawn from this statement only is that

    (A) discouragement sometimes leads to crime

    (B) in general, young men from minority groups are criminals

    (C) unemployment turns young men from crime

    (D) young men from minority groups are seldom employed.

38. "To prevent crime, we must deal with the possible criminal long before he reaches the prison. Our aim should be not merely to reform the law breakers but to strike at the roots of crime: neglectful parents, bad companions, unsatisfactory homes, selfishness, disregard for the rights of others, and bad social conditions." The above statement recommends

    (A) abolition of prisons

    (B) better reformatories

    (C) compulsory education

    (D) general social reform

39. "There is evidence which shows that comic books which glorify the criminal and criminal acts have a distinct influence in producing young criminals." According to this statement,

    (A) comic books affect the development of criminal careers

    (B) comic books specialize in reporting criminal acts

    (C) young criminals read comic books exclusively

    (D) young criminals should not be permitted to read comic books.

40. Suppose a study shows that juvenile delinquents are equal in intelligence but three school grades behind juvenile non-delinquents. On the basis of this information only, it is most reasonable to say that

    (A) a delinquent usually progresses to the educational limit set by his intelligence

    (B) educational achievement depends on intelligence only

    (C) educational achievement is closely associated with delinquency

    (D) lack of intelligence is closely associated with delinquency.

41. "There is no proof today that the experience of a prison sentence makes a better citizen of an adult. On the contrary, there seems some evidence that the experience is an unwholesome one that frequently confirms the criminality of the inmate." From the above paragraph only, it may be best concluded that

    (A) prison sentences tend to punish rather than rehabilitate

    (B) all criminals should be given prison sentences

    (C) we should abandon our penal institutions

    (D) penal institutions are effective in rehabilitating criminals.

42. "Many children who are exposed to contacts and experiences of a delinquent nature become educated and trained in crime in the course of participating in the daily life of the neighborhood." From this statement only, we may reasonably conclude that

    (A) delinquency passes from parent to child

    (B) neighborhood influences are usually bad

    (C) schools are training grounds for delinquents

    (D) none of the above conclusions is reasonable.

43. Old age insurance, for whose benefits city employees are now eligible, is one feature of the Social Security Act that is wholly administered by the Federal government. On the basis of this paragraph only, it may reasonably be inferred that

    (A) all retired city employees are now drawing old age insurance

    (B) all city employees favor becoming eligible for old age insurance

    (C) the city has no part in administering Social Security old age insurance

    (D) only the Federal government administers the Social Security Act.

44. "A peace officer's revolver is a defensive, and not offensive, weapon." On the basis of this statement only, a peace officer should best draw his revolver to

    (A) fire at an unarmed burglar

    (B) force a suspect to confess

    (C) frighten a juvenile delinquent

    (D) protect his own life.

45. "First aid by the Correction Officer is sometimes defined as the bridge between the accident and the doctor. It is the immediate and temporary treatment given in cases of accident or sudden illness before professional medical service can be obtained." This statement means most nearly that the Correction Officer administers first aid

    (A) when proper medical attention is not immediately available

    (B) to avoid accidents due to sudden illness

    (C) by providing professional medical services

    (D) to avoid the necessity for summoning a doctor.

End of Part One

If you complete your work before time is up, check your answers, making sure every question has only one answer. Do not go on to the next part until you are told to do so.

STOP

END OF PART ONE. IF YOU FINISH BEFORE 90 MINUTES IS UP, CHECK OVER YOUR WORK IN PART ONE ONLY. DO NOT GO ON TO PART TWO.

Part Two—Time: 80 Minutes—40 Questions

Directions: Study the three pictures which follow, noticing as many details as possible—people, clothing, activities, locations of objects, etc. Make no written notes but use ten (10) minutes to commit to memory as many of the details as possible. Later in the exam, you will be asked questions about these pictures.

Picture for questions 46 to 52.
At the Bank

Picture for Questions 58 to 63.
Meeting of the Board

Picture for questions 70 to 75.
Rap Session

Directions: Questions 46 to 52 are based upon the picture of people in line at the bank. Do **NOT** look back at the picture when answering these questions. Rely on your memory and mark the answer sheet with the letter of your choice.

46. The teller is

   (A) wearing a striped tie

   (B) wearing glasses

   (C) making change

   (D) left-handed

47. On the ledge in front of the teller is

   (A) a calendar

   (B) an ashtray

   (C) a bank book

   (D) a pen holder

48. The woman in the striped dress is

   (A) carrying a handbag

   (B) wearing a pendant

   (C) holding gloves

   (D) third in line

49. The man wearing a hat is also
    (A) handing money to the teller
    (B) wearing a bow tie
    (C) talking to another man in the line
    (D) smoking a pipe

50. All of the following statements about the picture are true EXCEPT
    (A) There are three people in line.
    (B) The man with the hat is wearing glasses.
    (C) The last man in line has dark hair.
    (D) There is no money in view.

51. The time of day is
    (A) early morning
    (B) lunchtime
    (C) mid-afternoon
    (D) late afternoon

52. The teller's name is
    (A) R. Smith
    (B) T. Jones
    (C) T. Smith
    (D) R. Jones

Directions: Each paragraph is followed by a number of questions. Read the paragraph carefully; then answer the questions on the basis of the information supplied in the paragraph. On your answer sheet, darken the letter of the answer you choose.

Paragraph for questions 53 and 54.

"There are at least two main difficulties in the field of Criminology. The first difficulty is the conflict between the objectivity needed for science and the ideology of reformers. While social concern was the mainspring of criminology from its beginning, applied criminology, a relatively new branch of the field, tries to bring about changes in both the offender and society itself to deal with the problems of crime. The second difficulty involves the criminologist's own feelings in responses and patterns which must be subjected to objective analysis. No scientist in any field can afford to let his personal values or the moral code of the times affect his search for truth."

53. According to the above passage, the aim of applied criminology is to
    (A) improve the attitudes of those dealing with the problems of crime
    (B) develop better conditions throughout the penal system
    (C) bring about changes in both the offender and society
    (D) eliminate the conflict between reformist feeling and scientific objectivity

54. It is indicated in the above passage, that one of the difficulties in the study of criminology is

(A) the tendency of individual criminologists to allow their opinions on morality to influence their scientific judgment

(B) an inability on the part of the offender to change his views about society

(C) duplication of the services offered criminals by the criminologists

(D) conflict among penologists as to the allocation of funds available for prison reform

Paragraph for questions 55 to 57.

At the receiving institutions newly committed inmates are confined to a separate wing or building for a definite period of time, usually one month. This quarantine period is partly to afford a convenient opportunity for case study without interrupting prison routine. It is during this period that the various examinations and interviews are carried on. The period also permits close observation, by picked officers, of personality traits and habits, relations to other inmates, and reaction to discipline. It prevents the social contamination which results from placing offenders by guess-work into situations where they may be injured or may cause injury to other inmates.

55. According to the preceding passage, the quarantine period

(A) begins after the medical examinations have been completed

(B) is used to study how the inmate behaves

(C) is used only if the disease is contagious

(D) is of different length for different inmates

56. According to the preceding passage, if there were no quarantine period, the study of the new inmate would probably

(A) not be possible

(B) interfere with other prison operations

(C) not get the full cooperation of all concerned

(D) require extra help

57. According to the preceding passage, an undesirable result that is avoided by keeping new inmates in a separate wing or building is

(A) the bad influence of other inmates

(B) poor discipline

(C) overcrowding in the institution

(D) the bad influence of unqualified officers

Directions: Questions 58 to 63 are based upon the picture of the meeting of the board. Do **NOT** look back at the picture when answering these questions. Rely on your memory and mark the answer sheet with the letter of your choice.

58. How many of the men at the table have glasses?

(A) one

(B) two

(C) three

(D) four

59. How many of the men are wearing dark suits?

(A) one

(B) two

(C) three

(D) four

60. Which of the following items is NOT shown on the table?

(A) file box

(B) water pitcher

(C) ashtray

(D) glass of water

61. The man at the head of the table is

(A) pointing to the map

(B) reading the papers in front of him

(C) looking at a man on his right

(D) looking at a man on his left

62. All of the following statements are true EXCEPT

(A) There are seven men at the table.

(B) The map is directly behind the man at the head of the table.

(C) The man who is speaking has a glass of water in front of him.

(D) One of the men is holding a pipe.

63. The man with the mustache is

(A) holding a pencil

(B) wearing a striped tie

(C) bald

(D) wearing a dark suit

Directions: Each paragraph is followed by a number of questions. Read the paragraph carefully; then answer the questions on the basis of the information supplied in the paragraph. On your answer sheet, darken the letter of the answer you choose.

Paragraph for questions 64 to 66.

"The final step in an accident investigation is the making out of the report. In the case of a traffic accident, the officer should go right from the scene to his office to write up his report. However, if a person was injured in the accident and taken to a hospital, the officer should visit him there before going to his office to prepare his report. This personal visit to the injured person does not mean that the officer must make a physical examination; but he should make an effort to obtain a statement from the injured person or persons. If this is not possible, information should be obtained from the attending physician as to the extent of the injury. In any event, without fail, the name of the physician should be secured and the report should state the name of the physician and the fact that he told the officer that, at a certain stated time on a certain stated date, the injuries were of such and such a nature. If the injured person dies before the officer arrives at the hospital, it may be necessary to take the responsible person into custody at once."

64. When a person has been injured in a traffic accident, the one of the following actions which it is necessary for the officer to take in connection with the accident report is to

   (A) prepare the report immediately after the accident, and then go to the hospital to speak to the victim

   (B) do his utmost to verify the victim's story prior to preparing the report of the incident

   (C) be sure to include the victim's statement in the report in every case

   (D) try to get the victim's version of the accident prior to preparing the report

65. When one of the persons injured in a motor vehicle accident dies, the above paragraph provides that the officer

   (A) must immediately take the responsible person into custody, if the injured person is already dead when the officer appears at the scene of the accident

   (B) must either arrest the responsible person or get a statement from him, if the injured person dies after arrival at the hospital

   (C) may have to immediately arrest the responsible person, if the injured person dies in the hospital prior to the officer's arrival there

   (D) may refrain from arresting the responsible person, but only if the responsible person is also seriously injured

66. When someone has been injured in a collision between two automobiles and is given medical treatment shortly thereafter by a physician, the one of the following actions which the officer must take with regard to the physician is to

   (A) obtain his name and his diagnosis of the injuries, regardless of the place where treatment was given

   (B) obtain his approval of the portion of the report relating to the injured person and the treatment given him prior to and after his arrival at the hospital

(C) obtain his name, his opinion of the extent of the person's injuries and his signed statement of the treatment he gave the injured person

(D) set a certain stated time on a certain stated date for interviewing him, unless he is an attending physician in a hospital

Paragraph for questions 67 through 69.

"After examining a document and comparing the characters with specimens of other handwritings, the laboratory technician may conclude that a certain individual definitely did write the questioned document. This opinion could be based on a large number of similar, as well as a small number of dissimilar but explainable, characteristics. On the other hand, if the laboratory technician concludes that the person in question did not write the questioned document, such an opinion could be based on the large number of characteristics which are dissimilar, or even on a small number which are dissimilar provided that these are of overriding significance, and despite the presence of explainable similarities. The laboratory expert is not always able to give a positive opinion. He may state that a certain individual probably did or did not write the questioned document. Such an opinion is usually the result of insufficient material, either in the questioned document or in the specimens submitted for comparison. Finally, the expert may be unable to come to any conclusion at all because of insufficient material submitted for comparison or because of improper specimens."

67. When a handwriting expert compares the handwriting on two separate documents and decides that they were written by the same person, his conclusions are generally based on the fact that

   (A) a large number of characteristics in both documents are dissimilar but the few similar characteristics are more important

   (B) all the characteristics are alike in both documents

   (C) similar characteristics need to be explained as to the cause for their similarity

   (D) most of the characteristics in both documents are alike and their few differences are readily explainable

68. If a laboratory technician carefully examines a handwritten threatening letter and compares it with specimens of handwriting made by a suspect, he would be most likely to decide that the suspect did not write the threatening letter when the handwriting specimens and the letter have

   (A) a small number of dissimilarities

   (B) a small number of dissimilar but explainable characteristics

   (C) important dissimilarities despite the fact that these may be few

   (D) some similar characteristics that are easily imitated or disguised

69. There are instances when even a trained handwriting expert cannot decide definitely whether or not a certain document and a set of handwriting specimens were written by the same person. This inability to make a positive decision generally arises in situations where

   (A) only one document of considerable length is available for comparison with a sufficient supply of handwriting specimens

   (B) the limited nature of the handwriting specimens submitted restricts their comparability with the questioned document

   (C) the dissimilarities are not explainable

   (D) the document submitted for comparison does not include all the characteristics included in the handwriting specimens.

Directions: Questions 70 through 75 are based upon the picture of the rap session. Do **NOT** look back at the picture when answering these questions. Rely on your memory and mark the answer sheet with the letter of your choice.

70. The number of people in this picture is

(A) 5

(B) 6

(C) 7

(D) 8

71. The person wearing boots

(A) is lying down

(B) has blond hair

(C) has a mustache

(D) is smoking a cigarette

72. The person wearing white socks

(A) is commanding the attention of the rest of the group

(B) is also wearing a leather jacket

(C) wears glasses

(D) none of these

73. The man who is reclining is

(A) raising one hand for attention

(B) leaning on his right elbow

(C) leaning on his left elbow

(D) taking notes

74. The man who is wearing sneakers is

(A) looking at his watch

(B) rubbing his left eye

(C) speaking

(D) cannot tell from this picture

75. The men are seated on

(A) small mats

(B) folding chairs

(C) bare floor

(D) thick carpeting

> **Directions:** Each passage is followed by a number of questions. Read the passage carefully; then answer the questions on the basis of the information supplied in the passage. On your answer sheet, darken the letter of the answer you choose.

Passage for questions 76 to 79.

Crime and the Criminal

"Criminology is more than the study of one type of prohibited behavior called crime; it is also the study of the individual who engages in this behavior—the criminal. This criminal must, in a court of law, be proved guilty of the offense with which he is charged and then convicted. As for the subject of crime, since the police are the first to learn of the commission of a crime, they are the source of the best, if still imperfect, data on crime. After the crime becomes known to the police, the next stage consists of the detection and apprehension of the suspected criminal through informers, fingerprints, modus operandi files, or the use of devices like the polygraph (lie detector). The appearance of the accused before the magistrate and the matter of bail come next. Surprisingly, many people think that bail payment is required as proof of a person's honesty, or as a test of a person's interest in his case. The sole function of bail, however, is to guarantee the appearance of the defendant at the time of his trial."

"Not all individuals who engage in criminal actions are considered by the law to be criminals. For example, some of these individuals are adjudged insane. Unfortunately, insanity is not the same as psychosis: the latter is a medical concept, while the former is a legal term. The famous Durham Rule, now the law for federal jurisdictions, holds that if the crime is the product of a mental disease, the individual is insane."

76. Which of the following is closest in meaning to the definition of criminology given in the above passage? Criminology is the study of

    (A) the behavior known as crime

    (B) the criminals who commit crimes

    (C) courts of law

    (D) crime and criminals

77. According to this passage, the only purpose of bail is to

    (A) serves as evidence of a person's financial reliability

    (B) test a person's honesty

    (C) make sure that the arrested person will show up for his trial

    (D) find out if a person thinks his case is serious

78. According to the passage, "psychosis" is

    (A) a medical concept

    (B) a legal term

    (C) a diagnostic term

    (D) the same as insanity

79. The "Durham Rule" referred to in the passage states that

    (A) insane individuals will commit more crimes than will sane people

    (B) certain crimes are so strange that they must have been committed by someone insane

    (C) if an insane person commits a crime, he will be freed under the law

    (D) a person committing a crime as a result of a mental illness is insane

Passage for questions 80 through 82.

"Group counseling may contain potentialities of an extraordinary character for the philosophy and especially the management and operation of the adult correctional institution. Primarily the change may be based upon the valued and respected participation of the rank-and-file of employees in the treatment program. Group counseling provides new treatment functions for correctional workers. The older, more conventional duties and activities of correctional officers, teachers, maintenance foremen and other employees, which they currently perform, may be fortified and improved by their participation in group counseling. Psychologists, psychiatrists, and classification officers may also need to revise their attitudes toward others on the staff and toward their own procedures in treating inmates to accord with the new type of treatment program which may evolve if group counseling were to become accepted practice in the prison. The primary locale of the psychological treatment program may move from the clinical center to all places in the institution where inmates are in contact with employees. The thoughtful guidance and steering of the program, figuratively its pilot-house, may still be the clinical center. The actual points of contact of the treatment program will, however, be wherever inmates are in personal relationship, no matter how superficial, with employees of the prison."

80. According to the above paragraph, a basic change that may be brought about by the introduction of a group counseling program into an adult correctional institution would be that the

    (A) educational standards for correctional employees would be raised

    (B) management of the institution would have to be selected primarily on the basis of ability to understand and apply the counseling program

    (C) conventional duties of correctional employees would assume less importance

    (D) rank-and-file employees would play an important part in the treatment program for inmates

81. According to the above paragraph, the one of the following that is NOT mentioned specifically as a change that may be required by or result from the introduction of group counseling in an adult correctional institution is a change in the

    (A) attitude of the institution's classification officers toward their own procedures in treating inmates

    (B) attitudes of the institution's psychologist toward correction officers

    (C) place where the treatment program is planned and from which it is directed

    (D) principal place where the psychological treatment program makes actual contact with the inmates

82. According to the above paragraph, under a program of counseling in an adult correctional institution, treatment of inmates takes place.

    (A) as soon as they are admitted to the prison

    (B) chiefly in the clinical center

    (C) mainly where inmates are in continuing close and personal relationships with the technical staff

    (D) wherever inmates come in contact with prison employees

Passage for questions 83 through 85.

"As a secondary aspect of this revolutionary change in outlook resulting from the introduction of group counseling into the adult correctional institution, there must evolve a new type of prison employee, the true correctional or treatment worker. The top management will have to reorient their attitudes toward subordinate employees, respecting and accepting them as equal participants in the work of the institution. Rank may no longer be the measure of value in the inmate treatment program. Instead, the employee will be valuable whatever his location in the prison hierarchy or administrative plan in terms of his capacity to relate himself constructively to inmates as one human being to another. In group counseling all employees must consider it their primary task to provide a wholesome environment for personality growth for inmates in work crews, cell blocks, clerical pools, or classrooms. The above does not mean that custodial care and precautions regarding the prevention of disorders or escapes are cast aside or discarded by prison workers. On the contrary, the staff will be more acutely aware of the cost to the inmates of such infractions of institutional rules. Gradually, it is hoped, these instances of uncontrolled responses to overpowering feelings by inmates will become much less frequent in the treatment institution. In general, men in group counseling provide considerably fewer disciplinary infractions when compared with a control group of those still on a waiting list to enter group counseling, and especially fewer than those who do not choose to participate. It is optimistically anticipated that some day people in prison may have the same attitudes toward the staff, the same security in expecting treatment as do patients in a good general hospital."

83. According to the above paragraph, under a program of group counseling in an adult correctional institution, that employee will be most valuable in the inmate treatment program who

    (A) can establish a constructive relationship of one human being to another between himself and the inmate

    (B) gets management to accept him as an equal participant in the work of the institution

    (C) is in contact with the inmate on work crews, cell blocks, clerical pools, or classrooms

    (D) provides the inmate with proper home environment for wholesome personality growth

84. According to the above paragraph, a result that is expected from the group counseling method of inmate treatment in an adult correctional institution is

    (A) be more acutely aware of the cost of maintaining strict prison discipline

    (B) discard old and outmoded notions of custodial care and the prevention of disorders and escapes

    (C) neglect this aspect of prison work unless proper safeguards are established

    (D) realize more deeply the harmful effect on the inmate of breaches of discipline

85. According to the above paragraph, a result that is expected from the group counseling method of inmate treatment in an adult correctional institution is

   (A) a greater desire on the part of potential delinquents to enter the correctional institution for the purpose of securing treatment

   (B) large reduction in the number of infractions of institutional rules by inmates

   (C) a steady decrease in the crime rate

   (D) the introduction of hospital methods of organization and operation into the correctional institution

END OF EXAM

ANSWER KEY FOR MODEL EXAMINATION 5

1. C	18. A	35. A	52. D	69. B
2. C	19. C	36. B	53. C	70. B
3. B	20. A	37. A	54. A	71. C
4. D	21. B	38. D	55. B	72. A
5. A	22. A	39. A	56. B	73. B
6. B	23. D	40. C	57. A	74. D
7. A	24. A	41. A	58. C	75. C
8. B	25. A	42. D	59. C	76. D
9. A	26. C	43. C	60. B	77. C
10. D	27. D	44. D	61. D	78. A
11. B	28. D	45. A	62. D	79. D
12. B	29. B	46. B	63. A	80. D
13. D	30. C	47. D	64. D	81. B
14. C	31. B	48. B	65. C	82. D
15. B	32. D	49. D	66. A	83. A
16. D	33. D	50. B	67. D	84. D
17. B	34. D	51. B	68. C	85. B

Explanatory Answers for Model Examination 5

Questions 1 through 6: If you missed any of these questions, look back at the pictures and observe more closely.

7. **(A)** When the sentence has been completed, the offender is no longer under the authority of the state *for that particular offense* and is not subject to any further restraint or punishment in connection with that offense.

8. **(B)** If the use or sale of prison-made items is limited to the institution where manufactured or to other state institutions and agencies, these items cannot be sold on the open market.

9. **(A)** The statement makes it clear that the classification of crimes is based upon the length of sentence and that there is no overlap. Obviously, the more serious crime draws the longer sentence. Choice (B) introduces a subject not covered in the statement. If you chose (C), reread the quotation more carefully.

10. **(D)** Prisoners must have benefited from their treatment and training, in other words, must be deemed to have been rehabilitated before being considered for parole. This is the only condition mentioned in the quotation. Scrving a minimum part of the sentence and good behavior are important factors in the granting of parole, but questions must be answered on the basis of the paragraph alone.

11. **(B)** No other aspect of prison life has interested the public as much as punishment, but the public is interested in other aspects.

12. **(B)** The word "changed" in the quotation is the key to the answer.

Questions 13 through 18: If you got any of these wrong, study the picture again.

19. **(C)** Physical and mental health refer to body and mind.

20. **(A)** Teamwork is cooperation.

21. **(B)** The last sentence makes this statement.

22. **(A)** The paragraph is telling us that criminal behavior is learned from one's friends.

23. **(D)** The first sentence makes this statement. The remainder of the paragraph amplifies the statement.

24. **(A)** The definition of a crime is that it is an act or an omission that is forbidden by law.

Questions 25 through 30: If you missed any of these questions, look back at the pictures and observe more closely.

31. **(B)** Unrestricted sale of firearms leads to ease of securing weapons.

32. **(D)** If a person is arrested during the commission of a crime, the reason for his or her arrest is so obvious that the person need not be told why he or she is being arrested.

33. **(D)** If a duty of the court officer is to keep order in the court, then maintenance of order is important for conduct of court business.

34. **(D)** All prisoners do not need the same type of custody, so a correctional system should provide several different types of institutions to serve the variety of needs.

35. **(A)** Busy inmates are less likely to be bored and have less time to cause trouble. The other choices may or may not be true, but they have absolutely nothing to do with the paragraph.

36. **(B)** All the statement says is that delinquency and neglect are found everywhere, in rural areas as well as in the city. Transportation, communication, and industry are the means by which delinquency is transmitted, not the delinquents themselves.

37. **(A)** Unemployment leads to hopelessness and discouragement, leading in turn to crime to satisfy needs.

38. **(D)** The list of roots of crime constitutes areas in which social reform is needed.

39. **(A)** Comic books which glamorize crime can influence young people towards a life of crime.

40. **(C)** The statement correlates poor academic achievement with delinquency, specifically stating that delinquents, despite their equal intelligence with non-delinquents, are behind in school.

41. **(A)** If a person comes from prison no better a citizen than when he or she entered, the prison has not rehabilitated, but it most certainly has still punished that person. The statement refers only to adults, so the conclusion of choice (C) is unwarranted.

42. **(D)** Every child is exposed to many influences, so choice (A) is incorrect. Schools and neighborhoods are the training grounds and daily experiences of children, but most children do not become delinquents, so most of these influences are not bad.

43. **(C)** If old age insurance is wholly administered by the Federal government, the city has no part in its administration. Choice (D) is incorrect because old age insurance is only one feature of the Social Security Act administered by the Federal government; other features of the act may well be administered by other authorities.

44. **(D)** A defensive weapon is used for self-protection.

45. **(A)** First aid is emergency, temporary treatment until the doctor arrives.

Questions 46 through 52: If you missed any of these questions, look back at the pictures and observe more closely.

53. **(C)** This statement is made in the third sentence.

54. **(A)** Scientific objectivity requires that personal values and judgments not enter into observation and analysis.

55. **(B)** Observation of personality traits and habits, of relations to other inmates, and of reaction to discipline is study of behavior.

56. **(B)** The quarantine allows for this observation to occur outside of prison routine so as not to interfere with other prison operations.

57. **(A)** Keeping new inmates separate and out of situations in which they may be injured implies that other inmates might injure them, either physically or by influencing them to behave in ways which would immediately create a bad prison record.

Questions 58 through 63: Any errors should lead you back to the picture for another look.

64. **(D)** Prior to writing the report, the officer should try to obtain a statement from the injured person or persons, that is, the officer should try to get the victim's version of the accident.

65. **(C)** See the last sentence.

66. **(A)** This answer is made very clear in the next to last sentence.

67. **(D)** The answer is in the second sentence.

68. **(C)** The third sentence explains the significance of dissimilarities.

69. **(B)** Any one of the answers might be correct, but the answer based on the passage is found in the last sentence.

Questions 70 through 75: Look at the picture to confirm the correct answer.

76. **(D)** The definition is given in the first sentence of the paragraph.

77. **(C)** The answer is in the last sentence of the first paragraph.

78. **(A)** *Psychosis* is a medical concept; *insanity* is a legal term.

79. **(D)** See the last sentence of the second paragraph.

80. **(D)** The whole point of the group counseling program is that all employees of the prison will be involved in the treatment and rehabilitation of inmates.

81. **(C)** The passage specifically states that the "pilot-house," the place in which the program is planned and from which it is directed, would NOT be changed.

82. **(D)** Since everyone working in the institution is involved in the counseling program, treatment takes place wherever there is contact between inmates and prison employees.

83. **(A)** The employee most valuable to the treatment process is the employee who is most able to develop human, one-to-one relationships with inmates, regardless of the employee's position in the institution.

84. **(D)** Because of their personal interest in inmates as human beings, the staff will be concerned with setbacks to growth and eventual freedom created by discipline infractions.

85. **(B)** A result, shown by some studies, is that inmates in the group counseling program will not create as many disciplinary breaches as those not in such a program.

Answer Sheet for Sample Promotion Questions

1. Ⓐ Ⓑ Ⓒ Ⓓ	21. Ⓐ Ⓑ Ⓒ Ⓓ	41. Ⓐ Ⓑ Ⓒ Ⓓ	61. Ⓐ Ⓑ Ⓒ Ⓓ	41. Ⓐ Ⓑ Ⓒ Ⓓ
2. Ⓐ Ⓑ Ⓒ Ⓓ	22. Ⓐ Ⓑ Ⓒ Ⓓ	42. Ⓐ Ⓑ Ⓒ Ⓓ	62. Ⓐ Ⓑ Ⓒ Ⓓ	82. Ⓐ Ⓑ Ⓒ Ⓓ
3. Ⓐ Ⓑ Ⓒ Ⓓ	23. Ⓐ Ⓑ Ⓒ Ⓓ	43. Ⓐ Ⓑ Ⓒ Ⓓ	63. Ⓐ Ⓑ Ⓒ Ⓓ	83. Ⓐ Ⓑ Ⓒ Ⓓ
4. Ⓐ Ⓑ Ⓒ Ⓓ	24. Ⓐ Ⓑ Ⓒ Ⓓ	44. Ⓐ Ⓑ Ⓒ Ⓓ	64. Ⓐ Ⓑ Ⓒ Ⓓ	84. Ⓐ Ⓑ Ⓒ Ⓓ
5. Ⓐ Ⓑ Ⓒ Ⓓ	25. Ⓐ Ⓑ Ⓒ Ⓓ	45. Ⓐ Ⓑ Ⓒ Ⓓ	65. Ⓐ Ⓑ Ⓒ Ⓓ	85. Ⓐ Ⓑ Ⓒ Ⓓ
6. Ⓐ Ⓑ Ⓒ Ⓓ	26. Ⓐ Ⓑ Ⓒ Ⓓ	46. Ⓐ Ⓑ Ⓒ Ⓓ	66. Ⓐ Ⓑ Ⓒ Ⓓ	86. Ⓐ Ⓑ Ⓒ Ⓓ
7. Ⓐ Ⓑ Ⓒ Ⓓ	27. Ⓐ Ⓑ Ⓒ Ⓓ	47. Ⓐ Ⓑ Ⓒ Ⓓ	67. Ⓐ Ⓑ Ⓒ Ⓓ	87. Ⓐ Ⓑ Ⓒ Ⓓ
8. Ⓐ Ⓑ Ⓒ Ⓓ	28. Ⓐ Ⓑ Ⓒ Ⓓ	48. Ⓐ Ⓑ Ⓒ Ⓓ	68. Ⓐ Ⓑ Ⓒ Ⓓ	88. Ⓐ Ⓑ Ⓒ Ⓓ
9. Ⓐ Ⓑ Ⓒ Ⓓ	29. Ⓐ Ⓑ Ⓒ Ⓓ	49. Ⓐ Ⓑ Ⓒ Ⓓ	69. Ⓐ Ⓑ Ⓒ Ⓓ	89. Ⓐ Ⓑ Ⓒ Ⓓ
10. Ⓐ Ⓑ Ⓒ Ⓓ	30. Ⓐ Ⓑ Ⓒ Ⓓ	50. Ⓐ Ⓑ Ⓒ Ⓓ	70. Ⓐ Ⓑ Ⓒ Ⓓ	90. Ⓐ Ⓑ Ⓒ Ⓓ
11. Ⓐ Ⓑ Ⓒ Ⓓ	31. Ⓐ Ⓑ Ⓒ Ⓓ	51. Ⓐ Ⓑ Ⓒ Ⓓ	71. Ⓐ Ⓑ Ⓒ Ⓓ	91. Ⓐ Ⓑ Ⓒ Ⓓ
12. Ⓐ Ⓑ Ⓒ Ⓓ	32. Ⓐ Ⓑ Ⓒ Ⓓ	52. Ⓐ Ⓑ Ⓒ Ⓓ	72. Ⓐ Ⓑ Ⓒ Ⓓ	92. Ⓐ Ⓑ Ⓒ Ⓓ
13. Ⓐ Ⓑ Ⓒ Ⓓ	33. Ⓐ Ⓑ Ⓒ Ⓓ	53. Ⓐ Ⓑ Ⓒ Ⓓ	73. Ⓐ Ⓑ Ⓒ Ⓓ	93. Ⓐ Ⓑ Ⓒ Ⓓ
14. Ⓐ Ⓑ Ⓒ Ⓓ	34. Ⓐ Ⓑ Ⓒ Ⓓ	54. Ⓐ Ⓑ Ⓒ Ⓓ	74. Ⓐ Ⓑ Ⓒ Ⓓ	94. Ⓐ Ⓑ Ⓒ Ⓓ
15. Ⓐ Ⓑ Ⓒ Ⓓ	35. Ⓐ Ⓑ Ⓒ Ⓓ	55. Ⓐ Ⓑ Ⓒ Ⓓ	75. Ⓐ Ⓑ Ⓒ Ⓓ	95. Ⓐ Ⓑ Ⓒ Ⓓ
16. Ⓐ Ⓑ Ⓒ Ⓓ	36. Ⓐ Ⓑ Ⓒ Ⓓ	56. Ⓐ Ⓑ Ⓒ Ⓓ	76. Ⓐ Ⓑ Ⓒ Ⓓ	96. Ⓐ Ⓑ Ⓒ Ⓓ
17. Ⓐ Ⓑ Ⓒ Ⓓ	37. Ⓐ Ⓑ Ⓒ Ⓓ	57. Ⓐ Ⓑ Ⓒ Ⓓ	77. Ⓐ Ⓑ Ⓒ Ⓓ	97. Ⓐ Ⓑ Ⓒ Ⓓ
18. Ⓐ Ⓑ Ⓒ Ⓓ	38. Ⓐ Ⓑ Ⓒ Ⓓ	58. Ⓐ Ⓑ Ⓒ Ⓓ	78. Ⓐ Ⓑ Ⓒ Ⓓ	98. Ⓐ Ⓑ Ⓒ Ⓓ
19. Ⓐ Ⓑ Ⓒ Ⓓ	39. Ⓐ Ⓑ Ⓒ Ⓓ	59. Ⓐ Ⓑ Ⓒ Ⓓ	79. Ⓐ Ⓑ Ⓒ Ⓓ	99. Ⓐ Ⓑ Ⓒ Ⓓ
20. Ⓐ Ⓑ Ⓒ Ⓓ	40. Ⓐ Ⓑ Ⓒ Ⓓ	60. Ⓐ Ⓑ Ⓒ Ⓓ	80. Ⓐ Ⓑ Ⓒ Ⓓ	100. Ⓐ Ⓑ Ⓒ Ⓓ

TEAR HERE

Sample Promotion Questions from Previous Exams

A Correction Officer who plans a career in the corrections field can look forward to promotion to positions of greater responsibility. In most corrections departments the job title directly above Correction Officer is Correction Captain. Other departments promote to Sergeant or Corporal. Whatever the intermediate titles, the final promotional goals are to the positions of Deputy Warden and Warden. Promotions are based on a combination of factors including: effectiveness as a Correction Officer, attendance record, perceived enthusiasm, recommendations of supervisors, seniority, and score earned on a promotional examination.

Just as initial entry exams vary widely from jurisdiction to jurisdiction, promotional exams show a great deal of variation also. All promotional exams require the Correction Officer to demonstrate thorough knowledge of the field of corrections and of the daily duties of a Correction Officer. In addition, most exams require total mastery of the rules and the ability to use sound judgment in corrections situations. Many exams attempt to measure the Correction Officer's natural grasp of supervisory principles and methods. Beyond these basic topics tested by all promotional exams, many include questions which involve reading interpretation, report writing, scheduling, and mathematics. In some jurisdictions, Correction Officers seeking advancement must take promotional courses. In these instances, the promotional exam will be based on course content. Other systems assume that a person who aspires to a corrections career has done extensive reading on the subject. These systems include questions based on correctional theory found in the literature. Still other systems include "in-basket" tests that demonstrate administrative skills or situational role playing to show ability to deal with novel stressful situations.

The questions that follow have been selected from among those asked on many promotional corrections exams administered over a number of years. The questions have been included here because of their universal and timeless relevance. Topics such as scheduling and budgeting have been omitted in favor of questions that get to the heart of corrections and supervisory knowledge and judgment.

> **Directions:** Choose the best answer to each question and darken its letter on the answer sheet. Official answers to these questions appear in the correct answer key following the last question.

1. The fundamental responsibility of prison management is the

    (A) secure custody and control of prisoners

    (B) development of work programs for prisoners

    (C) training of prisoners

    (D) classification of prisoners

2. The basic function of a correctional institution is

    (A) to operate at maximum efficiency

    (B) to make certain every department understands that teamwork is vital and that all departments are important

    (C) the protection of society and the rehabilitation of inmates

    (D) the recognition that correctional institutions face more difficult problems than at any other time in our history

3. Strict limitation and control of telephone calls made by inmates of a correctional institution is

    (A) desirable; it is a necessary security precaution

    (B) undesirable; it causes a loss of incentive for good behavior

    (C) desirable; the number of available telephones is limited

    (D) undesirable; it destroys morale

4. Of the following, the main purpose of the tool shadow board is to

    (A) enable employees to locate needed tools quickly

    (B) indicate when a tool is missing

    (C) provide a central place for storage of tools

    (D) reduce accidents by storing tools in a safe place

5. A correction officer in a court pen searches police cases delivered there for temporary detention before he or she assumes custody of these prisoners. The prisoners are later taken before a judge. For the correction officer to search the prisoners again when they are returned to the pen is

    (A) foolish, because the prisoners have not been out of the building and have been under surveillance at all times

    (B) sensible, because the prisoners may have acquired contraband when they were out of the pen

    (C) foolish, because the prisoners were thoroughly searched the first time

    (D) sensible, because prisoners in court pens should be searched regularly several times each day

6. A correction officer patrolling a cell block at night sees an inmate writhing on the floor in apparent pain. In this situation, the correction officer should

    (A) bear in mind that the inmate may be feigning and take necessary precautions

    (B) enter the cell immediately to get the inmate back on the bed and give first aid

    (C) notify the officer in command of the tour right away

    (D) summon a doctor immediately and wait for him to arrive

7. Correctional institutions where there is good morale generally have fewer escapes and escape attempts than those where morale is poor. Morale can be controlled by the manner in which the institution is administered. Of the following, the most important element in the control of morale is

   (A) elimination of mail censorship

   (B) improvements in prison sanitation

   (C) liberal visiting provisions with emphasis on open visits

   (D) well-trained and capable prison personnel

8. Decision making can be defined as the

   (A) delegation of authority and responsibility to persons capable of performing their assigned duties with moderate or little supervision

   (B) imposition of a supervisor's decision upon a work group

   (C) technique of selecting the course of action with the most desired consequences and the least undesired or unexpected consequences

   (D) process principally concerned with improvement of procedures

9. "The form that a riot takes determines what measure will be used to suppress it. New forms of rebellion will require good judgment and great restraint by staff since a standard revolutionary technique is to provoke authorities into overreacting." Of the statements below, the one that follows best from this passage is that

   (A) most riot situations can be readily controlled when personnel are adequately trained

   (B) a large percentage of offenders ordinarily take part in serious riots and therefore immediate suppression is sometimes difficult

   (C) control must be regained very quickly in situations where power has already been assumed by inmates

   (D) it is wise to take an estimate of the situation during riots before determining a course of action

10. If one of the correction officers you supervise does an exceptionally fine piece of work, it is usually best to

    (A) say nothing to him lest he become conceited

    (B) tell him that none of his co-workers could have done as well

    (C) explain how the work could have been even better so that he will not become complacent

    (D) praise him for the work he has done so that he knows his efforts are appreciated

11. Of the following, the most serious problem facing a captain when supervising new correction officers is that, for the most part, these officers

    (A) are afraid to face up to the responsibilities of their position

    (B) are overconfident and have a "know-it-all" attitude

    (C) have accepted this employment only as a stopgap until they find other work

    (D) have had no extensive formal training in this field of work

12. It has been suggested that the in-service training of employees in the correctional field should continue from the time they start until the time they leave the department. Of the following, the chief justification for such a continuous program of in-service training is that

    (A) a person's capacity for learning increases with age

    (B) because of a natural tendency to forget what one has learned and not put into practice, training must be repeated at regular intervals

    (C) employees are usually capable of further development on the job during the entire period of their employment

    (D) for learning to be effective, successive stages in the learning process must be correlated and coordinated

13. When explaining to a subordinate the importance of the tier officer's initial contact with new admission, the captain should stress most the

    (A) constructive influence this initial contact can have on the inmate's future adjustment to confinement

    (B) desirability of getting the inmate to talk freely and without interruption

    (C) harmful effect on the inmate's morale of a businesslike approach to conducting this initial interview

    (D) value of this initial interview to impress the inmate with the fact that violations of the rules will not be tolerated.

14. When explaining to a correction officer why an unvaried routine in the conduct of tier post inspections is not desirable, a captain should stress most the fact that

    (A) a method of work that may be entirely acceptable in one situation generally proves to be unacceptable when transferred without modification to another

    (B) inmates seeking to violate the institution's rules study the officer's habits so that they can time their activities to forestall detection

    (C) it is important to have a clear understanding of the purposes of tier post inspection in order to be able to carry it out efficiently and intelligently

    (D) the discovery of contraband is not the sole purpose of a tier post inspection.

15. A captain instructed subordinates that at all times the tier officer going off duty was to notify the on-coming officer of any inmate who should be particularly watched. The captain's instructions were

    (A) good because the on-coming officer will not be surprised if a particular inmate behaves strangely

    (B) poor because alertness and initiative on the part of the on-coming officer may be reduced

    (C) good because the on-coming officer will benefit from the experiences and observations of the off-going officer

    (D) poor because all inmates should be given careful custody and close supervision

16. "A cautious and observant officer seldom becomes involved in litigation initiated by an inmate who is injured during confinement on a tier." This statement is most probably based on the principle that such an officer will

 (A) avoid and prevent situations that might cause injury to an inmate

 (B) avoid any and all disputes with inmates

 (C) be able to persuade the inmate that litigation is not justified

 (D) make sure that any injury to an inmate is the result of the inmate's own negligence

17. A captain is summoned by a correction officer to the cell of a newly committed inmate who has been taken suddenly ill. After observing the inmate, the captain thinks that the inmate's condition is due to nervous excitement resulting from commitment to the institution. The captain should

 (A) speak quietly to the inmate until a normal condition is restored

 (B) give the inmate a mild sedative

 (C) make the inmate comfortable and instruct the officer to keep a close watch

 (D) secure medical assistance for the inmate

18. "From the standpoint of custody, the first concern of the correction officer in the court pen should be to lock the inmate in the pen as soon as possible." Of the following, the chief justification for this statement is the fact that the officer

 (A) can more easily take an accurate count of inmates confined in the pen

 (B) may be the only obstacle between the inmate and escape

 (C) can then give undivided attention to other important duties

 (D) does not know how soon the inmate will have to be produced in court again

19. When a correction officer asks a certain captain's advice about handling specific work problems, the captain occasionally responds by first asking the correction officer what he or she thinks should be done. This practice by the captain is generally

 (A) bad, since subordinates may be discouraged from asking questions in the future

 (B) good, since it motivates subordinates to think about possible solutions

 (C) bad, since correction officers will question the motives of the captain

 (D) good, since poorly thought out action can lead to undesirable results

20. Of the following, the best technique for a captain to use in training correction officers is to

 (A) encourage them to ask questions at all times

 (B) change their assignments frequently

 (C) teach them how to analyze important facts in order to make their own decisions

 (D) teach them how to evaluate inmate morale

21. Captain A, just before instructing a correction officer how to correctly search a cell for contraband, explained to the officer why it was important to follow the correct procedure. The captain's action was

    (A) good; a procedure is less likely to be forgotten if its purpose is understood

    (B) poor; since the importance of searching for contraband is obvious, the explanation is a waste of time

    (C) good; repetition is an effective aid in learning an operation

    (D) poor; such an explanation distracts the correction officer from the main points in the instruction

22. If a correction officer wants to talk to the captain about a personal problem, the captain should

    (A) be willing to discuss the matter with the officer

    (B) refer the officer to the assistant deputy in order to keep the captain–correction officer relationship impersonal

    (C) tell the officer to discuss the matter with another correction officer with whom he or she is friendly

    (D) tell the officer that personal problems should not be discussed on the job.

23. Assume you are a correction captain. Another captain has been newly assigned to your institution. For you to tell this new captain the strengths and weaknesses of some of the correction officers he or she will supervise is

    (A) bad; bias will be introduced unknowingly into the work situation

    (B) good; the new captain will be able to make various assignments of officers more intelligently

    (C) bad; it will delay the new captain's adjustment to new responsibilities

    (D) good; the abilities of a correction officer change from day to day due to the various factors

24. The term "malingerer" is most correctly applied to an inmate who

    (A) bears an officer a grudge for a long time

    (B) is a habitual liar

    (C) pretends to be ill in order to avoid working

    (D) takes a long time to recover from an illness

25. "The person who makes an ideal inmate in the penitentiary frequently does not make an ideal parolee when released." Of the following, the best justification for this statement is that

    (A) adjustment to prison life is, in many respects, more complex than adjustment to civilian life

    (B) high moral standards tend to remain well established once they have been developed

    (C) prison-wise inmates are often on their best behavior while they remain in prison

    (D) prison constitutes an acid test and no person is ordinarily paroled unless he or she passes this test

26. A representative group of young criminals in a certain state were found to be normal in intelligence, but 86 percent had been held back one to six grades in school. Of the following, the best inference from these data is that

    (A) lack of intelligence is closely associated with delinquency

    (B) criminals should be removed from the school system as soon as possible

    (C) educational maladjustments are closely associated with delinquency

    (D) the usual rate at which criminals progress educationally represents the limit of their learning powers

27. "One can only see what one observes, and one observes only things that are already in the mind." Of the following, the chief implication of this statement for the correction captain is that

    (A) observation, to be effective, should be directed and conscious

    (B) all aspects of a situation, unless the correction captain exercises caution, are likely to strike him or her with equal forcefulness

    (C) memory is essentially perception one step removed from observation

    (D) observation should be essentially indirect if it is to be accurate

28. "A promise to a subordinate is more important in a system of discipline than a promise to a superior." Of the following, the best justification for the above statement is that

    (A) subordinates are generally in no position to make promises to superiors

    (B) there is no obligation to make promises to subordinates

    (C) discipline cannot be maintained if promises are broken

    (D) discipline rests essentially on the respect of subordinates for their superior

29. Suppose you are a captain. A correction officer under your supervision submits a written recommendation concerning administrative procedure. You believe that the objective is worthwhile but that certain precautions are necessary. Of the following, the best action for you to take is to

    (A) submit the correction officer's memorandum to the warden along with a statement of your own opinion

    (B) submit the correction officer's memorandum to the warden without additional comment

    (C) advise the correction officer to submit the memorandum to the warden directly

    (D) advise the correction officer to withdraw the memorandum

30. "When assigned to duty in a large mess hall during inmate mess, it is important for officers to station themselves in such a way that they can see and be seen by their superior at all times." This statement is justified mainly because the

    (A) inmates will not attempt to create any disturbance when they see that the officers and their superior are in ready communication with each other.

    (B) officers will be able to show their superior that they are performing their jobs properly

    (C) officers will be able to tell if the superior has left the mess hall

    (D) superior might suddenly need to transmit an order to them quickly by means of a signal

31. It has been recommended that the work week of inmates employed in a program of prison industries be the same as the work week for similar employment in private industry. From the standpoint of the major objectives of a prison industries program, the adoption of this recommendation is desirable mainly because

(A) it will make possible the inclusion of a wider variety of employment in the prison industries program

(B) it will tend to make the deterrent objective of imprisonment more effective

(C) the rehabilitative process will be aided if conditions of work approach those in real life

(D) the prison industries will then be more profitable to operate since production will be greater

32. An important rule in carrying out an institutional program of inmate activities and privileges is the following:

(A) Do not curtail or revoke any inmate activity or privilege after it has been instituted.

(B) Do not give privileges to one inmate that cannot be earned in the proper way by any other inmate.

(C) Do not make any activity or privilege too pleasurable for the inmate.

(D) Do not use the program to help maintain discipline.

33. Of the following, the most important reason why psychiatric social workers have difficulty achieving success in prisons is that

(A) psychiatry and social work are not exact sciences

(B) neither inmates nor correctional officials are in sympathy with their work

(C) no precise goals have been established to guide them in their work

(D) they must tackle cases with which other treatment services have previously failed

34. "Contraband" in a correctional institution is best defined as any article

(A) that has been smuggled into the prison by an inmate

(B) that may be classified as a drug or alcoholic beverage

(C) the presence of which within the prison may jeopardize its safety and good order

(D) that may be sold or exchanged by an inmate for personal favors from the uniformed staff or other inmates

35. A correction officer under your supervision regularly submits considerably more infraction reports against inmates than other officers with similar posts. Of the following, the most desirable action for you to take is to

(A) direct this officer to be fairer toward the inmates

(B) give this officer additional training in order to strengthen his or her disciplinary control over the inmates

(C) reprimand this officer for his or her poor control over the inmates

(D) take no special action since in any such ranking there must always be one officer at the top and one at the bottom

36. An officer under your supervision reports that he suspects a certain inmate of suicidal tendencies. Of the following, the best action for you to take *first* is to

    (A) have the officer prepare a report to forward to your superior

    (B) rearrange the inmate's program so that he is always in the company of another inmate

    (C) talk to the inmate and keep him under observation for a while or order to verify the accuracy of the officer's suspicions

    (D) transfer the inmate to another cell where he may be kept under constant observation

37. A captain sees a correction officer deny an inmate's request to go to the medical clinic. This inmate has made similar requests in the past without cause and appears to have nothing the matter with her now. The captain should evaluate the officer's action as

    (A) unsound, because if the inmate is really sick, the denial of the request may have serious consequences

    (B) unsound, because an officer should never be influenced by an inmate's previous record

    (C) sound, because if the inmate is really sick she will let the officer know it soon enough

    (D) sound, because it takes into account the inmate's previous record

38. On a tour of the posts, you observe that in a cell block supervised by a new officer, the lineup of inmates is proceeding in a slow and disorderly manner. In this situation, it is most desirable that you, as captain

    (A) call the officer's attention to the fact that the lineup is not proceeding properly and then continue with your tour of posts

    (B) issue a mild reprimand and take personal command of the lineup in order to prevent further confusion

    (C) make a mental note of the situation and discuss the proper way of conducting a lineup at the next conference with your officer

    (D) take the officer aside and instruct him or her in the immediate action to take in order to correct this situation

39. Suppose that on organized searches for contraband more contraband is usually found on the post of one officer under your command than on the post of any other. The one of the following most likely to be an important contributing factor to the situation is the

    (A) amount of time this officer has devoted to the study of the rule book

    (B) amount of training you have given your staff in the detection and control of contraband

    (C) special problems inherent in the type of post commanded by this officer

    (D) thoroughness with which the different types of posts are searched

40. Suppose that a captain is required to review disciplinary reports against inmates prepared by correction officers before forwarding them to the disciplinary officer. Of the following, the report the captain should return to a correction officer for rewriting is one that

    (A) fails to employ a high standard of written English

    (B) fails to recommend an appropriate punishment

    (C) is incomplete as to main details

    (D) relates to more than one inmate

41. Suppose an inmate has made an unjustified complaint about you to your superior officer. The best of the following plans for you to follow is to

    (A) make him work harder and treat him roughly

    (B) see that he gets all the dirty, disagreeable jobs

    (C) spread the word among the other inmates that he is a "stool pigeon"

    (D) go to your superior officer and tell him the truth

42. A correction officer assigned to some clerical duties accidentally destroys an important document that was to be presented in court as evidence in a few days. The best action for him to take first in this situation is to

    (A) suggest that the case be postponed until more evidence can be obtained

    (B) immediately contact the person from whom the document was obtained and request another copy

    (C) say nothing at this time, but admit the destruction of the document if asked for it by his superior

    (D) notify his superior of the destruction of the document

43. Assume you are a captain. A newly appointed correction officer asks you what action she should take if, when patrolling a cell block at night, she notices that a prisoner has suddenly been taken violently ill. Of the following, the best advice for you to give this correction officer is that she should

    (A) open the cell immediately and apply first aid as soon as possible

    (B) summon another guard before opening the cell

    (C) open the cell immediately, examine the inmate quickly, and summon a doctor if the illness seems real

    (D) carefully check on the circumstances of the case before opening the cell

44. Suppose a correction officer coming on duty reports to you that a prisoner is missing from the cell block. Of the following, the best reason for sounding an alarm immediately, even before checking the officer's count, is that

    (A) the inmate may still be on the prison grounds

    (B) the escaped prisoner may have had an accomplice

    (C) there is no indication how long the inmate may have been missing from his cell

    (D) responsibility for the escape should be fixed immediately

Questions 45 through 47 are based on the following example of a correction officer's report. The report consists of sixteen numbered sentences some of which are not consistent with the principles of good report writing in correctional matter.

(1) On January 5, I was assigned as the "A" officer on the third floor of Institution Y during the 12 midnight to 8 a.m. tour of duty.   **(2)** At about 1:30 a.m. on said date, I heard a cry for help coming from the lower "A" section of the floor.   **(3)** I immediately ran into the section and found inmate John Doe in cell number 5 holding up inmate Robert James who was hanging from the light fixture of the cell by a bedsheet.   **(4)** One end of the bedsheet was tied to the outer frame of the light fixture, and the other end was tied around the neck of inmate James.   **(5)** I immediately ran to the telephone to notify the control room and ask for assistance. **(6)** While waiting for assistance, I notified Correction Officer Harold Smith who was assigned as the "B" officer on the floor and instructed inmate Doe to keep holding the hanging inmate in an upward position. **(7)** Correction Officer Thomas Jones arrived at the scene together with Dr. Walker Frazer who was the physician on duty in the institution at the time. **(8)** Correction Officer Smith and I then ran to cell number 5 while Correction Officer Jones operated the "A" section locking mechanism to open the door to cell number 5. **(9)** When the cell door was opened, I, together with Correction Officer Smith and Dr. Frazer, entered the cell where I cut the bedsheet with my pen knife to let the hanging inmate down. **(10)** I found no suicide note in the cell. **(11)** Dr. Frazer ordered the inmate to be placed on the floor outside of the cell so that he could inject emergency medication into the inmate's chest and administer artificial respiration. **(12)** Both Correction Officer Smith and I assisted in administering artificial respiration under the physician's supervision. **(13)** After the administration of artificial respiration for a period of approximately one-half hour, Dr. Frazer pronounced inmate James dead. **(14)** The dead inmate's cell partner, inmate John Doe, stated that he awoke from his sleep and saw his cell partner hanging from the ceiling with a sheet tied around his neck. **(15)** There were no pictures anywhere in the cell which would give information as to the deceased's family ties. **(16)** It is believed that inmate James committed suicide because of his concern about the sentence he would receive when he appeared in court for sentencing on January 6.

45. A good report should be arranged in logical order. Which of the following sentences does not appear in proper sequence?

    (A) Sentence 2

    (B) Sentence 10

    (C) Sentence 3

    (D) Sentence 13

46. Only material relevant to the main thought of a report should be included. Which of the following sentences contain material that is *least* relevant to this report?

    (A) Sentence 2

    (B) Sentence 11

    (C) Sentence 14

    (D) Sentence 15

47. Good reports should contain accurate statements based upon definite information. Which of the following sentences contains material that is not based on definite information?

    (A) Sentence 5

    (B) Sentence 6

    (C) Sentence 9

    (D) Sentence 16

48. Assume that you are a captain. An inmate comes to you with a request arising out of a grievance that he believes to be legitimate. You can see that the inmate is making a request that is important to him. You consider the inmate's request carefully and decide that you cannot grant it. It is best for you to

    (A) give the inmate a firm "no" answer and your reason for doing so

    (B) grant the inmate's request because of its importance but point out to him that there were very good reasons for not granting the request

    (C) tell the inmate that his request is an important one and you will let him know in the not too distant future whether the request can be granted

    (D) tell the inmate that there are two sides to granting his request and that you will ask the deputy warden to frame a written response to the inmate

49. To schedule an official count at or near the time of officer shift changes is usually found to be a

    (A) bad practice since officers coming on duty resent being held up while a previous shift makes its count

    (B) good practice since a large number of officers will be on hand if discrepancies in the count are found

    (C) bad practice since officers responsible for the count are too easily distracted

    (D) good practice since accuracy in the count is assured and interference with inmate activities is avoided

50. The three major ideologies affecting law enforcement and court and correctional activities are the punitive, therapeutic, and preventive ideologies. Of the following, the most correct statement is that

    (A) the therapeutic ideology rather than the punitive or preventive ideology is recognized as offering the ultimate promise for reducing crime

    (B) the preventive ideology seeks to promote development of a healthy personality by means of immediate and drastic social changes so that criminals will engage in socially approved conduct

    (C) the therapeutic ideology considers the criminal to be a victim of defective personality conditioning and, consequently, generally seeks a lifetime clinical treatment approach by specially trained psychiatrists

    (D) the punitive ideology has as its major objective the protection of society, and severe punishment is viewed as useful in reforming criminals

51. Increases in recidivist rates can result from

    (A) more liberal enforcement of parole supervision

    (B) increased use of probation by the courts

    (C) stricter enforcement of probation supervision

    (D) more liberal law enforcement

52. If a correction officer were to attend a preparatory class on supervisory techniques, he or she would most likely be instructed that a good supervisor is one who

    (A) believes in strong and centralized administrative control

    (B) is extremely ambitious

(C) maintains a favorable attitude toward those he or she encounters

(D) maintains his or her own method of handling problems

53. Of the following, the most important consideration for recommending a promotion to captain should be the correction officer's

(A) capacity to take disciplinary action

(B) ability to control inmate movement

(C) detailed knowledge of departmental rules and regulations

(D) seniority

54. A correction officer under your supervision as captain attempts to conceal the fact that he or she has made an error. You should proceed on the assumption that

(A) evasion may well be overlooked if the error occurred in a matter of no great importance

(B) a desire for concealment indicates an antisocial attitude

(C) the correction officer was ignorant of proper procedures and that the matter should be dropped

(D) the evasion indicates something wrong in the fundamental relationship between the correction officer and his or her captain

55. If a correction captain is to be an effective leader of those under her, she must

(A) utilize whatever motives she is able to discern in the officers working under her

(B) develop the assets of the officers and encourage them to work for the good of the organization as a whole

(C) avoid the use of regular conferences lest her officers be deprived of initiative

(D) outline repeatedly and in great detail the work to be performed by each member of the group

56. Inmates generally find their place within some group in the institution. A certain correction officer makes it a practice to find out as much as he can about such groups and the reasons for changes in their composition. The correction officer's practice in this regard is

(A) bad; a correction officer who develops a reputation for not minding his own business will be taken hostage in the event of a disturbance

(B) bad; within institutional rules, an inmate has as much right to a personal social life as anyone else

(C) good; institutional security may depend upon such observations

(D) good; most inmates are appreciative when correction officers show a personal interest in their activities

57. "It is generally accepted in the correctional field that society is best protected when a very high percentage of all releases are by parole." This is true primarily because

(A) it costs much less to handle inmates on parole than to incarcerate them

(B) the "bad risks" who need it most will be under supervision after release

(C) indeterminate sentences give correctional administrators maximum flexibility

(D) determining what constitutes success or failure on parole is relatively easy

58. Which of the following statements concerning riots and disturbances in correctional institutions is correct?

    (A) A system that provides for informal communications between staff and inmates is the best way to prevent riots and disturbances

    (B) Research studies have identified a set of causes that always precipitates a riot

    (C) Sudden or unexpected changes in institutional routines or policies may result in a major disturbance

    (D) The best way to prevent riots is to have an effective informant system

59. Penologists generally agree that the way a custodial prison maintains stability within its walls is

    (A) through the granting of privileges

    (B) through the exercise of total power by guards

    (C) by treating all inmates alike in order to destroy the influence of inmate leaders

    (D) by dealing with leaders chosen by the inmates

60. Chief Justice Warren E. Burger once stated: "It must be ironic to a prisoner to recall that society spared no expense to afford him three, four, or five trials and appeals at enormous cost but then proceeds to forget his plight." This statement implies that

    (A) more money should be spent for the treatment of prisoners and less for the adjudication of criminal cases

    (B) substantial sums of money are justifiably required to ensure that the innocent are not wrongly convicted

    (C) less money should be spent on the judicial process since it has not helped to reduce the rate of recidivism

    (D) more money should be spent for a prisoner's treatment in order to be consistent with the investment in convicting him or her

61. "Extra security precautions are generally advisable in the supervision of prisoners at mess." This is so mainly because

    (A) different classes of inmates mingle together freely at mess

    (B) large numbers of prisoners are concentrated together in one place

    (C) prisoners are usually dissatisfied with institution food

    (D) prison riots may begin anywhere

62. In a certain correctional institution, a captain discharging an inmate asked the latter some personal questions such as "Where do your parents live?" "What is your mother's name?" etc. The purpose of asking these questions was probably to

    (A) check the accuracy of the information on the discharge papers

    (B) motivate the inmate to renew family ties

    (C) prevent a substitution of inmates

    (D) show an interest in the inmate's welfare

63. Suppose that a study of prison inmates shows that the rate of recidivism increases as the number of offenses increases. That is, 10% of first offenders become second offenders, 30% of second offenders become third offenders, 70% of third offenders become fourth offenders, etc. If the findings of this study are valid, then it is most reasonable to assume that

   (A) environment plays a minor role in the predisposition towards criminal behavior

   (B) exposure to prison life inevitably leads to the commission of further crimes

   (C) first offenders represent the most fruitful field for intensive rehabilitation efforts

   (D) it would be desirable to house together offenders who have committed the same number of offenses

64. "Since inmate programs of work, recreation, vocational training, etc. have not been effective in reducing crime or the rate of recidivism, they should be abandoned." A basic weakness of this criticism is that it fails to take into account that these programs

   (A) are also needed to keep inmates occupied

   (B) are not intended to achieve the purposes stated

   (C) cannot influence the majority of criminals since they are not apprehended

   (D) have been tried for only a very short time

65. Of the following, the best reason for using tear gas in the event of a serious disturbance in a correctional institution is that it

   (A) permanently disables the ringleaders

   (B) teaches the inmates that disturbances will not be permitted

   (C) effectively curbs the disturbance without harm to the inmates

   (D) is what the public expects in a case of disturbance in a correctional institution

66. Suppose that you are a correction captain, and a newly appointed correction officer reports to you for duty. Of the following, the best procedure for you to follow to assure his rapid orientation to his work is to

   (A) ask him to briefly survey his qualifications for the job

   (B) observe him carefully as he performs the routine aspects of his duties

   (C) make a careful study of his work record previous to his coming to the Department

   (D) review with him the important elements of the job he will be required to perform

67. A captain notices that one correction officer does not get along well with the other officers. Of the following, the best thing for the captain to do in such a situation is to

   (A) make an effort to learn the reason for the difficulty in order to resolve the problem

   (B) overlook the matter since the work will probably be unaffected

   (C) prepare a report of the situation to a superior officer and be guided by the latter's decision

   (D) tell all the officers they must work together harmoniously or risk disciplinary action

68. The practice of admitting a new prisoner to the institution without a complete strip shake-down is

    (A) desirable only if the officer delivering the prisoner gives written assurance that the prisoner has been frisked and is free of contraband

    (B) not desirable under any circumstances

    (C) desirable only if the prisoner has been brought directly from another institution

    (D) not desirable except with material witnesses

69. "A captain should patrol at irregular and unexpected times throughout his or her tour." This method of patrol is preferable to patrols at scheduled times mainly because

    (A) the captain has greater flexibility in scheduling the day's activities

    (B) patrols will not be forgotten or reduced if they become habitual

    (C) officers on post know that the captain will be around to inspect their work

    (D) it gives a truer picture of actual conditions on the different posts

70. Of the following vocational training courses suitable for a women's institution, the one that has more value than the others because of its effect on institutional morale is a course in

    (A) beauty culture

    (B) homemaking

    (C) practical nursing

    (D) child care

71. Of the following, the best method for enforcing discipline among inmates of a penal institution is

    (A) reclassification of the offending inmates

    (B) transfer or reassignment

    (C) deprivation of privileges

    (D) use of duress or compulsion

72. In the institutions of the Department of Corrections, special security procedures are observed with an inmate sentenced to death or to a long term in a state prison. Such special procedures are advisable mainly because

    (A) the department is only temporarily responsible for someone who is actually a prisoner of the State

    (B) friends and accomplices on the outside may attempt to free such an inmate by force

    (C) isolation of such an inmate from the rest of the prison population is not practicable

    (D) the severity of the sentence may impel such an inmate to commit a desperate act

73. Assume that a new warden has been placed in charge of an institution. He is faced with the problem of deciding how strict or how relaxed discipline should be. It would be better for him to begin by setting standards of discipline that are

    (A) relaxed rather than strict because discipline should bear a direct relationship to the kind of violations committed and to the manner of their being committed

    (B) relaxed rather than strict since the good will of correctional personnel is a primary consideration

(C) strict rather than relaxed because it is easier to relax discipline than to tighten it

(D) strict rather than relaxed since both inmates and correction officers usually devise all manner of stratagems to see how far a new warden can be pushed

74. The principle of administration that states that the responsibility of higher authority for the acts of subordinates must be absolute means that

(A) each superior officer is held responsible for all the acts of his or her subordinates

(B) each subordinate is held responsible for his or her own acts

(C) the chief executive alone is not responsible for the acts of his or her subordinates

(D) coordinate officers are responsible for the acts of one another

75. The principal argument against the heavy weighting of seniority in a correction department promotional examination is the seniority credits

(A) tend to give credit for age

(B) create ill will among employees with shorter seniority

(C) violate the spirit of career service

(D) offer no positive assurance of competency

76. In planning courses for a correction officers' training program, it is most important to make the content of each lesson capable of being

(A) taught in one class meeting

(B) connected to something the trainee already knows and can do

(C) spread over a number of class meetings

(D) fully learned by the trainees as something entirely new

77. There is strong disagreement among correctional administrators concerning the use of inmate councils. The *most* feasible approach concerning the use of inmate councils is generally the

(A) elimination of inmate advisory groups since membership in such a group gives the inmate an opportunity to exploit other inmates

(B) formation of inmate advisory groups to deal with particular problems, with such groups dissolving as soon as the problems are resolved

(C) popular election by inmates of an inmate advisory group to meet at frequent periodic intervals

(D) taking of formal surveys by supervisory correction personnel to determine inmate attitudes

78. A major point of emphasis in the instruction of a correction officer concerns security and the causes of breach of security. Experience has shown that most escapes are traceable directly to

(A) relatives who smuggle escape instruments to inmates

(B) officers who smuggle contraband to inmates

(C) the haphazard handling of keys and tools

(D) the lack of knowledge among inmates as to the possible consequences of escape

79. "A good correctional program should be carried out in such a way that problem cases are revealed long before they reach a critical state." A correction officer could best help carry out such a program by

    (A) consulting with superiors as to the type of disciplinary action to be taken with problem cases

    (B) learning to recognize the signs of trouble and how to deal with them

    (C) preparing a good case against the inmates in the event a disciplinary hearing is held

    (D) getting the help of other correction officers in dealing with critical situations

80. Assume that as a correction captain you are assigned to conduct a refresher training course for correction officers. Of the following, the best reason for employing group discussion rather than routine lecture methods is that

    (A) learning is more efficient when officers participate actively in the process

    (B) the scope of a training course can be laid out more precisely when one person is responsible for the course

    (C) the more experienced the officers, the more likely they will benefit from a lecture course

    (D) less time has to be devoted to a course that has a well-defined purpose

81. "The competent correction captain attempts to develop respect rather than fear on the part of the officers under his or her supervision." Of the following, the chief justification for this statement is that

    (A) experience has demonstrated that negative incentives are more effective than positive ones

    (B) respect is based on the individual while fear is based on the organization as a whole

    (C) respect for officers is generally easier to develop than fear of penalty

    (D) officers who respect a supervisor are likely to give more than the minimum required performance

82. A captain advised a new correction officer not to permit inmates to address her by her first name. The captain's advice was

    (A) bad, because it creates a wider gap than necessary between officers and inmates

    (B) bad, because no rule is applicable in every situation

    (C) good, because familiarity between officers and inmates may lead to a breakdown of discipline

    (D) good, because the more impersonally an inmate is treated, the easier he or she is to control.

83. A new officer asks you what to do if an inmate refuses to carry out an order. As captain, you should advise the officer to

    (A) reconsider if the order was a reasonable one

    (B) avoid being drawn into a situation of this kind

    (C) immediately summon a superior for assistance

    (D) warn the inmate that he or she will be subject to disciplinary action

84. A correction officer is expected to report unusual situations to his superior and should use all of his senses. Which of the following statements regarding the use of sight by a correction officer is correct?

    (A) The officer should constantly watch inmates in his charge since observation is an effective medium for control and custody.

    (B) The officer should look just above inmates' heads (since this keeps them from becoming nervous) while his peripheral vision takes in that which is important.

    (C) The officer should not allow his eyes to rest on any one inmate since this is certain to provoke hostility.

    (D) The officer should train himself to concentrate on the hands of inmates since information gained from looking at inmate's faces is usually unreliable.

85. Which of the following guidelines is *least* appropriate for a key control system in a correctional institution?

    (A) All keys should be issued from a central location such as the institution control room.

    (B) Officers should not be permitted to withdraw keys unless they give receipts for them.

    (C) The key control center should have at all times at least one duplicate set of each bunch of keys.

    (D) Only reliable prisoners, such as "trusties," should be permitted to handle keys.

86. The degree of security needed to confine an inmate depends upon the

    (A) caliber of personnel assigned to the institution

    (B) personality and background of the inmate

    (C) type of programs available in the institution

    (D) type of security facilities within the institution

87. The essential features of good organizational structure for an institution for adult prisoners should include all of the following *except*

    (A) a constructive system of communication with inmates

    (B) a program of personnel development for correctional staff, including the classification of positions and in-service training

    (C) separate administrative controls for the personnel, inmates, and programs of the institution

    (D) a system for developing constructive community relationships

88. Where possible, the use of consolidated jails serving several jurisdictions has been recommended in lieu of individual local facilities. Of the following, the major advantage of consolidated jails is that

    (A) a more effective correctional program can be offered when funds and other resources are pooled

    (B) the population of local jails is reduced to more manageable proportions

    (C) specialized institutions can develop their separate treatment methods

    (D) community acceptance is more easily obtained for one large facility than for several smaller ones

89. A positive program of maintaining discipline is essential in preventing unrest or disturbances. A good disciplinary program is one that

    (A) is based on the use of disciplinary committees to punish all infractions of the rules

    (B) does not include punishment for violations of the rules except in extreme cases

    (C) maintains order with minimal friction and uses punishment in a constructive manner

    (D) uses administrative segregation as the basic method for controlling inmates

90. Which of the following statements concerning the relationship between custody and rehabilitative programs is *incorrect*?

    (A) Services and facilities for rehabilitative treatment operate effectively only in a climate where control is constant.

    (B) Positive programs of inmate activities generally weaken the effectiveness of security measures.

    (C) Rehabilitative services must be correlated with a system of sound custody, security, and control of inmates.

    (D) Security and control procedures produce maximum results when they are implemented in a manner that gains the cooperation of the majority of inmates.

91. The one of the following that has been a major obstacle to effective rehabilitation of prison inmates is the fact that

    (A) inmates have not been able to handle the permissiveness of the group approach to treatment

    (B) most correctional staff members are not interested in assuming new roles or in communicating constructively with inmates

    (C) the inconclusive results of treatment programs have reinforced doubts that prison inmates are capable of behavioral change

    (D) the inmate culture itself raises barriers against genuine participation of prisoners in treatment programs

92. While conducting a training session for correction officers, the most valid of the following points you can make on the subject of suicide is that

    (A) prisoners who are observed talking to themselves in a halting manner are suicidal and must be reported to the psychiatrist

    (B) those who try to commit suicide and fail often try again

    (C) the prisoner who tells a member of the staff that he is going to commit suicide should be ignored as he is engaging in a manipulative device

    (D) minor attempts at suicide, such as injuring an arm with shallow cuts, should be reported to the captain for disciplinary action rather than to a psychiatrist

93. The single most important factor when considering the problems involved in rehabilitating an offender is that the ultimate change sought

    (A) depends upon the inmate's becoming a self-disciplined person which, in turn, depends upon his or her accepting institutional discipline

    (B) is a harmonious adjustment to institutional life

(C) is adjustment to freedom in the community

(D) is making the offender aware that institutional life is not a penalty but an opportunity

94. Decision making is a rational process calling for a suspended judgment by the supervisor until all the facts have been ascertained and analyzed and the consequences of alternative courses of action studied. Then the decision maker

(A) acts as both judge and jury and selects what he or she believes to be the best of the alternative plans

(B) consults with those who will be most directly involved to obtain a recommendation as to the most appropriate course of action

(C) reviews the facts already analyzed, reduces all thoughts to writing, and selects the course of action having the fewest negative consequences in case the thinking has contained an error

(D) stops and considers the matter for at least twenty-four hours before referring it to a superior for evaluation

95. The correctional officer must master certain proven principles and techniques if he or she is to successfully supervise incarcerated offenders. One of these principles states, "A correction officer should not be too anxious to reveal completely to inmates what he or she knows and thinks." Which of the following is a reason for applying this principle?

(A) A correction officer should discipline him- or herself to think in terms of action rather than concepts.

(B) An inmate's action is often favorably influenced when the inmate fears the unknown.

(C) Inmate feelings of self-respect are enhanced if inmates believe they know something the correction officer does not know.

(D) To the greatest extent possible, a correction officer should speak to inmates only when spoken to.

96. Assume that you are a captain and that a correction officer with a long and excellent record has recently begun to exhibit laziness and a lack of interest in her work. Of the following, the best course of action for you as her superior officer to follow is to

(A) call the attention of the other officers to this case in order to demonstrate that good work requires constant, diligent application

(B) start disciplinary action immediately against this correction officer as you would against any other

(C) overlook the matter until the correction officer again demonstrates her usual high quality of work

(D) interview the correction officer and attempt to determine the reason for her unusual behavior

97. You observe that a correction officer under your command is not carrying out of specific assignment in accordance with the instructions you gave. Of the following, the most important reason why you should have this officer repeat your instructions is that

(A) instructions can be misunderstood even by excellent correction officers

(B) it will indicate that incorrect instructions were given

(C) inefficiency usually has serious consequences

(D) oral instructions should be repeated when issued to ensure that they are understood

98. Since a correction captain expects subordinates to carry out commands to the letter, it is most important for the captain to

    (A) check on the execution of all commands immediately

    (B) issue commands clearly and make sure they are understood

    (C) issue only commands that would seem reasonable to anyone

    (D) make only one officer responsible for the execution of any one command

99. Of the following, the one that is generally not a characteristic of individuals in a prison population is the

    (A) lack of ability to articulate feelings and ideas

    (B) inability to postpone gratification

    (C) orientation of the individual as receiver and a tendency to view others as givers

    (D) preoccupation with concrete and immediate objects, wishes, and needs.

100. A correction officer under your supervision comes to you to complain about a decision you have made in assigning the officers. You consider the matter to be unimportant, but it seems to be very important to him. He is excited and very angry. The best way to handle this case is to

    (A) tell him to take it up with the deputy warden

    (B) refuse to talk to him until he has calmed down

    (C) show him at once how unimportant the matter is and how absurd his argument is

    (D) let him talk until he "gets it off his chest" and then explain the reasons for your decision.

OFFICIAL KEY ANSWERS TO SAMPLE PROMOTION QUESTIONS FROM PREVIOUS EXAMS

1. A	21. A	41. D	61. B	81. D
2. C	22. A	42. D	62. C	82. C
3. A	23. B	43. B	63. C	83. D
4. B	24. C	44. A	64. A	84. A
5. B	25. C	45. C	65. C	85. D
6. A	26. C	46. D	66. D	86. B
7. D	27. A	47. D	67. A	87. C
8. C	28. D	48. A	68. B	88. A
9. D	29. A	49. B	69. D	89. C
10. D	30. D	50. D	70. A	90. B
11. D	31. C	51. C	71. C	91. D
12. C	32. B	52. C	72. D	92. B
13. D	33. D	53. A	73. C	93. C
14. B	34. C	54. D	74. A	94. A
15. C	35. B	55. B	75. D	95. B
16. A	36. C	56. C	76. B	96. D
17. D	37. A	57. B	77. B	97. A
18. B	38. C	58. C	78. C	98. B
19. B	39. C	59. A	79. B	99. A
20. C	40. C	60. D	80. A	100. D

Appendix—
Physical Fitness Course

In the law enforcement universe, much of the hiring decision is based upon the candidate's physical status. Considering the demands made upon the law enforcement officer's body, the emphasis on physical fitness is entirely reasonable. From your own standpoint as a serious candidate, it makes sense to devote at least as much attention to preparing your body for the physical test as to preparing your mind for the written exam.

Obviously, if you are considering yourself as a law enforcement officer candidate, you consider yourself a healthy, physically fit person. Even so, it would be wise to consult with your own doctor before proceeding. Tell your doctor about the type of work you have in mind, describe the physical demands, and ask for an assessment of your potential to withstand these rigors. If your doctor foresees any potential problems, either in passing the exams or in facing the demands of the job, discuss corrective measures and remedial programs right now. Follow the medical advice you receive concerning diet and general lifestyle. If the jurisdiction to which you are applying provides you with a description of the physical performance test you must take, describe it to your doctor. You may be able to pick up special tips to prepare yourself to do well on your exam. Your doctor may have a physical conditioning program to recommend. If not, design your own program. You may find the following suggestions prepared by the President's Council on Physical Fitness convenient to follow just as printed or helpful as you tailor-make a fitness program to your own needs and time requirements.

DEFINING FITNESS

Physical fitness is to the human body what fine tuning is to an engine. It enables us to perform up to our potential. Fitness can be described as a condition that helps us look, feel and do our best. More specifically, it is:

"The ability to perform daily tasks vigorously and alertly, with energy left over for enjoying leisure-time activities and meeting emergency demands. It is the ability to endure, to bear up, to withstand stress, and to carry on in circumstances where an unfit person could not continue and is a major basis for good health and well-being."

Physical fitness involves the performance of the heart, the lungs, and the muscles of the body. And, since what we do with our bodies also affects what we can do with our minds, fitness influences to some degree qualities such as mental alertness and emotional stability.

As you undertake your fitness program, it's important to remember that fitness is an individual quality that varies from person to person. It is influenced by age, sex, heredity, personal habits, exercise and eating practices. You can't do anything about the first three factors. However, it is within your power to change and improve the others where needed.

Knowing the Basics

Physical fitness is most easily understood by examining its components, or "parts." There is widespread agreement that these four components are basic:

CARDIORESPIRATORY ENDURANCE—the ability to deliver oxygen and nutrients to tissues, and to remove wastes, over sustained periods of time. Long runs and swims are among the methods employed in measuring this component.

MUSCULAR STRENGTH—the ability of a muscle to exert force for a brief period of time. Upper-body strength, for example, can be measured by various weight-lifting exercises.

MUSCULAR ENDURANCE—the ability of a muscle, or a group of muscles, to sustain repeated contractions or to continue applying force against a fixed object. Pushups are often used to test endurance of arm and shoulder muscles.

FLEXIBILITY—the ability to move joints and use muscles through their full range of motion. The sit-and-reach test is a good measure of flexibility of the lower back and backs of the upper legs.

BODY COMPOSITION is often considered a component of fitness. It refers to the makeup of the body in terms of lean mass (muscle, bone, vital tissue, and organs) and fat mass. An optimal ratio of fat to lean mass is an indication of fitness, and the right types of exercises will help you decrease body fat and increase or maintain muscle mass.

A WORKOUT SCHEDULE

How often, how long, and how hard you exercise, and what kinds of exercises you do should be determined by what you are trying to accomplish. Your goals, your present fitness level, age, health, skills, interest, and convenience are among the factors you should consider. For example, an athlete training for high-level competition would follow a different program than a person whose goals are good health and the ability to meet work and recreational needs.

Your exercise program should include something from each of the four basic fitness components described previously. Each workout should begin with a warmup and end with a cooldown. As a general rule, space your workouts throughout the week and avoid consecutive days of hard exercise.

Here are the amounts of activity necessary for the average, healthy person to maintain a minimum level of overall fitness. Included are some of the popular exercises for each category.

WARMUP—5–10 minutes of exercises such as walking, slow jogging, knee lifts, arm circles or trunk rotations. Low intensity movements that simulate movements to be used in the activity can also be included in the warmup.

MUSCULAR STRENGTH—a minimum of two 20-minute sessions per week that include exercises for all the major muscle groups. Lifting weights is the most effective way to increase strength.

MUSCULAR ENDURANCE—at least three 30-minute sessions each week that include exercises such as calisthenics, pushups, situps, pullups, and weight training for all the major muscle groups.

CARDIORESPIRATORY ENDURANCE—at least three 20-minute bouts of continuous aerobic (activity requiring oxygen) rhythmic exercise each week. Popular aerobic conditioning activities include brisk walking, jogging, swimming, cycling, rope-jumping, rowing, cross-country skiing, and some continuous action games like racquetball and handball.

FLEXIBILITY—10–12 minutes of daily stretching exercises performed slowly, without a bouncing motion. This can be included after a warmup or during a cooldown.

COOL DOWN—a minimum of 5–10 minutes of slow walking, low-level exercise, combined with stretching.

A MATTER OF PRINCIPLE

The keys to selecting the right kinds of exercises for developing and maintaining each of the basic components of fitness are found in these principles:

SPECIFICITY—pick the right kind of activities to affect each component. Strength training results in specific strength changes. Also, train for the specific activity you're interested in. For example, optimal swimming performance is best achieved when the muscles involved in swimming are trained for the movements required. It does not necessarily follow that a good runner is a good swimmer.

OVERLOAD—work hard enough, at levels that are vigorous and long enough to overload your body above its resting level, to bring about improvement.

REGULARITY—you can't hoard physical fitness. At least three balanced workouts a week are necessary to maintain a desirable level of fitness.

PROGRESSION—increase the intensity, frequency and/or duration of activity over periods of time in order to improve.

Some activities can be used to fulfill more than one of your basic exercise requirements. For example, in addition to increasing cardiorespiratory endurance, running builds muscular endurance in the legs, and swimming develops the arm, shoulder and chest muscles. If you select the proper activities, it is possible to fit parts of your muscular endurance workout into your cardiorespiratory workout and save time.

Measuring Your Heart Rate

Heart rate is widely accepted as a good method for measuring intensity during running, swimming, cycling and other aerobic activities. Exercise that doesn't raise your heart rate to a certain level and keep it there for 20 minutes won't contribute significantly to cardiovascular fitness.

The heart rate you should maintain is called your **target heart rate.** There are several ways of arriving at this figure. One of the simplest is: **maximum heart rate** (220 – age) × 70%. Thus, the target heart rate for a 40-year-old would be 126.

Some methods for figuring the target rate take individual differences into consideration. Here is one of them:

1. Subtract age from 220 to find **maximum heart rate.**

2. Subtract resting heart rate (see below) from maximum heart rate to determine **heart rate reserve.**

3. Take 70% of heart rate reserve to determine **heart rate raise.**

4. Add heart rate raise to resting heart rate to find **target rate.**

Resting heart rate should be determined by taking your pulse after sitting quietly for five minutes. When checking heart rate during a workout, take your pulse within five seconds after interrupting exercise because it starts to go down once you stop moving. Count pulse for 10 seconds and multiply by six to get the per-minute rate.

THE PROGRAM

The program below assumes that you have not been putting all of your muscles to any consistent use and that you are starting from close to "couch potato" status. If you are already in pretty good shape, you might be able to start more quickly. But do not overdo. A gradual build-up makes sense.

The program starts with an orientation or "get-set" series of exercises that will allow you to bring all major muscles into use easily and painlessly.

There are then five graded levels.

As you move from one to the next, you will be building toward a practical and satisfying level of fitness.

By building gradually, progressively, you will be building soundly.

What the Exercises Are For

There are three general types—warmup exercises, conditioning exercises and circulatory activities.

The warmup exercises stretch and limber up the muscles and speed up the action of the heart and lungs, thus preparing the body for greater exertion and reducing the possibility of unnecessary strain.

The conditioning exercises are systematically planned to tone up abdominal, back, leg, arm and other major muscles.

The circulatory activities produce contractions of large muscle groups for relatively longer periods than the conditioning exercises—to stimulate and strengthen the circulatory and respiratory systems.

The plan calls for doing 10 mild exercises during the orientation period and, thereafter, the warmup exercises and the seven conditioning exercises listed for each level. The first six exercises of the orientation program are used as warmup exercises throughout the graded levels.

When it comes to the circulatory activities, you choose one each workout. Alternately running and walking … skipping rope … running in place. All are effective. You can choose running and walking on a pleasant day and one of the others for use indoors when the weather is inclement. You can switch about for variety.

How You Progress

A sound physical conditioning program should take into account your individual tolerance—your ability to execute a series of activities without undue discomfort or fatigue. It should provide for developing your tolerance by increasing the work load so you gradually become able to achieve more and more with less and less fatigue and with increasingly rapid recovery.

As you move from level to level, some exercises will be modified so they call for increased effort.

Others will remain the same, but you will build more strength and stamina by increasing the number of repetitions.

You will be increasing your fitness another way, as well.

At level 1, your objective will be to gradually reduce, from workout to workout, the "breathing spells" between exercises until you can do the seven conditioning exercises without resting. You will proceed in the same fashion with the more difficult exercises and increased repetitions at succeeding levels.

You will find the program designed—the progression carefully planned—to make this feasible. You will be able to proceed at your own pace, competing with yourself rather than with anyone else—and this is of great importance for sound conditioning.

Note: Gradually speeding up, from workout to workout, the rate at which you do each exercise will provide greater stimulation for the circulatory and respiratory systems and also help to keep your workouts short. However, the seven conditioning exercises should not be a race against time. Perform each exercise correctly to insure maximum benefit.

How Long at Each Level

Your objective at each level will be to reach the point where you can do all the exercises called for, for the number of times indicated, without resting between exercises.

But, start slowly.

It cannot be emphasized enough that by moving forward gradually you will be moving forward solidly, avoiding sudden strains and excesses that could make you ache and hold you back for several days.

If you find yourself at first unable to complete any exercises—to do continuously all the repetitions called for—stop when you encounter difficulty. Rest briefly, then take up where you left off and complete the count. If you have difficulty at first, there will be less and less with succeeding workouts.

Stay at each level for at least three weeks. If you have not passed the prove-out test at the end of that time, continue at the same level until you do. The prove-out test calls for performing—in three consecutive workouts—the seven conditioning exercises without resting and satisfactorily fulfilling the requirement for one circulatory activity.

A Measure of Your Progress

You will, of course, be able to observe the increase in your strength and stamina from week to week in many ways—including the increasing facility with which you do the exercises at a given level.

In addition, there is a 2-minute step test you can use to measure and keep a running record of the improvement in your circulatory efficiency, one of the most important of all aspects of fitness.

The immediate response of the cardiovascular system to exercise differs markedly between well-conditioned individuals and others. The test measures the response in terms of pulse rate taken shortly after a series of steps up and down onto a bench or chair.

Although it does not take long, it is necessarily vigorous. Stop if you become overly fatigued while taking it. You should not try it until you have completed the orientation period.

The Step Test

Use any sturdy bench or chair 15–17 inches in height.

Count 1—Place right foot on bench.
Count 2—Bring left foot alongside of right and stand erect.
Count 3—Lower right foot to floor.
Count 4—Lower left foot to floor.

REPEAT the 4-count movement 30 times a minute for two minutes.

THEN sit down on bench or chair for two minutes.

FOLLOWING the 2-minute rest, take your pulse for 30 seconds. Double the count to get the per-minute rate. (You can find the pulse by applying middle and index finger of one hand firmly to the inside of the wrist of the other hand, on the thumb side.)

Record your score for future comparisons. In succeeding tests—about once every two weeks— you probably will find your pulse rate becoming lower as your physical condition improves.

Three important points:

1. For best results, do not engage in physical activity for at least 10 minutes before taking the test. Take it at about the same time of day and always use the same bench or chair.

2. Remember that pulse rates vary among individuals. This is an individual test. What is important is not a comparison of your pulse rate with that of anybody else—but rather a record of how your own rate is reduced as your fitness increases.

3. As you progress, the rate at which your pulse is lowered should gradually level off. This is an indication that you are approaching peak fitness.

Your Progress Records

Charts are provided for the orientation program and for each of the five levels.

They list the exercises to be done and the goal for each exercise in terms of number of repetitions, distance, etc.

They also provide space in which to record your progress—(1) in completing the recommended 15 workouts at each level, (2) in accomplishing the three prove-out workouts before moving on to a succeeding level, and (3) in the results as you take the step test from time to time.

A sample chart and progress record for one of the five levels is shown below.

You do the warmup exercises and the conditioning exercises along with one circulatory activity for each workout.

Check off each workout as you complete it. The last three numbers are for the prove-out workouts, in which the seven conditioning exercises should be done without resting. Check them off as you accomplish them.

You are now ready to proceed to the next level.

As you take the step test—at about 2-week intervals—enter your pulse rate.

When you move on to the next level, transfer the last pulse rate from the preceding level. Enter it in the margin to the left of the new progress record and circle it so it will be convenient for continuing reference.

SAMPLE	GOAL
Warmup Exercises	Exercises 1–6 of Orientation program
Conditioning Exercises	Uninterrupted repetitions
1. Bend and stretch	10
2. Sprinter	6
3. Sitting stretch	15
4. Knee pushup	12
5. Situp (fingers laced)	10
6. Leg raiser	10 each leg
7. Flutter kick	30
Circulatory activity (choose one each workout)	
Jog-walk (jog 50, walk 50)	$1/2$ mile
Rope (skip 30 secs.; rest 60 secs.)	3 series
Run in place (run 100, hop 25—2 cycles)	3 minutes
Water activities (see pages 361–362)	
Your progress record 1 2 3 4 5 6 7 8 9 10 11 12	13 14 15
Step test (pulse)	Prove-out workouts

Getting Set—Orientation Workouts

With the series of mild exercises listed in the chart which follows and described on the next two pages, you can get yourself ready—without severe aches or pains—for the progressive conditioning program.

Plan to spend a minimum of one week for preliminary conditioning. Don't hesitate to spend two weeks or three if necessary for you to limber up enough to accomplish all the exercises easily and without undue fatigue.

Note: The correction officer physical performance test is identical for both men and women because all correction officers must be able to perform all tasks. The demands of corrections work do not cater to weakness of any form. The women who can meet the physical standards take their places as full-fledged correction officers sharing equally in duties, responsibilities, risks and hard work.

There are, of course, real physiological differences between men and women. Some conditioning exercises are modified in recognition of these differences. Women with the potential to pass the correction officer physical performance test should find that the women's program described here, if followed faithfully, should prepare them well.

THE PROGRAM FOR WOMEN

ORIENTATION PROGRAM: WOMEN	GOAL
Conditioning Exercises	*Repetitions*
*1. Bend and stretch	10
*2. Knee lift	10 left, 10 right
*3. Wing stretcher	20
*4. Half knee bend	10
*5. Arm circles	15 each way
*6. Body bender	10 left, 10 right
7. Prone arch	10
8. Knee pushup	6
9. Head and shoulder curl	5
10. Ankle stretch	15
Circulatory activity (choose one each workout)	
Walking	¹/₂ mile
Rope (skip 15 secs.; rest 60 secs.)	3 series

The first six exercises of the orientation program will be used as warmup exercises throughout the graded levels.

Step Test Record—After completing the orientation program, take the 2-minute step test. Record your pulse rate here: _____. This will be the base rate with which you can make comparisons in the future.

1. Bend and Stretch

Starting position: Stand erect, feet shoulder-width apart.
Action: Count 1. Bend trunk forward and down, flexing knees. Stretch gently in attempt to touch fingers to toes or floor. Count 2. Return to starting position.
Note: Do slowly, stretch and relax at intervals rather than in rhythm.

2. Knee Lift

Starting position: Stand erect, feet together, arms at sides.
Action: Count 1. Raise left knee as high as possible, grasping leg with hands and pulling knee against body while keeping back straight. Count 2. Lower to starting position. Counts 3 and 4. Repeat with right knee.

3. Wing Stretcher

Starting position: Stand erect, elbows at shoulder height, fists clenched in front of chest.
Action: Count 1. Thrust elbows backward vigorously without arching back. Keep head erect, elbows at shoulder height. Count 2. Return to starting position.

4. Half Knee Bend

Starting position: Stand erect, hands on hips.
Action: Count 1. Bend knees halfway while extending arms forward, palms down. Count 2. Return to starting position.

5. Arm Circles

Starting position: Stand erect, arms extended sideward at shoulder height, palms up.
Action: Describe small circles backward with hands. Keep head erect. Do 15 backward circles. Reverse, turn palms down and do 15 small circles forward.

6. Body Bender

Starting position: Stand, feet shoulder-width apart, hands behind neck, fingers interlaced.
Action: Count 1. Bend trunk sideward to left as far as possible, keeping hands behind neck. Count 2. Return to starting position. Counts 3 and 4. Repeat to the right.

7. Prone Arch

Starting position: Lie face down, hands tucked under thighs.
Action: Count 1. Raise head, shoulders, and legs from floor. Count 2. Return to starting position.

8. Knee Pushup

Starting position: Lie on floor, face down, legs together, knees bent with feet raised off floor, hands on floor under shoulders, palms down.
Action: Count 1. Push upper body off floor until arms are fully extended and body is in straight line from head to knees. Count 2. Return to starting position.

9. Head and Shoulder Curl

Starting position: Lie on back, hands tucked under small of back, palms down.
Action: Count 1. Tighten abdominal muscles, lift head and pull shoulders and elbows off floor. Hold for four seconds. Count 2. Return to starting position.

10. Ankle Stretch

Starting position: Stand on a stair, large book, or block of wood, with weight on balls of feet and heels raised.
Action: Count 1. Lower heels. Count 2. Raise heels.

Circulatory Activities

WALKING—Step off at a lively pace, swing arms and breathe deeply.
ROPE—Any form of skipping or jumping is acceptable. Gradually increase the tempo as your skill and condition improve.

WOMEN: LEVEL ONE	GOAL
Warmup Exercises	Exercises 1–6 of Orientation program
Conditioning Exercises	Uninterrupted repetitions
1. Toe touch	5
2. Sprinter	8
3. Sitting stretch	10
4. Knee pushup	8
5. Situp (arms extended)	5
6. Leg raiser	5 each leg
7. Flutter kick	20
Circulatory activity (choose one each workout)	
Walking (120 steps a minute)	$^1/_2$ mile
Rope (skip 30 sec.; rest 60 secs.)	2 series
Run in place (run 50; straddle hop 10—2 cycles)	2 minutes
Water activities (see pages 361–362)	
Your progress record 1 2 3 4 5 6 7 8 9 10 11 12	13 14 15
Step test (pulse)	Prove-out workouts

1. Toe Touch
Starting Position: Stand at attention.
Action: Count 1. Bend trunk forward and down, keeping knees straight, touching fingers to ankles. Count 2. Bounce and touch fingers to top of feet. Count 3. Bounce and touch fingers to toes. Count 4. Return to starting position.

2. Sprinter
Starting position: Squat, hands on floor, fingers pointed forward, left leg fully extended to rear.
Action: Count 1. Reverse position of feet in bouncing movement, bringing left foot to hands, extending right leg backward—all in one motion. Count 2. Reverse feet again, returning to starting position.

3. Sitting Stretch
Starting position: Sit, legs spread apart, hands on knees.
Action: Count 1. Bend forward at waist, extending arms as far forward as possible. Count 2. Return to starting position.

4. Knee Pushup
Starting position: Lie on floor, face down, legs together, knees bent with feet raised off floor, hands on floor under shoulders, palms down.
Action: Count 1. Push upper body off floor until arms are fully extended and body is in straight line from head to knees. Count 2. Return to starting position.

5. Situp (Arms Extended)
Starting position: Lie on back, legs straight and together, arms extended beyond head.
Action: Count 1. Bring arms forward over head, roll up to sitting position, sliding hands along legs, grasping ankles. Count 2. Roll back to starting position.

6. Leg Raiser

Starting position: Right side of body on floor, head resting on right arm.
Action: Lift left leg about 24" off floor, then lower it. Do required number of repetitions. Repeat on other side.

7. Flutter Kick

Starting position: Lie face down, hands tucked under thighs.
Action: Arch the back, bringing chest and head up, then flutter kick continuously, moving the legs 8"–10" apart. Kick from hips and with knees slightly bent. Count each kick as one.

Circulatory Activities

WALKING—Maintain a pace of 120 steps per minute for a distance of 1/2 mile. Swing arms and breathe deeply.

ROPE—Skip or jump rope continuously using any form for 30 seconds and then rest 60 seconds. Repeat 2 times.

RUN IN PLACE—Raise each foot at least 4" off the floor and jog in place. Count 1 each time left foot touches floor. Complete number of running steps called for in chart, then do specified number of straddle hops. Complete 2 cycles of alternate running and hopping for time specified on chart.

STRADDLE HOP—*Starting position:* At attention.

Action: Count 1. Swing arms sideward and upward, touching hands above head (arms straight) while simultaneously moving feet sideward and apart in a single jumping motion. Count 2. Spring back to starting position. Two counts in one hop.

WOMEN: LEVEL TWO	GOAL
Warmup Exercises	Exercises 1–6 of Orientation program
Conditioning Exercises	Uninterrupted repetitions
1. Toe touch	15
2. Sprinter	12
3. Sitting stretch	15
4. Knee pushup	12
5. Situp (fingers laced)	10
6. Leg raiser	10 each leg
7. Flutter kick	30
Circulatory activity (choose one each workout)	
Jog-walk (jog 50, walk 50)	½ mile
Rope (skip 30 sec.; rest 60 secs.)	3 series
Run in place (run 80; hop 15—2 cycles)	3 minutes
Water activities (see pages 361–362)	
Your progress record 1 2 3 4 5 6 7 8 9 10 11 12	13 14 15
Step test (pulse)	Prove-out workouts

1. Toe Touch

Starting position: Stand at attention.

Action: Count 1. Bend trunk forward and down, keeping knees straight, touching fingers to ankles. Count 2. Bounce and touch fingers to top of feet. Count 3. Bounce and touch fingers to toes. Count 4. Return to starting position.

2. Sprinter

Starting position: Squat, hands on floor, fingers pointed forward, left leg fully extended to rear.

Action: Count 1. Reverse position of feet in bouncing movement, bringing left foot to hands, extending right leg backward—all in one motion. Count 2. Reverse feet again, returning to starting position.

3. Sitting Stretch

Starting position: Sit, legs spread apart, hands on knees.

Action: Count 1. Bend forward at waist, extending arms as far forward as possible. Count 2. Return to starting position.

4. Knee Pushup

Starting position: Lie on floor, face down, legs together, knees bent with feet raised off floor, hands on floor under shoulders, palms down.

Action: Count 1. Push upper body off floor until arms are fully extended and body is in straight line from head to knees. Count 2. Return to starting position.

5. Situp (Fingers Laced)

Starting position: Lie on back, legs straight and feet spread approximately 1' apart. Fingers laced behind neck.

Action: Count 1. Curl up to sitting position and turn trunk to left. Touch right elbow to left knee. Count 2. Return to starting position. Count 3. Curl up to sitting position and turn trunk to right. Touch left elbow to right knee. Count 4. Return to starting position. Score one situp each time you return to starting position. Knees may be bent as necessary.

6. Leg Raiser

Starting position: Right side of body on floor, head resting on right arm.

Action: Lift left leg about 24" off floor, then lower it. Do required number of repetitions. Repeat on other side.

7. Flutter Kick

Starting position: Lie face down, hands tucked under thighs.

Action: Arch the back, bringing chest and head up, then flutter kick continuously, moving the legs 8"–10" apart. Kick from hips with knees slightly bent. Count each kick as one.

Circulatory Activities

JOG-WALK—Jog and walk alternately for number of paces indicated on chart for distance specified.

ROPE—Skip or jump rope continuously using any form for 30 seconds and then rest 60 seconds. Repeat 3 times.

RUN IN PLACE—Raise each foot at least 4" off floor and jog in place. Count 1 each time left foot touches floor. Complete number of running steps called for in chart, then do specified number of straddle hops. Complete 2 cycles of alternate running and hopping for time specified on chart.

STRADDLE HOP—*Starting position:* At attention.

Action: Count 1. Swing arms sideward and upward, touching hands above head (arms straight) while simultaneously moving feet sideward and apart in a single jumping motion. Count 2. Spring back to starting position. Two counts in one hop.

WOMEN: LEVEL THREE	GOAL
Warmup	Exercises 1–6 of Orientation program
Conditioning Exercises	Uninterrupted repetitions
1. Toe touch	20
2. Sprinter	16
3. Sitting stretch (fingers laced)	15
4. Knee pushup	20
5. Situp (arms extended, knees up)	15
6. Leg raiser	16 each leg
7. Flutter kick	40
Circulatory activity (choose one each workout)	
Jog-walk (jog 50, walk 50)	¾ mile
Rope (skip 45 secs.; rest 30 secs.)	3 series
Run in place (run 110, hop 20—2 cycles)	4 minutes
Water activities (see pages 361–362)	
Your progress record 1 2 3 4 5 6 7 8 9 10 11 12	13 14 15
Step test (pulse)	Prove-out workouts

1. Toe Touch

Starting position: Stand at attention.

Action: 1. Bend trunk forward and down, keeping knees straight, touching fingers to ankles. Count 2. Bounce and touch fingers to top of feet. Count 3. Bounce and touch fingers to toes. Count 4. Return to starting position.

2. Sprinter

Starting position: Squat, hands on floor, fingers pointed forward, left leg fully extended to rear.

Action: Count 1. Reverse position of feet in bouncing movement, bringing left foot to hands, extending right leg backward all in one motion. Count 2. Reverse feet again, returning to starting position.

3. Sitting Stretch (Fingers Laced)

Starting position: Sit, legs spread apart, fingers laced behind neck.

Action: Count 1. Bend forward at waist, reaching elbows as close to floor as possible. Count 2. Return to starting position.

4. Knee Pushup

Starting position: Lie on floor, face down, legs together, knees bent with feet raised off floor, hands on floor under shoulders, palms down.

Action: Count 1. Push upper body off floor until arms are fully flexed and body in straight line from head to knees. Count 2. Return to starting position.

5. Situp (Arms Extended, Knees Up)

Starting position: Lie on back, legs straight, arms extended overhead.

Action: Count 1. Sit up, reaching forward with arms encircling knees while pulling them tightly to chest. Count 2. Return to starting position. Do this exercise rhythmically, without breaks in the movement.

6. Leg Raiser

Starting position: Right side of body on floor, head resting on right arm.

Action: Lift left leg about 24" off floor, then lower it. Do required number of repetitions. Repeat on other side.

7. Flutter Kick

Starting position: Lie face down, hands tucked under thighs.

Action: Arch the back, bringing chest and head up. Then flutter kick continuously, moving the legs 8"–10" apart. Kick from hips with knees slightly bent. Count each kick as one.

Circulatory Activities

JOG-WALK—Jog and walk alternately for number of paces indicated on chart for distance specified.

ROPE—Skip or jump rope continuously using any form for 45 seconds and then rest 30 seconds. Repeat 3 times.

RUN IN PLACE—Raise each foot at least 4" off floor and jog in place. Count 1 each time left foot touches floor. Complete number of running steps called for in chart, then do specified number of straddle hops. Complete 2 cycles of alternate running and hopping for time specified on chart.

STRADDLE HOP—*Starting position:* At attention.

Action: Count 1. Swing arms sideward and upward, touching hands above head (arms straight) while simultaneously moving feet sideward and apart in a single jumping motion. Count 2. Spring back to starting position. Two counts in one hop.

WOMEN: LEVEL FOUR	GOAL
Warmup Exercises	Exercises 1–6 of Orientation program
Conditioning Exercises	Uninterrupted repetitions
1. Toe touch (twist and bend)	15 each side
2. Sprinter	20
3. Sitting stretch (alternate)	20
4. Pushup	8
5. Situp (arms crossed, knees bent)	20
6. Leg raiser (whip)	10 each leg
7. Prone arch (arms extended)	15
Circulatory activity (choose one each workout)	
Jog-walk (jog 100, walk 50)	1 mile
Rope (skip 60 secs.; rest 30 secs.)	3 series
Run in place (run 145, hop 25—2 cycles)	5 minutes
Water Activities (see pages 361–362)	
Your progress record 1 2 3 4 5 6 7 8 9 10 11 12	13 14 15
Step test (pulse)	Prove-out workouts

1. Toe Touch (Twist and Bend)

Starting position: Stand, feet shoulder-width apart, arms extended over head, thumbs interlocked.

Action: Count 1. Twist trunk to right and touch floor inside right foot with fingers of both hands. Count 2. Touch floor outside toes of right foot. Count 3. Touch floor outside heel of right foot. Count 4. Return to starting position, sweeping trunk and arms upward in a wide arc. On the next four counts, repeat action to left side.

2. Sprinter

Starting position: Squat, hands on floor, fingers pointed forward, left leg fully extended to rear.

Action: Count 1. Reverse position of feet in bouncing movement, bringing left foot to hands, extending right leg backward—all in one motion. Count 2. Reverse feet again, returning to starting position.

3. Sitting Stretch (Alternate)

Starting position: Sit, legs spread apart, fingers laced behind neck, elbows back.

Action: Count 1. Bend forward to left, touching forehead to left knee. Count 2. Return to starting position. Counts 3 and 4. Repeat to right. Score one repetition each time you return to starting position. Knees may be bent if necessary.

4. Pushup

Starting position: Lie on floor, face down, legs together, hands on floor under shoulders with fingers pointing straight ahead.

Action: Count 1. Push body off floor by extending arms so that weight rests on hands and toes. Count 2. Lower the body until chest touches floor.

Note: Body should be kept straight, buttocks should not be raised, abdomen should not sag.

5. Situp (Arms Crossed, Knees Bent)

Starting position: Lie on back, arms crossed on chest, hands grasping opposite shoulders, knees bent to right angle, feet flat on floor.

Action: Count 1. Curl up to sitting position. Count 2. Return to starting position.

6. Leg Raiser (Whip)

Starting position: Right side of body on floor, right arm supporting head.

Action: Whip left leg up and down rapidly lifting as high as possible off the floor. Count each whip as one. Reverse position and whip right leg up and down.

7. Prone Arch (Arms Extended)

Starting position: Lie face down, legs straight and together, arms extended to sides at shoulder level.

Action: Count 1. Arch the back, bringing arms, chest and head up, and raising legs as high as possible. Count 2. Return to starting position.

Circulatory Activities

JOG-WALK—Jog and walk alternately for number of paces indicated on chart for distance specified.

ROPE—Skip or jump rope continuously using any form for 60 seconds and then rest 30 seconds. Repeat 3 times.

RUN IN PLACE—Raise each foot at least 4" off floor and jog in place. Count 1 each time left foot touches floor. Complete number of running steps called for in chart, then do specified number of straddle hops. Complete 2 cycles of alternate running and hopping for time specified on chart.

STRADDLE HOP—*Starting position:* At attention.

Action: Count 1. Swing arms sideward and upward, touching hands above head (arms straight) while simultaneously moving feet sideward and apart in a single jumping motion. Count 2. Spring back to starting position. Two counts in one hop.

WOMEN: LEVEL FIVE	GOAL
Warmup Exercises	Exercises 1–6 of Orientation program
Conditioning Exercises	Uninterrupted repetitions
1. Toe touch (twist and bend)	25 each side
2. Sprinter	24
3. Sitting stretch (alternate)	26
4. Pushup	15
5. Situp (fingers laced, knees bent)	25
6. Leg raiser (on extended arm)	10 each side
7. Prone arch (fingers laced)	25

WOMEN: LEVEL FIVE (Continued)	**GOAL**

Circulatory activity (choose one each workout)

Jog-run	1 mile
Rope (skip 2 mins.; rest 45 secs.)	2 series
Run in place (run 180, hop 30—2 cycles)	6 minutes

Water Activities (see pages 361–362)

Your progress record 1 2 3 4 5 6 7 8 9 10 11 12   13 14 15

Step test (pulse)   Prove-out workouts

1. Toe Touch (Twist and Bend)

Starting position: Stand, feet shoulder-width apart, arms extended over head, thumbs interlocked.
Action: Count 1. Twist trunk to right and touch floor inside right foot with fingers of both hands. Count 2. Touch floor outside toes of right foot. Count 3. Touch floor outside heel of right foot. Count 4. Return to starting position, sweeping trunk and arms upward in a wide arc. On the next four counts, repeat action to left side.

2. Sprinter

Starting position: Squat, hands on floor, fingers pointed forward, left leg fully extended to rear.
Action: Count 1. Reverse position of feet in bouncing movement, bringing left foot to hands, extending right leg backward—all in one motion. Count 2. Reverse feet again, returning to starting position.

3. Sitting Stretch (Alternate)

Starting position: Sit, legs spread apart, fingers behind neck, elbows back.
Action: Count 1. Bend forward to left, touching forehead to left knee. Count 2. Return to starting position. Counts 3 and 4. Repeat to right. Score one repetition each time you return to starting position. Knees may be bent if necessary.

4. Pushup

Starting position: Lie on floor, face down, legs together, hands on floor under shoulders with fingers pointing straight ahead.
Action: Count 1. Push body off floor by extending arms so that weight rests on hands and toes. Count 2. Lower the body until chest touches floor.
Note: Body should be kept straight, buttocks should not be raised, abdomen should not sag.

5. Situp (Fingers Laced, Knees Bent)

Starting position: Lie on back, fingers laced behind neck, knees bent, feet flat on floor.
Action: Count 1. Sit up, turn trunk to right, touch left elbow to right knee. Count 2. Return to starting position. Count 3. Sit up, turn trunk to left, touch right elbow to left knee. Count 4. Return to starting position. Score one each time you return to starting position.

6. Leg Raiser (On Extended Arm)

Starting position: Body rigidly supported by extended right arm and foot. Left arm is held behind head.
Action: Count 1. Raise left leg high. Count 2. Return to starting position slowly. Repeat on other side. Do required number of repetitions.

7. Prone Arch (Fingers Laced)

Starting position: Lie face down, fingers laced behind neck.
Action: Count 1. Arch the back, legs and chest off floor. Count 2. Extend arms fully forward. Count 3. Return hands to behind neck. Count 4. Flatten body to floor.

Circulatory Activities

JOG-RUN—Jog and run alternately for distance specified on chart.

ROPE—Skip or jump rope continuously using any form for 2 minutes and then rest 45 seconds. Repeat 2 times.

RUN IN PLACE—Raise each foot at least 4" off floor and jog in place. Count 1 each time left foot touches floor. Complete number of running steps called for in chart, then do specified number of straddle hops. Complete 2 cycles of alternate running and hopping in time specified on the chart.

STRADDLE HOP—*Starting position:* At attention.

Action: Count 1. Swing arms sideward and upward, touching hands above head (arms straight) while simultaneously moving feet sideward and apart in a single jumping motion. Count 2. Spring back to starting position. Two counts in one hop.

THE PROGRAM FOR MEN

About the Program

The program assumes you have not—recently and consistently—been exposed to vigorous, all-around physical activity ... which could be true even if you play golf once or twice a week or engage in some other sport; no one sport provides for balanced development of all parts of the body.

The plan starts with an orientation—"get-set"—series of mild exercises to limber up all major muscle groups and help assure a painless transition.

There are then five graded levels.

As you move up from one level to the next, you will be building toward a practical and satisfactory level of fitness.

By building gradually—progressively—you will be building soundly.

What the Exercises Are For

There are three general types—warmup exercises, conditioning exercises and circulatory activities.

The warmup exercises stretch and limber up the muscles and speed up the action of the heart and lungs, thus preparing the body for greater exertion and reducing the possibility of unnecessary strain.

The conditioning exercises are systematically planned to tone up abdominal, back, leg, arm and other major muscles.

The circulatory activities produce contractions of large muscle groups for relatively longer periods than the conditioning exercises—to stimulate and strengthen the circulatory and respiratory systems.

The plan calls for doing 10 mild exercises during the orientation period and, thereafter, the warmup exercises and the seven conditioning exercises listed for each level. The first six exercises of the orientation program are used as warmup exercises throughout the graded levels.

When it comes to the circulatory activities, you select one each workout. Alternately running and walking ... skipping rope ... running in place. All are effective. You can switch about for variety.

How You Progress

Right now, you have limited tolerance for exercise; you can do just so much without discomfort and fatigue.

A sound conditioning program should gradually stretch your tolerance. It should give unused or little-used muscles moderate tasks at first, then make the tasks increasingly more demanding so you become able to achieve more and more with less and less fatigue and with increasingly rapid recovery.

As you move from level to level, some exercises will be modified so they call for more effort. Others will remain the same but you will build strength and stamina by increasing the number of repetitions.

At level 1, your objective will be to gradually reduce, from workout to workout, the "breathing spells" between exercises until you can do the seven conditioning exercises without resting.

You will proceed in the same fashion with the more difficult exercises and increased repetitions at succeeding levels.

You will find the program designed—the progression carefully planned—to make this feasible. You will be able to proceed at your own pace, competing with yourself rather than with anyone else—and this is of great importance for sound conditioning.

Note: Gradually speeding up, from workout to workout, the rate at which you do each exercise will provide greater stimulation for the circulatory and respiratory systems and also help to keep your workouts short. However, the seven conditioning exercises should not be a race against time. Perform each exercise completely to insure maximum benefit.

When and How Often To Work Out

To be most beneficial, exercise should become part of your regular daily routine—as much as bathing, shaving, dressing.

Five workouts a week are called for throughout the program.

You can choose any time that is convenient. Preferably, it should be the same time every day—but it does not matter whether it's first thing in the morning, before dinner in the evening, just before retiring, or any other time.

The hour just before the evening meal is a popular time for exercise. The later afternoon workout provides a welcome change of pace at the end of the work day and helps dissolve the day's worries and tensions.

Another popular time to work out is early morning, before the work day begins. Advocates of the early start say it makes them more alert and energetic on the job.

Among the factors you should consider in developing your workout schedule are personal preference, job and family responsibilities, availability of exercise facilities, and weather. It's important to schedule your workouts for a time when there is little chance that you will have to cancel or interrupt them because of other demands on your time.

You should not exercise strenuously during extremely hot, humid weather or within two hours after eating. Heat and/or digestion both make heavy demands on the circulatory system, and in combination with exercise can be an overtaxing double load.

Your Progress Records

Charts are provided for the orientation program and for each of the five levels.

They list the exercises to be done and the goal for each exercise in terms of number of repetitions, distance, etc.

They also provide space in which to record your progress—(1) in completing the recommended 15 workouts at each level, (2) in accomplishing the three prove-out workouts before moving on to a succeeding level, and (3) in the results as you take the step test from time to time.

A sample chart and progress record for one of the five levels is shown below.

You do the warmup exercises and the conditioning exercises along with one circulatory activity for each workout.

Check off each workout as you complete it. The last three numbers are for the prove-out workouts, in which the seven conditioning exercises should be done without resting. Check them off as you accomplish them.

You are now ready to proceed to the next level.

As you take the step test—at about 2-week intervals—enter your pulse rate.

When you move on to the next level, transfer the last pulse rate from the preceding level. Enter it in the margin to the left of the new progress record and circle it so it will be convenient for continuing reference.

SAMPLE	GOAL
Warmup Exercises	Exercises 1–6 of Orientation program
Conditioning Exercises	Uninterrupted repetitions
1. Toe touch	20
2. Sprinter	16
3. Sitting stretch	18
4. Pushup	10
5. Situp (fingers laced)	15
6. Leg raiser	16 each leg
7. Flutter kick	40
Circulatory activity (choose one each workout)	
Jog-walk (jog 100, walk 100)	1 mile
Rope (skip 60 secs.; rest 60 secs.)	3 series
Run in place (run 95, hop 15—2 cycles)	3 minutes
Water activities (see pages 361–362)	
Your progress record 1 2 3 4 5 6 7 8 9 10 11 12	13 14 15
Step test (pulse)	Prove-out workouts

Getting Set—Orientation Workouts

With the series of preliminary exercises listed in the chart which follows and described on the next two pages, you can get yourself ready—without severe aches or pains—for the progressive conditioning program.

Even if these preliminary exercises should seem easy—and they are deliberately meant to be mild—plan to spend a minimum of one week with them. Do not hesitate to spend two weeks or even three if necessary for you to limber up enough so you can accomplish all the exercises easily and without undue fatigue.

ORIENTATION PROGRAM: MEN	GOAL
Conditioning Exercises	*Repetitions*
*1. Bend and stretch	10
*2. Knee lift	10 left, 10 right
*3. Wing stretcher	20

ORIENTATION PROGRAM: MEN (Continued)   GOAL

Conditioning Exercises	Repetitions
*4. Half knee bend	10
*5. Arm circles	15 each way
*6. Body bender	10 left, 10 right
7. Prone arch	10
8. Knee pushup	6
9. Head and shoulder curl	5
10. Ankle stretch	15
Circulatory activity (choose one each workout)	
Walking	½ mile
Rope (skip 15 secs.; rest 60 secs.)	3 series

The first six exercises of the orientation program will be used as warmup exercises throughout the graded levels.

Step Test Record—After completing the orientation program, take the 2-minute step test. Record your pulse rate here: _____. This will be the base rate with which you can make comparisons in the future.

1. Bend and Stretch
Starting position: Stand erect, feet shoulder-width apart.
Action: Count 1. Bend trunk forward and down, flexing knees. Stretch gently in attempt to touch fingers to toes or floor. Count 2. Return to starting position.
Note: Do slowly, stretch and relax at intervals rather than in rhythm.

2. Knee Lift
Starting position: Stand erect, feet together, arms at sides.
Action: Count 1. Raise left knee as high as possible, grasping leg with hands and pulling knee against body while keeping back straight. Count 2. Lower to starting position. Counts 3 and 4. Repeat with right knee.

3. Wing Stretcher
Starting position: Stand erect, elbows at shoulder height, fists clenched in front of chest.
Action: Count 1. Thrust elbows backward vigorously without arching back. Keep head erect, elbows at shoulder height. Count 2. Return to starting position.

4. Half Knee Bend
Starting position: Stand erect, hands on hips.
Action: Count 1. Bend knees halfway while extending arms forward, palms down. Count 2. Return to starting position.

5. Arm Circles
Starting position: Stand erect, arms extended sideward at shoulder height, palms up.
Action: Describe small circles backward with hands. Keep head erect. Do 15 backward circles. Reverse, turn palms down and do 15 small circles forward.

6. Body Bender
Starting position: Stand, feet shoulder-width apart, hands behind neck, fingers interlaced.
Action: Count 1. Bend trunk sideward to left as far as possible, keeping hands behind neck. Count 2. Return to starting position. Counts 3 and 4. Repeat to the right.

7. Prone Arch

Starting position: Lie face down, hands tucked under thighs.

Action: Count 1. Raise head, shoulders, and legs from floor. Count 2. Return to starting position.

8. Knee Pushup

Starting position: Lie on floor, face down, legs together, knees bent with feet raised off floor, hands on floor under shoulders, palms down.

Action: Count 1. Push upper body off floor until arms are fully extended and body is in straight line from head to knees. Count 2. Return to starting position.

9. Head and Shoulder Curl

Starting position: Lie on back, hands tucked under small of back, palms down.

Action: Count 1. Tighten abdominal muscles, lift head and pull shoulders and elbows up off floor. Hold for four seconds. Count 2. Return to starting position.

10. Ankle Stretch

Starting position: Stand on a stair, large book or block of wood, with weight on balls of feet and heels raised.

Action: Count 1. Lower heels. Count 2. Raise heels.

Circulatory Activities

WALKING—Step off at a lively pace, swing arms and breathe deeply.

ROPE—Any form of skipping or jumping is acceptable. Gradually increase the tempo as your skill and condition improve.

MEN: LEVEL ONE	GOAL
Warmup Exercises	Exercises 1–6 of Orientation program
Conditioning Exercises	Uninterrupted repetitions
1. Toe touch	10
2. Sprinter	12
3. Sitting stretch	12
4. Pushup	4
5. Situp (arms extended)	5
6. Leg raiser	12 each leg
7. Flutter kick	30
Circulatory activity (choose one each workout)	
Walking (120 steps a minute)	1 mile
Rope (skip 30 secs.; rest 30 secs.)	2 series
Run in place (run 60, hop 10—2 cycles)	2 minutes
Water activities (see pages 361–362)	
Your progress record 1 2 3 4 5 6 7 8 9 10 11 12	13 14 15
Step test (pulse)	Prove-out workouts

1. Toe Touch
Starting position: Stand at attention.
Action: Count 1. Bend trunk forward and down keeping knees straight, touching fingers to ankles. Count 2. Bounce and touch fingers to top of feet. Count 3. Bounce and touch fingers to toes. Count 4. Return to starting position.

2. Sprinter
Starting position: Squat, hands on floor, fingers pointed forward, left leg fully extended to rear.
Action: Count 1. Reverse position of feet in bouncing movement, bringing left foot to hands and extending right leg backward—all in one motion. Count 2. Reverse feet again, returning to starting position.

3. Sitting Stretch
Starting position: Sit, legs spread apart, hands on knees.
Action: Count 1. Bend forward at waist, extending arms as far forward as possible. Count 2. Return to starting position.

4. Pushup
Starting position: Lie on floor, face down, legs together, hands on floor under shoulders with fingers pointing straight ahead.
Action: Count 1. Push body off floor by extending arms, so that weight rests on hands and toes. Count 2. Lower the body until chest touches floor.
Note: Body should be kept straight, buttocks should not be raised, abdomen should not sag.

5. Situp (Arms Extended)
Starting position: Lie on back, legs straight and together, arms extended beyond head.
Action: Count 1. Bring arms forward over head, roll up to sitting position, sliding hands along legs, grasping ankles. Count 2. Roll back to starting position.

6. Leg Raiser
Starting position: Right side of body on floor, head resting on right arm.
Action: Lift left leg about 24" off floor, then lower it. Do required number of repetitions. Repeat on other side.

7. Flutter Kick
Starting position: Lie face down, hands tucked under thighs.
Action: Arch the back, bringing chest and head up, then flutter kick continuously, moving the legs 8"–10" apart. Kick from hips with knees slightly bent. Count each kick as one.

Circulatory Activities
WALKING—Maintain a pace of 120 steps per minute for a distance of 1 mile. Swing arms and breathe deeply.
ROPE—Skip or jump rope continuously using any form for 30 seconds and then rest 30 seconds. Repeat 2 times.
RUN IN PLACE—Raise each foot at least 4" off floor and jog in place. Count 1 each time left foot touches floor. Complete the number of running steps called for in chart, then do specified number of straddle hops. Complete 2 cycles of alternate running and hopping for time specified on chart.
STRADDLE HOP—*Starting position:* At attention.
Action: Count 1. Swing arms sideward and upward, touching hands above head (arms straight) while simultaneously moving feet sideward and apart in a single jumping motion. Count 2. Spring back to starting position. Two counts in one hop.

MEN: LEVEL TWO	GOAL
Warmup Exercises	Exercises 1–6 of Orientation program
Conditioning Exercises	Uninterrupted repetitions
1. Toe touch	20
2. Sprinter	16
3. Sitting stretch	18
4. Pushup	10
5. Situp (fingers laced)	20
6. Leg raiser	16 each leg
7. Flutter kick	40
Circulatory activity (choose one each workout)	
Jog-walk (jog 100; walk 100)	1 mile
Rope (skip 1 min.; rest 1 min.)	3 series
Run in place (run 95, hop 15—2 cycles)	3 minutes
Water activities (see pages 361–362)	
Your progress record 1 2 3 4 5 6 7 8 9 10 11 12	13 14 15
Step test (pulse)	Prove-out workouts

1. Toe Touch

Starting position: Stand at attention.

Action: Count 1. Bend trunk forward and down keeping knees straight, touching fingers to ankles. Count 2. Bounce and touch fingers to top of feet. Count 3. Bounce and touch fingers to toes. Count 4. Return to starting position.

2. Sprinter

Starting position: Squat, hands on floor, fingers pointed forward, left leg fully extended to rear.

Action: Count 1. Reverse position of feet in bouncing movement, bringing left foot to hands, extending right leg backward—all in one motion. Count 2. Reverse feet again, returning to starting position.

3. Sitting Stretch

Starting position: Sit, legs apart, hands on knees.

Action: Count 1. Bend forward at waist, extending arms as far forward as possible. Count 2. Return to starting position.

4. Pushup

Starting position: Lie on floor, face down, legs together, hands on floor under shoulders with fingers pointing straight ahead.

Action: Count 1. Push body off floor by extending arms, so that weight rests on hands and toes. Count 2. Lower the body until chest touches floor.

Note: Body should be kept straight, buttocks should not be raised, abdomen should not sag.

5. Situp (Fingers Laced)

Starting position: Lie on back, legs straight and feet spread approximately 1' apart. Fingers laced behind neck.

Action: Count 1. Curl up to sitting position and turn trunk to left. Touch the right elbow to left knee. Count 2. Return to starting position. Count 3. Curl up to sitting position and turn trunk to right. Touch left elbow to right knee. Count 4. Return to starting position. Score one situp each time you return to starting position. Knees may be bent as necessary.

6. Leg Raiser

Starting position: Right side of body on floor, head resting on right arm.

Action: Lift left leg about 24" off floor, then lower it. Do required number of repetitions. Repeat on other side.

7. Flutter Kick

Starting position: Lie face down, hands tucked under thighs.

Action: Arch the back, bringing chest and head up, then flutter kick continuously, moving the legs 8"–10" apart. Kick from hips with knees slightly bent. Count each kick as one.

Circulatory Activities

JOG-WALK—Jog and walk alternately for number of paces indicated on chart for distance specified.

ROPE—Skip or jump rope continuously using any form for 60 seconds and then rest 60 seconds. Repeat 5 times.

RUN IN PLACE—Raise each foot at least 4" off floor and jog in place. Count 1 each time left foot touches floor. Complete number of running steps called for in chart, then do specified number of straddle hops. Complete 2 cycles of alternate running and hopping for time specified on chart.

STRADDLE HOP—*Starting position:* At attention.

Action: Count 1. Swing arms sideward and upward, touching hands above head (arms straight) while simultaneously moving feet sideward and apart in a single jumping motion. Count 2. Spring back to starting position. Two counts in one hop.

MEN: LEVEL THREE	**GOAL**
Warmup Exercises	Exercises 1–6 of Orientation program
Conditioning Exercises	Uninterrupted repetitions
1. Toe touch	30
2. Sprinter	20
3. Sitting stretch (fingers laced)	18
4. Pushup	20
5. Situp (arms extended, knees up)	30
6. Leg raiser	20 each leg
7. Flutter kick	50
Circulatory activity (choose one each workout)	
Jog-walk (jog 200; walk 100)	1½ miles
Rope (skip 1 min.; rest 1 min.)	5 series
Run in place (run 135, hop 20—2 cycles)	4 minutes
Water activity (see pages 361–362)	
Your progress record 1 2 3 4 5 6 7 8 9 10 11 12	13 14 15
Step test (pulse)	Prove-out workouts

1. Toe Touch

Starting position: Stand at attention.

Action: Count 1. Bend trunk forward and down keeping knees straight, touching fingers to ankles. Count 2. Bounce and touch fingers to top of feet. Count 3. Bounce and touch fingers to toes. Count 4. Return to starting position.

2. Sprinter

Starting position: Squat, hands on floor, fingers pointed forward, left leg fully extended to rear.
Action: Count 1. Reverse position of feet in bouncing movement, bringing left foot to hands, extending right leg backward—all in one motion. Count 2. Reverse feet again, returning to starting position.

3. Sitting Stretch (Fingers Laced)

Starting position: Sit, legs spread apart, fingers laced behind neck, elbows back.
Action: Count 1. Bend forward at waist, reaching elbows as close to floor as possible. Count 2. Return to starting position.

4. Pushup

Starting position: Lie on floor, face down, legs together, hands on floor under shoulders with fingers pointing straight ahead.
Action: Count 1. Push body off floor by extending arms, so that weight rests on hands and toes. Count 2. Lower the body until chest touches floor.
Note: Body should be kept straight, buttocks should not be raised, abdomen should not sag.

5. Situp (Arms Extended, Knees Up)

Starting position: Lie on back, legs straight, arms extended overhead.
Action: Count 1. Sit up, reaching forward with arms encircling knees while pulling them tightly to chest. Count 2. Return to starting position. Do this exercise rhythmically, without breaks in the movement.

6. Leg Raiser

Starting position: Right side of body on floor, head resting on right arm.
Action: Lift left leg about 24" off floor then lower it. Do required number of repetitions. Repeat on other side.

7. Flutter Kick

Starting position: Lie face down, hands tucked under thighs.
Action: Arch the back, bringing chest and head up, then flutter kick continuously, moving the legs 8"-10" apart. Kick from hips with knees slightly bent. Count each kick as one.

Circulatory Activities

JOG-WALK—Jog and walk alternately for number of paces indicated on chart for distance specified.

ROPE—Skip or jump rope continuously using any form for 60 seconds and then rest 60 seconds. Repeat 5 times.

RUN IN PLACE—Raise each foot at least 4" off floor and jog in place. Count 1 each time left foot touches floor. Complete number of running steps called for in chart, then do specified number of straddle hops. Complete 2 cycles of alternate running and hopping for time specified on chart.

STRADDLE HOP—*Starting position:* At attention.
Action: Count 1. Swing arms sideward and upward, touching hands above head (arms straight) while simultaneously moving feet sideward and apart in a single jumping motion. Count 2. Spring back to starting position. Two counts in one hop.

MEN: LEVEL FOUR	GOAL
Warmup Exercises	Exercises 1–6 of Orientation program
Conditioning Exercises	Uninterrupted repetitions
1. Toe touch (twist and bend)	20 each side
2. Sprinter	28

MEN: LEVEL FOUR (Continued)	GOAL
3. Sitting stretch (alternate)	24
4. Pushup	30
5. Situp (arms crossed, knees bent)	30
6. Leg raiser (whip)	20 each leg
7. Prone arch (arms extended)	20

Circulatory activity (choose one each workout)

Jog	1 mile
Rope (skip 90 secs.; rest 30 secs.)	3 series
Run in place (run 180, hop 25—2 cycles)	5 minutes

Water activity (see pages 361–362)

Your progress record 1 2 3 4 5 6 7 8 9 10 11 12   13 14 15

Step test (pulse)   Prove-out workouts

1. Toe Touch (Twist and Bend)

Starting position: Stand, feet shoulder-width apart, arms extended overhead, thumbs interlocked.
Action: Count 1. Twist trunk to right and touch floor inside right foot with fingers of both hands. Count 2. Touch floor outside toes of right foot. Count 3. Touch floor outside heel of right foot. Count 4. Return to starting position, sweeping trunk and arms upward in a wide arc. On the next four counts, repeat action to left side.

2. Sprinter

Starting position: Squat, hands on floor, fingers pointed forward, left leg fully extended to rear.
Action: Count 1. Reverse position of feet in bouncing movement, bringing left foot to hands, extending right leg backward—all in one motion. Count 2. Reverse feet again, returning to starting position.

3. Sitting Stretch (Alternate)

Starting position: Sit, legs spread apart, fingers laced behind neck, elbows back.
Action: Count 1. Bend forward to left, touching forehead to left knee. Count 2. Return to starting position. Counts 3 and 4. Repeat to right. Score one repetition each time you return to starting position. Knees may be bent if necessary.

4. Pushup

Starting position: Lie on floor, face down, legs together, hands on floor under shoulders with fingers pointing straight ahead.
Action: Count 1. Push body off floor by extending arms, so that weight rests on hands and toes. Count 2. Lower the body until chest touches floor.
Note: Body should be kept straight, buttocks should not be raised, abdomen should not sag.

5. Situp (Arms Crossed, Knees Bent)

Starting position: Lie on back, arms crossed on chest, hands grasping opposite shoulders, knees bent to right angle, feet flat on floor.
Action: Count 1. Curl up to sitting position. Count 2. Return to starting position.

6. Leg Raiser (Whip)

Starting position: Right side of body on floor, right arm supporting head.
Action: Whip left leg up and down rapidly, lifting as high as possible off the floor. Count each whip as one. Reverse position and whip right leg up and down.

7. Prone Arch (Arms Extended)

Starting position: Lie face down, legs straight and together, arms extended to sides at shoulder level.

Action: Count 1. Arch the back, bringing arms, chest and head up, and raising legs as high as possible. Count 2. Return to starting position.

Circulatory Activities

JOG—Jog continuously for 1 mile.

ROPE—Skip or jump rope continuously using any form for 90 seconds and then rest for 30 seconds. Repeat 3 times.

RUN IN PLACE—Raise each foot at least 4" off the floor and jog in place. Count 1 each time left foot touches floor. Complete number of running steps called for in chart, then do specified number of straddle hops. Complete 2 cycles of alternate running and hopping in time specified on chart.

STRADDLE HOP—*Starting position:* At attention.

Action: Count 1. Swing arms sideward and upward, touching hands above head (arms straight) while simultaneously moving feet sideward and apart in a single jumping motion. Count 2. Spring back to starting position. Two counts in one hop.

MEN: LEVEL FIVE	GOAL
Warmup Exercises	Exercises 1–6 of Orientation program
Conditioning Exercises	Uninterrupted repetitions
1. Toe touch (twist and bend)	30 each side
2. Sprinter	36
3. Sitting stretch (alternate)	30
4. Pushup	50
5. Situp (fingers laced, knees bent)	40
6. Leg raiser (on extended arm)	20 each side
7. Prone arch (fingers laced)	30
Circulatory activity (choose one each workout)	
Jog-run	3 mile
Rope (skip 2 mins.; rest 30 secs.)	3 series
Run in place (run 216, hop 30—2 cycles)	6 minutes
Water activity (see pages 361–362)	
Your progress record 1 2 3 4 5 6 7 8 9 10 11 12	13 14 15
Step test (pulse)	Prove-out workouts

1. Toe Touch (Twist and Bend)

Starting position: Stand, feet shoulder-width apart, arms extended overhead, thumbs interlocked.

Action: Count 1. Twist trunk to right and touch floor inside right foot with fingers of both hands. Count 2. Touch floor outside toes of right foot. Count 3. Touch floor outside heel of right foot. Count 4. Return to starting position, sweeping trunk and arms upward in a wide arc. On the next four counts, repeat action to left side.

2. Sprinter

Starting position: Squat, hands on floor, fingers pointed forward, left leg fully extended to rear.

Action: Count 1. Reverse position of feet in bouncing movement, bringing left foot to hands and extending right leg backward—all in one motion. Count 2. Reverse feet again, returning to starting position.

3. Sitting Stretch (Alternate)

Starting position: Sit, legs spread apart, fingers laced behind neck, elbows back.
Action: Count 1. Bend forward to left, touching forehead to left knee. Count 2. Return to starting position. Counts 3 and 4. Repeat to right. Score one repetition each time you return to starting position. Knees may be bent if necessary.

4. Pushup

Starting position: Lie on floor, face down, legs together, hands on floor under shoulders with fingers pointing straight ahead.
Action: Count 1. Push body off floor by extending arms so that weight rests on hands and toes. Count 2. Lower body until chest touches floor.
Note: Body should be kept straight, buttocks should not be raised, abdomen should not sag.

5. Situp (Fingers Laced, Knees Bent)

Starting position: Lie on back, fingers laced behind neck, knees bent, feet flat on floor.
Action: Count 1. Sit up, turn trunk to right, touch left elbow to right knee. Count 2. Return to starting position. Count 3. Sit up, turn trunk to left, touch right elbow to left knee. Count 4. Return to starting position. Score one each time you return to starting position.

6. Leg Raiser (On Extended Arm)

Starting position: Body rigidly supported by extended right arm and foot. Left arm is held behind head.
Action: Count 1. Raise left leg high. Count 2. Return to starting position slowly. Do required number of repetitions. Repeat on other side.

7. Prone Arch (Fingers Laced)

Starting position: Lie face down, fingers laced behind neck.
Action: Count 1. Arch back, legs, and chest off floor. Count 2. Extend arms forward. Count 3. Return hands to behind neck. Count 4. Flatten body to floor.

Circulatory Activities

JOG RUN—Alternately jog and run the specified distance. Attempt to increase the proportion of time spent running in each succeeding workout.
ROPE—Skip or jump rope continuously using any form for 2 minutes and then rest 30 seconds. Repeat 3 times.
RUN IN PLACE—Raise each foot at least 4" off floor and jog in place. Count 1 each time left foot touches floor. Complete number of running steps called for in chart, then do specified number of straddle hops. Complete 2 cycles of alternate running and hopping for time specified on the chart.
STRADDLE HOP—*Starting position:* At attention.
Action: Count 1. Swing arms sideward and upward, touching hands above head (arms straight) while simultaneously moving feet sideward and apart in a single jumping motion. Count 2. Spring back to starting position. Two counts in one hop.

Staying Fit

Once you have reached the level of conditioning you have chosen for yourself, you will wish to maintain your fitness.

To do so, continue the workouts at that level.

While it has been found possible to maintain fitness with three workouts a week, ideally, exercise should be a daily habit. If you can, by all means continue your workouts on a five-times-a-week basis.

If at any point—either after reaching your goal or in the process of doing so—your workouts are interrupted because of illness or other reason for more than a week, it will be best to begin again at a lower level. If you have had a serious illness or surgery, proceed under your physician's guidance.

Broadening Your Program

The exercises and activities you have engaged in are basic—designed to take you soundly and progressively up the ladder to physical fitness without need for special equipment or facilities.

There are many other activities and forms of exercise which, if you wish, you may use to supplement the basic program.

They include a variety of sports; water exercises you can use if you have access to a pool; and isometrics—sometimes called exercises without movement—which take little time (6–8 seconds each).

ISOMETRICS

Isometric contraction exercises take very little time, and require no special equipment. They're excellent muscle strengtheners and, as such, valuable supplements.

The idea of isometrics is to work out a muscle by pushing or pulling against an immovable object such as a wall ... or by pitting it against the opposition of another muscle.

The basis is the "overload" principle of exercise physiology—which holds that a muscle required to perform work beyond the usual intensity will grow in strength. And research has indicated that one hard, 6- to 8-second isometric contraction per workout can, over a period of six months, produce a significant strength increase in a muscle.

The exercises described in the following pages cover major large muscle groups of the body.

They can be performed almost anywhere and at almost any time.

There is no set order for doing them—nor do all have to be completed at one time. You can, if you like, do one or two in the morning, others at various times during the day whenever you have half a minute or even less to spare.

For each contraction, maintain tension no more than eight seconds. Do little breathing during a contraction; breathe deeply between contractions.

And start easily. Do not apply maximum effort in the beginning.

For the first three or four weeks, you should exert only about one-half what you think is your maximum force.

Use the first three or four seconds to build up to this degree of force—and the remaining four or five seconds to hold it.

For the next two weeks, gradually increase force to more nearly approach maximum. After about six weeks, it will be safe to exert maximum effort.

Pain indicates you're applying too much force; reduce the amount immediately. If pain continues to accompany any exercise, discontinue using that exercise for a week or two. Then try it again with about 50 percent of maximum effort and, if no pain occurs, you can go on to gradually build up toward maximum.

Neck
Starting position: Sit or stand, with interlaced fingers of hands on forehead.
Action: Forcibly exert a forward push of head while resisting equally hard with hands.
Starting position: Sit or stand, with interlaced fingers of hands behind head.
Action: Push head backward while exerting a forward pull with hands.
Starting position: Sit or stand, with palm of left hand on left side of head.
Action: Push with left hand while resisting with head and neck. Reverse using right hand on right side of head.

Upper Body

Starting position: Stand, back to wall, hands at sides, palms toward wall.
Action: Press hands backward against wall, keeping arms straight.
Starting position: Stand, facing wall, hands at sides, palms toward wall.
Action: Press hands forward against wall, keeping arms straight.
Starting position: Stand in doorway or with side against wall, arms at sides, palms toward legs.
Action: Press hand(s) outward against wall or doorframe, keeping arms straight.

Arms

Starting position: Stand with feet slightly apart. Flex right elbow, close to body, palm up. Place left hand over right.
Action: Forcibly attempt to curl right arm upward, while giving equally strong resistance with the left hand. Repeat with left arm.

Arms and Chest

Starting position: Stand with feet comfortably spaced, knees slightly bent. Clasp hands, palms together, close to chest.
Action: Press hands together and hold.
Starting position: Stand with feet slightly apart, knees slightly bent. Grip fingers, arms close to chest.
Action: Pull hard and hold.

Abdominal

Starting position: Stand, knees slightly flexed, hands resting on knees.
Action: Contract abdominal muscles.

Lower Back, Buttocks and Back of Thighs

Starting position: Lie face down, arms at sides, palms up, legs placed under bed or other heavy object.
Action: With both hips flat on floor, raise one leg, keeping knee straight so that heel pushes hard against the resistance above. Repeat with opposite leg.

Legs

Starting position: Sit in chair with left ankle crossed over right, feet resting on floor, legs bent at 90 degree angle.
Action: Forcibly attempt to straighten right leg while resisting with the left. Repeat with opposite leg.

Inner and Outer Thighs

Starting position: Sit, legs extended with each ankle pressed against the outside of sturdy chair legs.
Action: Keep legs straight and pull toward one another firmly. For outer thigh muscles, place ankles inside chair legs and exert pressure outward.

WATER ACTIVITIES

Swimming is one of the best physical activities for people of all ages—and for many of the handicapped.

With the body submerged in water, blood circulation automatically increases to some extent; pressure of water on the body also helps promote deeper ventilation of the lungs; and with well-planned activity, both circulation and ventilation increase still more.

The water exercises described on the following page can be used either as supplements to, or replacements for, the circulatory activities of the basic program. The goals for each of the five levels are shown in the chart below.

Women

Level	1	2	3	4	5
Bobs	10	15	20	50	100
Swim	5 min	10 min	15 min	—	—
Interval swimming	—	—	—	25 yds. (Repeat 10 times.)	25 yds. (Repeat 20 times.)

Men

Level	1	2	3	4	5
Bobs	10	15	25	75	125
Swim	5 min	10 min	15 min	—	—
Interval swimming	—	—	—	25 yds. (Repeat 20 times.)	50 yds. (Repeat 20 times.)

Bobbing

Starting position: Face out of water.
Action: Count 1. Take a breath. Count 2. Submerge while exhaling until feet touch bottom. Count 3. Push up from bottom to surface while continuing to exhale. Three counts to one bob.

Swimming

Use any type of stroke. Swim continuously for the time specified.

Interval Swimming

Use any type of stroke. Swim moderately fast for distance specified. You can then either swim back slowly to starting point or get out of pool and walk back. Repeat specified number of times.

WEIGHT TRAINING

Weight training also is an excellent method of developing muscular strength—and muscular endurance. Where equipment is available, it may be used as a supplement to the seven conditioning exercises.

Because of the great variety of weight training exercises, there will be no attempt to describe them here. Both barbells and weighted dumbbells—complete with instructions—are available at most sporting goods stores. A good rule to follow in deciding the maximum weight you should lift is to select a weight you can lift six times without strain.

SPORTS

Soccer, basketball, handball, squash, ice hockey and other sports that require sustained effort can be valuable aids to building circulatory endurance.

But if you have been sedentary, it's important to pace yourself carefully in such sports, and it may even be advisable to avoid them until you are well along in your physical conditioning program. That doesn't mean you should avoid all sports.

There are many excellent conditioning and circulatory activities in which the amount of exertion is easily controlled and in which you can progress at your own rate. Bicycling is one example. Others include hiking, skating, tennis, running, cross-country skiing, rowing, canoeing, water skiing and skindiving.

You can engage in these sports at any point in the program, if you start slowly. Games should be played with full speed and vigor only when your conditioning permits doing so without undue fatigue.

On days when you get a good workout in sports you can skip part or all of your exercise program. Use your own judgment.

If you have engaged in a sport that exercises the legs and stimulates the heart and lungs—such as skating—you could skip the circulatory activity for that day, but you still should do some of the conditioning and stretching exercises for the upper body. On the other hand, weight-lifting is an excellent conditioning activity, but it should be supplemented with running or one of the other circulatory exercises.

Whatever your favorite sport, you will find your enjoyment enhanced by improved fitness. Every weekend athlete should invest in frequent workouts.